THE
ARCHBISHOP
WORE
COMBAT
BOOTS

FROM COMBAT, TO CAMELOT, TO KATRINA

THE ARCHBISHOP WORE COMBAT BOOTS

MEMOIR OF AN EXTRAORDINARY LIFE

Archbishop Philip Hannan
with Nancy Collins and Peter Finney, Jr.

Our Sunday Visitor Publishing Division
Our Sunday Visitor, Inc.
Huntington, Indiana 46750

Our Sunday Visitor Publishing Division
Our Sunday Visitor, Inc.
200 Noll Plaza
Huntington, IN 46750

bookpermissions@osv.com
1-800-348-2440

ISBN 978-1-59276-697-0 (Inventory No. T1018)
LCCN: 2010922943

Interior design by Sherri L. Hoffman
Cover design by Lindsey Luken

Cover images:
John F. Kennedy — Shutterstock/Getty Images
Jackie Kennedy — Michael Stroud/Hulton Archive/Getty Images
Boots — Shutterstock

PRINTED IN THE UNITED STATES OF AMERICA

Contents

Acknowledgments

It is impossible to simply acknowledge the friendship and love of the thousands of people who have supported me over my ninety-seven years. As such, I will try to say a few words about the folks who have helped me with this book. To any whom I may have omitted, I offer my deepest apologies and my heartfelt thanks to you also.

I want to first extend a thank you to Peter Finney, Jr., and Nancy Collins, who have helped me every step of the way; this book as is much theirs as mine. I thank them for their incredible help and assistance.

My secretary, Alma Cartagena, has helped me with the typing, transcription, and collection of materials and photographs through the years related to this book. I credit her custodial skills in keeping together a 1,200-page manuscript that could have become scattered!

My publisher, Our Sunday Visitor, and their team were enthusiastic supporters of this project from the time when we approached them; my thanks to them, and especially to Jacquelyn Lindsey.

My close friends, the Garvey Brothers and Dorinda Bordlee, have been tireless supporters of the Pro-Life cause and helped on those portions of the book.

My friends here in New Orleans provided encouragement and support (and in some cases food!) at every opportunity; Anne and King Milling, Garic and Susie Schoen, Mr. and Mrs. Drago and Clara Cvitanovich, Phillip Brooks, the late Deacon Paul Nalty, V.M. Wheeler, Joe and Sue Ellen Canizaro, Tom and Gayle Benson, the late Pat Taylor, Phyllis Taylor, and my best friend Alden "Doc" Laborde.

My medical and personal support staff: Dr. Charles Mary, Dr. Angela Buonagura, Dr. Eric Ehrensing and, most importantly, Dr. Bill and Anita Barfield for their almost daily attention and care in recent years. A very heartfelt and personal thanks to my sitter Millie Boihem and especially to my caregiver and friend Kent Bossier, who has gone far beyond the call of duty with my daily care. Thank you for everything; I could not have done it without you.

My brother priests have provided me with wonderful spiritual and intellectual support in this endeavor and in many others, especially Rev. Msgr.

Clinton Doskey, Rev. Msgr. Charles Duke, Rev. Msgr. Crosby Kern, Rev. Adrian Hall, and Deacons Butch Shartle, Nelvin Luke, Jack Finn, Ricky Suprean, Rusty Read, and Acolytes Jay Frantz and Jay Weil. These men have also helped me with the daily celebration of Mass in recent years, and I thank them.

Archbishop Francis Schulte, Archbishop Alfred Hughes, and Archbishop Gregory Aymond have been confidants and great friends. May the Lord continue to bless them and the people of Louisiana.

And finally my wonderful family — my nieces and nephews, especially those who have spent time with me in New Orleans over the last several years, including Peggy Hannan Laramie, Michael and Kathy Hannan, Tom Hannan, Paul Hannan, J.T. Hannan, Kara Hannan McGinn, and Kate Hannan.

My brothers and sister provided much of the material for this book, and I love them for it — Thomas Hannan, Dr. Francis Hannan, Mary Hannan Mahoney, William T. Hannan, Denis Hannan, and John Hannan.

My brother Patrick "Jerry" Hannan has helped me in more ways than I can count; profuse thanks to him.

And, finally, this book is dedicated to my parents, Patrick F. Hannan and Lillian Hannan. I still think about them every day.

CHAPTER 1

The Funeral of
President John Fitzgerald Kennedy

November 25, 1963. As I slowly climbed the familiar, winding steps to the elevated pulpit in the Cathedral of St. Matthew in Washington, D.C., I felt as numb and emotionally exhausted as every other American struggling to make sense of the stunningly brutal murder of the thirty-fifth President of the United States, John Fitzgerald Kennedy.

My own grieving, however, would have to wait. First Lady Jacqueline Kennedy had asked that I deliver the eulogy for her husband — and my friend. Though I had presided over hundreds of funerals in my thirty years as a priest and bishop, nothing had prepared me for today. More than a religious good-bye, this was the world's wake, a seminal moment in American history, beamed by television to every corner of a globe still reeling in shock and disbelief. Three days earlier John Kennedy — America's first Catholic, and, arguably, most charismatic president, a statesman of vigor, vision, virtue, and vice — had been brutally gunned down as his motorcade crawled along the cheering, crowd-lined streets of Dallas, killed by a twenty-four-year-old sharpshooter brandishing a rifle.

And though, of course, he was my President, ours had been a more personal relationship. Having met the dashing war hero and wealthy, if unknown Massachusetts congressman in the late forties, our friendship had continued into the White House where — when Catholic doctrine jousted with political instincts — I, secretly, counseled him. And now, at just forty-six, four years younger than I, he was dead from three fatal gunshots.

Taking my place behind the raised pulpit, I glanced down on his coffin, draped in the American flag, resting in the center aisle at the foot of the sanctuary. To get my bearings, I scanned the sea of black, searching for Jackie who with Bobby on one side, Ted the other, sat erect and composed, her fatigued, red eyes concealed behind a nearly opaque ebony veil. The remainder of the pew, meanwhile, was filled with sisters: Jack's — Eunice, Jean, and Pat — as well as Jackie's — Lee Radziwill — all so youthful it was hard to fathom that they were attending the funeral of a husband, brother, peer.

Behind the Kennedy family, a staggering array of the world's powerful, accomplished, wealthy, famous (and not), headed up by newly sworn-in President Lyndon Johnson and his wife Lady Bird, were packed into every conceivable corner of St. Matthew's. Rushing to Washington, they had gathered on this brilliant, sun-saturated fall day to sit in somber attendance on the lone casket in the center aisle — with the exception, that is, of French President, Charles De Gaulle. Having insisted on honoring the French tradition of standing during a Requiem Mass, the six-foot, five-inch De Gaulle loomed, a Gallic lighthouse in the storm, over those around him — ignoring FBI warnings that (due to threats on his life) he presented the perfect target for an assassin's bullet.

To the millions transfixed on the television coverage, the seating arrangement undoubtedly seemed perfectly choreographed. But that was hardly the case. As mourners filed into the cathedral, confusion reigned. Not having buried a sitting president since Franklin Roosevelt in 1945, the woefully unprepared State Department had scrambled to stage an event of this magnitude and speed. With only three days to issue — and RSVP — invitations, the harried officials had no idea which dignitaries would actually show up, resulting in a rash of security and diplomatic *faux pas* — my own included. Overwhelmed, the ushers and Secret Service accidentally sat two former presidents — Harry Truman and Dwight Eisenhower — on a side, not center aisle, unable to be seen. Consequently, I left both out of my salutation.

But then, I wasn't supposed to be standing here in the first place. Had the Kennedys followed church protocol, it would have been the archbishop of Washington, Archbishop Patrick J. O'Boyle not I — a chancellor serving under him — giving the eulogy. In truth, my seven years as the auxiliary bishop of the Washington Archdiocese placed me squarely on the lower end of the ecclesiastical totem pole. And, per church hierarchy, the archbishop of Washington should have been asked to deliver the eulogy for the archdiocese's most important Catholic. But Jackie had other ideas. Because of my long-standing, personal relationship with her husband, she sent word through Sargent Shriver, husband of Jack's sister Eunice, that she wanted me to deliver the remarks. And it was definitely her call. Behind Jackie's gentle, demure demeanor was a will of iron, readily enforced, if necessary, in the strongest possible terms. The First Lady wanted neither a lengthy service nor sermon — ten minutes at most. So when Sarge pointed out (during a family discussion) that, technically, it was Archbishop O'Boyle's job, she dug in her heels.

"Absolutely not," she snapped, dismissing his second attempt. "It's going to be Hannan or no one. If they ask, just tell them I got hysterical and you couldn't straighten me out." Though incredibly honored, if flabbergasted, to learn of her decision, it put me in a real bind — immediately alleviated by the graciousness of Archbishop O'Boyle. Deep down, he must have been deeply hurt at being passed over in this sacred responsibility for his auxiliary bishop. But, if so, he shared none of his personal disappointment with me. From start to finish, he was completely noble.

As fate would have it, the Archbishop and I had been together in Rome, attending the second session of the Vatican Council, when I heard the terrible news that President Kennedy had been assassinated. As a member of the American Bishops Committee, I conducted a daily afternoon press conference, along with a panel of U.S. bishops and church experts, for the hundreds of media covering the Council. That day, after finishing, I headed back to the Hotel Eden. Walking into the lobby, I was assaulted by the palpable rage and frustration in the air. Spotting me, an elegant Frenchman, trailed by four others, rushed up, asking in perfect English, "What does this mean? This tragedy is an outrage. Is it a Communist plot?"

"What happened?" I asked.

"President Kennedy was killed. He was shot. Did the Communists do it?" Before I could answer, a second voice piped in, and a third, all echoing the same question, same lament.

Immobilized by inertia, I could not, did not, want to believe what I was hearing. My first instinct was to deny. Surely, there had been a mistake... these people didn't know what they were talking about! But their anger was real — and convincing. "No... no... I don't know who did it," I finally stammered. "As you can see, I'm coming from a session of the Council." We stood in bewildered silence. Seconds later, as if snapping out of a trance, I suddenly became aware of other clusters of puzzled, panicked faces... the instantaneous camaraderie being forged among strangers, united by their need to know: *"Who did it? Was it the Communists?"*

Threading through the crowd to the reception desk, several people pulled at my cassock sleeve, saying, "Very sorry, very sorry." Behind his desk, the clerk forked over my key in mute sympathy. Stepping into the elevator, I was alone, as other guests apparently opted to stay downstairs in the information flow. Entering my room, I saw the telephone was flashing, indicating a message was waiting. It was my brother Bill in Washington, D.C. "I guess you've heard the news," he said. "Get the hell back here as soon as you can."

Hanging up, I started to dial Archbishop O'Boyle at the Hotel Michelangelo near St. Peter's Square, when several chambermaids, awash in tears, appeared at my half-open door. Desperate to express their astonished sorrow to the only American available, they broke down. "He was such a good man," they cried, repeating, chant-like, *Buono, buono, buono.* Sobbing, they stood rooted to the spot, unable to move. It took all I had not to cry with them. "Please pray for him and his wife," I got out before becoming overwhelmed myself. Slowly closing the door, I wept silently and alone.

Despite the jammed communications, I finally got hold of Archbishop O'Boyle, who had been trying to reach me. Assuring him that I'd get our plane tickets, I set off. The taxi driver, indeed, everyone at the travel office, posed the same questions again: "Who killed him? Wasn't it the Communists?" (This consensus of Italian opinion was such that the Soviet embassy was forced to issue an emphatic denial of any participation.)

Fortunately, the travel office clerk was very sympathetic. Not that it mattered, frankly. Though I loathe to do so normally, in this instance I was more than willing to use whatever pull I had. Recognizing my urgency, the clerk quickly secured two tickets. Back at the hotel, I tried to telephone my rectory at St. Patrick's Church in Washington, but the lines were solidly tied up.

Cabling notification of our arrival time, I raced to the Hotel Michelangelo where the Archbishop was in a state of total shock. Assuming the funeral would be held at St. Matthew's Cathedral, a few blocks from the White House, Archbishop O'Boyle finally notified Sargent Shriver that we were en route. With funeral plans still being determined, Sarge said that he'd be in touch once we landed. Knowing that capable, trustworthy Sarge was our contact was a great relief. He would get things done properly with the Archbishop.

Finally, boarding a plane full of other confused foreign officials, heading to Washington for the same reason, we took off. Two Moroccans, swathed in distinctively elaborate, Middle Eastern garb, sat in front of us, while the seat across the aisle almost swallowed up the diminutive Emperor of Ethiopia, Haile Selassie. One Swiss official, part of a congregation representing Western European countries, told us that he, more or less, got ordered to make the trip. Dining in a hotel the night of the assassination, several guests had accosted him. "Why are you here?" they demanded. "Aren't you going to Washington to represent us at the funeral of President Kennedy?"

At thirty-five thousand feet, my conversation with the Archbishop focused on Jackie and the family, whom we feared, given the brutal, public nature of Kennedy's death, might well be inconsolable. Eventually, the Archbishop dozed off, but I couldn't. Though physically exhausted, my adrenalized mind wouldn't shut down. Wide eyed in the darkness of the cabin, Jack Kennedy's Boston accent dancing in my head, I leaned back against the head rest, involuntarily rewinding the series of events that brought this extraordinary man — and his equally extraordinary wife — into my life.

Back in Washington

By the time we landed at Dulles Airport — teeming with foreign officials desperate for information — it was the evening of November 22. Spotting a particularly desolate soul, dressed in the flowing robes of a Muslim, I asked, in my halting French, if I could help. As it turned out, he had flown from Morocco with neither hotel reservations nor instructions as to the funeral's time and place. Seeking out a U.S. representative, we discovered there were only two beleaguered, uninformed State Department officials, surrounded by indignant potentates and a gang of reporters demanding to know why things weren't better organized. Offering to drop my new acquaintance at a hotel where he would have to fend for himself, we rounded up the Archbishop and took off.

It was around nine when we finally arrived at our rectory, much to the relief of the housekeepers and priests who had been fielding a barrage of questions. Sending them to bed, I took over. Two hours later, answering most inquiries, but barely unpacked, I got a call from Archbishop O'Boyle. His voice was tired, his words to the point: "I have been in touch with Sargent Shriver who is representing Jackie and the rest of the family in making arrangements for the funeral. Jackie wishes you to give the eulogy. Somebody will be in the sacristy at ten thirty tomorrow morning to give you material that's to be included." You could've blown me over with a feather — or less — given my exhausted state. I started to protest, but the Archbishop interrupted. "You'd better get to work." "Of course. Thank you," I replied. The honor at being chosen was quickly eclipsed by its reality. I had only a few hours to prepare what may well be one of the most important homilies of my life.

Fortunately, I couldn't dwell on it. By the time I sat down to even think about what to say — much less to whom I'd be saying it — I drew an emotional blank. With everything happening so quickly, my dominant feeling was still disbelief. Moreover, I'd picked up a ferocious sinus infection. My brothers Bill and Jerry feared that whatever I said might not be understood anyway. With all these strikes against me, I'd certainly have to rely on the Holy Spirit.

Protocol demanded that a speaker, delivering a major address, acknowledge the dignitaries in their proper order. But who would be present? I certainly didn't know, and at this hour, how could I find out? Who would have the list? From what I'd seen at the airport, even the State Department didn't know.

The key to an effective, edifying homily is knowing your audience; only then can you come up with what they need to hear. But that intelligence wasn't available. Surely, the fellow I was meeting in the sacristy the next morning would fill me in on everything I needed to know. "Right now, Hannan," I thought, "the only thing you *CAN* control about tomorrow is what you write and say. So get going." I started making notes, hoping that the congregation would realize I hadn't had much time to prepare.

The first thing that came to mind was Jack's Inaugural Address — the ideals and character espoused in those magnificent few words. But a eulogy should also speak to his distinct, powerful personality, notable to anyone who ever saw, heard, or met him — as many at the service probably had. Moreover, how could I say anything vaguely personal without divulging that I was a close friend, known, albeit, to only a handful of insiders? Tomorrow my audience would extend far beyond the walls of St. Matthew's Cathedral to millions of Americans as well as the citizens of over ninety countries, each seeking solace in the words of the funeral's participants. Most importantly, I had no real idea what Jackie and the family expected.

By midnight, it was clear that I simply wouldn't have time to come up with a good, lengthy sermon. So I returned to my original notion: let the president speak for himself, in his own stirring words: the Inaugural Address of January 20, 1961. On the day ending his presidency forever, I would cite passages from the day it had begun. Lyndon Johnson may have taken the oath, but to everyone else in that Cathedral, John Kennedy was still the President of the United States — at least for a few more hours. Since I couldn't possibly write anything better, why even try to outdo what Jack had done so brilliantly? I started scribbling notes. When I looked up it was after 1:00 a.m. If I had any hope of fighting off sinus congestion and jet lag in time for the funeral, I had to get some sleep.

At ten the next morning I walked into the controlled bedlam of St. Matthew's Cathedral. The church, tightly cordoned off by the Secret Service, FBI, Army, and local police, prompted Father Hartman, an assistant priest at the Cathedral, to approach me at the door. "Would you please get me into the rectory?" he pleaded. "I came outside to meet someone, and the Secret Service won't let me back because my name's not on the list." Vouching for my friend to the suspicious agent manning the door, we entered together. As promised, a representative of the State Department, standing in for the president's family, showed up in the sacristy at ten thirty, carrying an envelope of scriptural quotations used by Kennedy in his recent speeches. Since the list was short, I decided to include all of them in the eulogy. But now we had a bigger problem.

Archbishop O'Boyle, Bobby Kennedy, Mrs. John F. Kennedy, and myself at Arlington National Cemetery following President John F. Kennedy's funeral Mass.

"Where's the list of guests for the salutation?" I asked. "Besides the Kennedy family, I don't know who's coming."

The man just looked at me. "There is no list," he said, weary and exasperated. "We've been overwhelmed by calls, telegrams, and questions but, frankly, we just don't have the personnel to handle something this huge."

"Well, do you at least know which kings and heads of state are coming?"

"No, but you'll be standing at the cathedral door, waiting for the casket," he replied. "The principal guests will be walking behind Jackie, so just watch and see who they are. That's all I can say." It was almost as shocking as hearing that I'd be delivering the eulogy! How could I ever be expected to identify kings and heads of state whom I had never met or seen? Suddenly, a trick, picked up during decades of speechmaking on the D.C. banquet circuit — that is, memorizing the State Department's entire protocol list, delineating the rank of every member of the administration, judiciary, and Congress — popped to mind. Would that help? Probably not when it came to ascertaining the rank of kings, ambassadors, and heads of state.

Nevertheless, that was now my job. The Secret Service and FBI couldn't help; they were too busy restricting entry into the sanctuary. The only people authorized to be admitted were Boston Cardinal Richard Cushing, principal celebrant of the Mass by virtue of his longtime association with the Kennedys; Archbishop O'Boyle; Archbishop Egidio Vagnozzi, the Apostolic Delegate of Pope John XXIII; an auxiliary bishop from New York; the master of ceremonies, Father Walter Schmitz, S.S.; the altar servers; and myself. But that wasn't the case. Several adventurous "chaplains" attached to American Legion delegations had boldly talked their way into the sacristy — and the Secret Service wanted me to get rid of them. Extending our apologies, "so very sorry, these seats are taken," most cooperated, especially when I herded them into pews offering a good view of the altar. However, one recalcitrant Legionnaire chaplain refused to budge. "My group paid my way from Iowa to attend this Mass," he railed. "And they expect me to be seated in the sanctuary." This called for the "Big Guns." Motioning to the gray-suited Secret Service agents, I turned to our intruder. "Sorry, they're in charge. I have no authority over them." Faced with a god momentarily even more menacing than his own, the chaplain reluctantly capitulated.

The Secret Service had reason to be touchy. Not only had a president of the United States just been killed; but the previous day, there had been another scare during a Cathedral walk-through by FBI agents. Meticulously scouring the church's expansive dome, they happened upon a tangle of suspicious wires with no beginning nor end. Several hours of heightened anxiety later, agents nailed the "culprits": two mischievous Cathedral schoolboys. Happening upon the dome's entrance and stray wire, simultaneously, the pair simply dragged it with them and left it there. (Much of the Cathedral was a security nightmare.

The cavernous basement with its convoluted heating system — boilers generating hot air, delivered via pipes and floor openings — was rife with hiding places for bombs.)

With the "undocumented" visitors finally settled, we faced another dilemma: Archbishop Egidio Vagnozzi, the Apostolic Delegate of the Holy Father, had vanished. Futilely, we cased the Cathedral until the master of ceremonies signaled the approach of the official mourners. Sprinting to the front of St. Matthew's, we slid into position to receive the body of the president of the United States. Minutes later, I caught my first heart-wrenching glimpse of the iconic panorama, forever after burned into our consciousness: the riderless black stallion ... the boots slung backward ... the regal, horse-drawn caisson which, having once borne the body of Abraham Lincoln, now carried the flag-draped casket of yet another slain president, John Kennedy.

Following closely behind, escorting their husband and brother, Jacqueline, Bobby, and Ted Kennedy led the procession of luminaries walking down Connecticut Avenue toward the Cathedral, including President Lyndon Johnson and Lady Bird, and . . . was it possible? . . . our lost Apostolic Delegate to the United States, Archbishop Vagnozzi, dressed in civilian clothes, per his contention that, as the Pope's representative, he was ambassador as well as priest. Crowding both sides of the concourse, taking in this grave spectacle, the splendor of the fall season radiating on them, thousands of forlorn spectators, united in respectful silence, stood watching.

Most Rev. Philip M. Hannan, D.D.

will please present this card at

St. Matthews Cathedral
Rhode Island Ave. NW. between 17th and 18th Sts.

Monday, November 25th, 1963
at twelve noon

NOT TRANSFERABLE

Entrance card to the funeral of President Kennedy

As this extraordinary assemblage descended on St. Matthew's, this church where I grew up — partially funded by my Irish immigrant father, site of my own First Communion — I was suddenly awash in nostalgia, recalling my days as an altar boy for its creator, Monsignor Thomas Sim Lee, a descendant of Robert E. Lee. Determined to build, mere blocks from the White House, a Cathedral worthy of celebrating Mass for the someday first Catholic president, Monsignor Lee had done just that. And, now, that first Catholic president was being brought to his final Mass, albeit Requiem, at the Monsignor's Cathedral. "May the good God grant," I prayed, "that there never will be such a funeral again."

Watching it all, I was filled with an unexpected rush of pride — and apology. As much as I'd admired and believed in my friend, I had greatly underestimated Jack's power and influence, so evident now in the admiration and love so freely being exhibited toward this man, this President, who had touched the minds and hearts of rulers and citizens alike. But sentiment would have to step behind the task at hand; that is, memorizing the names and countries of those approaching.

In front of us, the casket, precision-lifted by representatives from each of the military services, was being carried, step by step, up to the Cathedral door and down the center aisle, the measured, military gait of the pallbearers announcing the dramatic finality of this journey. Once the coffin was securely resting near the sanctuary, Cardinal Cushing stepped forward, pronouncing the prayer for the reception of the body. As world leaders and Irish maids alike settled into their seats, Cardinal Cushing began the celebration of the Mass in ancient Latin, its sublime and sacred character so very apropos for this stellar, international congregation.

All too soon, however, it was time for the eulogy. Passing by Archbishop O'Boyle, I may have looked composed but I was not. Though humbled to be fulfilling Mrs. Kennedy's request, I was plagued with the feeling that Archbishop O'Boyle should be ascending the pulpit stairs. Instead, it was I, by far the youngest bishop in the sanctuary, poised to address the most august audience in the history of the Cathedral at a service of unequalled drama and significance.

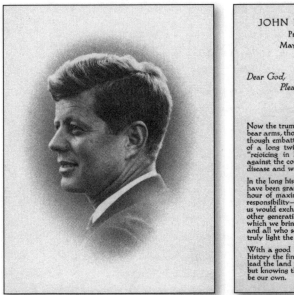

Prayer card from the funeral of President John F. Kennedy

The Eulogy

Once behind the pulpit, I relaxed a little. At its best, speaking from a pulpit creates unity and friendliness with those to whom you are talking. Taking a breath, I recited the salutation (per my afore-learned State Department protocol) without a hitch. Having decided to open with the President's favorite scriptural passages, I began reading from Proverbs and the Prophet Joel which had been included in Kennedy's dinner speech in Houston, the night before he was killed. "Your old men shall dream dreams, and your young men shall see visions…. And where there is no vision the people perish" (Joel 2:28, Prov 29:18). Moving

```
    MOST REVEREND PHILIP M. HANNAN
    Auxiliary Bishop of Washington, D. C.
    Saint Patrick's Rectory
    619 Tenth Street, Northwest
    Washington 1, D. C.

         Your Eminence, Cardinal Cushing, Your Excellency the

    Most Reverend Representative of the Holy Father, Your Excellency

    The Archbishop and Bishops, Mrs. Kennedy and children, members

    of the family, The President of the United States and distinguished

    Heads of State, and Representives of the Heads of State,

    distinguished friends of President Kennedy all:

         It was thought that the most appropriate commemoration

    of the heart-breaking event would be the expression of President

    John Fitzgerald Kennedy's ideals and sources of inspiration in

    his own words.

    Reading--Biblical Passages:

         President John Fitzgerald Kennedy was fond of quoting

    the Holy Bible.

         In the last dinner of his life, in Houston, Texas, last

    Thursday night, he applied to a friend--as it should be applied to

    him--this combination of passages from the Proverbs and the Prophecy

    of Joel:

         "Your old men shall dream dreams, your young men shall see
         visions. . . (and) where there is no vision, the people
         perish."

         And to those who shared his vision, in this land and

    abroad, he had said two months ago to the United Nations:

         "Let us complete what we have started; for, as the Scriptures
         tell us, 'No man who puts his hand to the plow and looks
         back is fit for the Kingdom of God.'
```

Original transcript of my homily for President John F. Kennedy's funeral. Requests for copies of it came from all over the world.

on, I referred to the President's speech to the United Nations on September 20, 1963: "Let us complete what we have started," I quoted, "for as the Scriptures tell us, no man who puts his hand to the plow and looks back is fit for the kingdom of God." It was the evocative third chapter of Ecclesiastes, however, that provoked audible sobs. "There is an appointed time for everything, and a time for every affair under the heavens," I slowly recited, "A time to be born, and a time to die. A time to plant, and a time to uproot the plant. A time to kill, and a time to heal. A time to tear down, and a time to build. A time to weep, and a time to laugh…" But today there could be no laughter. "Oh, how our country,"

At this time of sorrow and burden he would have us remember the passages from Joshua and Isaiah he had used in accepting the Presidential nomination:

"Be strong and of good courage; be not afraid, neither be thou dismayed. . . . They that wait upon the Lord shall renew their strength; they shall mount up with wings as eagles; they shall run and not be weary."

Finally, in his last hours, President Kennedy had prepared these words for Dallas and for the nation:

"The righteousness of our cause must always underlie our strength. For as was written long ago: 'unless the Lord keep the city, he watcheth in vain that keepeth it.'"

Ecclesiastes, Chapter 3

There is an appointed time for everything, and a time for every affair under the heavens. 2. A time to be born, and a time to die; a time to plant, and a time to uproot the plant. 3. A time to kill, and a time to heal; a time to tear down, and a time to build. 4. A time to weep, and a time to laugh; a time to mourn, and a time to dance. 5. A time to scatter stones, and a time to gather them; a time to embrace, and a time to be far from embraces. 6. A time to seek, and a time to lose; a time to keep, and a time to cast away. 7. A time to rend, and a time to sew; a time to be silent, and a time to speak. 8. A time to love, and a time to hate; a time of war, and a time of peace. (New Confraternity Ed.)

READING -- INAUGURAL ADDRESS (Excerpts) JANUARY 20, 1961

"We observe today not a victory of party but a celebration of freedom -- symbolizing an end as well as a beginning -- signifying renewal as well as change.

I thought, "in this bleakest moment of its history, needed the spiritual solace and firm promise of that timeless wisdom."

Pausing, I gazed out on the sad, confused eyes staring back as I evoked the powerful words of the principal passage from President John F. Kennedy's Inaugural Address. With its unique gravity, sacred tone, and solemn ending — a restatement of the pledge made by our forefathers — the words brought, full circle, the philosophy Kennedy had promised at the speech's beginning. "We observe today not a victory of a party but a celebration of freedom — symbolizing an end, as well as a beginning — signifying renewal, as well as change. For I have sworn before you and Almighty God the same solemn oath our forebears prescribed nearly a century and three quarters ago." I paused, filled with a sense of privilege to read aloud Kennedy's iconic, final challenge on the

-3-

"Let the word go forth from this time and place, to friend and foe alike, that the torch has been passed to a new generation of Americans -- born in this century, tempered by war, disciplined by a hard and bitter peace, proud of our ancient heritage -- and unwilling to witness or permit the slow undoing of those human rights to which this nation has always been committed, and to which we are committed today at home and around the world.

"Let every nation know, whether it wishes us well or ill, that we shall pay any price, bear any burden, meet any hardship, support any friend, oppose any foe to assure the survival and the success of liberty.

"Let both sides unite to heed in all corners of the earth the command of Isaiah -- to 'undo the heavy burdens . . . (and) let the oppressed go free.'

"All this will not be finished in the first one hundred days. Nor will it be finished in the first one thousand days, nor in the life of this Administration, nor even perhaps in our lifetime on this planet. But let us begin.

"In your hands, my fellow citizens, more than mine, will rest the final success or failure of our course. Since this country was founded, each generation of Americans has been summoned to give testimony to its national loyalty. The graves of young Americans who answered the call to service surround the globe.

unique responsibility of being an American. "And so, my fellow Americans, ask not what your country can do for you, ask what you can do for your country. With a good conscience our only sure reward, with history the final judge of our deeds, let us go forth to lead the land we love, asking His blessing and His help but knowing that here on earth God's work must truly be our own."

Looking up, I saw a congregation momentarily uplifted. Having heard again their President's visionary proclamation for our country, their faces registered both justifiable pride and reverent acceptance. Descending the pulpit stairs, I was struck by my own sense of inadequacy in the face of such a monumental occasion. However, lest I forget that this was also the funeral of an iconoclastic Irishman, I was reminded by another of the breed. Returning to my seat, I passed in front of Cardinal Cushing who, breaking the silence

4.

"Now the trumpet summons us again -- not as a call to bear arms, though arms we need -- not as a call to battle, though embattled we are -- but a call to bear the burden of a long twilight struggle, year in and year out, 'rejoicing in hope, patient in tribulation' -- a struggle, against the common enemies of men: tyranny, poverty, disease and war itself.

"In the long history of the world, only a few generations have been granted the role of defending freedom in its hour of maximum danger. I do not shrink from this responsibility -- I welcome it. I do not believe that any of us would exchange places with any other people or any other generation. The energy, the faith, the devotion which we bring to this endeavor will light our country and all who serve it -- and the glow from that fire can truly light the world.

"And so, my fellow Americans: ask not what your country can do for you -- ask what you can do for your country.

"With a good conscience our only sure reward, with history the final judge of our deeds, let us go forth to lead the land we love, asking His blessing and His help, but knowing that here on earth God's work must truly be our own."

whispered *sotto voce*: "Not bad." Jack would have loved it. (In the weeks and months afterwards, I received requests from all over the world, asking for a copy of my eulogy, which I gladly sent. Theodore Sorensen, special counsel to the President, who worked with Kennedy on the Inaugural Speech, sent an extremely thoughtful letter. "The dignity and grace of your participation in last week's services will be remembered by many of us for a long time," he wrote. "As you may know, I had a hand in putting together the material you read — and, while my work is not usually used by Bishops, no one could have lent it more distinction and eloquence.")

At the end of the Mass, the pallbearers reclaimed the casket, carrying their charge, followed by Jackie, Caroline, and John-John, back out the grand doors of St. Matthew's. As they lifted the flag-draped coffin into position on the caisson, I noticed Jackie bending down to whisper in John-John's ear. With a slight nudge from his mother, the little boy in the blue coat tentatively stepped forward. Raising his tiny right hand to his forehead, he snapped history's most famously poignant salute to his father. Released from restraint, the crowds erupted in an earthquake of pent-up emotion: groans, yelps, uncontrollable sobbing. Though photographers and TV cameras, naturally, zoomed in on John Jr., most missed the equally moving shot of regular human beings, disassembling in pain. Forty years later, my mental snapshot of that moment, a searing image of indescribable anguish, remains stunningly vivid.

Slowly, deliberately, the majestic funeral procession, with its Green Beret military guard, began its long, elegant procession past the thousands of bystanders packing the streets and bridge leading to Arlington National Cemetery. Reaching its final destination, the casket was lifted off the caisson by the precision-perfect American soldiers, who, in perfect lockstep, carried the casket to the mechanical platform suspended over the newly dug grave. Moments later, Cardinal Cushing stepped forward to read the prayers of interment, followed by a detachment of Irish soldiers whose stirring rendition of the traditional, "Military Salute to a Fallen Leader" harkened back to the heritage of this beloved Irish-American, himself now in the pantheon of tragedy-plagued Irish heroes.

When they were finished, Cardinal Cushing lightly touched Jackie's arm: "Now for Bobby's remarks," he murmured, adhering to the funeral plans approved by the First Lady. But she didn't budge. "No," she said quietly, "No." Thinking she had simply forgotten the lineup, the Cardinal repeated his verbal cue. "No," Jackie repeated, her tone firm and irrevocable. "No. I said, 'No.'" With unerring instinct, Jackie had correctly judged that enough had been said. Anything else would be anticlimactic. Adhering to his sister-in-law's directive, Bobby unobtrusively slipped a piece of paper back into his suit pocket. Moving purposefully away from the others, the former First Lady walked over to the unlit Eternal Flame where, handed a torch, she reached down and ignited the flame. The impact was immediate, as a collective murmer rippled through the crowd.

After returning to her place, the Army officer in charge of the interment detail gently presented Jackie with the casket's crisply folded American flag. Taking our cue, Cardinal Cushing, Archbishop O'Boyle, and I approached Mrs. Kennedy to offer our own final words of condolence. Exhausted, her lovely face streaked with dried tears, she, nevertheless, clasped my hand. "Thanks for the sermon," she said. "I thought it was great." My own swirl of emotion did not permit a response.

Offering condolences to Mrs. John F. Kennedy at her husband's funeral

It was after five when, after dropping Cardinal Cushing and Archbishop O'Boyle off at St. Patrick's rectory, I finally made it back to St. Matthew's to retrieve my civilian clothes. As my limousine reached the corner of Rhode Island Avenue and 17th Street, I noticed a lone, worn-out soldier still standing duty, left behind, no doubt, by his detail leader, who had forgotten him and returned to the barracks. Quiet and dejected-looking, the soldier reflected the confused feelings and loss of innocence that many of us shared — the confused feelings of a bereaved nation. At home, I telephoned his outfit. This weary guardsman could finally stand down.

That night, slumped in my chair at the rectory, my fatigued mind tried to sort out the jumble of paradoxes, at least as I knew them, in the life and death of John Kennedy. On the one hand, he was brilliant, witty, charming, a man navigating life with the utmost confidence. Though dominating every situation, he was never domineering. On the other hand, Jack was a complicated soul, incredibly talented, yet, flawed, categorizing his actions in a manner often hurtful to those who loved him. Though he never had to worry about money, he had forged a close bond with the poor, especially poor blacks, whose love and admiration for their President was visceral and responsive, thanks to his knack for being solicitous without condescension. Handsome and virile, he was attractive to women; a symbol (by virtue of his war record) of bravery and courage to men.

Above all, Jack challenged everyone — especially the young — to be his or her best self. "Ask not what your country can do for you, ask what you can do for your country" had called to action the children whose fathers fought and won World War II, challenging them to do something important with that hard-earned freedom. I, personally, knew scores of engineers, architects, lawyers, and plumbers who, infused with Kennedy's optimism, went on to get a masters, doctorates — or open their own businesses. Unlike no president before him, Jack Kennedy instilled in Americans that most imperative of all things: hope.

Though I was immensely privileged to have been his trusted friend and consultant, even more meaningful was having had a priest's relationship with the President. God knows, we didn't always agree on religious matters. But he never tried to change or twist my decisions. Flashing back to that whirlwind presidential campaign, I smiled, recalling his long, involved questions on church policy . . . my, undoubtedly, equally long-winded answers which he always accepted. We might argue like the devil but no verbal skirmish was ever disrespectful of either of our identities. Oh, how I would miss that intellectual parrying — miss my friend, Jack. (Even now, a half century later, I still marvel that God saw fit to bring John Kennedy and me into each other's lives at that particular moment in America's history. In the end, I have only the most inexpressible wonder and gratitude for having enjoyed such a remarkable relationship with such a remarkable man — one of America's truly great leaders.)

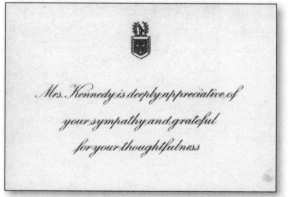

Thank you note from Jacqueline B. Kennedy

The next morning, my usual ride from the rectory to the chancery presented a startling, if reassuring, example of our incredibly resilient system of government. Motoring past 1600 Pennsylvania Avenue, there were no crowds, demonstrations, nor protests — merely two gardeners, raking leaves, on the White House lawn. The sight recalled the excited, worried questions that I'd encountered in Rome a few days earlier: "Is it a Communist coup?" "Will there be an attempt to overthrow the government?" Despite our national broken heart, the machinery of democracy neither fell apart nor ground to a halt, providing, instead, one of the finest hours in our national history.

Reinterment of Babies

Nine days after her husband's funeral, I got a call from Jackie who was still living in the White House. She had decided to bring the bodies of the children whom she had lost — a stillborn daughter in 1956 and Patrick, who died three days after his birth in August of 1963 — from the Kennedy Family cemetery in Hyannis, Massachusetts, to join their father in Arlington Cemetery.

"Could you be ready on Wednesday (December 4)," she asked, "for the reinterment of the bodies of our two babies at Arlington?"

"Certainly."

"All right," Jackie said. "It will be very secret. An Army staff car will pick you up at the rectory. The driver will know where to take you but not why you're there. Expect him about eight o'clock."

Jackie was insistent that only a very small group attend the ceremony: her mother, Janet Auchincloss; sister, Lee Radziwill; and three or four other close friends. Though I thought about suggesting she increase the number, I decided against it. A larger ceremony, recalling Jack's so-recent funeral, might be too hard on her. And, of course, I told no one, not even Archbishop O'Boyle. At the appointed hour the car arrived, and I got in with the driver. "Do you know where to take me?" "Yes sir." Heading towards Arlington, I asked the young soldier where he was from. "I don't like talking about it," he replied haltingly. "I'm not proud. I'm from Dallas."

Reaching our rendezvous, just outside the gates of Arlington Cemetery, I found Jackie, Lee, and the few friends who could fit in a limousine (Caroline and John were left back at the White House). Getting into her car, I drove with Jackie to the Kennedy plot. "Since I wanted to keep this secret," she explained, "I've spread the rumor that the reinterment will be tomorrow at noon." (Her plan worked.)

Driving as close as possible to where Jack now lay, we parked and got out. The sight of two such tiny, white caskets (holding such tiny, little bodies) was truly heart-wrenching. Before starting the ceremony, Jackie and I placed each on the ground near her husband's fresh grave. Seeing the three — father, daughter, son — back together again, albeit in death, was a stark reminder of the Herculean effort made by their parents to bring these babies to term. Both Kennedys desperately wanted more children and, losing these dear, little ones, had only increased the value of the two who survived. Though this tender scene cried out for soliloquy — conscious of Jackie's fragile emotional condition — I decided to offer only the prescribed, short prayers of the ceremony.

When we were finished, Jackie's sigh was deep and audible. Turning to me, she began talking as if her life depended on it — which perhaps it did. In a little under two weeks, the world as this courageous thirty-four-year-old woman knew it had spun out of control on its axis. That she was even here tonight, able to momentarily put aside her own exquisite suffering to bring together her deceased family in their final resting place, was nothing short of a miracle. Trying to understand, to come to terms with this senseless tragedy, would take a lot of talking — and I was more than happy to listen.

Walking back to her limousine, she asked if she could have the ritual book and stole that I'd used for the service. As I gladly handed them over, they seemed to unleash a torrent of spiritual concerns that only a priest could possibly help her work through: Why had God let this happen? What could possibly be the reason? Jack had so much more to give, was just hitting his stride. What was our destiny in heaven? Did I think he was there? How would the children ever understand? What should she tell them?

Eventually the conversation turned more personal. How was she to carry on? With the public's feelings about her, how would she ever be able to live even a semblance of a normal life? She didn't disdain those who tried to see and touch her, as if doing so would somehow secure a souvenir of the President. She understood that she was forever destined to have to deal with public opinion, the differing, not always flattering, feelings toward her. But she did not want to be a public figure. In one pull of a trigger, her identity as both wife and First Lady had been wiped out. And though she appreciated the good will and love being lavished on her, she desperately wanted to be private, someone whose character would be shaped by herself and her family. Already, however, it was clear that the world viewed her, not as a woman, but as a symbol of its own pain, expecting her to carry a torch not of her own making.

The more she talked, the more that Jackie's real feelings surfaced, her comments frank and to the point. Particularly galling, she confided, was the public's surprise at her stoicism while preparing — and during — the funeral. Why had so many columnists marveled at her composure? It was the least she could do for Jack. He would have expected nothing less. Given the presence of her mother and sister, I thought it might be more appropriate if she and I, privately, continued our conversation at my rectory or the White House. But Jackie was undeterred. "I don't like to hear people say that I am poised and maintaining a good appearance," she said, resentfully. "I am not a movie actress. I am a Lee . . . of Virginia." Just then, in a far gloaming, the imposing statue of General Robert E. Lee came into view, a fitting reminder that those with Lee's blood in their veins did not crumble in the face of adversity.

It was a strength she would need more than ever. Jacqueline Kennedy, America's most glamorous First Lady, was now the most famous widow — and single mother — on the planet. Yet even as she mourned the end of her old life, she was determined to be in full control of creating a new, secure one for her children and herself. Besides grappling with the death of a man whom I believe that she truly and deeply loved — who literally died in her arms, his blood and brain matter spattered on her lady-like white gloves — the sheer rawness of profound loss was finally beginning to set in.

That evening, as we strolled together through the beautiful if melancholy reality of Arlington, death was much on her mind — not only that of her husband, but also the children they had conceived, and lost, together. More urgently than ever before, any kind of afterlife — the Church's view as well as her own — weighed heavily. Having been traumatically, involuntarily wrenched from her known reality, Jackie Kennedy was suddenly faced with the stark reality of her next chapter: Life after Jack. Life alone.

Our conversation that evening marked the beginning of many such discussions between Jackie and me. Aside from our separate, if newer relationship, her trust in me sprang from the knowledge that Jack also set store in my counsel. As a result, I was one of the few people to whom she could turn to express the desolation and despair felt over the loss of her husband. In the months following the assassination, Jackie frequently put her agony and confusion down on paper in handwritten letters. While candidly describing her tumult of emotions, her words always reconfirmed a deep love for her husband, the loneliness without him.

Moreover, they illustrate the degree to which her life had been, inextricably, intertwined with his. Jack was her future. Having never realistically visualized an existence without him, she now faced an appalling emptiness. Even more importantly, her letters present a resounding refutation of the rumors and innuendo that the marriage of John and Jacqueline Kennedy was more one of convenience than affection. That is simply not the case — which is why, after much soul searching, I have decided to include some of her correspondence in this book. In the long run, these anguished notes prove, despite opinions to the contrary, that her husband's infidelity had not irreparably harmed their marriage, that theirs was a relationship grounded in deep, emotional conviction until the very end. Moreover, Jackie's letters reveal a tenderness and love which, in my opinion, is almost heroic. Despite all of Jack's faults, Jackie loved her husband — as her words prove.

Sixteen days after the interment of her children, I received this letter from Jackie, dated December 20, 1963 (original punctuation).

Dear Bishop Hannan,

I have meant to write to you for so long — to thank you for the most moving way only you could have read those words at the funeral, to thank you for the book and cloth from the children's burial — for asking me to the December 22 Mass — for your help always to my husband in seeing the world the way he did.

If only I could believe that he could look down and see how he is missed and how nobody will ever be the same without him. But I haven't believed in the child's vision of heaven for a long time. There is no way now to commune with him. It will be so long before I am dead and even then I don't know if I will be reunited with him. Even if I am I don't think you could ever convince me that it will be the way it was while we were married here. Please forgive all this — and please don't try to convince me just yet — I shouldn't be writing this way.

With my deep appreciation.

Respectfully,
Jacqueline Kennedy

One of the greatest regrets of my priesthood is that, in the immediate months following the President's assassination, I did not make even more of an effort to sit down and encourage Jackie to talk about her feelings. Given her condition, it should have been a priority. Of course, as the Auxiliary Bishop of Washington, assistant to Archbishop O'Boyle, pastor of St. Patrick's, and editor of the archdiocesan newspaper, responsible for the weekly editorials — not to mention fielding endless phone calls about Mrs. Kennedy — my hands were incredibly full. In retrospect, however, hiring someone competent to answer those calls, I should have put those hours, instead, into listening and hearing the woman who elicited them. To my eternal regret, I neither had, nor made, enough time to provide Jackie with the spiritual direction that she needed before moving to New York.

Very important letter from Jacqueline Kennedy expressing grief over her husband's death

Two weeks after the assassination, the former First Lady and her children moved out of the White House into Averell Harriman's house on N Street in Georgetown where it became rapidly apparent that any hope of privacy for the three would be impossible. The minute the family took up residence, their home turned into a tourist attraction — buses clogging the street, cameras aimed at every window — hoping to catch a glimpse of Jackie or the children. (The only safe route, as a result, was the back door leading to the alley.) Finally, fed up with this wretched existence, Jackie decided to move to New York, where she found an apartment on 5th Avenue not far from the Convent of the Sacred Heart, where Caroline would attend school.

The typed note she sent, in reply to mine, describing the reasons for her move, was both poignant and sad:

July 27, 1964

Dear Bishop Hannan:

I do want to thank you for your kind letter and the knowledge that I am in your prayers is a great source of comfort to me.

The decision to leave Washington was not easy, however, I do feel it the wisest one for both my children and myself at this time.

I shall never forget all you did to help me through those first tragic days and hope I will see you again before too long.

Respectfully,
Jacqueline Kennedy

After a natural paralysis, following the death of the President, all kinds of projects were proposed to commemorate JFK. In the end, Jackie and the Kennedy family finally approved two: the Kennedy Center in Washington, D.C., and the Kennedy Library at Harvard University in Boston. On both projects, I was asked to be a member and, though honored, knew it impossible to be an active member on more than one. At the insistence of Polly Wiesner, a great friend of Jackie and her mother, Janet Auchincloss, I ultimately chose the Kennedy Center. Eventually, however, Polly — confiding that Jackie favored the Kennedy Library as having more educational value and staying power — asked that I try to convince her differently, as I did whenever we saw each other at meetings for the Center. (Her love for her husband compelled the former First Lady to, at least, be involved in the planning of something celebrating his accomplishments and vision.) At one such gathering, Jackie's own sketches and watercolors of angels (demonstrating undeniable talent) were shown. Subsequently, I suggested that she design the cover for the proposed Register containing the Center's donor names. Jackie loved the idea, promising to follow up since, as she put it, "a simple cover didn't need a designing genius." However, due to her other demands, Jackie's "Memory Book" never came to fruition.

As President Kennedy's May 29 birthday approached, Jackie decided it would be appropriate to pray for the repose of his soul at a Mass — including friends and cabinet members — at St. Matthew's Cathedral. When she asked that I give the homily as well as celebrate the Mass, I decided on the same one

I gave at the Funeral Mass on November 25, 1963. (The Knights of Columbus, meanwhile, having organized their own Memorial Mass for Jack on the same day at the Shrine of the Immaculate Conception, were hurt that no one from the Kennedy family would be present. So, at the behest of Archbishop O'Boyle, I rounded up Sarge and Eunice Shriver who showed up to save the day — and feelings — of all concerned.)

During the Cathedral Mass, Jackie was extremely emotional and teary-eyed. In fact, she was so choked up that, when I approached her to exchange the peace of Christ, she could neither speak nor shake hands. Later, in a hand-written note, she explained that being back in St. Matthew's had simply been overwhelming.

June 1, 1964 (original punctuation):

Dear Bishop Hannan:

I do wish to thank you for the Birthday Mass — for making it so beautiful and so moving — For what you said about President Kennedy.

I am afraid that that — then hearing the Star Spangled Banner sung by the choir — were more than I could bear — and I felt as if time had rolled back 6 months — and I was in the same place in the same church I had been in in November — and all the efforts one had made since then

Letter from Jacqueline Kennedy that describes her state of mind after the assassination of her husband

— to climb a little bit of the way up the hill, had been for nothing — and I had rolled right back down to the bottom of the hill again.

That is why I could not bear to look at you when you came to speak to me — as I did not think I could control my tears — but I wanted you to know that was the reason.

You must know how grateful I am to you every day — for believing in and being a friend of John Kennedy when he was alive — and for bringing meaning out of the despair at his funeral and birthday Masses — and for the night in Arlington with our two children — and for your work now at the Center. You will always be working for all the things he believes in — and I will always know that and be comforted.

I will try so hard to recover a little bit more myself — so that I can be of more use to my children — and just for the years that are left to me — though I hope they won't be too many — And maybe one day soon I will feel strong enough to come and talk to you — With my deepest appreciation.

Respectfully,
Jacqueline Kennedy

In the years following, other than periodic Kennedy Center board meetings — I didn't see Jackie that much which, of course, was my loss. In 1965 when the ground was finally broken for the Kennedy Center — attended by President Johnson — Bobby and Jean Kennedy Smith asked that I give the invocation. (The site, a former public golf course where my brothers and I, using tees fashioned from a handful of sand in a nearby bucket, each played for five cents, carried its own memories for me.) When the ceremony was finished, an enterprising cameraman snapped a photo of our collective profiles — Johnson, Bobby, Jean, and I — dubbing it "Profiles in Courage." Though less interested in the Kennedy Library, I attended one meeting in New York where architect I.M. Pei presented his plans for the building. The curious ensemble of personalities included Chief Justice Earl Warren, who took great pride in

Groundbreaking of the Kennedy Center on December 2, 1965. A photographer snapped a picture of the profiles of Jean Ann Kennedy Smith, me, Robert Kennedy, and President Lyndon B. Johnson – dubbing it "Profiles in Courage."

protecting Jackie, as well as crude types like the Texas donor who, thrilled at being in close proximity to the former First Lady, decided to bullhorn her own pet theories on saving the country. Polite but deliberate, Jackie smoothly cut her off, eliciting such raucous applause that the woman gave up.

Though Jackie never talked to me about her second marriage to Greek shipping magnate Aristotle Onassis in October 1968, I viewed it strictly as one of convenience. Of course, I totally disagreed with her decision (as did most of the world) which no doubt she sensed — perhaps why I wasn't consulted. As a result, I was both surprised and deeply honored when Caroline asked that I preside over her mother's burial following her death from cancer on May 19, 1994, at the age of sixty-four.

After her Funeral Mass at St. Ignatius Loyola Church in New York, Jackie was laid to rest next to her husband, her children, and the Eternal Flame in the Kennedy burial plot in Arlington Cemetery. (On that brutally hot day, I was the only priest in attendance.) Caroline Kennedy Schlossberg, coordinator of her mother's last good-bye, was determined to keep reporters and photographers as far away as possible and did so — a half mile away, to be exact. Like her mother at her father's funeral, Caroline wanted things kept short.

Before we started, I noticed her looking at the interment service's first draft, indicating that President Clinton would "address" the mourners. Scratching out "address," she penciled in "remarks." The last thing Caroline needed was Bill Clinton on a verbal tear. As a result, the grave-side ceremony lasted just over ten minutes: Handsome, young John Jr. read from the fourth chapter of St. Paul's First Letter to the Thessalonians: "We would not have you ignorant, brethren, concerning those who are asleep," he said, his voice strong, "that you may not grieve as others do who have no hope. For since we believe that Jesus died and rose again, even so, through Jesus, God will bring with him those who have fallen asleep" (verses 13-14). Caroline then followed with Psalm 121: "The LORD will keep you from all evil; he will keep your life. The LORD will keep your coming out and your coming in from this time forth and for evermore" (verses 7-8).

When Jackie's beloved children had finished, I offered my own few words, that Jackie, "so dearly beloved, would be so sorely missed" . . . concluding with the prayer of committal: "O, God, the author of the unbought grace of life, you are our promised home. Lead your servant Jacqueline to that home bright with the presence of your everlasting life and love, there to join the other members of the family. Console also those who have suffered the loss of her mortal presence. Give them the grace that will strengthen the bonds of the family and of the national community. May we bear your peace to others until the day we join you and all the saints in your life of endless love and light. We ask this through Christ our Lord. Amen."

Across the Potomac, a bell tolled sixty-four times, once for each year of Jacqueline Bouvier Kennedy Onassis's extraordinary life. The most famous woman in the world was then

Jacqueline Kennedy Onassis is laid to rest in 1994 (Reuters photo)

laid in her final resting place, attended by fewer than a hundred close family and friends — exactly what this private, enigmatic soul would have wished.

CHAPTER 2

In the Beginning

The bed I sleep in today is that in which I was born — as were my sister and six brothers — on May 20, 1913, at 1501 17th Street in Washington, D.C. In those days babies didn't enter the world for free — but almost, as the doctor charged my parents, Lilian and Patrick Hannan, a mere ten bucks for this momentous, in their opinion, house call. Undoubtedly, it was the same fee they forked over for the arrival of each of their other children: my oldest sister Mary as well as my brothers John, Frank, Bill, Tom, Denis, and Jerry. I came along fifth. Given its familial pedigree, our communal birthing bed hardly needed anything further for me to cherish it as I do. However, in 1987 even that sentimental game got upped when Pope John Paul II slept in it for two nights on his historic visit to New Orleans. (In case anyone gets the urge to have a garage sale one day, I put a plaque on the headboard making that clear.) And though I love my bed, I never spent more time in it than my necessary five or six hours of sleep a night.

Like many of the Irish, we were immigrants. My father, Patrick Francis Hannan — P.F. or "the Boss" — was born on March 8, 1870, to an impoverished family in Kilfinny, County Limerick, a village so small it's not even on the map. Since his father was sickly, Patrick attended the local school, a thatched building with a sod floor, for only three years before going to work at the nearby estate of the English Lord Adair where future prospects were slim. Indeed, thanks to the area's English, viciously anti-Catholic landowners, the Irish were legally prohibited from even buying any property — no doubt a driving force prompting my father, at 18, to strike out for America where he subsequently snapped up every piece of land he could lay his hands on.

Patrick Hannan set foot in America on February 29, 1888, just in time for the famously paralyzing blizzard of 1888 (as a result detesting snow for the rest of his life) and signed on as an apprentice plumber for $2.50 per day. Foregoing even streetcar fare by walking three miles to and from work every day, he supported his family on Capitol Hill as well as Ireland on his weekly salary. When he had saved up a modest stake, he went into business on his own — a great success thanks in large part to his philosophy of working hard and saving money.

My mother, Lilian Louise Keefe, born in Washington on August 16, 1881, was the daughter of an Irish immigrant, John Keefe, and a German-descent Lutheran, Louise Kaufman. Three weeks after giving birth, Louise died. Consequently, my mother's father, a successful saloon owner, agreed to have his new daughter raised by her late mother's Lutheran family. Their agreement, a written contract, stipulated that though John Keefe would never seek to regain custody of Lilian, even if he remarried, she was nevertheless to be raised a Catholic. As a result, my mother matriculated at the The Immaculate Conception Academy, ate fish every Friday, attended Mass every First Friday, showed up at Mass every Sunday and attended all the parish missions.

The man who raised her — Uncle Charlie Smithson — was the chief mechanic of the Navy Yard who prided himself, even if forced to arise at two, on making it to work by eight, never having been late to work a day in his life. Growing up we were equally devoted to our relatives, both Catholic and Protestant, with whom we shared many similar values. (Citing moral lessons learned from her Lutheran relatives on sexual morality, for instance, my mother remarked: "I was told that it was better to have ten children on your pillow," she said referring to abortion, "than one on your conscience.")

My parents were married on June 22, 1905, in Washington's Immaculate Conception Church. Considering the early 1900s, the Hannans were a typical Irish Catholic family: our parents were devoted to God, each other, and their eight children, stressing the importance of faith, sacrifice, love, and hard work. Mary, the eldest, and only girl, was the family darling. (According to the Boss, Mary's brilliance, talent, and patience with her unruly brothers were worth at least three boys!) Born on February 25, 1906, Mary weighed only one pound, fourteen ounces. Two months premature, the doctor said there was faint hope that she would survive. But he didn't know the Boss. Refusing to accept his daughter's death sentence without a fight, my father, like the plumber he was, rigged up a radiator heating system in her room to serve as an incubator, raising the temperature to eighty degrees. Bringing in goat's milk to supplement that of my mother, he proved the doctor wrong as Mary got bigger and stronger. A few months later, she was completely out of the woods.

Mary was always a supremely gifted student — beginning in the second grade when she started studying French at the Visitation School, current site of the Mayflower Hotel. Moreover, she was in the vanguard of multitasking, practically raising my youngest brother, Jerry, born in 1922. Sitting on the bottom step of the porch, Mary, crooking a leg around the axle, would rock him to sleep while reading a book and knitting a sweater. Later, after graduating from Trinity College, she became the first laywoman student at Catholic University of America to secure a doctorate, majoring in mathematics, Greek, and Latin. During my seminary years, I leaned a lot on my sister who knew more Latin than most of my professors. When it was time to choose my episcopal motto — "*Caritas Vinculum Perfectionis*" ("Charity Is the Bond of Perfection") — I ran it past just one person: Mary liked it, which was good enough for me. From my perspective, if she wasn't the most wonderful creature God ever made, she was darn close.

Positioned in the middle of seven boys, I was the fourth son. The eldest, John, born in 1907, unfortunately suffered a serious brain injury when he was hit by a truck riding his bicycle — so unnerving our parents that they forbade the rest of us to go anywhere near one. After graduating from high school, John joined my father in the plumbing business. The second son, Frank, born in 1909, graduated from Georgetown Medical School and, following World War II, in thanksgiving for making it out alive, devoted himself to caring for the sick (charging $2 for an office call and $5 for a home visit) with patients ranging from top names in government to anyone who walked in his office door. Bill came along next in 1911, going on to become a prominent D.C. trial lawyer and partner in the law firm of O'Connor and Hannan. Advising me on difficult cases when I was a bishop, Bill refused to take on a divorce — except when I asked that he help a priest who, having married, wished to return to the Church.

Tom followed me in 1915, eventually graduating from Catholic University's School of Engineering; while Denis, born four years later, was inducted into the Army on the first draft following high school graduation, serving in six major World War II campaigns from North Africa to Italy, including the terrible battles near the Benedictine Abbey at Monte Cassino. Returning home, he went into the rug business, eventually working for the federal government. (Although Denis, Frank, and I all served in the Army during WWII, none of us, by the grace of God, was wounded, with Frank hauling home the best show-and-tell piece: a large chunk of the shell that grazed his helmet.) The youngest Hannan, Jerry, born in 1922, was a brilliant student, speeding through elementary school in six years to graduate from Catholic University's School of Science. Exempted from the draft to work at the Carnegie Institution's Geophysical Laboratory, Jerry spearheaded a study that improved the service life of gun barrels.

Sitting around the dining room table, we joked that we had everything covered but an undertaker.

All the boys in the family attended nearby St. John's College High School where the Christian Brothers had developed a college-prep curriculum specializing in science and mathematics (four years) and Latin (two years). I even learned how to type — a skill that came in handy later when I got involved in Catholic journalism. I fared well in my studies (was valedictorian) — along with being cadet captain — and at the end of the four years received a scholarship to Catholic University.

Large families naturally develop into sections. In ours, I teamed up with my older brother Bill, who was good-looking, sociable, a great singer, and never bashful or cautious. We often went to parties and dances together, sometimes double dating. One night, after attending an event at St. John's High School (therefore wearing a cadet corps uniform, gray with scarlet trimming, much like West Point's), we passed by the Mayflower Hotel where a dance for West Point cadets was in progress. "Our uniforms look just like theirs. Let's try to get in," Bill said. Naturally, I tagged along. We made it in until an ominous-looking officer approached and escorted us out. Bill's advice was not always perfect.

Parents

Despite their opposing temperaments, my parents were extraordinary role models. Lilian, dedicated to Catholicism and education, firmly believed that it was the mother who was responsible for the family's direction. Not only did she keep the books for the plumbing business, she cooked, sewed, heard our lessons, gathered us for Rosary, and made sure we were never late to serve Mass on the altar at St. Matthew's. Moreover, she was a gracious hostess, constantly hosting meetings and encouraging women to attend retreats as well as holding dances, since both parents loved to celebrate. (When I was fifteen, declaring it was high time I learned to rhythmically negotiate my feet, she pushed me around the floor of our spacious parlor. "It's important for you to know how to dance," she insisted. "You'll need it.") She was also great with a buck. Her economy in running our home not only guaranteed each of us any education we wanted but also allowed my father to acquire any property he wanted for additional income — not only for himself.

Charity was the supreme virtue of my father's life — starting with his own people. Encouraging any Irish immigrant who crossed his path to buy a home as soon as he got a job, he opened his own Savings and Loan. Each week, these hopeful, newly minted Americans would bring their deposits — and books — to our house where a special box on the hall mantle was reserved as the bank. Once their weekly "board meetings" adjourned, my father deposited their fistfuls of money into their bank. The immigrants trusted my father, and he, in turn, honored their trust. One "regular," a maid pulling in $30 a month, saved enough to buy a small house in Georgetown where, at that time, property was cheap. Upon her death, she left everything to the archdiocese, which sold it for unimaginable profit. Years later, when I was chancellor, another maid whom my father helped purchase two houses on M Street near 18th also willed both to the archdiocese, which turned them around for $250,000. (A lifelong member of the St. Vincent de Paul Society, Dad, opposing those who advocated keeping "a safe balance of funds on hand," always voted to give any that was available to the poor. "The money was given by people who want it used to aid the less fortunate," he argued at the Society's weekly appeals meeting. "Leaving it on a balance sheet doesn't help them.")

Altruism aside, my father certainly wasn't above flashes of Irish temper. When it came to the delays by city bureaucracy in granting his frequent applications for plumbing work, he would take on anybody. "As soon as Frank Hannan comes through the door," district building officers were heard to remark, "there's going to be a fight." They were wrong. The Boss had his fists up before walking through them. When it came to his employees, however, almost anyone was given a chance to prove himself. "I'll always remember," he said to us again and again, "that I was once a greenhorn, needing help."

Growing up, we were surrounded by aunts, uncles, and cousins — all of whom lived within a five-block radius.

The "other" Hannan family, my father's older brother, Will, and his nine children, lived down the block. The operator of a large, prosperous grocery store, Uncle Will saved every penny to bring his family, including my father, over from Ireland. A devout Catholic and member of every known parish organization (including the Nocturnal Adoration, where as group leader he would read aloud every word in the prayer pamphlet, including "Now be seated"), it was almost fitting that Uncle Will was killed crossing 17th Street on his way to confession at St. Matthew's.

My father's sister, meanwhile, Molly Ryan, and her two sons, lived on P Street; while the big house on the corner of 17th and T Street was home to the Boss's other sister, Margaret "Maggie" Collins, her husband, Aeneas Patrick, and their children: Margaret, Mary, Bill, and Aeneas Patrick' — called "Collie" — with whom my brother Paul and I paled around. Smart, fun-loving, and witty, Collie, after serving in the Coast Guard during World War II, signed on at the fledgling National Institutes of Health as a medical librarian, where he helped build the institution's world renowned library. Always full of surprises, Collie and his beautiful southern wife, Elsie, shocked our Washington clan (almost as much as I did when announcing that I wanted to be a priest) by moving their family in 1954 to what we considered the genuine wild west — that is, Hamilton, Montana — to take over the medical library at The Rocky Mountain Laboratory, a branch of the NIH. (Their son, Pat, a Bronze Star recipient in Vietnam and a Republican campaign manager, in 1980 at age 35 was appointed the Undersecretary of Energy in the Reagan Administration, at the time one of the youngest undersecretaries in any department. Later, it was his sister, Nancy — a respected print and TV journalist whose interviews have appeared in *Vanity Fair*, *Rolling Stone*, and *Architectural Digest*, as well as on ABC's "Primetime Live" and "20/20" — to whom I turned to help me write this book.)

Though our Irish enclave — the Hannans, Collins, and Ryans — boasted no shortage of memorable characters, my cousin Francis, *raconteur extraordi-*

naire, probably topped the list. Following a "private graduation" from sixth grade, he briefly worked for my dad before opening, close to the Lincoln Memorial (the sight of today's Kennedy Center), a riding school — famous for housing congressional horses and staffed by a conglomerate of relatives and horse-crazy volunteers who always included several beautiful, female government employees. Not that Francis was any smooth talker. Indeed, "Hey, get me something to eat. I'm hungry" was the closest he ever got to a flirtatious overture.

He, did, however, have a soft spot which could backfire on him. At one point, he let a black youth, claiming his parents never cared for him, eat and sleep in the stable. As a result, several months later, Francis was hauled into court on a charge of "involuntary slavery," the first such case since the Civil War. Being an equal-opportunity pin cushion, he was also once charged — by the Society for the Prevention of Cruelty to Animals — with mistreating his goat. The animal, it seems, had a daily habit of ambling to nearby Heurich's Brewery where he'd be given mash to nibble. Following a six-pack lunch, he'd lurch, happily, back home to the stable — until, that is, the day he got nabbed by a zealous SPCA officer who charged Francis with cruelty to animals. Francis' final foray into misunderstood good will took place in a more public forum: a Washington Redskins football game in Griffith Stadium. Always up for the theatrical, Francis and a parachutist, dressed as Santa Claus, cooked up a surprise entrance onto the field during the game's halftime. Just as Paratrooper Claus was about to hit the ground, Francis, driving a Santa sleigh, would speed onto the field in time to scoop up Kris Kringle and drive off. Alas, the best laid plans of mice and merriment often go awry — and did here. Instead of gracefully landing on the grass, as planned, a sudden gust of wind blew Santa into the nearby parking lot, where, landing unceremoniously, he sprained an ankle, leaving getaway-driver Francis racing, inexplicably, toward mid-field in front of hundreds of fans. Needless to say, the family dined out on that one for years.

Immaculate Conception School

All the Hannan boys, and most cousins, attended the Immaculate Conception Parish School, at 8th and N Streets. In 1920 carpooling fashion, Dad trundled us to school in the family's horse-drawn carriage, clip-clopping along the asphalt, picking up any kids, regardless of race or nationality, along our route. In those days, Catholic boys were taught by male teachers, in this case the Brothers of Mary, advocates of those tried-and-true basics: education and discipline, the latter dispensed, if necessary, by a determined principal wielding a stout ruler. Complaining at home about a paddling simply guaranteed getting another from the Boss. Contrary to horror stories of parochial school punishment, nobody I knew ever complained. Most of us, after all, were the offspring of immigrants, seasoned believers that when it came to seizing opportunities afforded by this wonderful country, you did whatever it took — and took whatever resulted — without complaining. It was action that mattered. When it came to bullying, for instance, that hot button issue generating hours of discussion among today's school administrators, the Brothers of Mary suggested, shall we say, a more hands-on approach. "The next time an older kid beats up on a younger one," they instructed, "defend the little guy and beat the devil out of the big."

I liked school — sports and studies which my mother monitored tenaciously. Every evening, sitting around the dinner table, our kitchen turned into a one-room school house overseen by Mother making sure that we did our homework. If anyone got stumped, we simply shouted across the table to our sister, Mary who knew everything. When it came to sports, meanwhile, baseball — played during recess and lunchtime — was my game (I was an outfielder). Growing up, my hero was Walter "The Big Train" Johnson, who, pitching for the Washington Senators from 1907 to 1927, wound up with 417 victories, second only to Cy Young in major league history. Sportswriter Ogden Nash wrote that he was called "The Big Train" because, fast and overpowering, "he could throw three strikes at a time." I don't know about that, but he certainly was my hero. When I was eleven, I wrote Johnson a letter, praising his pitching and sportsmanship. When he sent back a quick response, I couldn't believe it: "Dear Philip, I am very grateful for your kind letter and appreciate your support of me." In the seventh game of the 1924 World Series, Johnson, coming in as a reliever, pitched four scoreless innings, ensuring the Senators' victory over the New York Giants. For me, it was one of the greatest nights of my young life, sitting in the stands, listening as my dad, literally, did play by play in the dark (in those days baseball parks weren't lit at night). He explained that batters, hampered by nightfall and seeing only his release, not delivery, knew they struck out only after hearing the ball pop into the catcher's mitt. Strike three!

Unfortunately, my grammar school years weren't all World Series and hero worship. In fact, in the summer of 1919, Washington's Seventh Street race riots resulted in the worst memory of my young years. After World War I, the African-American veterans who had to fight for the right to serve in actual combat roles in the Army returned home hoping that their proud military service would promote fair treatment as full-fledged U.S. citizens. It did not. Indeed, the civil rights situation worsened, causing clashes to break out between white and black veterans. It got so bad, in fact, that President Woodrow Wilson, in order to stop the riot, mobilized 2,000 troops who patrolled Seventh Street in armored cars. Even now, eighty years later, that scene — we small boys being protectively convoyed home by larger ones — remains vivid in my mind.

Blacks may have been persecuted in other parts of the city, but not where we lived. As an underdog growing up, my father favored the downtrodden. Unlike the prejudice of most whites toward blacks, Irish immigrants of that era retained a sense of kinship with Negroes, as they were then called, as fellow sufferers under tyranny. (Never did I hear the "N" word used in our home, church, or school.) In fact, my maternal grandfather, John Keefe, financially helped St. Cyprian's Parish, a black Catholic parish; my own folks considered it a duty to contribute money to St. Augustine's, a 15th Street parish for African-Americans, continuing a tradition started in the 1860s by President Lincoln who allowed St. Augustine to use the White House lawn for a fund-raising fair to build a new school. (Politically, my parents, though conservative, were, like most Catholic immigrants, Democrats. Though I never officially joined the Democratic Party, I always felt it was my party.)

In our family, meanwhile, any black workers or maids whom my father hired for business or home were always treated like family, in fact, were respected, mythic figures to my siblings and me: Old Joe, carrying a piano on his shoulders into our home, and Charlie Tatum from North Carolina, who could shovel dirt with one hand. (For the record, the Boss always used an African-American notary public.) One Thanksgiving — then the auxiliary bishop of Washington — I showed up at the family dinner to scant fanfare; while my parents' maid garnered a near-standing ovation. "I've married into a strange family," remarked my newlywed sister-in-law. "When the son, a bishop, arrives, nobody pays any attention; but the maid shows up and everybody cheers."

An International Neighborhood

It helped, of course, that we lived in such a truly international neighborhood, starting with the public school where both black and white students were enrolled (among them the future General Douglas MacArthur). Adjacent to our house was my father's plumbing shop, whose backyard was cluttered with discarded sinks, stoves, and pipes, the perfect place, as it turned out, for my first — and only — encounter with tobacco. Egged on by older cousins, I confidently stuck a cigar, undoubtedly purloined from Uncle Will's store, into my mouth. Seconds later, I spit it out. It didn't take a surgeon general to tell me that tobacco was a lousy idea! The next-door laundry shop, meanwhile, was owned by a Chinese man who was also proprietor of a nearby restaurant where each year he hosted an elaborate dinner attended by my parents and their friends. It was not his only custom. Every night at six, sitting in a chair in front of his shop, the Chinaman calmly filled his pipe with opium and smoked it — a ritual paid no heed by the neighbors nor police. Further down the block, a white man lived with his Japanese wife, while the black Protestant church belted out Christmas carols all year long, including August. Across the

FAMILY PHOTOS

My mother Lilian in her wedding dress that was handcrafted by nuns who made the dresses to earn money for their community

Father Philip Hannan, September 1951

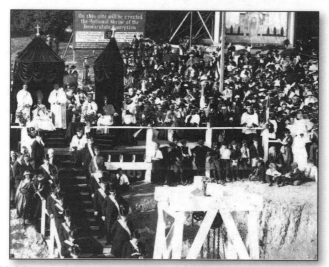

Seven-year-old Philip Hannan, seated with older brother Bill just to the right of the main wooden stairs, was present at the September 23, 1920, groundbreaking for the Basilica of the National Shrine of the Immaculate Conception in Washington, D.C. Cardinal James Gibbons, seated beneath the main tent at left, presided over the ceremony.

A Hannan family photo taken at my twenty-fifth anniversary of episcopal ordination in 1981.

Family picture at Hannan family farm taken in 1943

Photo of the handsome Hannan family taken around 1923, when I was nine or ten years old. Front row: Tom, Jerry (on Mom's lap), Mom, Denis, and Dad. Back row: Me, Frank, Mary, John, and Bill.

Hannan family at the Mayflower Hotel, celebrating my parents' fiftieth wedding anniversary in 1955. Seated: Mary, my mom, and my dad. Standing: Frank, me, John, Denis, Jerry, Bill, and Tom.

Left: Mary Hannan, the only girl among seven Hannan brothers, was a brilliant student. She graduated from Trinity College and then became the first laywoman to earn a doctorate from the Catholic University of America in mathematics, Greek, and Latin. My father Patrick was so proud of his eldest child that he often remarked: "Mary was worth at least three boys." *Right:* 1929, St. John's College High School

Denis, Jerry, and Bill Hannan flank their brother at a reception in the St. Louis Cathedral rectory after a 1981 Mass celebrating my twenty-fifth anniversary of episcopal ordination.

Archbishop Patrick O'Boyle and my mother Lilian, with my brothers and me

My brother William Hannan reading at the 1981 anniversary Mass

My brother Jerry Hannan and I at Christmas 2009

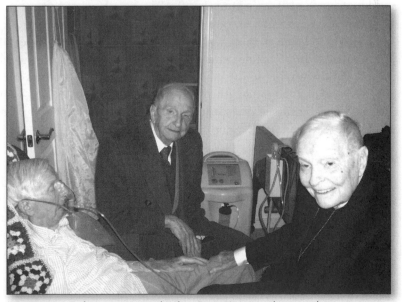

Jerry Hannan and I minister to our brother, Denis Hannan, who passed away on February 5, 2010.

street, a Filipino houseboy ran the home of a retired brigadier general; while his neighbors, a sun-worshipping Scandinavian couple, determining their off-spring benefit from sunshine, allowed their children to play naked in the front yard — much to the amazement of pedestrians heading to their offices in close-by government buildings.

With so many government officials living in the area, you never knew what celebrity might walk down our sidewalk, stopping — like one ramrod-straight Army officer, whom I later learned was General John J. Pershing — to pat our heads. (Pershing apparently never recovered from the traumatic loss of his wife and three young daughters in the tragic fire at San Francisco's Presidio in 1915.) My brother, Tom, in fact, may well be the only person in Washington to run down a sitting president with a scooter. One morning, President Cal-vin Coolidge, accompanied by a Secret Service agent, was enjoying his usual, early-riser constitutional up 17th Street (from the White House) when Tom, hell-bent on getting his scooter to fly across the pavement, suddenly scored an abrupt bulls-eye on the leg of the leader of the free world. Unperturbed, Coolidge, sidestepping his young assailant, simply continued on.

It would not be the last time that Tom — or the rest of us — would set eyes on the President of the United States. In 1927, due to White House renovations, Coolidge temporarily moved into the home of publishing heiress Cissie Patterson in Dupont Circle, two blocks from our house — wonderful serendipity, as it turned out, for the Hannan boys. When President Coolidge welcomed Charles Lindbergh to Washington, following his historic transat-lantic flight, he invited "Lucky Lindy" to the Patterson house where an excited crowd — my brothers and I among them — stood on the lawn's trampled bushes, cheering for the dashing aeronautics hero to make an appearance. Finally, Lindbergh and Coolidge emerged onto a second-floor balcony where Lindbergh, timidly waving to the noisy throng, allowed my brothers and me a bird's-eye view of the world's (then) most famous human being. Seconds later, he was gone, both men disappearing back into the house without saying a word. So much for public relations!

St. Matthew's Cathedral

Ultimately, everything of any importance in our family centered on the Church, in our case St. Matthew's Cathedral, four short blocks away on Rhode Island Avenue. I can still dimly recall the church's aged, aristocratic founding pastor, Monsignor Thomas Sim Lee, a Maryland cousin of Robert E. Lee. Autocratically deciding in 1897 that the parish church, whose bound-aries included the White House, should be worthy of a Catholic president of the United States, he set about making it a reality. As a result, the Monsi-gnor commissioned New York architect John Lafarge to design St. Matthew's imposing dome whose construction, exceeding the height restrictions established by zoning laws, required the city to change them. (The ornate interior, meanwhile, required thirty years to reach completion.)

The priests of St. Matthew's Cathedral were, like their leader, as varied as the neighborhood. Well into his eighties, Monsignor Lee still insisted on taking nighttime sick calls, while his successor, Monsignor Edward Buckley, an Episcopalian convert, set the gold standard when it came to "walking the parish" to visit every parishioner. Father Argaut, a member of the French Missioners of Paris as well as a wise, gifted counselor and confessor, found Washington's humid climate, after years spent in India, more than agreeable. What was not agreeable was anything that did not adhere to the "old France." One time, when the visiting French choristers, Les Petits Chanteurs a la Croix de Bois, sang the Marseillaise on the steps of the cathedral, Father Argaut huffed off in disgust. "I can't stand that revolutionary song." I was baptized by the English Father Mills whose father (an Oxford don) taught him to speak Latin and Greek. A thoroughly entrenched academician, Father Mills required every young First Communion candidate to pass a written exam — throwing my oldest brother John into a six-year-old sweat when it was discovered that he'd rejiggered a basic Catholic tenant: "There are," he confidently wrote, "two Gods."

"John, I'm shocked," my mother reportedly exclaimed hearing of this blasphemy. "You know there's only one God!"

"I know, Mom," he replied, "I just couldn't spell 'one'!"

Priests were as much a part of our social, as religious, life. Nothing pleased my mother, an excellent cook, more than inviting over the parish priests as well as any from Catholic University (a constant influence in our lives) where Father William Turner, her fourth cousin, was a professor of philosophy. "Tur" (from baby Jerry's inability to pronounce "Turner") was smart and forward thinking, undoubtedly the force behind convincing, years later, the University's powers-that-be to break tradition and allow my sister, Mary, to study for a doctorate in Latin and Greek. When Tur was named the Bishop of Buffalo, he delivered the exciting news to Mother via phone:

"Lil, how'd you like to have the Bishop of Buffalo as a dinner guest tonight?"

"Lord, no," she exclaimed. "I've nothing ready for a big dinner!"

"I'll come anyway," he laughed. "You're talking to him. I'm the new Bishop of Buffalo."

In the Hannan family, the boys became altar boys, choir members, or both. Though Tom, Denny, and Bill, whose beautiful tenor voice invariably assured him the solo in the "Gesu Bambino" carol every Christmas, sang in the celebrated St. Matthew's choir (under direction of Malton Boyce), I — better at hitting a curve ball than "high C" — never qualified. (Asked later to try out for a singing role with the Mutual Broadcast System radio network, Bill refused. "Fortunately, I had enough sense to turn down a part in a flimsy radio company," he always explained, "and became a lawyer.") When we weren't at

St. Matthew's serving Mass, we were on the altar of the Convent of the Sacred Heart at 1719 Massachusetts Avenue (now Georgetown University's School of Linguistics) where The Madames of the Sacred Heart ran a select school for young ladies. (At age four, watching my older brothers going off to Church for nightly May devotions, I burst into loud, protesting tears at being left behind. Grabbing me by the arm, my brother Frank offered sage, brotherly advice: "Listen, you little dummy," he said, "once you start going to Church you've got to keep it up for the rest of your life. Shut up and stay home as long as you can." And I did — quite happily.)

The Farm

By 1927 my parents, having already acquired the houses on either side of us, decided to buy a farm eleven miles outside of Washington near Norbeck in Montgomery County, Maryland. With sixty acres and a sturdy holly tree farmhouse, it would be, they felt, both the perfect summer escape from the city's oppressive heat as well as a new, educational venue for their children to learn the value of hands-on labor. And we did. The younger sons, including me, pitched hay, milked cows, and wrestled sheep for shearing which, lacking electric sheers, was done by hand — without question the hardest job of my life. (Properly sheering a sheep requires that he be flipped on his back and held down. If standing, you stand no chance since he'll wrestle and wriggle free.) It was also an important spiritual lesson. Thanks to those woolly devils, the Gospel image of the Good Shepherd came clearly into focus: sheep do need a shepherd to care for them; otherwise, they collapse in the heat. (Visiting the Roman catacombs as a seminarian, though, I saw plenty of pictures of sheep and the Good Shepherd. There wasn't a single image of one being sheared — a major oversight in Church tradition!) Besides this, we milked a couple of goats and five cows a day, developing, along the way, hands and forearms like rocks. Coupled with superb fresh food — corn, lamb, ice cream made from cream skimmed off the top of milk from Jersey cows — my appetite, and physique, blossomed.

Overseeing everything, was Milton, an African-American who lived with his wife Victoria, a large, dominant woman, in a house on the farm. Not only did we work under Milton, we also regarded him as family. In fact he was easier on us than our father, who brooked no distinctions when it came to color or class. Once, when a water system needed to be installed at the farm, my father sent out several black workers from Washington to do the backbreaking work — rendering my mother the only white woman within miles of the farm. I thought nothing of it until the day she surprised me with a comment. "Phil, people have been asking if I mind being the only white woman on the farm with all these blacks," She recounted in disgust. "Well, I trust these black men as much as I trust the white." Though I never mentioned our conversation to my brothers, the message was clear: whether white or black, those with whom you work deserve trust and respect — until proven otherwise.

In the country, our parish church was St. Peter's Mission Church in Olney, three miles from Norbeck, where Mass, celebrated every fourth Sunday of the month, was attended by the whole family. One night the pastor at St. Peter's came to dinner. Afterwards, strolling across the lawn, he announced that he was "measuring the distance for the light poles of a lawn fete." From this was born an annual summer celebration featuring fried chicken, fresh corn on the cob (from our farm), and cakes of every description. With the Hannan boys responsible for the shucking and hauling of farm produce, neighboring families showed up to help with the cooking and serving. Not about to be left out, friends from Washington caravanned out to take advantage of the Depression price of "seventy-five cents for all you could eat."

Blessedly, the Great Depression (1929-39) didn't significantly affect our family simply because those relying on my father's plumbing services, federal government workers, weren't fired during these dark economic times. Though business slowed, the Boss never faced a complete shutdown. (Moreover, he made himself available for odd jobs — hanging pictures and fixing floors and roofs.) His goal was keeping employees on the payroll and finding them work — still plentiful in the "big houses" of people like the Duponts who employed thirty to forty maids — all Irish whom they knew wouldn't steal. As a teenager, I learned my own personal lesson in Depression-era economics. In grammar school, the Brothers, stressing thrift and saving for the long haul, encouraged students to open a bank account with whatever coins they could scrounge up. When I left the eighth grade, my account boasted $100 which, thanks to the crash, plummeted to $6. Devastated, I simply started saving all over again.

In 1965, the Boss, having always planned to give ten of our choicest acres to the archdiocese for a church, finally did so in the name of our sister Mary, who died from breast cancer at age fifty-three. As a result, St. Patrick's Parish in Norbeck, canonically established in 1966, was dedicated in December 1968 with my mother and her sons present (Dad had long since gone to his reward). Of course, there was no doubt about the name of the church — St. Patrick's — though whether it was after Irish saints, Patrick Cardinal O'Boyle or Patrick Hannan is yet to be determined.

Like all families, we had our share of trauma, sorrow, and loss — most notably the early death from breast cancer of our venerated sister Mary in 1959. Although Mary desperately wanted children, she and her husband, Robert Mahoney were never able to have any of their own. As a result, she simply spread her love across the world, starting in Tanzania where she established eight maternity clinics. While her husband was head of the public schools in Hartford, Connecticut, Mary was a member of the Hartford Housing

Authority and President of the National Conference of Catholic Women. To avoid a conflict of interest, she turned down several political opportunities — an offer from Connecticut Governor Abraham Ribicoff to be his secretary of state, as well as Republican and Democratic requests to run for Congress. The Mary Mahoney Village in Hartford, apartments for the elderly poor, are named in her honor. All of these charitable acts were performed in the same quiet way that our father performed his charity work through the parish's St. Vincent de Paul Society.

Mary's death — a huge loss for her husband — devastated all of us. I still recall the tenderness with which my mother personally cared for my sister in her final days spent in one big bedroom of the family home. As mentioned earlier, this was little Mary, the "preemie" who had survived long odds at birth, nursed to health in a room that my father had turned into an incubator. Life had come full circle. Thanks to my brother Frank's brilliant diagnostic ability, I was graced to be with Mary when she died. Calling on a Sunday evening Frank told me, "Mary will die on Tuesday evening. You should be there for her comfort as well as Mom's." And, gratefully, I was. Mary died around nine o'clock that very date.

Early Thoughts of a Vocation

When it came to their children, my parents prayed for a doctor or lawyer — not a vocation. In fact, ironically enough, no one in our large, Irish Catholic family ever had a calling to the priesthood or religious life. Consequently, when I dropped the bomb at the dinner table, conversation ground to a halt — no small feat in a loquacious gang like ours. When someone asked if I planned to accept the scholarship offered by Catholic University (and follow my brother Bill studying law), I decided that the moment of truth was at hand: "No," I replied, "I don't intend to go there." My father was aghast. "What do you mean?" "I'm thinking," I continued slowly, "about going into the seminary." My God, did forks drop onto plates! My announcement was a complete and utter surprise.

I can't recall exactly when or how the idea of a religious vocation began simmering in my mind. Certainly, there was no Eureka moment. Like all boys growing up, I had a million ideas about what I wanted to do. Though I loved sports, especially baseball, I was too small to make the high school team. Eventually, my activities, like the Catholic Students Mission Crusade, generally combined a mixture of social and pious goals. Though geared toward assisting missions, the organization had other attractions as well: meetings and a yearly dance attended by representatives from all Catholic high schools, including the girl schools — a big draw for a guy like me who, enjoying girls, had the usual dates and prom nights, usually at the glamorous Shoreham Hotel.

If anything, the birth of my vocation involved a long, if spasmodic, labor — a struggle more apparent to others than to me. In one instance, Brother Luke, my "homeroom" teacher at St. John's High School, broached the subject after class. And his advice was chillingly candid: "You ought to think about the permanence of the commitment in becoming a priest. It's forever. There isn't any turning back." On another occasion he put it a little differently. "Hannan, you get too many ideas. Skip every third one" (advice seconded, apparently, by many).

During my senior year, a friend of the family, Admiral Washington Lee Capps, offered to let me take the examination for the U.S. Military Academy at West Point. Admiral Capps, head of the Board of Strategy for the Navy in World War I as well as supervising contractor at the Union Iron Works in San Francisco (overseeing the construction of the Battleship Oregon and Battleship Wisconsin), was a staunch, flinty patriot married to an elegant Catholic lady. Since the Capps lived in St. Matthew's parish and had no children, they took great interest in the Hannan boys. Nevertheless, I turned down the Admiral's invitation to "audition" for West Point.

"Why didn't you take the examination to West Point?" my mother asked.

"I just didn't feel like it," I said evasively. At that time, the U.S. Army with a mere 50,000 troops, was practically an endangered species, offering no future. And though I'd thought about becoming a doctor, lawyer, even architect, I simply couldn't shake the idea of a religious vocation. I knew I had to make up my mind by graduation since, in our family, there was zero tolerance for drifting through life or taking a year to "think about it."

Finally, I took action. If I didn't settle the thought, really run it into the ground, I would never be content in any profession that I chose. Seeking out a friendly priest at St. Matthew's rectory, Father Edward Roach, I confided that I was thinking about becoming a priest. No sooner had the words passed my lips, than he considered it a done deal. "We have doubts about some young fellows who say they want to be a priest," Father Roach said, "but not you. However, the only way to find out whether or not you've actually got a vocation is to try it." Toward that end, he offered to take me to St. Charles College in Catonsville, Maryland, a minor seminary near Baltimore, at the beginning of the next session in September 1931.

Though stunned, my parents were obviously proud. While my father immediately told his brother Will how proud he was, my mother was far more cautious. "Of course we're pleased, Philip," she said, "but this is a very serious decision and you're very young," opening a door in case I changed my mind. I did not. Still, her remarks made it much easier to strike out to St. Charles College, located, ironically, on Maiden Choice Lane near Catonsville. Walking in the door, the only thing I knew about St. Charles was that I was entering a seminary.

CHAPTER 3

My Seminary Days

Having no idea of St. Charles' regimen, I had no expectations and, thus, no disappointments. Indeed, I experienced only a keen sense of exultation that I was coming to grips with my choice in life, resolving that most difficult of possibilities: the priesthood. Furthermore, I was proving my independence from the family, my brothers all having attended either Georgetown or Catholic University. Justifiably, the Hannans felt that Washington had everything one needed in life — and I had stepped out of that circle. St. Charles College offered both a high school and two years of college. While the high school was called the "kids' side," the college was divided into the "Poets" and the "Rhets" (Rhetoric) emphasizing English, poetry, and writing. The real Mason-Dixon line, however, was your knowledge of Greek and Latin, still the language of the Church in the liturgy as well as philosophical and theological studies. Since my Latin courses at St. John's hadn't prepared me for such an onslaught of the language, it took a year of struggle to catch up with my classmates. (Not only were the academics demanding, the professors were tough, if helpful. Father "Tug" Dyer, for instance, in charge of seminary finances, taught bookkeeping by beginning each class reciting, mantra-like: "When you're priests, your people will want to know what you're doing with the money they give you. So learn how to give an accounting.")

The architecture at St. Charles, meanwhile, was impressive, especially the beautiful chapel, a large, separate building with magnificent mosaics and marble work. The first time I saw it, I couldn't believe that the Jenkins family had given this gorgeous edifiice — a source of inspiration and meditation where we began each day in reflection before Mass — to such a minor seminary. The campus also had excellent athletic facilities — baseball diamonds, tennis courts, a swimming pool, and an indoor gym where I boxed, conscious that my large knuckles could protect me. Though there were lots of good athletes on campus, sheer athleticism was held in check by the study-conscious Sulpician Fathers who believed in testing character as a means of developing spiritual lives. Most surprising to me, however, was how readily the seminarians accepted the stiff regimen: religious reading during dinner; grand silence extending from night prayers to the end of Mass the following morning; and expulsion for smoking cigarettes. While Christmas vacation lasted a week, and summer three months, parents were only allowed to visit one Sunday afternoon a month, when my folks would regularly show up with cakes to share with my friends.

Represented in the student population was every country in Europe as well as Latin America. As such we were all "equals" — basic training for my later Army life. My main job, however, was determining if I truly had a vocation. As the months wore on, though I grew increasingly comfortable with my decision, I saw no reason to "rush the cadence." By the end of my second year, realizing I probably did have a religious vocation, I had to make a decision: continue in the seminary, and, if so, enter the Basselin curriculum at Catholic University; or take my courses at St. Mary's Seminary in Baltimore. While the Basselin required three years of philosophy studies, ending with an MA in philosophy, the courses at St. Mary's Seminary, requiring only two years, delivered an AB in philosophy. Not surprisingly, my sister Mary, a devotee of higher education, urged the Basselin, where I could take advantage of Catholic University's superior library and wider academic choices. Her wisdom naturally won out. I chose the Basselin, named in honor of a Canadian lumberman who, on the advice of St. Augustine Bishop Michael J. Curley, established a foundation providing seminary courses to develop "better preaching" by priests.

Happily, I was again back in Washington. Basselin students lived on the fifth floor — with no elevator — at the Theological College, called the Sulpician Seminary, at the corner of Michigan Avenue and Fourth Street. All total, I would be living in the Theological College for seven years — three for the Basselin courses, four for theology — a daunting prospect indeed. The difference between seminary life at St. Charles College and Catholic University was the difference between ROTC and military combat. The heart of the Sulpician seminary was Father "Jus" Vieban, a pious, saintly, unassuming, and learned priest trained in his native France who loved nothing more than mingling with his students. Following dinner, when the students walked around the "boardwalk" behind the seminary building, Jus invariably joined them — and their conversations. In more spiritual matters, Jus wisely exhorted us to persevere with caution. "Now don't be too worried," he admonished, "about whether you are worthy of becoming a priest." We understood what that caution meant. Our prayers meanwhile were vintage French Sulpician. "Look down upon me, a less than nothing..." (to which my roommate invariably remarked: "God must really have good eyesight").

The faculty, mostly Sulpicians, alternated with Jus in delivering the spiritual talks. Almost all were inspired speakers, except for Father Hemelt, the treasurer, who gave only one speech a year before we left on summer vacation.

"Don't play mixed doubles in tennis," as he cautioned us one summer, "with the opposite sex." We got the point.

I suppose students of every era like to play little tricks on their teachers, and Father Hemelt was an easy target. We gathered one night for common prayer, and the prayer service included a time for Father Hemelt to read the prayer intentions for sick relatives that seminarians would write down on small pieces of paper and submit to him. Father Hemelt unwittingly led a prayer for Gypsie Rose Lee, the famous burlesque star of the 1930s: "Please pray for Rose, who is suffering from pneumonia." Everyone burst out laughing, and he didn't know what in the devil was going on. That's called seminary humor.

The main seminary courses were in philosophy taught by Father Jules Baisnee, who had lost his left arm while serving in the French Army in World War I. He used his physical loss to prove that the brain was the center of feeling as well as of thought. "Today I can feel the nerves in my left hand (which was missing) as if I still had it," he would say.

One of the most practical courses taught us how to properly project our voices so the congregation could hear us. I'm convinced this could help today's seminarians, who often rely too much on sophisticated sound systems. What happens if the sound system goes haywire, which is not an isolated occurrence? Our professor, Mr. Wisniewski, first sized us up with a rough physical exam — as though he were measuring us for a suit. We always called him "The Tailor." The exam was to see if we had strong enough lungs and diaphragms. Then we received individual attention in how to enunciate clearly and project our sound. After class we were encouraged to walk into the woods behind the seminary and yell loudly to develop our vocal strength. He didn't want us staying inside because you get used to the sound of your own voice. The key was to breathe from your abdomen to provide the proper support. I'm glad there were no neighbors around. I'm convinced after hearing a lot of television announcers these days that they could have profited from having Mr. Wisniewski as their teacher.

We had advanced courses in Latin and the usual studies for a bachelor of arts degree, but the course in English, taught by Father Speer Strahan, dwarfed all the other offerings. Father Strahan was a recognized poet and a graduate of Yale who really believed in the goals of a classical education set by Mr. Basselin. His special quarters in Caldwell Hall included space for a grand piano, which he could play without unduly affecting the other residents.

We had to submit a theme for each of the three classes a week during the first semester. His minute criticisms savaged the products of our minds. The next semester we engaged in writing a novel. First, we composed an outline of the novel. In successive weeks we wrote the first chapter, the climactic chapter, and the final chapter. Before the year was over, we had performed other substantial assignments. In later years Father Strahan admitted he had "overdone" our assignments. He didn't have to let me know that. My classmates and I had come to that same conclusion years before.

Catholic Evidence Guild

Seminary training didn't come only inside the seminary walls. Seminarians could join the Catholic Evidence Guild, a group that started in London's Hyde Park in 1918 and specialized in defending the Catholic faith in the public square. We would prepare talks on different aspects of Catholicism and then go to a public park, set up a light pulpit, and begin speaking. Before long, a crowd would gather. My area of expertise was the development of the Bible and how the Church determined what books would be included in it. After my talk I had to answer any questions and objections the crowd would have. That was great practice defending the faith, and I still can't understand why we didn't continue it.

We attended the special lectures presented by the university on current topics, generally held in the auditorium of McMahon Hall. We were in the Roosevelt days of the NRA (National Reconstruction Act), and one evening Monsignor John A. Ryan, a renowned champion of social rights, gave a witty and effective talk justifying FDR's Agricultural Administration Act that resulted in the slaughter of six million young pigs in order to drive up pork prices and get more money into the hands of farmers.

Shortly thereafter, Father Fulton J. Sheen, then an assistant professor in philosophy at Catholic University, criticized FDR's program, citing the killing of the pigs as a sign of a skewed program in view of the widespread hunger in the country. Sheen was becoming the orator of the nation, and his words went far beyond the classroom.

Of course, Father Sheen was better known for his sermons than his academic courses, but one of his lectures always produced an immense audience. It was his annual lecture on "The Hound of Heaven," the famous poem by Francis Thompson and arguably the best religious poem in the English language.

The nuns and the lay students came in droves. As the classroom overflowed with people, Father Sheen would announce, "The word has gotten out that we are giving away samples. The class will be held in the auditorium." Then ensued a mad scramble to get good seats in the auditorium. Father Sheen spoke about the poem so often he could quote passages of it without having to refer to any paper, and he would read the phrases in his dramatic fashion and explain the philosophical content. The audience feverishly recorded every word he spoke, even the most banal. I always attended accompanied by a seminarian from Milwaukee named McGrath. We marveled at the spectacle, making remarks about the audience but always astounded by the power of Father Sheen's drama.

Many of my classmates at St. Charles were also Basselin students, which made the transition very easy. One was Marty Killeen from Atlantic City, a very intelligent and personable fellow, with whom I was a fellow student all through our seminary days, including the North American College in Rome.

I had very congenial, if different, roommates each year. Vince Sullivan, a real "brain" and later a Sulpician, was my first-year roommate. Next year was "Bonny" Herbeck, named for his blond hair, who was a consistent sleepwalker. Every night of the full moon he would walk around the room but could be coaxed back rather easily: "Bonny, get back to bed. No, don't just sit on the bed. Get into the bed."

The third year Dick Ginder, from Pittsburgh, was my roommate. He was an extraordinary musician and a fellow of the guild of organists, and he really rattled the establishment the first time he was allowed to play the organ for our Sunday High Mass in the Shrine of the Immaculate Conception. He played for the recessional a rousing, hopping Bach piece. Father Baisnee didn't approve at all, but Father Vieban was understanding. The music lovers were rapturous.

Our recreation consisted of taking walks on Wednesday afternoon and playing baseball, for the sports-minded, after dinner. The walks took us all over Washington. I remember a walk with Wilbur Wheeler, a converted Episcopal minister, who was really intrigued with the library in the Masonic Temple on 16th Street. We made our entrance, dressed in Roman collars, and that

Seminarians at the Sulpician Seminary in Washington, D.C., taken in May 1934. I am in the third row, fourth from the left

caused a sensation among the library attendants. Worse yet, Wilbur wanted to see the anti-Jesuit section of the library. It was impressive. The attendant showed it to us and then made a suggestion about seeing another part of the library, but that didn't budge Wilbur. The attendants seemed very relieved when we left.

Baseball was the center of the recreational program. I played center field for the team, and our chief rivals were the team from the famed Dominican House of Studies, next door to the seminary. Once a year we played St. Mary's Seminary from Baltimore. They had a couple of famous hitters, but we had an ace pitcher from Hartford. Before the game he would caution me, "I'll use my fastball on them. Play way back. In fact, play in the center of the tennis court (which was behind me in the outfield)." At the appointed time, I'd go back to the center of the tennis court. To my relief, he struck out most of the opposing batters.

The development of the spiritual life of the students was strongly nurtured and closely watched. My spiritual director was Father Collins, who believed in student initiative, and I cannot remember his ever pressuring me to continue studies for the priesthood. Of course, attendance at all the spiritual exercises — morning prayers and meditation, Mass, spiritual reading, and night prayers — was mandatory, and the cassock was the required "uniform" of the seminary.

We had a wonderful opportunity to hear outstanding Catholic scholars speak at the university. There was plenty of controversy, heightened by the crisis of the Depression and the terrible drought in the early 1930s. We students certainly learned that the basic social principles of the Church could be debated strongly without any acrimony.

Naturally there were many prominent politicians who seized the opportunity to advertise their views through university lectures. President Roosevelt, who felt a great kinship with the ideas of Monsignor Ryan, was the principal speaker at one of the graduations. He was trundled onto the stage in his wheelchair. It was the time when Communism was being debated on many American university campuses, and Roosevelt wished to demonstrate his anti-Communist stand through his presence at the university.

I did have some free time during the summers, and that was when my mother would take me and several of my siblings on pilgrimages to some of the great shrines in Canada. We went to Montreal one summer, and I actually got to meet Blessed Brother André, who is responsible for building the incredible Oratory of St. Joseph on the slope of Mount Royal. Blessed Brother André was a simple porter for forty years at the College of Notre Dame-du-Sacré-Couer in Cotes-des-Nieges. He did not know how to read or write until he was twenty-five years old, but he had a renowned spiritual gift for healing. He shook hands and talked with everyone at the doors of the oratory, and he always concluded his remarks with, "Pray to St. Joseph." He was a very holy, very simple man.

In 1935, I received my AB degree in philosophy after completing a dissertation on "The Concept of Immortality in the Writings of Samuel Taylor Coleridge." The following year, I received my master's degree in philosophy. That commencement marked a new era in my life. Each year the Archdiocese of Baltimore — including at the time Washington, D.C. — would send two seminarians (with stellar academic records) to the North American College in Rome to complete their studies for the priesthood. At the end of my final year at the Basselin, I knew, thanks to my good marks, that there was a possibility that I could be sent to Rome. Following normal procedure, Archbishop Curley decided that Johnny Linn, a student from Baltimore, and I would make the cut. I was completely thrilled. My sister Mary, knowing the value in seeing the heart of the church and expanding my world view, had encouraged me to focus and do my best. And, as usual, Mary was right.

CHAPTER 4

Four Years in Rome

Johnny Linn and I embarked for Rome in September 1936 from Hoboken, New Jersey, aboard the S.S. Exochorda, a combination freighter-passenger vessel of the Export Line. It was the season for the equinoctial storms. These are violent rainstorms that occur at or near the time of the equinox (where the sun is directly above the earth's equator), normally occurring around March 20 and September 23 each year. Just a half-day out of port we encountered a hurricane that blew us almost all the way to southern Europe. Few meals were eaten, and the porthole in our cabin, punched open by a swell, left us swamped. The ship's roller coaster movement was so intense that the dining room staff had to wet tablecloths to keep plates and cups from slipping off the table and crashing to the deck. Eventually, we arrived at Naples, where we were escorted to Rome by Charlie Gorman, a third-year seminarian from Baltimore (stopping long enough in Naples to see Mount Vesuvius and visit the Shrine of Our Lady of Pompeii where, inside the door, a mother breast fed her baby while saying her prayers — welcome to Europe).

The North American College in Rome was located in a 400-year-old building at Number 30 Via dell' Umiltà, named after a stunningly beautiful painting in the chapel, Our Lady of Humility, by Guido Reni. Following a brief stay there, we traveled to the College's summer villa for seminarians — the Villa Caterina — located close to Castel Gandolfo, the pope's summer residence. Besides a swimming pool and tennis courts, the view of Rome from the main building was spectacular. Though peaceful, the feeling among the Italian populace was anything but serene. Adolf Hitler, in the midst of his rabid campaign to conquer the world, had convinced Benito Mussolini, following "jackal-like," to share in the spoils of his conquests. The war in Spain, meanwhile, also winding up, had unleashed divisions of soldiers throughout Europe. Everyone, it seemed, proclaimed a political aim and wore a uniform — myself included. While each seminary had its own distinctive garb, ours, a black cassock, trimmed in light blue with a red sash, was particularly so. As a result, we dubbed ourselves "bags," derived from the Italian world *bagarozzi* (meaning cockroaches), a derisive term used by anticlerical Italians.

In October, we packed up and left the villa to return to Rome and the North American College, where we would begin our studies. "Packing up," in this instance, was literal: that is, picking up your actual mattress and clothes, which were loaded onto a truck and, entering via the rear of the college, dumped on the ground. Instantly, a mad scramble ensued as seminarians fought to grab a good mattress and haul it off to their room. Our first Christmas at the College, meanwhile, taught us to be thankful for small favors. Due to inconsistent heat and electricity, we were forced to wash and shave in water so cold it barely remained liquid. As it turned out, the College, aiming to impress visitors to the annual ordinations, turned on the heat only in December. All classes at the Gregorian — an old Jesuit university commonly called the "Greg" — were conducted in Latin, as well as Hebrew, which was also taught from a Latin text. Both the College and the "Greg" were a mere stone's throw from the famous Palazzo Venezia, the office of Mussolini.

Mussolini, a classic demagogue, was a real piece of work. Only five feet seven, he never addressed his troops from street level, instead, elevating himself

Seminarians from the Archdiocese of Baltimore in the North American College. I am standing on the far left

in the public eye by sitting on a horse or standing on the second-floor balcony of the Palazzo Venezia, where he would whip his audience into a frenzy. When Italian soldiers appeared in the piazza below his balcony, he would incite them. Since each carried a short sword, the end of Mussolini's orations, detailing his plan to restore the former glory of Rome, were marked by soldiers, trained to punch their swords into the air, shouting: "Duce! Duce! Duce!" If the cheers weren't loud enough, Mussolini disappeared inside. Seconds later, when one of his stooges popped out on the balcony, the people would cheer, and Mussolini, depending on how he felt, would return for an encore — or five or six. While overrating Hitler, Mussolini underrated England and France. Moreover, he had his own goals: restoring the Roman Empire, where he would be enshrined in the pantheon of famous Roman emperors.

My first walk in Rome was, of course, to St. Peter's Basilica, which was simply overpowering. Exhausting every faculty of my mind and heart, I tried to grasp its enormous scale and breathtaking beauty. St. Peter's was not only an unbelievable work of art, engineering, and history, it was, above all else, an inexhaustible source of inspiration. It is not simply the size of St. Peter's that is the source of its grandeur but also the congruity of every unique element of the whole piazza: the stupendous church that stands like a creed (credo) of faith; the arc of the Colonnade of Bernini, which welcomes the human family to its place of worship; the paved surface of the piazza that conveys charm to its visitors. Of course, the Scavi — or underground excavations — attest to the presence of St. Peter, the first Vicar of Christ on earth and our pastor in the faith. As a Washingtonian, the dome of St. Peter's bespoke the capitol of the United States. Not surprisingly, there was an architectural legacy responsible for that similarity. Christopher Wren had Michelangelo's dome of St. Peter's in mind when he designed St. Paul's Cathedral in London in the late seventeenth century, and Thomas Ustick Walter, the architect of the Capitol dome in the 1850s, was inspired by Wren's design. Not surprisingly, all roads led back to Michelangelo.

After a few visits and prayer sessions, I finally began to comprehend St. Peter's. And it became a home — one that never dulls but continually uplifts the soul with a fresh surprise or thrill. In short, it possesses the spirit of God, never lacking inspiration, never growing old. The tomb of St. Peter, the Pieta, the Blessed Sacrament chapel, the underground excavations (*Scavi*), mosaics, and marble were stunning. But the discreet feature that truly epitomizes St. Peter's is the near invisible mosaic directly above the central front door — the Navicella (little boat) — a respresentation of Christ rescuing St. Peter during the storm on the lake. Having bade St. Peter to come to Him across the water, Christ is saving Peter as he begins sinking from lack of faith. As such it typifies the history of the Church: "It is battered but never sinks." That treasured mosaic was preserved from the old St. Peter's and placed in the new basilica (dedicated in 1626). Because of its great message of the power of faith, it was placed in the vestibule as a final inspiration to the faithful leaving the cathedral.

St. Peter's Basilica

One must live with St. Peter's on a daily basis to truly appreciate its majesty. One of my favorite stories is that of the Egyptian obelisk in the center of the piazza. Following the custom of the time, the Emperor Caligula brought it to Rome, erecting the obelisk at a spot near the Palace of Nero before relocating it near the first St. Peter's Church. After the completion of the "new" basilica in 1586, Pope Sixtus V decided to place the obelisk in the center of the piazza. Moving it, of course, was perilous, requiring the efforts of 800 men, 150 horses, and 150 cranes — all supervised by Domenico Fontana. To ensure calm during the delicate operation, the Pope decreed that any bystander making an outcry would be subject to the penalty of excommunication. As the men tried to lift the obelisk in place, it became apparent that the ropes were not strong enough, eventually becoming so taut they were unable to lift the spire, prompting a sailor named Byesca from Bodighera to yell out: "Water to the ropes!" His sage advice salvaged the operation, and the obelisk settled into place. In thanksgiving for the savvy seaman's advice, the Pope awarded him the honor of having his village supply the palms to St. Peter's on Palm and Easter Sundays.

As we new seminarians settled into our studies, there was an informal initiation ceremony at the North American College, a seminary which over the years garnered a reputation for being a bishop "factory." Upper classmen would take you aside — always very politely — and ask that you recite the obscure prayer said before putting on your surplice. Then, when they had you reeling, they would ask: "Which course of studies do you want to follow? Do you want to be in the advanced courses?" Of course, everyone said yes. "So you're saying you want to enroll in the course," they continued, intent on embarrassing the guys with any such ambition, "that teaches you to be a bishop?" At that moment, you knew you'd been had — albeit all in good fun.

Life at the College, organized according to a *camerata* system with roots in the old Florentine educational society, centered on small groups of students gathered for learning. Each afternoon a *camerata*, eight to ten students living in the same section of the college and led by an upper classman — a prefect assisted by a "beadle" — would take walks. And though our group might pass another *camerata* inside a church or on the street, we weren't allowed to mingle much less swap stories. My *cam* leader was Bob Arthur, a fellow student from the Archdiocese of Baltimore, who dutifully took us to all the important churches in Rome. Besides Bob, our diverse, congenial *camerata* was populated by types rebelling against the long-standing Roman traditions of behavior for seminarians studying in Rome. They included: George Spehar, a huge, Croat-descent from Crested Butte, Colorado; Frank Latourette from Denver, who, ultimately left the seminary to become a successful TV producer; Ed O'Connor and Marty Killeen from Atlantic City; Charlie Noll from Cincinnati; Tom Powers from Philadelphia; Jim Woulfe from Binghamton, New York; and Johnny Linn from Baltimore.

All Gregorian classes were in Latin, producing a challenging, immensely rewarding spectacle. Sessions in moral and dogmatic theology, for instance, were held in a huge aula seating, arena style, around 300 students from almost every nation in the world. There were no textbooks. The professors simply delivered their lectures in Latin as we, scribbling furiously, tried to keep up. Needless to say, three or four months were required to become capable of understanding and recording a whole lecture.

Although we had outstanding professors — each an expert in his field — we never really met them. Leaving as soon as the lecture was finished, they discouraged any attempts at conversation. If a seminarian happened to be late, the professor gave everyone permission to make a hissing sound, which I found rather childish. During class, meanwhile, the silence and solemnity were never interrupted except, that is, by an intrepid English seminarian whose raucous rooster cackle invariably provoked utter disgust in our lecturer. Though a few dared laughing, the culprit was never apprehended thanks to his neighbors concealing his identity. The courses, prepared for an international student body of nearly every race and nationality, were taught by equally diverse professors: Italian, Spanish, German, Dutch, French, Hungarian, and a lone American. As a result, teaching, emphasizing principles applicable to individual cases and problems, was, nonetheless aimed toward a worldwide Catholic congregation, ultimately making it impossible to conclude that there could ever be an American, French, or African Church. (Later in my priesthood, encountering diverse problems in diverse national and ethnic contexts, I thanked God for my education at the Gregorian.)

Examinations, held once a year in July, were a sheer terror. Students were summoned by name to sit in a chair opposite one of several professors, also seated and giving the oral exams which, being public, were open to any student who wished to observe. Inevitably, a group of Italian students, fluent in Latin, would gather to wallow in the discomfort of the less-talented, especially the Americans. In my case, I never had an examiner from the United States nor one with whom I'd actually taken classes. Talk about a home-field disadvantage! Standing near the Greg's front door, a gaggle of pious, indigent women, begging and offering to say prayers on behalf of the nervous students, invariably pulled in a rich harvest of coins each day of scheduled exams. One first-year American student really cracked under pressure. Throwing him a softball question, the professor asked in Latin, *"Quid est philosophia?"* —

"What is philosophy?" Rattled, the poor guy gave the first answer that leapt to mind: "*Chi lo sa*" — "Who knows?" — causing loud, audible snickering from the Italians in the audience.

Food at the North American College was lousy, mainly because the English, trying to starve the Italians into quitting their cooperative agreement with Germany, posted part of their navy at Gibraltar and the Suez Canal. As a result, not many good food products were getting in — resulting in delicacies like sardine soup for lunch. It got so bad, in fact, that the rector, firing the cook, allowed a committee including the seniors to search for a new chef, proving true the adage that "God so loved the world that he did not send a committee." Ultimately, the rector hired a fellow from Hungary who was told that American seminarians liked pies. Finally, the big day arrived. The new cook was finally in charge and out came his pies — filled with spaghetti! It was the end of his — and almost the rector's — career.

I became so intrigued with the current events and history of Rome that, aided by Ed Latimer, a seminarian from Erie, Pennsylvania, we published an annual magazine called "Roman Echoes" (dropping off the magazine at the printer, Vatican City's famous Polyglot Press, afforded me the chance to get a snack and drink at the bar — a liqueur costing six cents — a rare treat in the days of food blockades). For one issue, besides normal stories about prominent visitors and major events, I decided to interview Giovanni, the elderly, respected waiter at the head table. "Of everyone you've ever served, cardinals, statesmen, presidents, and movie stars," I asked, "who was the most outstanding?" Giovanni didn't hesitate. "Buffalo Bill," he shot back. "Now that was an extremely gallant man."

Traveling through Europe

Each July, exams over, I traveled through Europe, often with my mother and father — always generously paying for traveling as part of my education — or brother Bill. Though mother was thrilled by European life, the Boss desperately missed his home-cooked meals back in Washington. In the summer of 1937, his first encounter with Italian coffee engendered instant pity for his son. Joining my parents for breakfast at a good hotel on Rome's Via Veneto, I watched with amusement as Dad, inveterate "Irish breakfast" addict, ordered coffee, two eggs, and a small steak. "*Si, si,*" the waiter replied. When the java arrived, his first sip made him grimace. "Son, is this what they give you to drink every morning?" "Actually, our College coffee isn't this good." Subsequently, he slipped me extra cash to buy real coffee outside of the seminary.

In fact, the Boss made only one transatlantic trip, combining a visit to Rome with a pilgrimage to his native Ireland. Though he liked seeing St. Peter's and the Pope up close, the hundreds of other churches and art galleries didn't much impress him. As a result, we had to fool him into visiting Venice, which Mother desperately wanted to see, saying we'd merely pass by on the road to Ireland. Once in Venice, Dad hated the Venetian gondolas, seeing no sense in using canals as streets. Since he couldn't swim, being in a town that was virtually underwater was a constant trial. As we walked through the glories of Venice, all Pop could say was: "When do we get out of here?"

Eventually, we made it to Adare, Ireland, the nearest town to Kilfinny where my father was born. (Surprisingly, I learned it had been the center for the revival of Irish literature, familiar territory for the likes of Yeats and Keats.) Hiring a car, we drove up to the house of our relatives in Kilfinny, a village so small it had a school and a church, but no resident pastor. My folks were overjoyed, however, when, upon seeing us, everyone shouted: "Glory be to God, look who's here." Immediately, my father's cousins insisted that we move out of the hotel and live at their thatched roof cottage — a wonderful experience with food boiled atop the fireplace, tea served at every meal. That first day, however, we spent little time eating since Dad wanted to show us his "college" — a two-room, thatched-roof shack with sod floor that served as grammar school for his three years of formal education. Having to leave school to help support his family, he ended up on an estate in Adare, receiving a shilling — twenty-five cents — a day from the English lord who, owning even the broad stream, declared it illegal for an Irishman to fish in it. Nevertheless, Dad never expressed any anti-English sentiment since the lord had allowed his father, though infirm and unable to work, to live with the family in a small hut. Though the family's abysmal poverty eventually forced Dad and his older brothers and sisters to immigrate to America, none ever bore a grudge against the English. As the Boss told me: "The English lord never forced my sickly father out of his home." Standing there that day, I was never prouder of my father.

The trip really tapped into my father's charitable leanings, albeit not always successful with the proud Irish. After visiting his cousin Mary Leo, we called on the parish priest. "I'm worried about my cousin Mary," he told the pastor. "She doesn't complain or ask for help, but I don't know how she lives or who supports her. If you'll accept it, I'll be glad to send money to you each month for her living expenses." Fixing my father with a withering glance, the priest replied: "Glory be to God, man, doesn't she have any neighbors?" whereupon our visit ended. (In the evenings we caught up on everyone's lives. Though most had close relatives in the United States, sending a sizable check each month, our Irish relations were extremely concerned about the decline in morality among the youth. "Don't you know that they're drinking cocktails now," they said. "Did you ever hear of such a thing?")

All too quickly, our stay came to an end, and we drove to Cork where my parents were catching their boat back home. As it turned out, it was the first time I saw my mother crying. "We're leaving Phil all alone," she sobbed. Though sorry to see my parents leave, I was raring to move on with the rest of my European travels. Given Mother's passion for art and architecture, I knew she'd be back the following summer unless war broke out. And I wasn't wrong. In July 1938, she indeed returned, this time with my brother, Bill. Boundlessly curious, insatiably interested in art, we hit every museum and cultural site we could find. After visiting the basilicas and Vatican museum, we traveled to Florence, Venice, and Dresden, fulfilling mother's lifelong desire to see Raphael's Sistine Madonna housed in the town's art gallery where we rushed straight from the train. My Lord, was it worth it! That glorious painting, the Blessed Mother holding her Divine Child in heaven, the sole object in a grand room, was instantly spellbinding, arresting one's entire being.

It was in Dresden that we got our first taste of life in Nazi Germany. At the registration desk of a nice hotel, Bill started signing his name on the register. Just then two Nazi officers came up, brusquely shoving him aside. Bill, ever the impetuous lawyer, shoved back, hard. I intervened, stopping the set-to. "You and I can't handle the whole German Army," I told him as he calmed down. That evening, as we were leaving the room to join Mother for dinner, the hotel manager appeared at our room. "I saw what happened today," he said. "Here are the keys to my car. You may use it as long as you are in Dresden." Clearly, not all the Germans were pro-Hitler. My German extraction mother, meanwhile, was appalled at the behavior of the soldier and Hitler Youth. "These are not the Germans," she said nearly once an hour, "that were in our family."

My most enlightening — and frightening — experience happened when I was traveling alone on the Rhine steamer en route from Cologne to Coblenz. I was seated next to an elderly German woman when a group of boisterous, arrogant Hitler Youth passed by. Cautiously, my seatmate turned to me, asking, "You are an American, are you not?" Answering yes, I showed her my passport. When I said that I came from a family of one sister and seven brothers, she happily revealed that she, like my mother, had had seven sons. "We older people," she sighed, "will never have peace in this country until we have killed our own sons!" Her devastating description of Nazi Germany haunts me to this day. It also confirmed my conviction, based on my visits, that a conflict with Germany was unavoidable. The country was preparing for war with everything, and everyone was under surveillance. Once your train left Italy and stopped in the first German town, German soldiers jumped onboard, rifling through identity papers, books, and magazines, confiscating all reading material, especially foreign-language publications. Even more unnerving, once having crossed the border, everybody greeted each other with: "Heil, Hitler!" a salutation I certainly never returned.

Eventually, we made our way to Paris, then onward to my favorite cathedral in France in Chartres. Keen to see the Cathedral's world-renowned stained glass windows, the moment was bittersweet as we watched workmen taking them down in order to protect them from bombs. Fervently, we prayed for peace.

In the United States, meanwhile, many intellectuals, including Father Fulton Sheen, were convinced that there would be no war because, as Sheen put it, the "people would not permit it." Obviously, he had never been to Germany. Had he, he would have realized that the German people had already given their permission — to the Nazis.

For me, the turning point in the rise of Hitler was the collapse of Austria — the Anschluss — in March 1938, since it enabled Hitler to prove to himself, his people, and the world that he could take another nation with neither France nor England coming to its rescue. Certainly he fooled the Viennese Cardinal Theodor Innitzer who, giving in, signed a declaration supporting the Anschluss with the fateful words: "Heil Hitler!" Though Pope Pius XI later forced Cardinal Innitzer to recant his statement, the damage was done. In the summer of 1938, fellow seminarian Butch Burke and I visited Vienna, which was bereft of tourists. The city was dead. At the famous Rathskeller, we were the only dinner guests. Being such rare birds, we got super treatment. When we departed the restaurant, the crowd cheered, leaving us agape and not knowing what to do — a history lesson I'll never forget. When Winston Churchill called the approaching war "The Gathering Storm," his image perfectly matched my personal observations. In recent years, trying to evaluate why I am so troubled by hard rock music — especially its constant, pounding beat — I suddenly realized that it reminds me of young Nazi soldiers, pounding along the pavement in unison, intoxicated by their percussive sound.

I suppose that's the reason that to this day I am always a bit distraught over the utter incapability of the people of our time — the younger people — to comprehend the evil of the tyranny of Communism. Perhaps theoretically they can acknowledge its danger, but it is to be appreciated only in the fullness of its experience — the degradation and torture of people. A complete degradation of the dignity of humanity, a total disregard of human rights. No one can see how bad it is from a book. One has to see it in action.

Mussolini's efforts to partner with Hitler were pitiful. The Italians could not be fanaticized and always retained an appreciation of Christian culture. In a barbershop in Naples I heard a customer lecture the barber about the advantages for him to join the Fascist party. Finally the man told the barber triumphantly, "The Party would send your son to college without any charge." The barber replied without a pause, "Yes, and at that point, whose son is he?"

I always enjoyed watching groups of Fascist students demonstrate against the United States. I would stand across the street as they shouted, "Down with the U.S.," and return their wave as they finished. Then they would walk off, having done their duty for that day. Not surprisingly, I received an anxious letter from my mother. "The papers here say there is rioting in Rome against

American students. Are you safe?" Writing back, I assured her that there was no cause for worry.

Mussolini did know how to curry favor with Catholics. He destroyed the power of the Masons, restored crucifixes to Italian classrooms, and agreed to pay the salaries of the clergy.

Yet even Mussolini could not dim my enthusiasm about being in Rome and St. Peter's Basilica. In my seminary days, the papal Masses were resplendent affairs, the pope being carried into St. Peter's in the richly adorned *sedia gestatoria*, or portable throne, always to an avalanche of excited clapping and yelling from the assembled congregation.

And the beatification Masses raised the excitement level a notch higher. At one of my firsts, I was standing next to a group of Austrian nuns. As Pope Pius XI was carried in, they flew into a fury of excitement and joy. Unfortunately, however, their view of the Pope was partially blocked by several tall men standing along the aisle. Desperate, one tiny Sister spied me and marched right up: "Pick me up!" she demanded. Dumbfounded, I didn't immediately react. "Pick me up!" she firmly repeated, grabbing my arm. Obeying orders, I did as I was told, discovering, much to my chagrin, that the little nun was not so little in gerth. Still unable to satisfactorily see the Pope, she yelled again, "Higher!" Exerting myself to the max, I finally managed to raise her a few inches higher, whereupon, applauding loudly, she screamed like a Beatles fan: "*Viva il Papa!*" and crossed herself as the Pope extended his blessing to the nearby crowd. At that point, I dropped her. As she half smiled in thanks, I quickly and prudently moved a safe distance from the Sisters. As I soon learned, when it comes to St. Peter's, expect anything, especially the odd, sometimes hilarious question. One day, standing in the Piazza San Pietro, I was approached by a stylish American woman. "Which denomination," she asked, "owns that church?" My answer was most polite.

Pope Pius XI and Pope Pius XII

I shall never forget the "audience" that Pope Pius XI granted the seminarians from the Archdiocese of Baltimore. Making his five-year report to the Holy Father, Archbishop Michael Curley of Baltimore asked that the seminarians from his city be allowed to see the Pope and receive his blessing. Gathering in the anteroom of the Pope's office while the Archbishop gave his report, the door suddenly opened and we were allowed to enter. Upon entering, we knelt in response to the order of the Archbishop, who asked the Pope to give us a blessing — which he did along with a medal for each of us. Arising, we departed, awash in gratitude.

The rector of the North American College, Bishop Ralph Hayes, always understood that seminarians were in Rome to profit from all these opportunities. As a result, we were able to attend the funeral of Pope Pius XI in February

1939 and the election of Cardinal Pacelli as Pius XII. The change in pontificates began one morning before Mass with the simple announcement by our spiritual director, Monsignor Fitzgerald, that the Pope had died. (In Rome, His Holiness is always well until the moment he dies.) During each day of the conclave to elect a new Pope, we raced to St. Peter's, watching for the "white smoke" from the burning ballots signifying a completed election. Since the Cardinal electors indignantly rejected the Nazi threats to harm the Church if Cardinal Pacelli got in, the election of Pope Pius XII was very quick. And, of course, they voted him in largely because, having been a nuncio in Germany, the Cardinal was famous for his opposition to Hitler.

When it came to announcing the results, however, there was a glitch. When one of the cardinals, in an operatic voice boomed out: "I announce to you a great joy. We have a Pope, Cardinal Eugene..." a burst of thunderous applause broke out among a group of French students and visitors, who, standing in St. Peter's Square, were convinced that their famous French Cardinal Eugene Tisserant had gotten the bid. Pausing until silence returned, the Cardinal continued, "... Pacelli, who has taken the name Pius XII" eliciting even more raucus cheers from the Italians. As Americans, we felt that a friend had been elected. Cardinal Pacelli had not only visited the United States, but had held an important meeting and dinner at the North American College with the Under-Secretary of State of the United States in a last-ditch effort of the United States and the Vatican to avert the coming World War. That night at the College, there was celebrating indeed.

In the summer of 1939, with war inevitable, my folks did not make the trip to Europe. But free for the summer, I was determined to see Budapest, whose national feast day was reputed to be the most beautiful of any national celebrations in Europe. The only difficulty was the date — August 20 — by which time the trip could be too dangerous. Undaunted, I enlisted my intrepid classmate Butch Burke, from a Kansas diocese, to accompany me to Budapest.

During the train ride, I was seated next to an elderly lady loaded down with an abundance of packages and baggage. Arriving in Budapest, I helped her with her belongings. When it became apparent that she had no money for a taxi, I gave her enough to take care of the fare. She then drew me aside. "Are you really an American?" she asked. I showed her my passport. "All right," she said. "You did me a big favor. I'll do one for you. I am fleeing from Germany, where I saw railroad cars full of our troops going to the Polish border. The war will start in a few days. If you're here for the holiday celebration, get out as soon as it's over, get out of here. Go to the west, anywhere in the west. But leave."

When I told Butch about our conversation, he wasn't impressed. Armed with the name of a modest hotel, we went to register, learning that the heart of the celebration, a big parade, was scheduled for that afternoon. It did not disappoint. The parade and its attendant festivities were grand and gorgeous.

The relics, including the royal crown and the remains of King Stephen, who led the Hungarian conversion to the Church, were carried in procession, followed by the Regent and the Cardinal in his flowing robes.

Adding to the spectacle were detachments of the Hungarian military, each representing an epoch in the history of Hungary, beginning with the soldiers of the time of King Stephen. That gave a unique splendor to the event. They were followed by peasant representatives of the various regions of Hungary, each with the brilliant and varied colors of their festive costumes.

Mindful of the elderly woman's admonition to leave Budapest, we spent just one night in our hotel before Butch returned to Rome and I headed for Paris the next morning. I figured if I was in Paris when the war started, I would be able to secure a boat ticket back to the United States or get back to Rome if the war did not disrupt the college program.

My route to Paris was via Munich. When the train pulled into Munich on the way to France, a large agitated crowd was milling around the station. As I looked out the window from the train, an excited German, sizing me up as an American, rushed over to me and shoved a copy of a newspaper, the *Voelkischer Beobachter*, into my hands. The headline read: "Germany signs an agreement with Soviet Russia." "This very same newspaper reported yesterday that Germany was condemning the Communists," he said, "How can this new headline be true?" Of course, I had no answer, only a better understanding of Nazi perfidy. After a four hour delay in Munich, we left for Paris.

The City of Light was grim, quiet, and uneasy. At the office of American Express only three customers were ahead of me. By the time I got to the teller my remaining German marks had dropped by 50 percent.

Blitzkrieg

On September 1, the Nazi blitzkrieg hit Poland. For safety reasons, I decided to return to Rome via Switzerland where, along with another student, Henry Cosgrove, I decided to climb the Matterhorn. Though the day was gorgeous, "very unusual weather," they said, its beauty waned when, hiking up the mountainside, we encountered Swiss troops walking to machine gun emplacements on the mountainside.

Back in Rome, the city was feverish with expectation. Everyone in Italy was delighted that the terms of the Axis agreement did not require Italy to go to war. For its part, gallant Poland immediately rejected the Nazi ultimatum, the only European country to do so sans hesitation; ultimately Poland was overpowered and divided up between Germany and Russia. Thus began the year of the "phony" war — "No action on the Western Front."

As the 1939 academic year approached, my focus was more on my upcoming ordination to the priesthood than world peace. In the vortex of excitement about war, the twelve members of my class and I prepared diligently for our December ordination in the chapel of the North American College.

None of us, truthfully, found the situation that troubling. To live in Rome, even during a War, is to live in the company of saints. Our daily walks took us to churches dedicated to heros of Christ who literally lived the phrase of St. Paul: "It is no longer I who live, but Christ who lives in me" (Gal 2:19). The lives of saints' mirroring the troubles of all humans, are often characterized by family turmoil, hatred or conflict. Recalling them we were consoled and directed.

Since every church is also a temple of Christ, whose Presence in the Blessed Sacrament in the tabernacle is the center of, and reason for, its existence, so every visit was also its own sermon on the Presence of Christ, brought to that altar by the Mass. Therefore, the focal point of our visits was the recitation of prayers, spontaneous or traditional, directed to Christ the High Priest.

A few yards away from the College, an added source of inspiration, was a Perpetual Adoration chapel where two Sisters consecrated every moment of the day to Christ with prayers and dedication. To avoid any distraction the Sisters wore slippers. "They come in and out like snowflakes,"as someone said. Frequently during those days I slipped into the chapel to add my personal intentions. In retrospect, the beginning of the war was the best preparation we could receive for our ordination and service in the priesthood. In fact, every event of the War was a source of spiritual education. Even now, I recall the succinct, three-word opinion of an old, Italian priest during speculation about Hitler's designs on conquest: "*Superbia semper ascendit*" ("Pride always increases or expands.") He was correct. Neville Chamberlain had no clue.

Since the U.S. State Department decreed that it would issue no visitor visas, travel to Italy was now impossible. This prevented any of my relatives from attending the ordination. We neither mailed invitations nor made plans for a party. Our focus was singular — ordination to the priesthood of Christ to be given by the Rector in the venerable chapel of the College.

Ordination Day

Ordination was conferred on December 8, 1939, the Feast of the Immaculate Conception. It was the beginning of a new life. The words of the famous hymn, "You are a priest forever" (*Tues sacerdos in aeternum*), sung beautifully, expressed the whole transcendent reality.

Only one outsider managed to find her way into the ordination Mass, a disturbed but gentle woman known as "The Abbess." A convert from Richmond, Virginia, whose wealthy family allowed her to stay in Rome, she frequently wandered in and out of the chapel. Following the ceremony, the newly ordained priests gathered in a room at the College for a reception, where we entertained friends and classmates from the Gregorian University. Kneeling for a blessing, they then rose to receive the most prized gift that we could impart at the time — a cigarette.

I celebrated my first Mass on December 9, 1939, in the Greek Chapel of the Catacombs of St. Callistus, which I had discovered during one of my early walking tours of Rome. The oldest picture of the Mass in the Greek Chapel — all the inscriptions are in Greek — illustrates the Eucharistic celebration being offered at a table with the patron, a woman, seated next to the celebrant. Reminding me of an old, respected family picture, I came to think of the people in it as my nameless, saintly ancestors. Consequently, celebrating Mass there was both thrilling and humbling. Today that is no longer allowed. In fact, I was turned down, to my great disappointment, when I pleaded with the Benedictine Sisters, the caretakers of the Catacombs of St. Callistus, to celebrate Mass there during my 60th year of ordination in 1999.

On the occasion of that first Mass, I wrote this poem.

First Mass
By Father Philip M. Hannan
Rome, December 1939

Boyhood dreams of long ago
saw an altar fair
consecrated, trembling hands
lifted there in prayer.

And those dreams have led me on
dreamlike though they seemed.
Now, dear friends, thank God with me,
I am what I dreamed.

Other dreams have I today,
brighten spite of fears
that this human heart may be
Christ-like thru the years.

Think of me when on your knees
that this dream comes true,
bowed before that altar fair,
there I'll think of you.

On December 10, 1939, I celebrated my second Mass at a side altar of St. Peter's Basilica. St. Peter's is the heart of the Church, and there could be no more appropriate place for a priest to consecrate the Eucharist. My third Mass was at the Basilica of St. Mary Major, the oldest and greatest church in Rome dedicated to the Blessed Mother, built in 432. What is believed to be relics from the crib of Christ rest under the high altar. The ceiling of this magnificent church is decorated with the gold Christopher Columbus brought back from the New World.

After Mass and breakfast each day, we went to the Greg for the remaining classes of those days. We were ordained for a purpose, and nothing was allowed to infringe on that purpose. Ordinations for our class were held in two sections — one on December 8 and the other early in the next year. In subsequent years I have often thought about the grim circumstances of our ordination and the remarks that it was "a shame" to have such war-time deprivations. But, I have always come to the same conclusion — the whole class consisted of thirty-seven students, and only one of them left the ministry of the priesthood; that one student received a dispensation and has led a very Christian life. That record speaks for itself.

The dignity of the priesthood certainly resulted in our being more attentive in class, and, for me, it was the best scholastic year of my life. We remained at the College for another semester to complete our theological studies. Somehow I contracted rheumatism for two weeks in April 1940, and I was so sick the doctor came to pay me several visits. His prescription was one for the ages: I was to drink red wine, and not only that, I had to make sure I heated it up first. When the pain increased, I increased the level of the red wine "cure," but to no avail. The rector decided I should be admitted to the hospital, staffed by the Irish "Blue Nuns," aptly named for the color of their habit.

The Sisters were very supportive, but they put me on a no-salt starvation diet, and I was getting weaker by the day. Finally, the doctor, accompanied by the Sister Superior of the hospital, came to my room and solemnly told me I must resign myself to the prospect of not being able to walk for two years. The diet had no effect except to make me very hungry. The pain increased to the point of affecting even my eyes, so the electric lights in the room were turned off and a candle with a shade was installed. A few nights later, I felt the pain spike noticeably, and it seemed to be gradually approaching my heart. I prayed very intently. Before morning, the pain began to subside from my heart, and I was convinced I was on the mend. Now I uttered some prayers of very deep gratitude.

Convinced that my salt-free diet was useless, I arranged for one of my classmates, Henry Cosgrove, to come to the infirmary with several bananas. Henry performed like a true secret agent, stashing the bananas beneath his cassock. When he gave them to me I voraciously wolfed a few down and saved some for later. "But you've got to help me get rid of the evidence," I told him. "Before you go, open the window." Even though I was still too weak to get out of bed, my baseball arm was equal to the task — I threw every peel out of the window onto the lawn below. As soon as I ate the bananas, I felt very invigorated. Even though the doctor had said I would collapse if I tried to get out of bed, I began walking around just fine.

The next day when the doctor came to see me, I told him I was feeling great and I showed him so by walking around the bed. He said simply, "It's a miracle!" When I told him I didn't really think it was a miracle, he replied, "It *is* a miracle. You've got to believe that, and if you don't, you're a bad priest." He was implying that I wasn't thankful for what God had done to heal me. Just then the gardener came into the infirmary in a white-hot rage and said, "I clean this place up every day, and now I'm picking up banana peels on the lawn. It's coming from a room near here." By that time I put on my overcoat and told the sister who was the floor nurse, "Sister, it's time for me to go back to the seminary."

Weak from the ordeal, I got permission from the Rector to take a week of convalescence in Sicily. I went to a good pensione in Taormina, with its dramatic setting on the sea and directly in front of snow-capped Mount Etna. The homegrown food was even better than the bananas, and I recovered fully.

Incidentally, upon returning to the United States, I asked my doctor-brother Frank to examine me, and I told him the whole story. After a thorough exam, he said, "I can't find a thing wrong with your heart. I don't know if it was a miracle or a bad diagnosis. Anyway, be grateful to God for the cure." I agreed.

In the hectic first year after the conquest of Poland, Myron C. Taylor, President Roosevelt's personal representative to the Vatican, hosted a special banquet at the North American College at which there were several special guests, including United States Under Secretary of State Sumner Welles and a representative of the Holy Father. There were various rumors about the nature of the event, and later it was learned that it was a last-ditch effort by the Pope to end the war.

It was obvious from the very animated conversation among the special guests, who disregarded their food, that some unusual proposal was being discussed. No explanation was ever offered about the nature of the banquet meeting, but eventually it became known that the papal entreaties were in vain. The reason given for the unusual site of the meeting was that the College was neutral territory, neither Italian nor Vatican.

I stayed in Rome until May 1940. The last few weeks of class were very hectic. Rumors circulated of a new campaign by the Nazi forces to increase the military tension, and I studied mightily to pass my forthcoming exams for my licentiate in theology. The Nazis finally opened their Blitzkrieg against Belgium and France, to the dismay and shock of the rest of Europe.

At that point, Secretary of State Cordell Hull had notified everyone that the United States could no longer guarantee the safety of its citizens in Italy after June 1940, and he gave a final, stern warning to leave the country. Exams were hurriedly prepared. Bishop Hayes, the rector, had anticipated this emergency and had been gathering cash to help any seminarians who didn't have the money on hand to secure boat passage back to America on the S.S. *Manhattan*. Italy was desperate for American currency, and even those seminarians who had bought their tickets with Italian lira were told they had to buy new tickets with American dollars. This gave me a problem. I had received a $50 gold piece at the time of my ordination from a member of our family. Now I had to dispose of it, and so I went to the bank, presented it to the teller, who immediately bounced out of his chair and took it to the manager's office. The manager came out and locked the door of the bank. It was illegal in Italy to hoard gold coins. Nevertheless, the manager was delighted to arrange an exchange and did so. I received for the gold piece $500 in Italian currency.

I believe the vice rector may have stayed behind temporarily at the College to keep an eye on the building. But after war broke out officially, the Italians converted the seminary into an orphanage, which I was finally able to visit toward the end of the war in 1944.

The only difficulty in the College's evacuation plans involved an Italian-American seminarian born of Italian parents in Italy. The Italian authorities had sent him a notice that he should report for military service, which, of course, he had no intention of doing. The only alternative was to sneak him onto our boat in Genoa, the S.S. *Manhattan*. Practically the whole college got on that boat. We stayed in a tightly packed group and gave our tickets to the boarding agent, and he did not hold us up to find out where the tickets had come from. The students, priests, and seminarians all slept in the main ballroom, which was converted into a dormitory. The boat was filled with passengers. The transatlantic voyage was uneventful except for the lurking presence of a German submarine that tailed the *Manhattan* the entire way, leaving us only when we entered the coastal waters of the United States. If the United States had declared war on Germany, the German submarine, under the laws of naval warfare, could have seized our ship. An American woman passenger expressed the sentiments of many on board the *Manhattan*: "It's a bit uncomfortable to have so many seminarians aboard, but maybe their prayers will guard us."

As the *Manhattan* passed the Statue of Liberty in New York harbor, all the refugees knelt on the deck in prayer to thank God for the safe passage. My parents had been extremely concerned about my safety. No matter how much I had reassured them I was okay, they were getting a different story in the local newspapers, so, of course, they were beside themselves. But my arrival set their minds at ease. My parents and my brother Tom met me at the dock in New York, and we had a tearful reunion. When I later met my youngest brother, Jerry, at Union Station in Washington, D.C., I didn't recognize him. When I left, he was four or five inches shorter than I; now he was several inches taller!

In New York I prayed with the passengers for the many blessings that God had showered me with over the previous four years — the blessing of my studies in Rome, a growing realization of the freedom and opportunities I had been given to serve God, and the inestimable gift of the priesthood of Jesus Christ.

My life was a gift! My four years in Rome constituted a four-year retreat in preparation for the priesthood, and now I was being called to begin that ministry for God's people in my home country. Father Jean Baptiste Lacordaire, a nineteenth century French Dominican, summed up my feelings as I embarked on my priesthood in America:

> To live in the midst of the world without wishing its pleasures; to be a member of each family, yet belonging to none; to share all sufferings; to penetrate all secrets; to heal all wounds; to go from men to God and offer Him their prayers; to return from God to men to bring pardon and hope; to have a heart of fire for charity and a heart of bronze for chastity; to teach and to pardon; console and bless always. My God, what a life! And it is yours, O Priest of Jesus Christ!

What a supreme gift!

I was also convinced America would be drawn into international conflict. I hoped that I, who had seen some of the terrible sources of the war, would someday be able to serve as a chaplain for our troops, preferably in combat, where chaplains are needed the most.

CHAPTER 5

My First Parish Assignment

As much as I longed to see combat, I first needed to get my clerical feet wet back home. Just before I returned to the United States, Baltimore Archbishop Michael Curley came to Rome to meet with his priests and seminarians studying at the North American College.

"Just because I know your father, don't expect any favors," the Archbishop warned me. His bluntness dashed any hopes of requesting an assignment to a predominantly African-American parish, a desire born out of my father's struggle for equal rights which had instilled in me a love for African-American Catholics. Growing up in Washington, D.C., I knew, firsthand, the terrible history of the Catholic Church as it related to slavery. In southern Maryland, during the seventeenth through nineteenth centuries, the Jesuits owned thousands of acres and hundreds of slaves, with those who ran the parishes selling slaves and breaking up families, a historical stain on the Church that I can never forget. (This is one of the reasons, in fact, that I have been particularly sensitive to the needs of African-American Catholics throughout my entire priesthood — a wrong, I am happy to say, with God's grace, that I was able to address in a small way as Archbishop of New Orleans.)

Determined to do my best wherever I landed, I was very pleased when I found out that I had been appointed an assistant to the pastor of St. Thomas Aquinas Parish in the Hampden area of Baltimore, effective ten days after returning to the United States. Knowing nothing about Baltimore, much less St. Thomas Aquinas Parish, I, nevertheless, trusted that God was sending me exactly where I needed to be. As indeed He did.

My ten-day vacation allowed me to celebrate my first Mass in my own parish of St. Matthew's in Washington, D.C. My family and fellow parishioners, forgetting that I had been doing this since my ordination six months prior, were awed that the "new priest" was so relaxed and calm. What those present that day did not see were my intensely profound, if hidden, feelings — that I, a former altar boy, was now being served at the altar by two of my brothers in the presence of the whole family, a truly overwhelming experience.

Rev. Philip M. Hannan blessing a seminarian after his ordination to the priesthood

Afterward, at a cheerful family reunion and party at Norbeck farm, my future pastor in Baltimore, Father Francis D. McGraw, surprised me by showing up.

St. Thomas Aquinas Parish

After a hurried round of visits to relatives where I was inevitably asked my opinion of the war, I reported to Baltimore and the rectory of St. Thomas Aquinas, located at 37th and Hickory Streets, and founded in 1837 by Father Thomas Foley, whose patron saint was St. Thomas Aquinas. The plain, well-built, gothic-style church, surprisingly large for a neighborhood full of Methodists, boasted an ample rectory as modestly furnished as a monastery. The sitting room of my suite consisted of two straight-backed chairs, with a third in the adjoining bedroom, whose bathroom I shared with the other assistant, Father Herb Howley, who informed me forthwith that Father McGraw, a pious, simple priest, harbored a secret — a nickname, that is, of "Muggsy," a moniker of unknown origin never to be used in his presence. Though spare, my new digs were a veritable Taj Mahal compared to my room in Rome.

Once ensconced at St. Thomas Aquinas, it became clear that Father McGraw's main worry was the $40,000 still owed on the new parish school building. Though a monstrous sum to him, it wasn't to me since the weekly collection averaged around $1,000. Still, almost as soon as welcoming me to the rectory, I was informed that I would be in charge of the annual drive to retire said debt, as there was obvious tension between the pastor and first assistant, Father Howley, a sociable, carefree sort who loved to entertain with his splendid baritone voice. Though he had tried to smooth his relationship with the pastor, it hadn't worked out.

Dealing with difficult personalities in, and out, of the priesthood is an essential part of the life, the sacrifice you make. The good Lord gives no assurances that upon ordination you will be serving with consistently pleasant people. And though I got along well with both men, the pastor was admittedly a worrier, overly devoted to schedules like our written-in-stone evening routine. Every night, following dinner, we would adjourn to the second floor, listen to the news on the radio, and the minute it ended, go downstairs to take care of requests from the people. (I was also assigned to celebrate the 6:00 a.m. daily Mass.)

The first time that I celebrated a Sunday Mass there, I was surprised when parishioners unable to secure a seat simply walked into the sanctuary and stood for the duration of the service. They, in turn, were equally stunned when this upstart, new assistant from Rome delivered a short homily on the need for charity in every aspect of our lives, including toward other nations. After Mass, the senior altar boy, a bright-looking lad of fifteen, made me chuckle when he asked where, being Roman, I had learned English.

The next day, after the collection was counted, Father McGraw asked that I accompany him to the bank. "Since the parish is big, you'll need a car," he announced, adding that despite its size, the percentage of Catholics was small. "We have a lot of Ku Klux Klan in this area," he nonchalantly added, "but they don't cause us any trouble."

Hearing that I needed an automobile, I called my father who knew of a convent selling a secondhand Dodge, which I promptly bought. Driving around with Father McGraw, he explained that the parish was divided into three distinct sections: Hampden, Woodbury, and Roland Park, home to many of Maryland's first families who opted to attend Mass downtown at the Jesuit church, St. Ignatius, rather than St. Thomas Aquinas in middle-class Hampden. For their part, Hampden residents were devoted to their area, as I later discovered visiting a sick policeman at Mercy, who was born in Hampden and said it was "the first time in my life that I've been out of it for more than a week. I'm lonesome."

"Well, thank God that you had the good fortune to live here so long," I responded. "Offer up your loneliness and tell your wife how much you miss her."

In Roland Park, meanwhile, with grand St. Mary's Seminary as well as the Anglican church, St. David's, religious boundaries were often ignored among friends. Being introduced to one family guaranteed entrée to all, as I found out when the MacSherrys, one of the oldest, most devout Roland Park families, invited me to dinner, introducing me to their group, including the Shriver family, whose cousin Sarge married John Kennedy's sister, Eunice. (Favorites of Cardinal James Gibbons, the legendary Catholic prelate, Mrs. MacSherry was the only female that the cardinal let drive him around in a car.)

Unlike many Roland Park residents, the MacSherrys chose to attend St. Thomas Aquinas, and it was through them that I ended up regularly taking Holy Communion to Mrs. Shriver, who was infirm. Meeting me at the door, Mrs. Shriver's maid, bearing a lighted candle and walking backward, so as not to turn her back on the Blessed Sacrament, would dutifully lead me to Mrs. Shriver's bedroom. (Later, in Washington, I jokingly told Sarge that I expected the same devotion from him as from his Maryland relatives.)

Woodbury, meanwhile, site of the mills making cotton duck (a Fabric) for the war effort, was the poorest section, where I was thrilled to begin my work — and learning curve. When I hit the ground in Maryland, being a priest was far more theoretical than practical. Though the fortunate recipient of brilliant academic preparation on the subject of a vocation, I knew little about the day-to-day, person-to-person, soul-to-soul work of helping other human beings walk in the grace of God. Knowing the Scriptures by heart means nothing if you cannot make them live in the hearts of others. For someone like myself, who had grown up schooled, trained, and loved by devoted Catholic parents as well as the Catholic Church, believing in its teachings — indeed believing in God — was like breathing: automatic, life-giving, trusted. If I worked hard, perhaps I could help others find their own spiritual confidence.

Parish Census

My initial duties in Woodbury would be to help take the census that the parish was conducting as well as contacting couples who were invalidly married. (More than a hundred families, of the four hundred registered on our books, were not in a valid marriage. And, of all the evangelizing missions given me by Father McGraw, this would be my most beneficial pastoral opportunity, particularly in terms of own my spiritual development.)

On both counts, I was complimented that my first efforts would be among our poorest parishioners — many from Appalachia. Though not always Catholics, they welcomed advice and help from anyone offering, including a Catholic priest. Shortly after arriving, a tall, strongly built Appalachian man asked to speak with me at the rectory. After an awkward beginning, a surfeit of missing teeth impairing his speech, he asked me to convince his wife to return to him, giving the address of a married daughter with whom he thought she was staying.

Imbued with optimism, I arrived at the door early the next morning to a curt reception. "I don't know where my mother is," a young woman scowled, as I heard a scurrying noise upstairs. "Well, your father," I said, raising my voice, "wishes your mother to return to their home. I can guarantee you that he will neither bite nor harm her." Suddenly, a woman appeared at the head of the stairs. "How do you know that?" she asked. "Because he has lost his teeth," I replied. The wife wound up returning to her husband.

With their open, guileless manner, the people in Woodbury soon made me feel at home as I trudged door to door asking them personal questions about their lives for the census. For the new guy in town the assignment turned out to be a wonderfully unexpected shortcut to becoming known among my new parishioners. A priest's most important task is to know the spiritual needs of his parishioners, which requires getting out among them. You learn how to be a priest by doing the work of one — most importantly, listening. And census-taking ended up being just the spiritual-engagement short course needed by this rookie. To get to their heart, you must (first) get through their door. And humor helped. One elderly lady, asked her age, responded: "Like the hills, I have no age." "So shall I write down 'old as the hills'?" Suppressing a giggle, she asked me in.

Of course Woodbury also had its share of tough customers. Walking up the stairs at one modest house, I thought I saw a pair of eyes watching me. After I knocked, a gruff, unkempt man answered the door. "Get out of here. If you don't, I'll knock you down the stairs." "Listen, mister," I replied, "I'll leave, but I guarantee that you're not going to knock me down." Later, when he was visited by the FBI, I learned that the man had been harboring an escaped convicted murderer.

Meanwhile, following up with the unmarried parishioners turned out to be a delicate task indeed. Any success that I might have had in helping couples depended on making friends with them first. In those days, most wives, being homemakers, were at home during the day, which meant talking to them before meeting their husbands. In this regard, children were my greatest allies.

"Mom, the priest is here," invariably signaled a mother's headlong rush to the parlor before their kid could blab every family secret crammed in his little head to a priest. However, once Johnny had been sent from the room, talking about him was always a conversation starter. Whatever the state of her own immortal soul, a mother was always anxious about the spiritual and physical development of her child, providing the perfect opening to inquire about the spiritual status of the couple.

It didn't take long to figure out that when it came to getting married, women were the prime movers. (Times haven't changed!) Men, on the other hand, were procrastinators. "All right," the husband would say. "We'll fix it sometime. But what's the rush?"

With women, you could appeal to their conscience. With men, you appealed to, well, whatever got their attention. Approaching the home of one couple, I purposefully started chatting with a neighbor standing in her yard. It wasn't long before the man in question came out of his house and joined us, eventually inviting me in to see the weight room where he and his four sons engaged in weightlifting — a sport holding zero interest for me. After several minutes of demonstrating how to bench-press two hundred fifty pounds, he looked at me and said: "You know, we don't have any religious beliefs in this family. Maybe we ought to talk about that." We did. And, eventually, he, his wife, and their four, buff sons joined the Church.

Roland Park Catholics weren't always so hospitable. Hearing from a Catholic friend that his neighbor's wife was gravely ill, I made a house call, bringing the holy oils. At the door, her husband was matter-of-fact. "Thank you, Father, for coming, but we have called a Jesuit priest," he said without inviting me in to bless his wife.

That evening, at dinner, I told the story to Father McGraw, who became uncharacteristically angry. "What did you say to him?"

"I didn't know what to say, so I said nothing," I replied.

"If it happens again," he continued, "tell them that since they live in our parish, you have a duty to care for them spiritually, even if they insist on having their own priest present." Father McGraw's years on the job had taught him when to vent righteous "holy anger" and "moral indignation" — and when to turn the other lip, as it were. Being an effective priest takes experience — and I had none. Clearly, I had a lot to learn.

Bringing non-Catholics into the faith, of course, was always a priority. Never knowing when God was going to drop a potential believer in my path, I was always on the lookout. Serving as a substitute chaplain at Johns Hopkins Hospital, I met a young doctor who was interested in becoming Catholic. An avid, quick learner, within a week he asked to see a confessional. Surprised, I was also anxious, since he had expressed an interest in psychiatry. (Johns Hopkins had pioneered studies in the development of the science.)

Fearing he may have been influenced by anti-religious ideas perpetrated by the field's early practitioners, I carefully explained the history and method of Confession before showing him an actual confessional. He was enthralled.

"This is the perfect way to deal with sin," he exclaimed. "Complete anonymity. No embarrassment, and a good opportunity to instruct people. Who invented this?" His fresh observations subsequently made me reinvent my own approach to teaching converts how to confess their own lapses in judgment.

Youth Ministry

A year after my arrival at St. Thomas, it became clear to me that if we didn't engage the young people in the parish, we would lose them. This led to one of my biggest, most successful projects. What St. Thomas Aquinas needed was a youth program geared to teenagers and those in their early twenties; but how to make it happen? And where? The only available auditorium, located in the school basement, was already reserved for the weekly Bingo Night, which is exactly where I hatched up my grand plan.

Wanting to be accessible, I made it a point to attend Bingo Nights — a cruel and unusual penance unrecorded in any spiritual text acceptable to the good Lord, who understands all the vagaries of human nature. However, compared to spending three hours answering questions — "Why are you eating so many peanuts? Don't they feed you in the rectory?" "Peanuts help me think" — dreaming up an entire youth program was a trip to the beach.

And the peanut-thinking paid off. With Father McGraw's permission, I investigated the interiors of the former parish school, shunted aside for our indebted newer model. Solidly constructed with classrooms, a cafeteria, and toilets, the space could handily be converted into a sizeable meeting hall. Moreover, according to my brother Tom, our *pro bono* contractor, a stage could also be added at the far end of the bingo hall so plays could be produced to raise funds and reduce the school debt. In short order a gang of volunteers turned our old facility into a new reality.

Figuring nothing sells like success, I asked the school's most popular girls and boys to meet with me and figure out a program. (Naturally, the girls were the magnets.) The program we hammered out was simple and practical: every other Saturday night, we would hold a dance; and during intermission, there would be a discussion based on questions submitted by teens to what we called "The Question Box."

To get the evenings rolling, a welcome committee of attractive, sociable teens would introduce everyone. On one point, however, I was emphatic: there were to be no wallflowers. Any girl who came had to have at least a few dances. If the boys didn't ask on their own, I'd introduce them to the wallflowers on my own. Conversely, if a girl got "stuck" with an unattractive boy, I would swoop in and rescue her, saying I needed to see her about something. Overseeing the whole shebang would be officers, initially chosen by me, but eventually by the membership. When I presented my plan to Father McGraw, there was only one sticking point — he wanted dances to end at eleven; I, midnight. We compromised on eleven thirty.

The Youth Club was an instant hit. Kids poured in the door while the entertainment committee unearthed such impressive local talent that the Wurzburg jukebox quickly got junked in favor of a small but enthusiastic band.

But the real star of the show was "The Question Box." Our goal was relevancy, so after starting off with a couple of basic questions about the obligation to attend Mass and confession, we quickly crossed over to discussions about the war, when I was often asked to give my own observations on the situation in Europe.

Victory breeding victory, our sought-after Saturday nights woke up the athletic committee, who formed a basketball team, drummed up donations to buy uniforms, and organized a playing schedule. The dances grew so fast, meanwhile, that, issuing ID cards, we were forced to restrict them to Catholics, prodding complaints from members who wanted to bring Protestant friends. Ultimately, we agreed that they could on the condition that they would be totally responsible for their guests. The overwhelming success of our venture proved the wisdom of the principle of subsidiarity, stressed by Pope Leo XIII in his famous encyclical on the rights of labor and the evils of industrialization, *Rerum Novarum*. Moreover, I learned a lot; mainly, build a field and they will come — to God.

However, when youth from Roland Park started showing up in Hampden, I knew that this newly ordained priest needed the advice and assistance of older, wiser heads. As a result, I organized a group of priests who developed an all-parish program that included a large, multi-parish ballroom dance featuring a big band at Baltimore's biggest hotel. Ticket sales were so huge that we chartered a boat for an evening ride on the Chesapeake Bay. Acting as chaperone, Father Scalley, from St. Bridget's Parish, merrily spent the evening prowling the dark recesses of the vessel on behalf of Christian morality.

It was our poster for that dance, a picture of the *labarum* of Emperor Constantine, bearing the cross with the inscription, "In this sign you will conquer," that got me called into the chancery for a meeting with Monsignor Joseph Nelligan. Monsignor Nelligan, son of a wealthy banker, was spare, business-like, but approachable. Allowing me to fully explain why and how I began this youth apostolate, he had just one criticism. "I support everything you're doing," he said, "with the exception of the poster's cross and inscription which might be offensive to those outside our Church. It would be better to drop it." His kindness and helpful use of authority were a great lesson, not to mention a perfect example of the wisdom of my high school teacher: "Hannan, forget every third idea."

Capitalizing on the favorable publicity, Father McGraw gave the go-ahead for my brother Tom to build our stage in the bingo auditorium. Our first play, "Growing Pains," pulled in over $500, then a sizeable sum and a welcome donation to the parish.

Much more importantly were the parents' reactions to their children's performances. Couples who had shown no interest in the Church returned with enthusiasm to the practice of their faith. Unwittingly, the kids, having become the family evangelizers, were far more effective than any priest.

"Day of Infamy"

On December 7, 1941, the Japanese suddenly attacked Pearl Harbor, reigniting my desire to be an Army chaplain. Convinced that America belonged in the war, the Pearl Harbor attack only solidified my feelings, making me even more determined to get to the front and make my own small contribution to the war against Nazism.

In Baltimore, Archbishop Curley, a supporter of President Roosevelt's decision to join the war, announced that a priest would be permitted to become a chaplain in the armed forces if his pastor, agreeing not to expect a replacement, granted permission. It was all I needed to hear. Listening to the nightly radio reports with Father McGraw, I began remarking on the need for chaplains. Adding to the pressure, I highjacked dinner conversation, talking about the anti-Christian atrocities committed by the Nazis. Shoring up my case even further, I let my feelings be known to key parishioners who in turn talked to the pastor.

What sealed the deal, however, was the arrival of a new assistant, Father Dziwulski, replacing Father Herb Howley, who had been so kind and generous with his advice to a newcomer. Finally, biting the bullet myself, I knocked on Father McGraw's door. Seated at his desk, he immediately knew why I was there. Almost before I could ask, he gave me his permission to leave.

When I telephoned my parents, though not wanting another son to follow my brothers Frank and Denis into the war, they raised no objection. The Youth Club and parishioners, already aware of my ambition, were comforted that a young priest was eager to serve alongside their own sons.

Registering at the recruiting office, my physical revealed no vestige of rheumatic fever damage to my heart. After getting my uniform, complete with first lieutenant's bars and the chaplain's cross, I was ready to go. But the Army wasn't. Cooling my heels for several long weeks, my notice finally arrived in the mail. I was to report to the Chaplains' School at Harvard at the end of December 1942. (The only difficulty I encountered was getting accepted by the Military Ordinariate, the Catholic diocese in charge of chaplains, since a priest, generally, had to have three years of pastoral experience before joining the armed forces. Citing that I had been ordained on December 8, 1939, I managed to qualify as a candidate by December 1942.)

The parish's farewell party, though warm and fun, was a real tear-jerker. Held in the auditorium that I had helped build, we reminisced, laughed, and belted out the popular new Christmas song, "White Christmas." The parishioners gave me a generous purse and a new radio to keep in touch with the news. Fighting back my own tears, I thanked them for their infinite support, inspiration, and affection during my two and a half years at St. Thomas Aquinas. Arriving as an inexperienced priest, new to their ways, their acceptance of me had nurtured my education as a parish priest. Moreover, each person's reverence for the priesthood as well as our faith had made me realize the grandeur of my vocation. In that sense, this was a kind of graduation. Never had the words "good-bye and God's blessings" meant more.

The following day, as he walked me to my car, Father McGraw surprised me with an unexpected question. "Will you return to St. Thomas after the war?" I paused. "I don't think I can answer that," I said slowly, pausing again. "I just don't know."

CHAPTER 6

Into the Army

On a brisk day just after Christmas — December 28, 1942 — I left Washington to report to the U.S. Army Chaplain School at Harvard University in Cambridge, Massachusetts. The motto of the Chaplain School was *Pro Deo et Patria* ("For God and Country"), a simple statement that would define my life for the next three years.

It was cold in Boston, with a few patches of snow on the ground. The size of our class — more than a hundred men — was surprising, and I was delighted that one of the chaplains was a fellow diocesan priest as well as a fellow North American College graduate, Father Jack Albert. Having been a chaplain for some time, he promptly offered some useful advice: "It's easy to get overworked as a chaplain. There is too much to do. Don't knock yourself out." Being a popular, handsome priest, solid in his piety, I took his advice to heart.

I was billeted in Connate Hall, Room 44, along with seven other chaplains, Protestants of various denominations, all gregarious, friendly, and extremely interested in meeting a "Catholic priest."

Classes began immediately on December 29 with an address by the commanding officer, Chaplain (Colonel) William D. Cleary, nattily attired in his uniform and the polished boots of a cavalry officer. Just as surprising, he spoke with an Irish accent — a congenial, but no-nonsense Catholic officer and priest.

In addition to relatively easy classes on military law, military sanitation, military courtesy, and protection against chemical warfare, we had drilling and hiking exercises to teach us the rudimentary phases of "close-order drill." Thanks to my four years as a cadet at St. John's College High School in Washington, the drilling — and hikes — were hardly taxing.

My academic background as a student at the Catholic University had prepared me for Chaplain School. Having gotten such a superior education from my professors, I wasn't the least worried about embarrassing myself. In fact, my only difficult academic class was Graves Registration, involving, in case of significant casualties, laying out a cemetery on a map which required a solid knowledge of mathematics. Having studied algebra and trigonometry in high school, I tried to help chaplains with weak math backgrounds, since flunking

Graves Registration might wash them out of school. On test day, after finishing the cemetery problems, I went to the bathroom, leaving my exam paper on my desk so that anyone needing to take a look could. I don't know if it helped, but no one flunked. In the end, there was nothing to worry about because, as we later discovered, the Army forbade chaplains to bury any men killed in action. The ultra efficient Graves Registration Office had complete jurisdiction over the bodies of soldiers fallen in combat, securing and identifying the body as well as notifying the family.

Though we could have learned what we needed to know about being a chaplain in one afternoon, they dragged it out for three or four weeks, making sure we knew the drill. In the end, I think we got some kind of spurious recognition from Harvard University, allowing me to tell pals that I got through Harvard in four weeks.

Chaplain Philip M. Hannan

Personally, my only problem was the presence of some very pretty Irish cousins who, living in Boston, visited me on Sunday afternoons. Since I made the mistake of introducing them to my roommates, one young Presbyterian chaplain promptly asked if I could help him make a date with one of them. Since they, fortunately, all had steady boyfriends, I could say, with some mental reservation, that they were all engaged.

What we didn't learn in classes we made up for in our interesting discussions, the Protestant chaplains eager to understand Catholic moral teaching in matters such as "use and abuse." "How can you allow people to drink liquor?" they asked. "What do you think about smoking? Or gambling? Or dancing?" — a query from one handsome young man who, being a good musician and having an attractive wife, was forbidden to dance under penalty of discharge by his local authority. Carefully explaining the difference between properly acceptable versus sinful dancing, I saw relief flooding his face. In fact, he was so grateful — and scrupulous — that just before we completed our training, he approached me again: "Now, let's go over this another time. I've got to be able to convince my superior that there is a moral way to dance." Assuring him there was, I wished him well!

Having the utmost respect for each other, Catholic, Protestant, and Jewish chaplains interacted easily. Though the Catholics held informal group meetings to strengthen our camaraderie and support for each other, Chaplain Cleary politely and firmly reminded us of our great opportunity to be of service to our Protestant and Jewish confreres. At one such Catholic chaplains gathering, I met my first Cajun priest, who flashed the daring, fun-loving attitude that I would see close up many years later as Archbishop of New Orleans.

Finally, completing our initial training, we received our first assignments as rookie chaplains — our own preferences not part of the equation. With my fluency in Italian and knowledge of Europe, I expressed my desire to be assigned to a combat group, but the Army had other ideas, sending me instead to a basic training center of the Army Air Corps in Florida. "Well," I thought ruefully, "at least my parents will like the appointment." My older brother Frank, a doctor, who had no children, and my younger brother Denis were both in tough combat groups, so my safety was naturally of deep concern to my parents and family.

Basic Training Center, Miami Beach

My assignment was Basic Training Center No. 7 of the Army Air Corps in Miami Beach. At that time, Miami Beach was an exotic amalgam of humanity that only the frenetic haste of a world war could create, with at least one hundred thousand recruits packed into hotels built for winter snowbirds from the North. Moreover, there were no billets for chaplains. Fortunately, the senior Catholic chaplain, Father John Green from Philadelphia, invited me to move into the house that he and two other officers had rented at 5786 Pine Tree Drive. I gladly accepted and met the two other tenants, Captain Ed Hartung and Captain John Farrell. Their advice proved to be even more valuable than the living quarters.

Father Green informed me that forty-two thousand of the one hundred thousand recruits were Catholics, most drawn from large Eastern cities with substantial Catholic populations. Besides me, there was only one other Catholic chaplain, a brawny, athletic priest of Lithuanian descent who had his own apartment at the end of the beach. Since all accommodations were "war-time crowded," my office was the former "ladies room" in the Shelburne Hotel, where my first two visitors turned out to be the embarrassed female secretaries to a couple of high ranking officers. Except for a desk, the furniture had been removed, leaving me to scavenge for chairs and a typewriter not in use by other offices. Eventually, I got an assistant, a man in his thirties from Boston whose principal asset was that, being Catholic, he could serve Mass.

Meanwhile, Chaplain William H. Howell, a Methodist from Texas and the Protestant chaplain of Training Center No. 7, informed me that my first duty the next day would be to give an orientation talk, following his opening remarks, to a thousand new recruits gathered in a large hall. Sitting in the back of the room the following morning, I watched Chaplain Howell quickly enter the stage, salute smartly to the sergeant in charge and begin. Near the end of his talk, he said, "I wish you to remember this rule of sexual morality: Whatever I do not wish anyone to do to my mother or sister, I shall not do to any woman." In front of me, a recruit whispered to his neighbor, "I'm lucky. I don't have a sister or mother."

My speech emphasized the Ten Commandments for both Christians and Jews. Catholic soldiers were obligated to attend Mass on Sunday, confess their sins, and receive Holy Communion. For those with no religion, I stressed the voice of conscience as their rule, quoting St. Paul's famous instructions on this matter in 2 Corinthians 3:3 that the law of conscience is "written not with ink but with the Spirit of the living God, not on tablets of stone but on tablets of human hearts." Ending with the advice to "be honest in writing your letters back home. Don't tell them that everything in the Army is wonderful. They'll know that you're lying and won't believe anything you write"; I also admonished the soldiers "not even to consider marriage until the war is over." Talk about an unpopular remark!

My chief duty and problem was how to properly celebrate Mass for the thousands of Catholics in my training center. Fortunately, there was a Catholic Center, located on Collins Avenue within my territory, where daily Mass, confessions, and small events could be held. Also within our territory was an imposing Catholic Church, dedicated to St. Patrick and pastored by Monsignor William Barry, who also had a filial chapel dedicated to St. Joseph.

In the final analysis, however, the beach, though less than ideal due to the relentless trade winds constantly blowing sand, was the only location large enough to accommodate several thousand Catholics for Mass. Besides having sand blown in their faces, the recruits had difficulty concentrating on their devotions thanks to the distraction of an endless parade of beachcombers and female sunbathers. Though able to secure a wooden altar with a cover, I had no public address system. Since there were no "extraordinary ministers of Holy Communion," later made possible by the Second Vatican Council, giving Holy Communion to two thousand men with sand blowing in their faces was challenging indeed.

On Sundays, there was an early morning Mass in St. Joseph's Chapel, a 10:00 a.m. Mass on the beach, and a noon Mass inside a theater. At the beginning of every beach Mass, I cautioned the relatively informal congregation to try not to ogle the girls in their swimsuits. Despite my former practice of shouting in the woods behind the Sulpician seminary to strengthen my vocal cords, no voice was strong enough to convey a sermon to a congregation that size on a beach. Finally, an industrious sergeant came to my rescue. Though lacking public address systems, the Army did have copy machines. As a result, printing my sermons in huge numbers, I distributed them on the beach, which paid off. Some soldiers even mailed them home, prompting nice notes from their appreciative folks.

If I was overwhelmed by anything, it was the ambition of the officers and recruits. Determined to succeed, especially those who wanted to become pilots, their spiritual development was considered an essential element of their preparation. When they flunked a critical test, they turned to me as their sounding board, claiming they "deserved another chance. I was sick and nervous when I took the test, so worn out from physical training that I couldn't concentrate."

Among the officers was a large number of West Pointers who, setting a strict code of conduct, insisted on a high moral code. When an officer was found guilty of sexually abusing a young boy, they printed the story on the front page of the local newspaper and dismissed him from the service.

Although many questioned our alliance with Communist Russia, none questioned the morality of a war against Nazism — a sentiment I used to prod recruits who had slipped in their Mass attendance to return to church. "Hitler at least was honest when admitting that he disregarded the Church," I told the absentees, "but what excuse do you have for not attending Mass?"

Though officers generally cooperated with chaplains in setting aside reasonable time for recruits to attend church, there were exceptions. One former National Guard colonel ordered training marches on Sunday mornings, with the peculiar explanation that, "If you were on Guadalcanal, you wouldn't have a chance to go to church." "If you were on Guadalcanal," I answered, "you wouldn't be wearing that shirt or pants," which got me nowhere. So I turned to Army regulations, namely AR210-10, December 20, 1940, which stated: "Commanders will reduce military labor and duty on Sunday to the measure of strict necessity. Such duties will, if practicable, be so scheduled as not to interfere with attendance at services of worship." It got his attention.

One day in the officer's mess, an "old Army" officer wanted to know how the men were doing. "Chaplain, how is the morale of the men?" I answered honestly, "Great. They can't wait to get out of here to go where the action is." No more conversation.

Occasionally, we chaplains got together socially. Arriving early at one gathering, I found the only Jewish chaplain, Chaplain Harold Gordon, already there. "I have an extra bottle of Jewish wine, Manischewitz," he said. "Would you like it?" Thanking him, I put the bottle into a box. When everyone else arrived, a Protestant chaplain showed a short movie demonstrating the evils of even a tiny amount of alcohol. On screen, a scientist poured the amount of alcohol contained in a 3.2-percent bottle of beer into a goldfish bowl. At first swimming furiously, the fish suddenly turned belly up. As he did so, Chaplain Gordon flashed me a smile.

Challenges on the Beach

Of course, given the immense number of soldiers and officers on the beach, I knew as a chaplain I would have to deal with men involved in sinful sexual relations. In one case, a splendid lawyer, Herbert J. Kenarik of Newark, New Jersey, spent a long time at his expense searching for a soldier who had convinced a nineteen-year-old woman to back out of her wedding and then subsequently had gotten her pregnant. The soldier had used an assumed name, but Mr. Kenarik somehow traced him to Miami Beach. I was delighted to help the attorney find the soldier and confront him.

In another case, a woman from Chicago came to Miami Beach with her godchild, who had become pregnant after having relations with a soldier. When I discovered that the soldier had been shipped out to a camp in California, the godmother asked, "When does the next train leave for California?" That young lady was in good hands.

War puts emotional stress on everyone, and one recruit told me he had felt pressured to marry a girl he had only been friendly with before shipping off to basic training. "We dated occasionally, but I certainly was not in love with her," he explained. "The newspaper carried stories about draftees getting married to their sweethearts. The girl and her parents talked with my folks about a marriage. My folks agreed because they liked the girl, and then they urged me to marry her. Frankly, I didn't want to argue or hurt my parents or hers. So I got married, but I did not have the intention of getting married. What should I do?" I advised him, "Be careful of how you write to her. Avoid saying that you love her. After the war bring your case to the Catholic tribunal in your diocese and explain the case to them. You have a good case." War is never an excuse for a quickie marriage.

Some recruits were so anxious to pass their physicals they temporarily developed high blood pressure. My standard advice was, "Put yourself in the hands of God, and also say a prayer for the intercession of the Blessed Mother." The prayer worked well. But one day a Jewish soldier named Brock asked for advice because his sinuses would get inflamed as soon as he started the physical exam. "I need rest to control it," Brock said. "All right," I replied. "Here's the key to my apartment. Take a nap." That also worked.

Young, lovelorn soldiers were a special problem. One forlorn soul told me he had to go AWOL (absent without leave) because his girlfriend was being wooed off her feet by a neighbor. "I can't write well and tell her how much I love her," he pleaded. "Well," I replied, "sit down here and tell me how much you love her, and I'll tell you how to phrase it." He obeyed. A week later he came back, all smiles — and I discovered that writing an effective love letter and an inspirational homily isn't all that different, except for the audience.

An older soldier had a different problem. His wife left him, and he found, in searching her belongings, that her baptismal certificate indicated she was sixteen years older than she had admitted. "You mean to tell me you couldn't tell that she was sixteen years older than she claimed?" I asked. "No," the soldier replied sheepishly. "She was sunburned."

Some of the recruits were illiterate, and were taught to read, count, and write in an elementary manner. There were a few Catholics among them, but they all seemed to know that the Catholic chaplain could help them. Unfortunately, some "barracks lawyer" told them that if they were completely uncooperative, they would be dismissed by the Army and allowed to go home. A gullible victim of that nonsensical advice came to my office, disheveled and thoroughly dirty. "I'm sorry to tell you that the advice you got is all wrong," I said. "Let me explain how you can get a whole new life if you follow the recommendations of the Army." Surprisingly, my guidance worked.

Unbecoming Conduct

In general, the civilian population of Miami Beach generously provided volunteers for our Catholic Center (USO) as well as supplies for the use of the chaplains. There was, however, one group of storekeepers who gouged the soldiers for their ordinary needs. One of these was the Pancoast Drug Store, which sold soft drinks, sandwiches, and toiletries. I lodged a formal complaint with the Office of Price Administration but got nowhere. I concluded some direct action was needed.

I spoke to Chaplain McClay, the commanding officer of the men in the immediate area of the Pancoast Drug Store, and asked if he would give me permission to suggest to the men that they not patronize the store. Then, early in the morning, I stood in front of the store, diverting all the soldiers from entering. The effect was immediate. About ten thirty in the morning, trucks came to haul·out their perishable goods. Shortly thereafter, I received a telephone call in the store asking me to picket another store. The news spread.

While I was speaking to the store manager, an officer of the Provost Marshall arrived and hustled me off to his office. Chaplain Salango, a Protestant chaplain, had joined me, and so he came along. The Provost Marshall summarily ordered us to stop the boycott and said nothing could be done to put the store "off limits." At lunch, I was told to report to Colonel Parker, the elderly commanding officer of the entire operations at Miami Beach. He told me, "This is the most disgraceful exhibition of an officer I have ever seen in my life. Go down and be judged by your immediate commanding officer." I reported to Colonel Claggett, who chewed me out a bit, but did nothing further. A few hours later, I was ordered to report to the Air Force Inspector General, who informed me that I had been accused of starting a riot. I knew I had to be clear about what had happened, so I signed an affidavit stating the exact chain of events.

That night a young, polite officer of the Judge Advocate General's Office came to my apartment and told me, "I approve of what you did today, but I'm sorry to inform you that you are charged with conduct unbecoming an officer." I related what had happened. The boycott was so controversial that the newspaper carried an article about it. I decided to visit Monsignor William Barry, the courageous and effective pastor of St. Patrick Parish on the beach, who was considered by the mayor and chief of police as the unofficial manager of the bustling area. Whenever anything unusual happened on the beach, Monsignor Barry was there to offer advice to city authorities. A few years earlier Monsignor Barry had been offended by a drug store's practice of advertising that it had contraceptives for sale, and when he appealed to the pharmacy to remove the storefront ads, it flatly refused. On the following Sunday, he asked all of his parishioners to boycott the drug store. Very quickly, the drug store pulled the advertising. Monsignor Barry was equal to the task in defending my actions. He explained the situation to a colonel friend, and the colonel quashed the case.

Somehow, the word of what I had done got back to Archbishop Michael Curley in Baltimore, and he paternally ordered me to be more prudent in the future, pointing out that a charge of "conduct unbecoming an officer" could be very maliciously interpreted. I also received a letter from Father John Cronin, in charge of the Social Action Department of the National Catholic Welfare Council in Washington, D.C. — which later became the National Conference of Catholic Bishops and the United States Catholic Conference — inviting me to join him in his labor union work after the war.

That experience demonstrated I should be very careful about promoting any ideas to better the lives of the recruits except through my spiritual ministry, although there often is a political or social component to spreading the Gospel. I had my hands full in fulfilling my spiritual ministry on the Beach. The three Catholic chaplains decided to offer a weeklong "mission" for all the military personnel and any other Catholics who lived on the beach. We delivered a mission sermon every night at eight o'clock, followed by Benediction of the Blessed Sacrament. We heard confessions before and after the homily. At the solemn closing of the mission on Sunday afternoon, Monsignor Barry offered Benediction. It was very successful — about twelve thousand soldiers attended.

In the week leading up to Christmas in 1943, we heard confessions practically all day. I remember leaving the confessional on Christmas Eve at 11:50 p.m., just in time to put on the vestments for Midnight Mass. The reward was infinitely worth the effort. There was an intense feeling of family and religious unity among the men. I tried to tie it all together with my homily, which focused on unity with Christ in the Holy Family. I asked the men to remember their families at home and the families of all engaged in the war effort. After Mass, the soldiers were so enthralled they gathered in groups to continue singing Christmas hymns for hours. We really had the Christmas spirit. Many of the men were away from home for the first time, and they enjoyed our efforts to make this Christmas special. A soldiers' choir set an excellent tone for the Mass and led the caroling after Mass. We foraged for extra food to provide snacks for everyone after the Midnight Mass.

We priest chaplains were so busy that I was very happy when additional priests joined us as reinforcements. Father Edward Trower, a Redemptorist, reported in and was assigned officially to take care of the hospitals, but he generously gave us help at any time he could spare. A Carmelite priest from Chicago, Father Robert Burns, arrived and quickly became a great favorite with the enlisted men. He had taught English and coached the football team at a Catholic high school in Chicago. Father Burns was very zealous but refused to celebrate Mass on the beach, saying, "I can't stand seeing those lousy beachcombers gawking at the congregation of soldiers and making sneering remarks."

Father Burns was extremely athletic and devoted to physical training. Once, when he was forced to go to the hospital for an illness, he did his exercises in the bed. A sergeant made the mistake once of challenging him about his physical fitness, and he made the sergeant count the number of push-ups, sit-ups, and other exercises he could do. The test took so long the sergeant appealed to me to try to stop him. "Look, he's done over a hundred push-ups alone, and that's way above 100 percent of what we require. Now he's doing sit-ups, and I don't know how long this will go on. Can't you stop him?" My pleas to Father Burns fell on deaf ears until I told him, "Father, you have worn out the seat of your shorts, and you're showing." That did the trick!

Father Burns physically could outperform every man in his unit and was regarded as the champion of the enlisted men. He was equally strict about religious duties and had a very powerful effect on the soldiers' religious observance.

Father Burns also solved an unusual problem for a young married officer who had asked me, "I'm being sent overseas, and the hurricane season is approaching. I rented a house with two apartments. Could you find me somebody who is strong and reliable and who could live in the other apartment and who could help my wife in case of trouble?"

"I've got exactly the right man," I said, and I introduced him to Father Burns. A couple of weeks later I called the wife to ask how things were. "Wonderful," she said. "Father Burns came and introduced himself to me and gave me a bouquet of flowers and a quart of ice cream. The only trouble is that I tried to clean his apartment when he was on duty, but I couldn't move the heavy weight equipment he has. I couldn't even budge it." I told her not to worry: "He'd be disappointed if you could move it."

Another priest, Father Leo J. Schafer of Indianapolis, arrived about the same time, and he was accompanied by his widowed father. The two of them were a fantastic team. Father Schafer was a great asset, a very quiet and zealous priest. His father helped out in any way possible. He was a good juggler and entertained every new group of inductees.

I was even more thankful for the reinforcement of our chaplain ranks when I received an official order that I was to take care of the psychiatric patients at the huge Coral Gables Hospital, "in addition to my usual duties." The "hospital" was a converted massive hotel and was filled with wartime psychiatric cases. I soon discovered that it was best to visit the overworked staff and the struggling patients in the evening. A clever doctor determined that having them tend "victory gardens" could help many of the less troubled patients. There is no less likely site for a successful garden than the sand of Coral Gables, but the idea worked. The cycle of nature — the fascination of seeing the sprouting and growth of vegetables — had a very calming effect on the patients.

Some of the psychiatric cases were far more difficult. One young man was catatonic and impossible to make contact with. I was asked to help him. I thought that maybe he, like others, had found the effect of combat, including dropping bombs, to be shattering. He was a bed patient. I bent down and started to recite the Lord's Prayer in Latin. I saw his lips begin to quiver, then to fashion words. Next I said the Hail Mary in Latin. Finally, he responded. Those timeless words had broken through. I soon discovered that he was a former seminarian.

Breaking down barriers with another patient required my knowledge of Italian. The "patient" was a very healthy young foreigner who could not speak a word of English. After trying several phrases in the few languages I knew, he seemed to understand a bit of Italian. Soon I discovered he was a sailor from the Dalmatian coast who had been working on a freighter that had been sunk by a German submarine. He swam ashore and was picked up by the local police and taken to the local draft officer, who drafted him and dispatched him to the Army. Anything to fill the quota!

I tried to capitalize on the increased attendance at Mass for the feast days to teach Catholic doctrine about many matters. Whenever two or more soldiers are gathered during wartime, the discussion invariably centers on two topics: religion and sex. I redoubled my efforts to instill a better understanding of our Christian faith and the Sixth Commandment — "You shall not commit adultery" — including the dangers of venereal disease and infidelity. I also touched on stealing and the treatment of prisoners of war, as well as the Geneva rules of warfare. I found soldiers coming to me more often for Confession.

Naturally, my preaching also produced a large number of requests by soldiers to see me about their problems. Most of the problems dealt with their parents, or wife, or girlfriend back home. The most peculiar case was that of a married soldier from New York who was convinced that his wife was unfaithful. He secured a furlough, found indeed that his wife was unfaithful, and went to see a lawyer. The lawyer told him he did not have witnesses for a divorce. The soldier spied on his wife, saw a man entering his wife's apartment, and called the fire department. The firemen discovered the couple in bed — and no fire. The soldier secured the names of the firemen who saw the infidelity, paid the fine for a false alarm, and went to the lawyer with the names of the witnesses.

In one day, I received five applications for "shotgun" marriages. Despite the entreaties of the girls, I always investigated the circumstances to see if the marriage had a probability of success.

I had other minor difficulties, including correctly pronouncing Slavic names in marriages. An excellent young fellow came in for a marriage application and smiled as he wrote his name. "I dare you to pronounce it," he said. It was Szuszczewicz.

Then there was the poor fellow who could not stand the heat in Miami but who had made arrangements for his marriage. He landed in the hospital with heat exhaustion but still insisted on being married. He fainted three times after leaving the hospital to go to the church, went back to the hospital, was given two shots to stabilize him, and finally got to the church for the wedding. I was very pleased I was not the priest for the wedding.

Soldiers tried every trick in the book when it came to finding a way to get back home for an "emergency." One soldier asked me to recommend his application to go home "because my father needs me badly." I asked where his father was. "He's in the penitentiary," the soldier replied. "He needs me to cheer him up." I asked how long he had been in prison and how long his sentence was. He told me he'd been there for ten years and was sentenced to one hundred years for a murder. "I think he'll still be there when the war is over," I said. "He'll also need cheering up then." After listening to these inventive arguments, I always hoped the soldiers would expend as much energy and creativity in fighting the enemy.

Of course, I recorded all of these activities in my monthly reports to the military command and to the Military Ordinariate in New York City. I never knew if anyone read the reports until one day when an affable Protestant chaplain came to my office with an unusual offer. "My commanding officer has learned about all your activities, including the large number of confessions you have been hearing," he said. "He told me to help you out. I'll be glad to hear some confessions for you if you tell me what to say." I explained politely that I could not give him permission to hear confessions because it was a sacrament that required ordination to the priesthood. That explanation didn't stop him.

"Well, I'd like to see the words you use," he said. "Maybe I could change them and use them with our Protestant men." I showed him the words in Latin and firmly, but politely, asked him not to offer "confessions" to his men. We remained good friends.

Despite my overcrowded schedule, I intermittently tried to secure a decent portable altar for the Masses on the Beach. I finally located an "official artist" for the Army by the name of Guranowski. He had been brought over from Poland to decorate the Polish Pavilion for the 1939 World's Fair in New York and never found his way back to Poland. Guranowski said he needed an assistant to help him, and I suggested a number of men who were registered as artists. Guranowski brushed aside all the suggestions and said decisively, "There is only one artist here. He is Max Schnitzel." Max was an abstract painter who had painted enough "moods" to get him into our "Who's Who."

I accepted Max and then went to the office of engineers. The post engineer was Igor Polevitsky, who approved the sketch for the altar but insisted on some changes. I asked him to confer with Guranowski, but then a hitch developed. Schnitzel demanded that, before he begin the work, an application be submitted to the Smithsonian Institution to accept the altar as an exhibit there after the war. At that point, I decided to leave the project in Polevitsky's hands. The altar was finished and delivered just two weeks before I was given orders to leave.

In the midst of these negotiations, the Catholic chaplain for the Officers' Candidate School was changed and sent to another post, which gave me the added task of caring for the Catholic men in that school. The most demanding aspect of that appointment was taking care of the marriages of the newly commissioned officers immediately after their inductions as officers. This was no cursory task. There were fifteen marriages to be conducted in one afternoon. The marriages were scheduled to begin at fifteen-minute intervals. The men were inducted into the Army as officers in the morning, married in the afternoon, and left that night. Any couple that was late for its scheduled time was obliged to wait until all the other marriages were completed. True to their Army training, all were completed on time.

Meanwhile, I was growing increasingly restless about not being with a combat unit. I wrote on several occasions to the Chief of Chaplains of the Army Air Corps, and also to the Military Ordinariate, expressing my burning desire to join a combat unit in light of my European education and knowledge of foreign languages. Again, I received only negative replies. Finally, a wonderful Franciscan chaplain in the Chief of Chaplains Office, Lieutenant Colonel Constantine Zielinski, replied and assured me that my request had been received and that I would be given another assignment. I never forgot Father Zielinski, and after the war, when his Franciscan religious superior wished him to return to the Franciscans, I helped him to be formally accepted in the Diocese of Richmond, which allowed him to continue to be a chaplain in the Army.

In view of this good news, I decided I should get into better physical condition. My tonsils needed attention. I went to see an excellent young surgeon from the Boston area. He took a look and said, "They're hanging so loose that you don't need to go to the hospital." The next day, I returned, and the doctor seated me in a chair, gave me a local anesthetic and proceeded to extract the tonsils. Well, it didn't happen as expected. After a half hour of cutting, tugging, and additional shots of anesthetic, he said, "The complication is that you have some infection that I did not expect. I'll be finishing soon." In about fifteen minutes, he was finished, and so was I.

The doctor put me in the hospital to recover. It was late in the evening by the time I was bedded down and given a shot to put me to sleep. The next morning, I was awakened by a supervising nurse, who sternly informed me that I had broken a regulation by not having made my bed! Fortunately, I recovered rapidly and asked to be released. I received a flat denial. The hospital was scheduled for closing because of a low patient count — and I had to stay to bolster the count. We made a compromise. I agreed to return to my bed at night for the count while I returned each day to my work.

To my great surprise, I received a communication from the commanding officer that I was obliged to undergo training to become a rifle marksman. Of course, this was contrary to the Army regulations that forbade a chaplain to carry weapons. Nonetheless, I was not about to begin a discussion with the commanding officer about this matter. I dutifully reported to the commanding officer in charge of the shooting range, and on my first try succeeded in hitting the bull's eye, thus qualifying to be a marksman. I hope no record was ever made of my effort.

Finally, the time came for a reduction in the number of chaplains and, by attrition, I became the Chief Chaplain for the Training Center. My principal duty was to notify the chaplains of their orders to report to other posts, many of them being in foreign lands. Naturally, I appealed again for a new assignment. At last, there arrived a notice that a Catholic chaplain was needed in a "rainy, cool area," which meant England.

Promptly, I made out the order and delivered it to myself, glad to be leaving Miami Beach and hoping that I could somehow be assigned to a division bound for combat on the European continent. That U.S. Army Chaplain School motto, *Pro Deo et Patria* — "For God and Country" — was ringing in my ears.

CHAPTER 7

England and Combat

My transfer orders called for me to leave Miami for the embarkation camp at Taunton, Massachusetts, near Boston. While awaiting further orders, I was asked to celebrate Mass on Sunday at the coastal defense post guarding the Welland Canal. My curiosity was piqued as I spotted the gun emplacements on the coast. Were they there to repel Nazi submarines? I found that the coastal guns originally were placed to ward off invasion by the British fleet in 1812! Of course, now they would repel anything that the Nazis could send.

The crew at the coastal defense post was very friendly and appreciated my celebrating Mass. I had breakfast with two young officers, who complimented the crew. But one of the officers had an elitist complaint about the breakfast: it seems the sergeant in charge of the mess hall did not know how to properly "shirr" the eggs he had ordered. I was never more eager to serve my country — outside of the United States.

I was with a group of hastily trained, undisciplined infantry troops, and our hiking exercises took us across a pontoon bridge that crossed a small lake. The soldiers in front of me began to horse around on the bridge and their weight snapped the connection between two of the bridge sections, throwing me and another soldier into the lake. He screamed that he couldn't swim, so I pushed him onto the broken pontoon section, which could support only one person. Then I had to strike out for shore on my own. I certainly learned that boots and a field uniform are a poor swimsuit. I didn't complain about the incident because I feared any complaint might lead to a hearing, which would delay my embarkation.

Finally, we got the alert to board the *Mauritania*, a converted transatlantic passenger boat, for the voyage to England. At one time the *Mauritania* had held the speed record for crossing the North Atlantic; therefore, it required no armed convoy. It was supposed to be capable of outracing any German U-boat.

We had been told to expect cold and rainy conditions in the North Atlantic the next day, but when it turned out sunny and warm — and when we saw dozens of flying fish — we discovered that we had taken a circuitous route that brought us just north of the Bahamas, apparently to outrun a pack of German submarines.

The military had a solution for everything, especially for completing distasteful tasks. To ensure that every soldier received his proper shots before landing in England, medics would approach us with their loaded needles while we lined up in the mess hall for our two daily meals. That was a pretty efficient system.

In due time, we arrived in Liverpool. A group of dirty, hungry children gathered around us as we left the ship. As we stood in line for assignment to our camp, a Red Cross nurse went along the line cautioning us, "Don't touch the children. They all have lice." Well, we didn't think giving them some candy would give us lice.

Liverpool was an industrial port city that looked grimy from years of war and aerial bombardment, but there was a feeling of dogged and unflagging determination. There was no trace of defeatism, although the people looked tired. They were "bloody, but unbowed." The wartime atmosphere was completely different from that of the United States, where the rationing of some supplies and blackout regulations were daily inconveniences but not real privations.

To maintain their long-term resolve, the English were intransigent in holding onto their daily customs, such as a "spot of tea" in the afternoon. They were absolutely unrelenting in maintaining secrecy about anything relevant to the war. At times, they were even hesitant to tell you the distance to a port or an important manufacturing town. And, they didn't answer any questions or speculate about the timing or the method of attack that the Allies were certain to launch on the continent at some point in the coming months. We Americans experienced a bracing feeling that we were close to participating in the war, and we looked forward to making our contribution, big or small.

I was assigned to an airfield near Wantage, Oxfordshire, about ten miles southwest of Oxford: a small town graced by an imposing statue of King Alfred the Great, who was born there in the ninth century. I was assigned to serve the airplane maintenance mechanics, test pilots, and pilots for special bombing targets. I was given an assistant, Tom Getty, an excellent Catholic who was likable and very popular with all the men.

I hit it off immediately with the commanding officer, Colonel Harris, a solid, practicing Baptist from Montgomery, Alabama. Colonel Harris was a member of the old breed. He was extremely worried that his soldiers would become engaged to the local ladies. When he learned I demanded solid proof from the men of the prospects for an indissoluble marriage by both parties, he appointed me the investigator for all marriage applications. Army regulations required that permission for marriage be given by the commanding officer of the unit. I insisted on genuine proof from the men that they had prudently thought out their decision, and I devised a simple test that would indicate how well the soldier knew his fiancée. I had the soldier fill out a marriage application in triplicate, and often he would spell the name of his fiancée differently on each copy. That was an immediate red flag. If that happened, I would present the three copies to Colonel Harris and note the disparity. That was the end of that application.

One nineteen-year-old soldier was so convinced his rights were being infringed by these regulations that he bugged the Colonel for days about the supposed injustice. But the Colonel remained firm. Three weeks later, the soldier came back with an application to marry another girl!

The Catholic men regularly practiced their faith, and the Baptist colonel certainly encouraged them. "You can stop your work any time to go to religious services," he told his men. That standing order paid off in the soldiers being even more dedicated to their work.

The lack of immediate danger for our men at the airfield could have created a lethargic attitude among the troops. I decided to give the men lectures on the Catholic faith and encouraged them to get involved in helping a local beleaguered Catholic pastor. He had only a storefront for a church, and he needed help. As a preliminary step, I took up a collection of money among the men for his parish. It was a godsend to him and to his parish, as well as for our men. One week's collection by our soldiers was equal to a year's collection in his small parish.

Part of my duty was addressing the spiritual needs of the men when there was a plane wreck, and there were plenty of those. The airmen and aircrews had a Catholic chaplain at the airbase, but wrecks happened all over the area because of the frequently impenetrable fog conditions.

On my first night on duty, I was baptized into the life of an air chaplain. I received word that a bomber had crashed in pea soup fog while making an airfield approach. It was so foggy we couldn't even find the crash site. My jeep driver, Tommy Getty, and I started out on an invisible road. I took a flashlight and held the light just a few inches from the ground to keep the wheels on the road. We followed the road until we thought we were directly across from the crash site. I left Tom in the jeep — no jeep, not even in the fog, was ever left unattended — and trudged into the darkness.

I had plenty of time to pray for guidance. I coursed up and down the field and then slipped on a piece of metal. I smelled some acrid smoke and went in the direction of the smoke. Through the fog, not far away, I could see a macabre sight of crushed metal, with smoke swirling up to the sky. A terrific fire had engulfed the remains of the engines and part of the fuselage. I circled the remains, looking for any signs of the crew. I prayed earnestly, "God, Our Father, into your hands I commend all who were in this plane. Be merciful to them. They were sacrificing their lives for the cause of freedom you have given us."

I was hoping that somehow some of the bodies had been thrown from the plane by the force of the crash. I rummaged through the metal, looking for bodies or uniforms. I finally found a lone eagle insignia, completely torn away from the pilot's uniform by the force of the crash. I picked it up as though it were a relic — it was all that remained of the brave crew. I said a prayer and gave conditional absolution, hoping that perhaps in the fog there was a body that I had not discovered — knowing that only the good Lord knew for certain.

As I returned to the jeep, holding only the eagle insignia, I just shook my head at Tom, confirming his sad premonition that we would find only a grave with nothing in it. We turned over the insignia to the officer responsible for it and glumly walked over to the mess hall as the dawn brought another day of war.

There was no "getting used to" this grim price of war. Even when occasionally a whole flight would return, with some of the pilots waggling their planes' wings up and down as a sign of triumph as they landed, there was always the thought of what the next flight might bring — more victims, especially the civilians, left at the site of the bombing.

A less troublesome duty I took on was serving as the officer for the base dances. The colonel said he just hated doing it, and he asked me to take over as his delegate. I soon found out why he couldn't stand it. The dances were open to all the noncommissioned officers and privates in the area, including the soldiers from the nearby truck company. The girls were all English from the surrounding area. The colonel always dispatched a personnel carrier for my use. If any girl desired to leave the dance hall and return home because things got too rowdy, I could send her home in the personnel carrier, manned by a dependable sergeant. It gave the girls a sense of security to use it if needed.

Most of my time chaperoning dances was spent answering questions from the English girls. A favorite question was, "I've known this soldier for several months now, and he wants me to marry him. He says he comes from a nice town in Texas. Is it really like one of our English villages?" I would reply, "I don't know that town. My advice is for you to wait to get married after the war and for you to travel to take a look at the town and his family before you get married. Make him pay for the ticket, and be sure it's a two-way ticket, just in case. If he really loves you, he'll agree to do that."

I knew of one case in which a GI in England changed the final words of his marriage promise from "until death do us part" to "for the length of the duration"!

D-Day Invasion

D-Day — June 6, 1944 — changed the whole atmosphere in England. The Brits were liberated from bombing attacks and no longer had to hide under tables when the warning sirens for bombs went off. The Allied forces were on the attack, and the English people were eager for any bit of news from the Western Front. A new spirit swept the camp. The end of the war could not be far off.

I heard the news about D-Day over the radio in England, and I was praying hard because I knew the stakes were as high as they could be. My brother Frank, who was in the invasion, said everyone prayed crossing the Channel. A Ukrainian American prayed in his mother tongue. Italian Americans did the same.

Much later when I came to New Orleans, I met engineer Frank Walk, who was a green soldier of only twenty-two when he landed on the beach in the Normandy invasion. His commanding officer was supposed to be in charge of beach traffic, but he psychologically broke down. Undaunted, Frank took over and coordinated the traffic to save the day. It was acts of heroism such as his that won the war. Frank, by the way, much later designed the papal altar we used for the great outdoor Mass by Pope John Paul II in 1987 at the University of New Orleans. He is one of the true unsung heroes.

In July 1944 we received word we were being transferred to an airfield in France to service the planes attacking Germany. The airfield was near Melun, a pleasant town about thirty miles southeast of Paris. Incredibly, our movements were held up for a few days because we had run out of typing paper, and everything had to be recorded in quintuplicate. The most serious difficulty was the theft of a package that contained the warm-weather flying gear for the pilots.

Moving to France brought us closer to the war and increased our rapport with both the pilots and the French citizens. Despite the catastrophic impact of the war, the French civilians retained their Gallic sparkle. The new post also brought more duties for me.

Our camp was near a large convent with an attached boarding school for girls in elementary grades. Because the French population was predominantly Catholic, I naturally had more contact with the local residents, the local pastor, and the civil authorities. The sisters were the first to make a request — that I celebrate Mass occasionally for them and their students. After the Mass, celebrated in a beautiful chapel (a rare treat), the Sister Superior had a list of questions. In perfect English, she asked, "Why do the English, and I think some of the Americans, dislike General DeGaulle so much?" "What will be the attitude of your country toward France after the war?" "Can you get some of your soldiers to help repair some parts of our building?"

The last question was easy to handle — until the soldiers realized there were no older girls enrolled in the school.

Colonel Harris, our commanding officer, enjoyed the welcoming attitude of the French and accepted an occasional invitation to dinner by some of the wealthy citizens. This led to his request that I accompany him to Paris, where he was called on official business. When his business was finished, he asked me to help him buy some French perfume for his wife. He asked, "What does *Ma Peche* mean?" I answered, "My sin." He put the bottle down, saying, "No, never. My wife is back home by herself." He finally settled for something safe — Shalimar, named after the famous garden of Lahore in Pakistan.

With the perfume secured, we went to a restaurant, where I informed the maître d' how important the colonel was. The chef presented us with an exquisite filet mignon with a special béarnaise sauce that he had developed. After the chef made a personal presentation at the table and finished with a bow, the colonel asked, "Where's the ketchup?"

Despite the affluence of a few French families, the plight of the less fortunate was desperate. The Nazis had taken an immense toll on the food supply. Also, it was common to see French farmwomen walking with no stockings and wearing shoes made of cardboard and cloth.

Nevertheless, practically every French town that was liberated held a victory celebration, and I was asked to attend to represent the United States. At one celebration, the ostentatious mayor was dressed in his official sash and stood near the center of the town hall to receive guests and well wishers. He asked me to stand next to him. The dance was lively, and ironically, the most popular dance was the polka, which originated in central Europe, not in France.

The intermission produced a rush to the table for refreshments. Our mess sergeant had donated some hamburgers for the occasion, and the people were so hungry they devoured them immediately. After the intermission the mayor and I resumed our positions of honor. The first dance after the intermission was another polka. When a handsome airman with a beautiful young mademoiselle swished past us, all of a sudden a big hamburger popped out of her blouse, flopping down just in front of the mayor. With no hesitation, the mademoiselle bent down, snatched the hamburger from the floor, and slipped it back right between her breasts in her blouse. With no loss of dignity, the mayor stared straight ahead. Food is a precious commodity in a time of war.

The Catholic soldiers responded well to the lift that came from being in a Catholic country. Some politely asked me if it would be all right for them to attend Mass in nearby churches. I encouraged them to do so but also reminded them to be generous when the collection basket came around. As usual, I took up a collection for the benefit of the nearby church, which had been badly damaged. When I presented it to the pastor "for your church," he demurred. "I cannot touch the church building," he said. "It is a national monument. But I can take the money for the poor." All the prominent French churches were controlled by their government.

As the summer of 1944 wore on, anticipation grew that the war was reaching its conclusion. That gave me an opening to tell the men to get themselves in good spiritual condition to return home — and not to propose to those pretty French girls. I continued my successful method of forestalling marriages by making the soldier fill out the application in triplicate, one sheet at a time. The French names, especially, were a puzzle to them, and that tripped them up.

The pilots were a very friendly but extremely competitive group. I found this out one day when the chief test pilot asked me to join him on one of his test missions. After about twenty minutes of all kinds of gut-wrenching maneuvers — Immelmann turns, upside down flying, steep climbs followed by feathering the prop, and steep dives that left my stomach about a thousand yards behind my body — it occurred to me he was repeating the same maneuvers.

"Why are you repeating the same thing?" I shouted. He shouted back, "Are you sick?" I replied, "No, not yet." After several more maneuvers, the pilot asked again, "Are you sick now?" I answered, "No, but I don't want any lunch."

Finally, we came down, and when my brain had left my throat, I asked the pilot, "Why did you put me through all this?" Sheepishly, he replied, "The first time that I went through all those maneuvers, I got sick. I just wanted to prove that no chaplain was tougher than I." I shot back, "Why didn't you tell me that? I would have gotten sick for you in record time."

As the winter of 1944 approached, we believed that the reeling German army would certainly collapse and surrender. I was still strongly dissatisfied with serving outside the combat zone and told the colonel, who saw no reason why I should be permitted to leave his command to join a combat unit. Finally, in December, we received the surprising news that the German army, under Field Marshal von Rundstedt, had smashed a gaping hole in our front in the Ardennes Forest section in Belgium.

Immediately, I went to see the colonel, who admitted, "Those fellows are fighting for their lives. The two airborne divisions, the 82nd and the 101st, are in a terrible position. Okay, you can leave." Off I went to Paris, accompanied by my assistant Tom Getty, where I volunteered to join the Airborne. I was told that the 82nd needed a Catholic chaplain for its 505th Regiment, and orders were promptly cut assigning me to the 505th Parachute Infantry Regiment of the 82nd Airborne Division. Now the trick was to find out where they were. No one knew exactly. I was told to go to the headquarters at Rheims, and someone there could point me in the right direction.

The severe weather that had allowed the Germans to launch their offensive also affected the weather in France. It was a bitterly cold drive in the jeep to Reims, but Tom was delighted to be of service for this mission. As we approached Reims it was like approaching a different planet. Fresh units were mixed with retreating, despondent, and weary soldiers. Reims was total confusion. Troops were trying to dig fortifications near the town, fearing the Germans might get there soon. Spying the cross on my uniform, soldiers asked for a blessing and asked me, "What's the news? Where are the Germans?" I didn't know any more than they did.

We finally found the Army headquarters, and everything was crisp and businesslike. Someone took a look at my orders and handed me a slip that would get Tom and me billeting for the night. It was too late to go to the front. We were told to come back in the morning, and we would be given instructions on where they thought the 82nd and the 505th were located. And then, as an afterthought, they told us there were no supplies of warm clothing and that we should hold on to what we had. I had a trench coat and as much warm clothing as I could get. I managed to get an insignia, a shoulder patch of the 82nd, which I sewed on my trench coat.

The headquarters was close to the center of town, dominated by the huge and magnificent Notre-Dame de Reims Cathedral, which seemed to brood over and defend the anxious groups of soldiers. The cathedral had been badly damaged in World War I and had been rebuilt and fully reopened in 1938 through the generosity of the Rockefeller Foundation. I had visited the cathedral during a vacation as a seminarian at the North American College, and I felt as though I was coming back to a second home, not as a visitor but as a member of the family. This time, I was coming to try to defend it.

I said a long prayer, asking the good Lord, through the intersession of the Blessed Mother, to help me discharge my duties to the men I would be serving. I was thrilled to know I was about to participate in the war that I had foreseen and that I was entering the active period of my chaplaincy.

The billet was a haven for officers and soldiers en route to the front and a few coming back from the front. I didn't get much sleep because I was trying to get information from officers returning from the front. I needed to learn everything I could to understand how our troops were weathering the surprise attack.

The next morning at headquarters, I said good-bye to Tom, who decided he did not want to join the Airborne. I got into a truck that would take me to find the 82nd and the 505th. The driver was Lieutenant Solbjor of the 82nd Airborne, and to my surprise we were joined by a determined female war correspondent, Martha Gellhorn, the third wife of novelist Ernest Hemingway. We were seated on the front seat, which made conversation easy.

Lieutenant Solbjor did most of the talking, telling us that security was paramount because the Germans had taken a huge warehouse of American supplies at St. Vith. Many of the German officers and soldiers were dressed in our uniforms. Many Germans spoke English, making it easy for them to infiltrate the Allied lines. Some of the Germans were even dressed in cassocks, making it much easier for them to gain credibility. Therefore, the officers of the 82nd and their regiments placed a premium on secrecy concerning the exact location of the troops.

We had brought along "K" rations — 3,200-calorie nonperishable meals developed in the 1940s by physiologist Dr. Ancer Keys — and we stopped at one point to eat them. I learned that hunger was a good sauce; in fact, it was the only sauce that made "K" rations edible. Sometimes the only way to thaw out a frozen a "K" ration was to put it under your shirt. Thawing the food with your body didn't improve its taste but made it edible.

In the afternoon, we drove off the main road, and Lieutenant Solbjor threaded through roads in the Ardennes. The snow seemed to increase as we drove along, the majestic pine trees mantled in snow like Christmas trees. Then, piercing the winter air, we heard the booming of distant heavy artillery, the crackling of rifle fire.

Finally, through the trees, we came to a clearing and a snowy field in front of us. Solbjor stopped the truck. "We're in the territory of the 505th," he told me. "If you walk across that field, you'll find some elements of the 505th; they can take you to their headquarters. I've got to find the division headquarters. Good luck." And off he drove with Hemingway's wife.

I trudged across the open field carrying my Mass kit, wondering how to find the paratroopers. The snow was as high as my knees. It was very cold, and not a person, not a voice, was there to break the silence. As I neared the trees, a voice with a German accent rang out: "Halt!"

I halted. I thought to myself, "Was I to become a German prisoner before I even reached the 82nd?" Then I heard some muffled conversation, which I couldn't comprehend. There was a long silence and then a sentence in German. I had to respond. "I know very little German," I shouted, "but if you speak very slowly I might be able to understand."

Then there was a brief pause. "Okay, come forward," the voice said.

Two figures seemed to rise out of the snow. They were Americans: a lieutenant with piercing blue eyes and, next to him, a sergeant who seemed to be very unfriendly and distrustful. The lieutenant was of German descent from South Dakota, a Protestant, and very friendly. The sergeant was of Polish descent, a Catholic from the Midwest. I quickly showed them my orders, and the lieutenant explained the delay. "You're wearing a trench coat, and we were not issued any trench coats," he said. "The Germans got a lot of trench coats from the warehouses in St. Vith."

The sergeant, now relieved, spoke up. "I told the lieutenant, 'I'm a Catholic, and I know we don't have no Catholic chaplain. He's got to be a German. Why not shoot him?'"

The lieutenant finished the story. "I thought I'd try some German, and when I heard you talk I became convinced that you couldn't be a German. We'll get you up to the regimental headquarters." With sincere apologies to my excellent German teacher at Catholic University, Dr. Behrend, I was eternally grateful that my one year of German didn't stick!

Helping the Wounded

Regimental headquarters was in a small house. Colonel William Ekman, the commanding officer, was checking on some of the frontline positions. Sergeant Ernie Massei from Richmond, Virginia, had me sign in and then sent me to the medics, with Captain McIlvoy in command. Sergeant Massei told me that my assistant, Jacques Ospital, would be there.

There was very little difference between the front lines and the position of the medics. It seemed as though we were all at the front. I met Captain McIlvoy, who immediately introduced me to Jacques (pronounced "Jack"), who seemed to be a part of the medics. McIlvoy turned out to be a graduate of the Tulane Medical School in New Orleans, and he was a no-nonsense, efficient doctor.

Jacques was of Basque descent, raised on a sheep ranch in California, and a devout Catholic gifted with a wonderful personality. He had been a radio man in the invasion of Sicily and had become an assistant to the Catholic chaplain for the Normandy invasion, serving under the famous Father Connolly in that campaign and for his replacement in the Holland campaign. Jacques had taken a "bust" from sergeant to corporal to serve as the assistant for the Catholic chaplain. He was very popular with the men and seemed to know everybody.

Meanwhile, there was the immediate task of helping the wounded being brought into the first aid station. There was no Protestant chaplain, so I took care of all the wounded, including any German soldiers. I gave the Last Rites to two Catholic wounded paratroopers and then said the Lord's Prayer, an Act of Contrition, and a blessing with the one Protestant wounded trooper. I administered to the wounded as the medics were cutting off their boots. Expertly, the medics would bandage their bones and then give them an intravenous shot of blood. They placed them on a homemade ambulance, a jeep that had two stretchers, and promptly took them off to the field hospital some miles back.

As soon as they were finished, a jeep rolled up with a badly wounded American and a German, who had a piece of paper attached to his bloody uniform that read, "He did a favor for us." The dog tag of the American and the *Soldat Buch* ("soldier book") of the German showed that both were Catholic. Both were in very bad shape with multiple wounds as though from a hand grenade. I made an Act of Contrition with them (the *Soldat Buch* of the German had an Act of Contrition in it), anointed them, and gave them absolution. The story behind the note attached to the German's uniform was that he had helped a wounded American soldier.

Encouraging and consoling the wounded was demanding. A very strong trooper, a Mormon, had lost both feet to a shell blast. He could still feel his feet because of the nerves. "Tell me straight," he said to me, looking me squarely in the face. "What's wrong?" I replied, "I'll tell you straight. You have lost both feet but not your legs. They'll teach you to use artificial feet. You've got the guts to survive this, and soon you'll be able to walk. Now, I'll give you a blessing." The wounded men always wanted to know how they were wounded, even if it was bad news. I always told them the full truth and how to cope with their wounds.

To a dying Catholic who knew that he was mortally wounded, I assured him that I would write to his parents and tell them that I had given him the Last Rites. He smiled and said in a whisper, "They'll love that. God bless you." "And God bless you," I said. "You're in His hands."

My job was to give soldiers a reason to live. When you are seriously wounded, it is much easier to die than it is to live. Living involves pain and suffering, and I tried to get the wounded to make the most extreme effort of their lives to keep fighting and undergo the treatment.

I was, of course, a Catholic chaplain, but I certainly was not a chaplain just for Catholics. Every chaplain was trained to minister to every soldier, regardless of religious affiliation. But I do feel Catholic chaplains had an easier time taking care of Protestant soldiers than Protestant chaplains had caring for Catholic soldiers because we had sacramental rituals that could be easily modified to any situation. I would always say an Act of Contrition with a Protestant soldier — although he might not have known it as such. I would ask a Protestant soldier if he was sorry for his sins, and he would always say "yes." Then we would say the Our Father and I would give him a blessing and absolution. Rituals are very adaptable.

During noncombat days, if there was no Protestant chaplain around, I would conduct Protestant services as best I could. The soldiers were very nice about it as long as I gave them a good sermon and it didn't last too long! I spoke to them completely as if they were Catholics.

My assistant, Jacques, had to explain to all the medics the work of the Catholic chaplain and why we paid as much attention to the Germans as we did to the Americans. They understood. But a very slightly wounded and rookie paratrooper asked me, "Do you do exactly the same service for the Germans as you do for the Americans? Don't you give us a little extra?" I explained to him, "We're all equal in the sight of God. They all get the same." The paratrooper didn't seem satisfied with my explanation and simply shook his head. I regretted there wasn't enough time to explain my abrupt answer, but there were other wounded to care for.

All the wounded, regardless of nationality, were efficiently and quickly handled. Captain McIlvoy, the head of the medics, called me aside and said,

"I'm pleased that you don't expect any medic to stop caring for the men as you give them the Last Rites. You're very welcome here. Just don't get in the way."

There were also first aid stations for the battalions, and I always visited them. The fighting had reached a climax. The paratroopers were extended so far that each fighting man had about fifty to one hundred yards to cover.

The fighting at Cheneux was typical. This tiny village was atop a hill, its approaching road, snow banked on either side, strewn with the bodies of German soldiers prevented from decomposing by the bitter cold. The troopers, without artillery and good antitank weapons, had crouched in the snow as the German tanks trundled up the road, turrets open to enable the tank men to see. Jumping from the banks onto the turrets, troopers cut down the Germans with their knives. Eventually, Field Marshal Montgomery's headquarters ordered a fallback, leaving a lone paratrooper covering the retreat in his area. Armed with rifle and hand grenades, he heroically held off the German advance until finally being killed by a blast from a Nazi plane.

Visiting outposts meant crawling in the snow since anyone standing was a dead giveaway to the American position. To protect the men from Germans, often less than one hundred yards away, American GIs were issued, along with their warm winter clothing, white "smocks," guaranteeing near-perfect camouflage in the snow. When the bad weather giving Germans cover finally lifted, American planes swarmed over the battlefield, strafing, bombing, and killing, even, alas, some of our own. (Just how many became clear when, following that campaign, I wrote condolences to the families of those killed in action — many victims of friendly fire since the snow offered no distinguishing marks between the German and American positions.)

As important as reclaiming our dead from the battlefield was finding and helping the disabled and wounded — Americans and Germans alike — an effort that involved all available officers and men. With almost half of the upper-echelon officers West Pointers — believers in an ethical code of conduct, "the profession of arms" — the rules of war established by the Geneva Convention were staunchly upheld. The notion that "anything goes in war," never applied here — especially when it came to helping the wounded. Though American casualties took priority, the medics also cared for the enemy wounded. Because Hitler had ordered all available troops to stem the American counterattack, allowing what was left of his elite troops to escape, crowds of dejected, half-frozen, wounded soldiers were left plodding in the snow: aging men and too-young-to-shave youths in green Luftwaffe uniforms, even the occasional female machine gunners — a reality that didn't play well with our men. "An army ought to give up before it makes women fight as soldiers," one soldier replied when I asked how he felt about women in combat. "It wouldn't work with us. The men would be trying to protect the women instead of fighting the Krauts."

Any lull in working with the wounded gave me the chance to recite my breviary, the timeless book of prayers, psalms, and Scriptures to which priests are committed as a daily devotion (mine, printed in Latin, took about fifty minutes). I certainly wasn't alone in the need for prayer. The men wanted it, too, along with the Mass which I celebrated for small groups whenever — wherever — possible. The Ardennes being hilly, I chose a spot in the lee of a hill sheltered from artillery fire. My altar, often the case, was the hood of a jeep (if that wasn't available I settled for a cardboard box used for "K" rations). My greatest difficulty was preventing the wine from freezing, usually accomplished when a trooper, usually Jacques, held the bottle under his shirt next to his body. Though I insisted that the men wear helmets, I was more impressed that they insisted, despite my assurance they could stand, on kneeling to receive Communion. In fact, during that whole campaign, no soldier stood; everyone knelt in the snow and the ice.

A priest in a war zone quickly learns to improvise. For instance, the Mass Kit carried, per Catholic practice, by all Catholic chaplains originally contained a small, marble altar stone, embedded with the relic of a saint whose powers, however great, did not keep it from breaking in the field. As a result, the Military Ordinary got practical, replacing the stone with a piece of cloth also containing a relic. Beyond that, the Mass kit included holy oils for anointing and a small prayer book with the Last Rites. Celebrating Mass in the field, I learned to do so quickly, given the constant danger of enemy artillery shelling. However, I never sped through; the men didn't want you rushing things. But they also didn't want you to dawdle. Often Mass was celebrated in the opening in the woods — the men taking shelter in the trees. Once, heading for leafy shelter the third time, a sergeant spoke for them: "It's your turn to take shelter. You say Mass in the woods. We'll wait for you." (If requested, of course, I always heard confessions, ending each with a reminder to pray for the recently killed and wounded.)

One day following Mass, a friendly officer made a suggestion. "Being new, I wonder if you've been told to write a farewell letter to your folks in case you don't survive?" I had not. Thanking him, I decided that the best recipient for such a solemn missive would be my sister, Mary who, if necessary, could explain the situation to my folks to whom I could never adequately explain my reason for becoming a paratrooper. Subsequently, shortly after Christmas 1944, I wrote the following note to Mary (retrieving it after concluding our last campaign at the Elbe River):

Dear Mary,

As you see, I have a new home. An accident occurred to a Catholic chaplain (jump accident), and I received a very sudden call.

I have not yet explained to Dad and Mom that I am serving with the paratroopers. I gave the address only as the 505th Infantry, which is what it is. At present, we are only doing infantry work, and I did not wish to alarm them. I am in less danger than Frank or Denis, and since my regiment is considered the most experienced of even the Paratroop regiments, it is very, very unlikely that I shall ever find myself in bad shape. The men are all superb troops.

You are probably asking why I inflicted a fresh burden of worry on Dad and Mom. I did not do it unnecessarily. There was a need for a young Catholic chaplain, and I know they will understand that I inherited from them a sense of duty; they can't blame me for what I learned from them. And the minimum a Catholic Priest can do is to offer to assist Catholic soldiers in danger. That is why I was ordained, and it was a great pleasure to be able to serve with a combat group. I love it.

Love,
Phil

Since paratroopers were all volunteers, no griping was allowed about the terms of their service. And though grumbling could be loud and clear when it came to battle strategy or the cold, you never heard: "Why did they send me here?" In fact, given a paratrooper's extra jump pay — $50 for privates and noncoms, $100 for officers — any grousing was invariably countered with: "You get paid to die in this outfit. Why squawk?" The most lethal danger we faced were tree-level artillery barrages, shells designed to explode at the highest point of a tree before spraying shrapnel down across a wide area. Your only recourse to these treetop killers was standing very straight next to the biggest tree you could find, hoping its branches would block the shrapnel. Very often they didn't; and a lot of casualties ensued.

Shortly after Christmas 1944, a stable line of defense was established. It was quickly followed by a surprising order from Field Marshal Montgomery: because the British troops were even further back, the 82nd was to fall back to a line designated by Montgomery. General Slim Jim Gavin was outraged. "If you want to straighten out the line," he raged, "why don't you come forward to our position?" Finally, Slim Jim got a visit from English general Sir Miles Dempsey, who, a friend of the 82nd, persuaded him that obeying an order from the commanding general of the sector was his duty. As a result, for the first time in the history of the 82nd, we retreated and fell back. Slim Jim never forgave Montgomery for tarnishing our proud legacy.

A company's normal complement of officers was the captain and at least four lieutenants, each company having several squads of eight men each. However, the fiendish weather and fierce, unrelenting fighting had greatly reduced the strength of the regiment. Second Battalion, "D" Company had one officer left, Lieutenant Meyers, along with a six-man platoon; "C" Company had lost all its officers, leaving thirty-two men. "B" Company had its captain, executive officer, and twenty-four men; while "A" Company counted among its ranks only two officers and twenty men. Nevertheless, the regiment was still in shape for battle, and a counterattack was ordered for the night of January 3, 1945.

Following a dinner of "K" rations, Jacques and I headed out, driving silently through the night... the only sound the crunching of jeep tires on the heavy snow. Per orders, the windshield was down, allowing the wind-driven snow to lash across our faces. His scarf wrapped twice around his throat, Jacques kept our jeep directly behind the medics' truck.

As we crept into the village of Basse Bodeux, feverish activity broke out among the remaining civilian population as they hustled cattle, squealing pigs, and barking dogs into a safe spot. Upon finding the school, site for the first aid station, we promptly unloaded our supplies before searching for a spot to sleep — in my case a basement reserved for storing potatoes which, soft and spongy, provided a welcome impromptu mattress. Unrolling my sleeping bag, I bedded down. A few hours later, we were up, rearranging the first floor of the school. Walking to our jeep for supplies, I was surprised to see the snow covered in patches of black powder — deposits from artillery fire. Suddenly, from nowhere, we were surrounded by the crack of rifles, the thud of artillery.

Minutes later, the first casualties were brought into our makeshift first aid station. Walking toward the stove where bodies were placed, I rolled back the blanket on the nearest one. It was O'Brien, a "spotter" for our artillery, who'd advanced so far forward he'd been hit by one of our shells. Now his body, crisscrossed with deep, shrapnel-laden lacerations, was cold. Giving conditional absolution, I anointed him. The next body was that of DiGirolamo, a young, aggressive corporal who talked endlessly about his beautiful fiancée waiting for him to get married. Beside him, another trooper, just joined up at Theux, manfully tried to conceal the excruciating pain caused by the wicked gap laying bare his sciatic nerve. Medics, doing heir best, offered what they could: one shot of morphine.

Soon a steady stream of wounded and near-dead were pouring into the aid station. As fast as I could, I anointed and gave absolution to soldier after soldier — often before the medics got to them. As usual, there was no talk, no moaning — only the occasional barked order or comment among the medics. Since blood doesn't flow in icy cold weather, the near-zero weather usually plugged up the flow until a wounded soldier hit the station's warm air. As I bent over one GI, searching for his dog tag to find if he was Catholic, Protestant, or Jew, the captain tapped me on the shoulder. "Better get over there and take care of that captain," he said pointing to a man well known for being tough and gregarious. "He'll die of shock soon." Surprisingly, he appeared to have a mere nick on his chin. As it turned out, he'd been hit by a brand new, high-powered German cannon missile. "This will help you recover quickly," I said to the captain as I heard his confession and anointed him. Shortly there-after he died.

Among the wounded were Germans of all ages — old men conscripted into the people's army (the *Volkssturm*), scared, nervous teenagers trying to act more mature than their years... all deftly handled by the calm, practiced American medics. Suddenly in the midst of the melee, there was more shocking news: Lieutenant Colonel Vanderwoort had rushed into the aid station hold-ing a bloody cloth against one eye. Among his paratroopers who willingly fol-lowed him as a talisman of survival, Vanderwoort was legendarily immune to wounds and death, having, despite extraordinary valor, never been hit. "I think I've got a nick next to my eye," he said in no apparent pain. When the medic peeled back the blood-soaked rag, even he looked stunned. There was no eye in Vanderwoot's socket — only a gaping, bloody hole. The surge of combat adrenalin had overridden the pain the Colonel felt when his eye was shot out.

During the night, I was helping load a couple of badly wounded onto the back of the "ambulance" jeep when I slipped. Looking down at the blood all over my boots and clothing, I felt a surge of gratitude well up inside, a thanks for being in my position. "I am where I should be," I said to myself. "This is what I was ordained for. May God give me the grace to do what I should."

Though trauma continued to be the order of the night, it was not without levity. One trooper, still carrying his rifle, hand grenades dangling from his belt showed up with blood on his arm. "What happened to you?" snapped a medic. I got bit by a dog," the soldier replied unleashing a burst of gallows humor from everyone in earshot, as a straight-faced medic retorted: "Hell of a way to get a purple heart," then bandaged his arm.

As laughter died down, the Captain beckoned me over to his patient: "Look at this," he muttered, "Now I've seen everything." Lying on the stretcher was a wounded trooper, veteran of four campaigns, who though writhing in agony was still able to talk easily. Pulling me aside, the Captain said, "A bullet went right through his heart. We can't understand why he's alive." But indeed he was. After hearing his confession and giving him absolution, I looked him decisively in the eye: "I'll be praying for you." He survived.

It is impossible to adequately describe the bravery, competence, and com-passion of the medics — wounded and killed as often as their comrades. "They're better at this than a doctor," Dr. Franco, a battalion medical officer told me. "Doctors would stop and think about what should be the best treat-ment. These guys go right to work" — one reason they were treated with the utmost respect by other soldiers whose trust in this gutsy lot could be summed up in a sentence: "They'll help us no matter what." How could I forget Leland Heller and dental officer Captain Suer, both fatally mowed down as they ran to the aid of bullet-riddled soldier two hundred yards from the enemy? Or driver Howard Lee who dodged enemy fire to get bleeding soldiers into his jeep, carrying them to safety when its motor was shelled; and Fletcher Saxton, feet frozen, but refusing to quit ministering to soldiers under fire?

Finally, displaying its fantastic spirit and courage, the remnants of our regiment took all of its objectives — fighting its way to the Salm River. There, having lost almost everything but our fierce determination, it was decided, over the Colonel's misgivings, that the regiment should be sent to the Belgian village of Theux for a rest. Once there, with no previous warning to the populace, the 505th would be billeted in local homes. Knowing nothing more than the name of the town, Jacques and I arrived about 2:00 a.m. Driving down the main street, we spotted what we thought was a family home. Tentatively, I knocked on the door. After awhile, hearing stirring inside, I yelled, in my best French, "I'm the Catholic chaplain with the paratroopers, and my assistant and I need a shelter."

When the door finally opened, a fully dressed, middle-aged man appeared, his wife in the background. Explaining our presence, I asked for a room, creating a buzz of activity. Finally, our host spoke again: "*Entrez s'il vous plait*" ... "Have you eaten?" "No, but we have our 'K' rations." "*Mais non*," the father said. "We shall try to get you some eggs." Thirty minutes later, now surrounded by the whole family — Monsieur and Madame Pouplier, her parents, daughter Betsy, son Phonsy — Jacques and I sat down to a delicious meal of eggs and fresh bread. Afterwards, learning that the family, under constant threat of V bombs, had moved its beds to the cellars, we asked if we could use the main bedroom on the second floor, delighted when they said yes.

During the days we spent there, Captain Schenck, taking over a movie house, ran American movies, the Red Cross girls set up a doughnut factory, and I got to celebrate Mass on a real altar in a real church, a Gothic building dating back to the twelfth century, which though beautiful, had no heat. By the end of Mass, my feet were lumps of ice. The war, however, was never far from our thoughts, thanks in large part to the overhead buzz of V bombs on their way to Liège. If their motors started to sputter, we automatically headed for cover, since V bombs went down when their fuel ran out.

General Slim Jim Gavin

The highlight of our combat vacation was the arrival of General Slim Jim Gavin, who showed up in Theux to address each battalion of the regiment. I always marveled at his ability to arouse the fighting spirit of the men due in large part to his own quiet valor. An intrepid scout with endless endurance, he always packed a rifle and was an expert shot. His preternatural hearing, meanwhile, could determine the exact location of incoming shells. When Slim Jim took cover, the shell was right on top of him.

The veterans who had finished five rigorous, bloody campaigns had been promised more than once that they would be sent home after the next campaign. That promise was never kept — though it hardly diminished the men's spirit, especially after listening to Gavin. (I came to the conclusion that the law of self-exception governed all high-spirited young men: regardless of the high percentage of casualties, wounded, and killed, the feeling always was, "Everyone else may get it, but I won't.") At the end of his first pep talk, the waiting troopers yelled at those departing the general's remarks. "Did he say we're going home?" "No," came the reply. "He talked us into it again."

Slim Jim considered membership in the Parachute Division a paramount honor and passed that on to his men. One day a trooper came to see me, complaining that Slim Jim had been cruel to one of his buddies, notorious for being late and occasionally going AWOL. Slim Jim had decided to make an example of him. Lining up the regiment, he read out the trooper's list of offenses, dismissed him from the regiment and, as a parting shot, tore the paratroop insignia off of his uniform. Relating the story of his friend, the trooper broke down and cried.

"If my buddy did something really bad, okay, shoot him," the trooper pleaded with me. "But don't tear off his paratroop wings."

When our leave came to a close, there were no complaints. The men left Theux better prepared for battle, having received additional infantry and armored tactics training as well as being instructed in the use of new weapons like Panzerfausts, gammon grenades, and flame throwers. In addition, new replacements had arrived, wounded returned, and we had a new Protestant chaplain, William Byrd, eager to serve.

The 82nd's new mission was to pierce the Siegfried Line in the St. Vith-Malmedy sector, a mission presenting a great challenge. The famous 1st Infantry Division, the Big Red One, was on the flank of the 82nd, engendering a friendly but intense rivalry as each tried to reach its objectives first. The 1st, fully equipped with motorized elements, had the use of main roads for its vehicles while the 82nd, with scant motorized equipment, was relegated to back roads and trails. Nevertheless, the 82nd passed through the 7th Armored Division and, following a grueling march through deep snows, finally arrived in the woods near Meyerode. Barely had we put down our gear when, at ten thirty in the evening, we were ordered to attack!

This advance was the ultimate test since the whole 505th Regiment had to trek though huge snowbanks. The footing was slippery and the men, carrying equipment, exhausted. At one point, I noticed a small trooper pass out. As he gathered his strength and stood up, I said: "You've done all you can. Why not let me authorize you to go to the rear?" He bit his lip and replied, "I've made every day of combat that this regiment has had. I'm not giving up." I completely understood. So, picking up one of his pieces of equipment, I carried it until I found my jeep and threw it in. Later I learned from his lieutenant that the trooper, despite collapsing three times, had finally finished it.

The trucks meanwhile, battling snowdrifts, were forced to push already frozen troopers into snow banks in order to pass; while the trail, completely clogged, required the 1st Battalion to cool their heels for two hours at the start point before moving ahead. At five that morning, after fighting the snow all night, 2nd Battalion, positioning its frozen troopers atop a platoon of tanks, attacked, making short shrift of the enemy, taking over their improvised billets. Once in Germany, we found German civilians, fearful of the future, huddled in homes and institutions, among them a couple dozen terrified Catholic sisters whom I briefly greeted before continuing my rounds of ministry to the soldiers. Thrilled to see Americans, their superior summed up the elation of everyone there, clergy or not. "Now we are saved! God bless all of you!"

One enemy we hadn't planned on was the foul, freezing weather. Keeping warm enough to keep fighting was an ongoing, daily struggle. One soldier, having come upon a closetful of priest's vestments in a chapel, happily layered five sets of them over his uniform, presenting a bizarre sight indeed as red, green, white, and violet vestments, draped over his torso, flapped in the wind. The only thing odder than how he looked, was the expression on his face. Regretfully, I had to make him return them to the chapel, though my bigger disappointment was not having a camera to capture such innovative wartime attire.

A correlative of the cold, of course, was severe frostbite. It required stern discipline to make troopers sit in the snow, unbuckle boots, and knead toes to restore proper circulation. Though I fortunately managed to avoid the affliction, I did suffer one close call after celebrating Mass in an eleventh century church sans heating. By the time I told them *"Ite missa est"* (to go in peace), my feet and lower legs up to my knees felt like heavy pieces of ice, my circulation returning only after a vigorous rubdown. (My testiest battlefield *bête noire*, however, were lice which frequently required disappearing into the woods to completely strip and douse my body.)

The regiment, passing through the 325 Glider Regiment, attacked again, followed shortly by the 1st Battalion taking a village called Losheimergraben. When the 2nd Battalion followed suit, capturing a town called Neuhof, the 505th then commandeered a three-mile line looking down on the Siegfried Line with its awesome array of tank barriers and pill boxes, neatly arranged to cover the territory with murderous fire. Following a twenty-four-hour respite, the 2nd Battalion, storming the camouflaged pillboxes protected by mines and booby traps, opened the attack on the Siegfried Line.

The regiment, meanwhile, overdue for a much-needed rest, was pulled back to Salmchateau — a pile of rubble thanks to the fierce battle to be retaken by the 75th Division. No one much cared, however, once the engineers erected a large shower tent allowing men their first glorious bath in two months. It wasn't our only luxury. There was also a church which, though badly battered, looked like a piece of heaven to this priest who hadn't said Mass in a real one for weeks. After cleaning out the rubble, Jacques, ever the wise veteran, enlisted his network of town criers to get the word out that Mass was going to be celebrated in an actual church on a fixed altar with a few real seats. St. Peter's Basilica had nothing on us!

Antitank Shell

A few days later, we were ordered to Hürtgen, which rising temperatures had turned into a sea of mud — enveloping our jeep up to its floorboards as Jacques and I made our way to an intersection in the Hürtgen Forest, bereft of trees due to constant fighting. Stepping out of the jeep to ascertain our location, an 88-mm, antitank shell suddenly whizzed over the top of my head, landing directly in front my body and blowing me off my feet into a quagmire. Jumping up, an old adage sprang to mind: "If you ever see an 88 shell explode, you'll never live to tell the tale."

But, apparently, unbelievably I had. Surely, I must have been hit somewhere! Emotions, like blood bubbling in my veins, surged through me as I did a quick inventory, grabbing my uniform to search for signs of blood and holes. Nothing! Eyeing my body further, prayers of thanksgiving poured out of me when I, again, found nothing. Looking down at the swampy ground, I suddenly realized the source of my salvation: the shrapnel, flying away from me in the opposite direction, had been absorbed by the deep mud.

But Jacques! How was he? Calling out his name, he answered, miraculously protected by the body of the jeep from any injuries. Collapsing back in the mud, collecting my senses, I shouted out, in thanks and wonderment, "I'm alive!" "Well, then get up!" Jacques retorted, and I did, mumbling even more prayers. Leaping back into the jeep, we floored it out of there in a swirl of mud.

Looking back, my lucky brush with death turned out to be a prophetic prelude to the dangerous months ahead — a warning from God, in a sense, to be careful and pay attention. As incomprehensibly tragic and barbaric as what had gone before, it would be nothing compared to what I — all of the 82nd — would see, hear, smell, and feel now that we had entered into the heartland of Hitler, the personification of evil, for whom human life was nothing more than a pawn to be played in his psychotic, irrevocable chess game for international power and prestige.

The 82nd, having relieved the 8th Infantry Division, began marching though territory retaken by the Germans in their initial attack. Very quickly it became clear just how far Hitler was willing to go to win that game of chess. Passing on the road near Kommersheidt, a small village, we encountered our first grim reminder: "death valley"... strewn with the remains of the 29th Division... bodies in heaps... wrecked, abandoned trucks, twisted into hulks of metal in efforts to break a road through trees. Everywhere, before our astonished eyes, was the detritus of war: booby traps, mines, corrupting bodies, heroic resistance, defeat, death — a scenario so raw that one batch of new recruits cracked up and had to be sent back. Wherever we went, on unmarked roads or marching from Vossenack to a village called Schmidt where we gingerly traversed the largest minefield we had yet to confront, we invariably encountered hundreds of shattered bodies of American and German soldiers, mute but convincing proof of the German determination to impede our advance... to resist until the end.

In shockingly rapid order, it became clear that this was a new and terrible kind of warfare, fought in a country of towns and villages with confusing names, even to Jacques, who despite his fluency in four languages, found most German names, indeed the whole language, incomprehensible. Moreover, everywhere we went, the shelling was relentless and dreadfully accurate, killing men who had survived campaigns from Sicily to the Bulge. And now, on German soil, in sight of the end, these proud survivors were being massacred by subterranean enemies: mines, shells, and booby traps.

The Regimental Aid stations set up for business wherever we could — in one instance, a beer hall where I slept under the bar. When it was shelled for three successive days — and I escaped — I came to be regarded as something of a lucky piece, welcomed heartily wherever I went, including the front lines. Believing a chaplain should be available to the men, I left the Aid station every day to visit soldiers on the front.

Once, seeing several men hit by shells, I worked my way to one who'd been thrown between saplings — his legs blown off. Immediately anointing him, I desperately tried to free him from his position, finally noticing another trooper, running forward, rifle in hand. "Trooper," I yelled. "Come here and help me." But he kept on going. A second look revealed it was General Slim Jim Gavin racing forward to find the location of the artillery doing the shelling (many of which, I later learned, were German railroad gun shells, weighing a ton).

Priests and clergy were hardly immune. Visiting a Catholic rectory, I asked the young, resolutely anti-Hitler pastor, if there was a rift in the attitudes of priests about the Nazis. "We suffered a great deal from them," he told me. "Many of us were imprisoned and tortured. In this diocese of over a thousand priests, I know of only one who was favorable to them."

Finally, the regiment reached the Roer River, a tributary of the Rhine, feeding a large dam, which we were to seize before it could be blown up, flooding the neighborhood. Despite vigorous patrolling to determine the size and position of the enemy across the river, as well as consistent firing (with our limited firearms) against their mortars, the Germans weren't about to give in. Their shelling was unremitting, our casualties heavy, including young men like twenty-year-old Joe Melahn, who despite heavy fire, left his observation post to repair the communications line. He fixed it but never made it back. His loss was especially poignant as he had a twin brother, George, in the same unit. (The paratroopers were one of the few units allowing twins to remain together, a main reason, I thought, why the Melahn brothers signed up, joining several other sets of 82nd Airborne twins, each of which lost a brother.)

Sharing a deep faith with Joe — both attended Mass whenever possible — George was equally gutsy, suffering a wound that sent him back to the hospital, knowing nothing about the fate of his brother. When he returned, I knew I had to tell him the sad news but before I could, he began to cry, instinctively sensing what I was about to say. "We were very close," he explained through tears. "Often, we could tell what the other was thinking."

Later, after Jacques returned home, George took his place as my assistant. After the war, I met his parents, outstanding Catholics, and his mother said something I felt expressed the feelings of all Gold Star moms. When a neighbor complained that her son had come back from combat with a crutch, Mrs. Melahn didn't miss a beat: "If my son Joe could return with a crutch, I'd dance with it." (A footnote: returning from the war, George married Dolores Sarjeant. Their first son, born in 1951, was named Joseph.)

Combat Morality

Combat, of course, carried with it broad moral dilemmas on a daily basis. One day, an expert rifleman came to me with an unusual qualm. "With this telescopic sight, Father, I can kill an enemy soldier a mile away," he said. "He doesn't have a chance. Is that all right?" "It sure is," I replied. "It's not your fault." Another soldier, a lieutenant harbored lingering guilt over the Battle of the Bulge campaign. "Though we only had a few men in my platoon," he told me, "we gained the top of a hill. Below were a lot of Germans so we opened up, killing a good number. Suddenly, an officer yelled that he wanted to surrender but I couldn't let him because we had so few troopers. If he saw how few, I knew they'd come at us. So we shot some more, and then I let them surrender. Was that wrong?"

"At that time did you think it was wrong?" I asked.

"No, not at all," the lieutenant said. "I had to save my men."

"Well, don't worry about it," I said.

Of course, I wasn't immune from moral dilemmas myself. Chaplains were forbidden to carry guns, a rule with which I completely agreed. However, once, in the midst of severe combat, a colonel said I could ride in his jeep to another part of the front where German patrols, scouting out positions, had badly hit a number of our men. Getting into the jeep, the driver, just nineteen and adhering to the rule that the soldier riding shotgun was obligated to handle the machine gun assigned to every jeep, gave me an order: "You hold that machine gun and guard us. There are plenty of Germans around here."

"No, I'm not allowed to do that," I said. "Chaplains can't handle guns."

"What! I can't help that chaplain stuff," he replied, clearly irritated. "You're sitting where a soldier holds that machine gun. Grab it!" So, I did, placing my right hand on the handle, keeping it there during the entire ride. Though he felt safer, I had no intention of firing it. And, thank God, wasn't put to the test.

Once at the front, I learned that paratrooper bodies had been brought in and placed under a tent. With some still warm, I sought out the Catholics for conditional absolution, eventually spying a body with a rosary around the neck. As I started to anoint, it sat up: "Hey," asked the surprised trooper, "what are you doing?" Explaining that I thought he was a Catholic casualty, he said that not only was he not Catholic, but also only "had a very small hit. I was just taking a nap before getting attention." As for the rosary, he explained, his buddy wore one and it seemed to help; so he got one for himself. It wasn't an uncommon practice. In another instance, spying a rosary around the neck of a soldier and assuming he was Catholic, I began giving the Last Rites until, slipping momentarily back into consciousness, he announced that he was Jewish. Ultimately, I sent the rosary to his parents, who in a thank you letter, asked what they should do with it. "Keep it as a memorial to your son," I instructed.

Catholic medals, also popular, sometimes turned out to be literal lifesavers. (I, personally, wore a large Benedictine medal over my heart.) Father Sampson, a famous Catholic chaplain in the 101st Airborne Division, was captured and lined up to be executed until a German sergeant saw his intercessory medal and spared him. In his gratitude and excitement, Father Sampson, grasping for a prayer, could only come up with: "Bless us, O Lord, and these thy gifts, which we are about to receive from thy bounty," — our grace before meals.

Finally the word came down that the Regiment and Division were to be relieved. On February 19, assembled at Walsheim where there was a large Catholic church in good condition, I said Mass to an overflowing crowd. After two months of freezing, exhausting, costly campaigning, the Bulge was over. Our palatial transportation out harkened back to World War I — forty and eights (freight cars holding forty men or eight horses) with straw for bedding. But who cared? We were out of battle and headed for a rest at the camp in Suippes.

Suippes

Getting into Suippes, a former French military camp not far from Reims, I bunked in the officers' quarters, collapsing into the longest sleep of my life. The next day Jacques and I inspected the chapel, as plain and uninviting as a tool shed. "How do we get the men to Mass on Sunday?" I asked, conscious of their extreme fatigue. "No trouble," Jacques said. "I'll tell them that the Mass is for all their buddies who died in the campaign."

As usual, Jacques was right on the money. Troopers not only filled the inside, including aisles, but outside crowded to get a look through the windows. I have never had such a congregation. In fact, I was so impressed that it was difficult to battle my emotions. Each of them, officers and young soldiers, having survived the worst campaign of the war, were profoundly grateful to be there, grieving for their friends who weren't. My sermon was short and to the point. There was no need to explain sentiments shared by everyone.

As I set about making the chapel more inviting and devotional, I got plenty of help from men eager to get out of the training grind that began almost immediately. Concurrent with refurbishing the chapel, I had the excruciatingly painful duty of writing condolence letters to the parents of the men who had been killed, often reopening emotional wounds. The subsequent responses I received often renewed my own sorrow. Few parents could understand the conditions of battle. Beyond their profound loyalty to each other, a trooper's first duty is to defeat the enemy. In the danger, excitement, and chaos of combat, men often couldn't remember exactly what had befallen a stricken comrade.

One letter from a trooper's sister demanded to know every single circumstance leading up to her brother ultimately being killed in combat, along with the level of treatment he received after being hit. I understood her anguished questioning, her search for definitive answers, most of which I did not have. Such torment was not restricted to civilians. A general whose son had been killed just two hours into his first day of combat also came to me, wanting to know why.

Generally, I spared families any hurtful details. If a trooper was believed to have been the victim of "friendly fire," that supposition was never included in my condolence letter. Since our own Air Corps couldn't, in close combat, in the snows of Ardennes, distinguish between Allied lines and the enemy, we undoubtedly lost a number of men to errant fire — not to mention inexperience. One detachment, looking for German patrols in the basement of a house in the Rhine, was suddenly surprised by an armed man in uniform bursting through the door yelling, *"Hande hohe!"* ("Hands up!"). Naturally, they shot him. As it turned out, however he was an American sergeant who, slated for a promotion, wanted to prove his courage by capturing a Nazi with a hand gun. (It took hours of reassurance from me to convince the paratrooper who pulled the trigger that it wasn't his fault.)

Whatever the situation, it always relieved a family's burden of sorrow to be assured that their son, brother, or father had been able, as a result of my saying Mass during combat, to receive Holy Communion. In the end, I tried to tell parents as much as I could about the circumstances of their child's death. Typical is this letter I sent on April 23, 1945, to Mr. O'Dea whose son, First Lieutenant Clifford J. O'Dea, had been killed in action on April 12 in Germany. I wrote:

"Your son had crossed a large river into territory held by the enemy to recover the body of one of his men killed in combat. While carrying the body, he set off a mine and was killed instantly.

"Although your son had been an officer in this unit a very short time, he had won the good will and respect of both officers and men. His care for the welfare of the men was an outstanding characteristic, and he always exhibited a cheerful disposition under the most trying circumstances.

"... Please be assured that he did have the comfort and aid of his religion. All during the bitter weather of the winter campaign the men did continue to attend Mass and to receive General Absolution whenever it was possible; Mass was even said in the deep snow. I can assure you from personal experience that even those who do not have the opportunity of attending Mass certainly pray in time of danger; they are certainly ready to face God if called to meet Him.

"... He was given a Catholic, military funeral in one of our Army cemeteries."

If anything I wrote comforted them, I was equally moved by the replies I received from the parents of those killed in combat. Mrs. Josephine Melahn of Far Rockaway, New York, the mother of twin brothers Joe and George, wrote the following about Joe's death:

"My deepest gratitude to you, Father, for your kindness in writing to me about my dear son's death. Joseph certainly was always wonderful to us, and I could not write until I heard from George. Being twins and never separated for any length of time, I naturally felt anxious about George's reaction. I left it to Our Blessed Mother and today received George's letter. I know now that she did not fail either of us. His letter reassured me that he too can take it and come through this greatest blow with remarkable courage. Only with God's grace will he be able to stand the strain, and dear Father, please give him a helping hand. He is so young. The two years they have been away seem to bring us closer, even though thousands of miles apart.

"... With so many remarkable men in that outfit, we cannot fail, and God grant the day will come soon for all to return home to their loved ones."

Even though I was chaplain of a paratroop outfit, I, like other recruits who joined the 82nd for the Battle of the Bulge, never had any formal training for jumping out of an airplane. But that was about to change. The fateful announcement came from Colonel Ekman: "You can't be a member of this Division or this Regiment without qualifying as a jumper. You'll have the proper training and instruction from the officer in charge. We need you." As indeed they did, having lost so many jumpers in the Bulge. Nevertheless, I was hardly enthusiastic, especially considering that this group of twenty soldiers and one doctor were very young compared to my thirty-two-year-old self.

Our training started the next morning: four hours of calisthenics, push-ups, rope climbing, topped off by an hour's run, in boots, across rough countryside. The drill sergeant was omnipotent and remorseless, especially for slackers: "Twenty push-ups for not paying attention," he ordered the doctor. As we sweated, grunted, and groaned, I noticed the troopers eyeing me, hoping I'd be forced to quit, which only ignited my naturally competitive nature. "I'll bet somebody in this group," I thought to myself, "is weaker than I." I also thought, "This, just like saying Mass, is God's will." I almost convinced myself.

Next came brief instructions on how to gear up your harness, minus, I might add, the training aids and equipment used at Fort Benning, Georgia, home of the parachute training center. Here in the middle of war-torn Germany it was strictly the basics: how to put on the equipment, check that of the man in front of you, hook up with the static line, jump straight out into the propeller blast and do a half-turn to your left to ensure that the full force of the propeller blast would open your chute.

When I returned to my tent, Jacques's greeting was laced with irony: "How'd you like it?"

"I'm not obliged to like it. I can stand it."

The test of our potential skills came the next morning at six. "We jump early," the sergeant explained, "because there's less wind." Perhaps, but the air was nippy indeed as the truck hauled us out to the end of the runway where our plane, coughing and sputtering, sat warming up. Solemnly, we climbed into the C-32's side door near the plane's tail, open and ready for jumping. Carefully examining each man's jump pack, the jumpmaster squeezed the belts around our waists so tightly that the piece of wood, brought along solely for that purpose, could not be inserted. Carrying a makeshift pack, we climbed into the plane where I was put closest to the door. "Officers jump first to give the example," the jumpmaster said, "but I'll give the orders." When we were finally arranged to his satisfaction, he ordered the plane to take off, and we climbed into the morning. Circling the drop zone, the jumpmaster kept his eye on the ground as well as the light next to the door which would turn green when the pilot was over the drop zone.

"No use sitting down," our fearless leader yelled, "You won't be here long enough." Minutes later, over the motor's deafening roar, the wind rushing through the open door, he bawled: "Get ready!" — though apparently we were not as yet. He had a few more instructions: after jumping, count "one thousand, two thousand, three thousand"; if the parachute on our backs hadn't opened, pull the rip-cord on the reserve shoot strapped on our stomachs. Once descending, never let the chute oscillate and twist in the wind — you could land on your back, your side, or backwards. To correct oscillation, grasp the risers (cords leading from harness to canopy) and collapse the chute to make the body fall straight. Seventy feet above ground, let go of the riser and land properly — not standing up (you could break a leg) but using a "three-point" landing on the thigh, knees, and feet. As soon as your feet hit the ground, throw your body to the right so the ground collision could be partially absorbed by the right side of your body and hip. And, one more thing: immediately grab your chute so the wind doesn't drag you helplessly along the ground.

By this time, jumping without a chute looked easier than remembering the instructions on how to jump with one… not to mention enduring more of the push-ups and hour marathons that had preceded it. "You should have been in Fort Benning in the old days," the jumpmaster sniffed at our griping. "A squad had to lie on the ground and hoist a pine log over their heads while the sergeant walked down the row on their stomachs. Now that was real training."

Whatever you called what we did for training, it was now over. "Stand up and hook up," he barked scrutinizing each as we attached the static line going from our parachute to the steel cable running the plane's length.

"Check your equipment," he shouted, reminding us to do again what we had been doing for the last hour. Sound off for equipment check!" "Number eight, okay," yelled the rear trooper, slapping the thigh of the trooper in front of him, an assurance that the back of his equipment was okay. "Number seven, okay," and so it went until finally, it came to me: "Number one, okay," I yelled.

"Stand to the door," the jumpmaster ordered, checking the green light as he looked down at the drop zone. "Go!" he finally commanded, slapping my thigh. Easy for him to say! All I had to do was relax and forget my dignity.

Gripping the door's rim for leverage, I hurled myself into the air, doing a half turn. The propeller blast instantly ripped open my chute, followed by a terrific body wrench courtesy of my skin-tight harness. My helmet, already crunched into my head, added its own insult, delivering a powerful whack to the bridge of my nose. In seconds, my entire body was reacting to a forced sudden stop after going one hundred twenty miles an hour in a plane. Barely had I gotten my bearings before something, not covered by the jumpmaster, began to happen. Up here, alone in the quiet of the Universe, floating in God's ether, I was suddenly filled with an unexpectedly overpowering feeling of peace and harmony, a near celestial sensation of well-being. Maybe this was what heaven was like! If this was only my first jump, I couldn't wait to go again.

My second, alas, was far different. Deciding the men needed "morale boosting," the commanding officer gave me a field promotion from rookie to "jumpmaster." That's right. The day before, I had jumped out of a plane for the first time in my life, and now I was an expert — and a Catholic one at that! My faith, as it turned out, superseded my skills. Since most of the volunteers were Catholic, the commanding officer explained, "They'll respond better to a priest than an ordinary layman when it comes to remaining with the Airborne." (He wasn't wrong. Almost all of the volunteers stuck with us.) I, of course, too stunned to answer anything else, blurted out, "Yes." Still, I was more than thankful that Sergeant Jumpmaster would be at my side in the plane.

Though the wind had picked up, it wasn't enough to cancel the second jump. As the plane neared the drop zone, the sergeant nudged me. In as manfully a manner as I could muster, I started shouting over the motor's deafening roar. "Stand up and hook up." But in fact, we already were — standing that is. Maybe nobody noticed! Taking a deep breath, I continued bellowing commands: "Check your equipment!" "Check off!" After the man standing next to me weighed in, I paused. Per instructions from an Army psychologist, I was now to shout: "Are you happy?" Looking down the line at the taut, white faces of this gang of eighteen-year-olds, never in a plane before yesterday's jump, I thought: "What fool thought up this command?" Nevertheless, I delivered my question as convincingly as I could, "Are you happy?" Every mouth opened, but not a sound emerged.

"Let's go! Follow me!" And out I jumped. Thank God they all followed.

Filled with relief that my chute opened again, I landed with a short prayer of gratitude before quickly checking the others. All jumped, all chutes opened! However, perusing the sky, I noticed that one parachute inhabited by a slight, thin paratrooper and driven by a recalcitrant breeze was uncontrollably drifting over the chute of a beefier soldier whose own chute, creating a fleeting vacuum, collapsed the one above it. Instantly, the skinny soldier fell onto the one below. "Hold on!" I yelled, terrified. "Hold on!" He couldn't. Sliding off the canopy, he was hurtling straight toward the ground. Watching in horror, I prayed hard. Apparently it worked. Some fifty feet from the ground, his collapsed chute, catching a slight breeze, partially lifted, allowing the soldier to land, albeit tangled in his equipment. Rushing to him, I saw he was alive, but shaken, suffering only a broken leg. My prayer of thanksgiving was fervent indeed!

Not everyone, of course, was cut out to fly in the sky. One rookie, never having jumped, came to me, explaining his fear. Nothing I said eliminated his reservations. Finally, he asked what would happen if he refused to jump in combat. "Forget the idea. You don't want to go there." But he persisted. "Refusing to jump means you'll get a dishonorable discharge along with two years of hard labor at Fort Leavenworth prison. So don't even consider it. Jacques will take you to training exercise this afternoon." And off he went. It couldn't have gone worse. While the pair watched (a particularly large training jump involving hundreds of men) a plane lost power completely. Gliding helplessly, it cut through the pack of jumpers, killing several mid-air, confirming, of course, his worst fears. Jacques returned with the even more terrified trooper, who repeated his question: "Tell me again. What's the penalty for refusing to jump?" Assuring him there would be none in his case, I gave him my blessing and a transfer to a truck company.

Happily, the remaining five qualifying jumps were uneventful. After being presented our paratroop "wings," attesting to our new status, I was informed that new paratrooper officers were expected to attend the "Prop Blast," a tradition requiring newly decorated paratroopers to take one drink from a large flagon of brew prepared by the officer in charge. This "big gulp" had to last as long as it took to say the: "one thousand, two thousand, three thousand," used by troopers jumping out of planes. In a nod to its significance, the drink, a concoction of every alcohol imaginable or available, was served in an impressive silver bowl. The trick, of course, was the timekeepers who had wicked fun counting out the "one thousand, two thousand, three...." The first new "victim" got a count so slow he nearly drained the flagon. When it was my turn, the time keepers showed mercy, counting off "one ... two ... three" in quick succession — still far too long to have the stuff in my mouth.

Watch on the Rhine

Now that I was a qualified paratrooper, I strongly felt that I should jump in combat, a decision that solidified further when rumors began circulating that Slim Jim was arranging for the 82nd to do the "Rhine jump" — that is, an attack on the German forces who, retreating across the Rhine River, had formed a formidable pocket of resistance.

Once again on the road, our motor column wound its way toward the Rhine and Cologne where I'd visited during seminary vacations. Being Easter week, I had plenty of time that afternoon to read my breviary and say the rosary. Toward evening, however, I had the queasy feeling that the column was lost. Reading German signs was always a mystery, and sure enough, when night fell, we were still moving.

Sometime after dark, Jacques and I smelled smoke, but the column continued until, suddenly, minutes later, the night rang out with a blast of sparks and smoke. "Drive faster," an alert sergeant shouted, "and keep the cars jammed together." As it turned out, the road, abutting an open-pit coal mine, had been lit by some diehard Nazi determined to block our advance. By increasing speed and staying bumper to bumper, our tight-knit column prevented being surrounded by smoke and fire. At the wheel, Jacques kept our front bumper jammed up against the rear of the jeep ahead. For my part, I prayed hard, asking God for protection and quick wit for the drivers. Finally having escaped the fire, Jacques and I realized that we were alone, separated from the others. Filled with trepidation, we sped through the night, until to our utter relief, we pulled into Sachem, gratefully taking up quarters in a clean, neat home.

The Rhineland's rich, prosperous appearance — pristine homes, meticulously tilled fields, and vineyards — coupled with the populace's prevalent anti-Nazi sentiment confused our men. Should they believe Germans when warned about things like the "werewolves," a fanatical Nazi youth group who, dedicated to the disruption of the American occupation, snipped communication lines and changed road signs. The idea of American soldiers shooting German teenagers, of course, was unacceptable. "If we put a tank at every street corner," Colonel Ekman said, "we can't solve the problem."

If tanks wouldn't work, I thought, honor might. Why not appeal to the good, not suspicious, in people? So I suggested the following solution: in every newly occupied village we would appoint, without formality, a respected pastor as interim mayor — a Protestant for predominantly Protestant villages, a priest for those more Catholic. With "mayors" appealing to the people's consciences, order could be restored. And it was. The arrangement worked beautifully.

One of my first priorities was to see firsthand the condition of the massive Cathedral of Cologne. So one day, Jacques and I headed out for Cologne. What awaited us was stunning. The beautiful city I remembered had been reduced to an enormous pile of rubble. The only building standing was the cathedral, erect like a majestic symbol of the perpetuity of the faith. In the front around the Platz, burned-out Panzer tanks had been left abandoned at the edge of the Rhine, a nearby bridge buckled and broken.

I had to get inside the cathedral. With German troops across the Rhine, we parked the jeep at a safe spot. Creeping behind mountains of rubble, I reached the front door. Immediately, a machine gun nest across the water sent a volley across the Platz. Detouring, I finally managed to work my way inside, a sad but impressive sight. Though aerial bombs had blown gaping holes in the roof, the spires and walls, amazingly enough, were still intact. The floor meanwhile, covered with marble chips from destroyed altars, boasted a couple of brick bunkers.

Eventually, I located an exhausted, disheveled priest, who had hidden in the cellar to greet the Americans. Explaining I was a Catholic who visited the cathedral before the war, he told me that the famous artistic pieces, constituting the cathedral's treasury, were hidden in the bunkers. "Our men have been issued new gammon grenades that can easily break open these bunkers," I told him, "Having visited this cathedral, I'm anxious to try to protect it, especially the artistic pieces. If I can get permission from the archbishop to establish a guard cross here, I'll be glad to do it."

After eyeing my identity card, he revealed that Archbishop Josef Frings, the area's archbishop, was in a convent in Honnef, across the Rhine in territory held by the Americans. A day later, Jacques and I were crossing the pontoon bridge built by our engineers heading for Honnef. Perched on the river bank, the village's streets were pockmarked with destroyed Allied planes,

Chaplain Philip M. Hannan

During World War II as a chaplain

As a chaplain in the field

Celebrating Easter Mass in 1945 on the grounds of a camp in Germany before departing for a campaign on the Elbe River

An 82nd Airborne practice jump in France

With assistant Jacques Ospital

artillery, and bombshell explosives. Eventually we found the badly damaged convent where Archbishop Frings and an assistant priest shared a cellar with the convent's nuns. Earnestly, I explained my anxiety to the Archbishop, a thin, intense man who, listening carefully, dispatched his assistant to fetch a small typewriter in another room. Sitting down, he dashed off a letter officially making me the Administrator of the Cologne Cathedral!

Honnef, 16.April 1945
The Archbishop of Cologne
J.-Nr.

I hereby authorize the American Military Chaplain, the Reverend Philip Hannan, to protect from theft and destruction the liturgical objects and vestments as well as objects of Church art, located in the Cologne Cathedral and other churches of Cologne and not secured, for the time being as long as German priests are unable to take care of these things because of existing areas which are off limits.

+ Joseph
Archbishop of Cologne

Signing it, the Archbishop handed the letter to me. "Why didn't the Allies come into Germany by the north?" he then asked. "There were no fortifications there." That would have been a much better strategy, I agreed, one we tried to do — but failed — in the campaign to take Arnhem. Graciously, the Archbishop invited Jacques and me to lunch, consisting of a bowl of soup carefully prepared by the Sisters. Immaculately dressed in their religious garb, these good women were the triumph of order in a war of chaos. Upon leaving, the Archbishop gave me the address of his auxiliary bishop, asking that I inform him he was well, and I did.

With my new authority, we immediately established a guard at the cathedral. I also sent out word in the area, via Jacques, asking troops and citizens who might have taken anything from the cathedral to either return it to me personally or leave it in my tent. Though I collected from the cathedral a duffel bag of religious articles, prayer books, broken vessels, there were no artistically valuable items. A day later two nuns approached me in my tent at twilight. "We know you visited the Archbishop in a convent for Sisters and have a favor to ask. Being members of our Congregation, those Sisters should be here with us. Can you bring them?"

"I'm very sorry, but I can't bring them over here," I replied. "Since the Rhine is a security line, any German citizen who tries to cross it — not to mention anyone helping them — is liable to be shot."

"But our rule says they should be with us," insisted the Sister whose face fell when I had to refuse. Hearing our exchange, Sister Superior motioned to

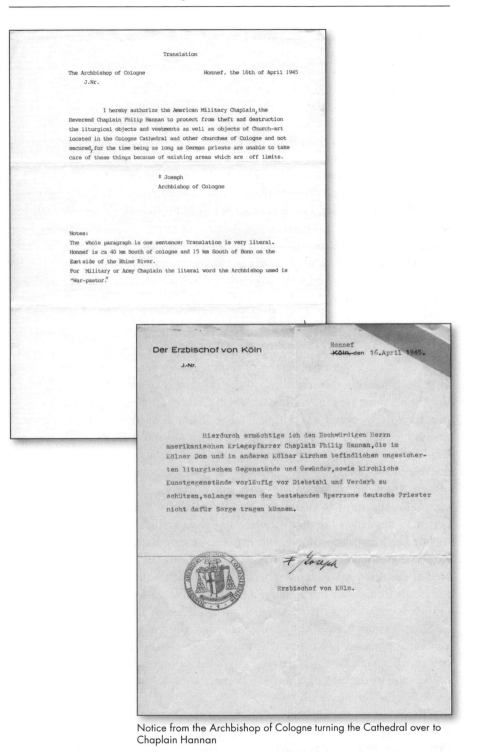

Translation

The Archbishop of Cologne Honnef, the 16th of April 1945
    J.Nr.

        I hereby authorize the American Military Chaplain, the
Reverend Chaplain Philip Hannan to protect from theft and destruction
the liturgical objects and vestments as well as objects of Church-art
located in the Cologne Cathedral and other churches of Cologne and not
secured, for the time being as long as German priests are unable to take
care of these things because of existing areas which are off limits.

                    ✝ Joseph
                    Archbishop of Cologne

Notes:
The whole paragraph is one sentence; Translation is very literal.
Honnef is ca 40 km South of cologne and 15 km South of Bonn on the
East side of the Rhine River.
For Military or Army Chaplain the literal word the Archbishop used is
"War-pastor."

Der Erzbischof von Köln Honnef
                             Köln, den 16.April 1945.
    J.-Nr.

        Hierdurch ermächtige ich den Hochwürdigen Herrn
amerikanischen Kriegspfarrer Chaplain Philip Hannan, die im
Kölner Dom und in anderen Kölner Kirchen befindlichen ungesicher-
ten liturgischen Gegenstände und Gewänder, sowie kirchliche
Kunstgegenstände vorläufig vor Diebstahl und Verderb zu
schützen, solange wegen der bestehenden Sperrzone deutsche Priester
nicht dafür Sorge tragen können.

                    ✝ Joseph
                    Erzbischof von Köln.

Notice from the Archbishop of Cologne turning the Cathedral over to
Chaplain Hannan

her crestfallen comrade, who produced from beneath her voluminous robes a pint of schnapps. Grabbing the bottle, the Sister Superior tried to give it to me. "Please do it," she pleaded.

"Sorry, Sister," I sighed, "not even for schnapps."

Not long after, Colonel Ekman ordered that I report to the Corps Headquarters to see the Chaplain of the Corps, who had summoned me. He also said to find a "Class A" uniform; I needed to look sharp for the meeting which he obviously thought was serious. "Make sure and report back to me why you were wanted." Decked out in my dress uniform, I dutifully reported to Corps Headquarters in the northern part of the Rhine where I looked like a real oddball. Everyone else was in combat fatigues though there was no fighting for miles. Showing my orders, I was ushered into the chaplain's office where I was stunned to see, sitting with the Corps chaplain, Father Speer Strahan, my former professor of English at Catholic University in Washington... the man who assigned us to write an entire novel in one semester. And he was dressed, very unconvincingly, in combat fatigues. This guy had never seen battle.

After initial pleasantries, he said he'd heard that the 82nd had been in the Rhineland and asked if I had visited the town of Munchen Gladbach. "No. Why do you ask?" Father Strahan's response stuns me to this day. "Having long been interested in the liturgy," he explained unapologetically, "I heard they made some very interesting fabrics for Mass vestments there." A few minutes later I left, eventually telling Colonel Ekman only that a former professor had looked me up. With Jacques, I was a tad more candid. "He was my English teacher and very demanding. But I think he's been overcome by his interest in the liturgy."

As American troops on the other side of the river squeezed the pocket of Germans, the need to patrol the Rhine gradually diminished. White flags began to appear as German troops as well as civilians fled across the river to our section. Since a large segment of the population was Polish, Father Kozak, a Catholic chaplain in the 82nd, fluent in Polish and Russian, officiated at fifty-two marriages of liberated Polish slave laborers. During the war, the Nazis forbade anyone to enter a Catholic church, so the Polish, extremely knowledgeable about their Catholic faith, conducted their own marriage ceremonies, in accordance with Canon law that a group of Catholics, unable to contact a priest, could marry themselves with two witnesses. Ultimately, of course, they wanted their marriage "blessed" along with a record certifying it was solid in the eyes of Church and state. It took Father Kozak two days to complete the ceremonies.

Being an occupying army with access to German homes, an occasional shakedown of the troops was necessary. Instructed to get together everything they owned, the unit was marched down the road into a field where they were ordered to open up all their gear. Standing close to the scene of a shakedown, I noticed that one young trooper seemed perfectly at ease. "You're not worried?" I asked.

"No. I can't steal."

"What do you mean?"

"Well, Father, I was taught by the Sisters, and anytime I get the urge to steal, I can see that Sister standing over me, ready to pull my ear off." I laughed. There's no moral deterrent like a Catholic nun ready to strike.

Eventually we were given orders to move to the Elbe River to serve under the command of the legendary Field Marshal Bernard L. Montgomery, commander of the Allies' northern front. Now finished, our stay in the Rhineland — blessed by meeting so many good Catholics and Protestants — continuously made me ponder the rise of Nazism, as seen in these thoughts I recorded in my journal:

> "We are now in a Catholic part of Germany. The contrast between the horrors of Nazism and the quiet, pious life of the individuals here naturally prompts the question, how did it happen? How could Nazism be forced upon these people; how could they let it grow? We see the full-blown, stark horror of Nazism but forget they did not accept it in this stage; they accepted it as a seedling that grew irresistibly to its present terrible size. Their great sin, it seems, was toying with temptation. They did not reject it promptly... or at all because it had pleasurable aspects — bread, work, security.... (A)n evil system develops quickly, like a cancer, in time of disorder or unrest..."

Epinal

Given orders to return to France as a temporary assignment camp, we passed through the German town of Munster where the ancient cathedral had been reduced to a pile of rubble — the sole memorial to Bishop Clemens August von Galen, the Lion of Munster. A stalwart and effective anti-Nazi spokesman, the Bishop, in a series of 1941 homilies, bravely unmasked the twisted ideology of Nazism, publicly railing against the forced closure of convents, the arrests of clergy and religious, the deportations, and the destruction of human lives that the Nazis deemed unworthy to be lived. When the Nazis stormed his rectory to arrest him, the Bishop, forewarned, donned full liturgical vestments and put on his miter. Standing six feet, six inches, towering over his captors, he directly confronted them: "You may have come to arrest me, but I insist on going to jail fully dressed as the Bishop because as the Bishop of this area, I am being arrested because of my stand against you." Knowing his popularity, they fled in abject confusion. (Blessed Bishop von Galen truly bore witness for the Gospel of Life and in 2005 was duly rewarded with beatification.)

Since Stapel, near Munster, had a displaced persons' camp filled with Poles, French, Flemish, and a few Germans, I scheduled Mass at 5:30 p.m. in the yard of the Protestant church, the only clean and unoccupied space nearby. A sturdy Flemish woman approached asking if she could go to Confession. In my poor German, I explained that since I'd be giving general absolution, everyone could receive Holy Communion. She broke in, obviously disappointed: *"Ach, ein Evangelischer"* ("Oh, a Protestant"), and turned to leave, followed by the whole contingent of worshipers. Rushing to the front of the church, I blocked the door, saying in German and French: "I'm a Catholic priest. I was ordained in Rome." Fortunately, some people understood, explaining that I was, indeed, an authentic Catholic priest. Convinced of my religious bona fides, they returned to their pews. Giving general absolution to this diverse crowd, I began Mass. When it came time for Communion, they came up, haltingly, but with great joy like children. I had never seen such devotion in receiving the Body and Blood of Christ. For the Poles, it was their first Communion in five years.

At the end of Mass, I asked if there was a hymn that everyone knew, but no one could agree. Finally they decided on a well-known Polish hymn. The streams of song welled up from the depth of their souls. It rose in volume as the people recalled more firmly the words and the tune. It swelled to a steady, heady volume, interrupted only by intermittent sobs as emotion overpowered the singers. I didn't understand a word, but everyone understood the meaning of the hymn. It was the expression of the joy of Catholic Poland, a hymn of resurrection from the dead. Later the Catholics sang in German "Holy God We Praise Thy Name" with ear-breaking volume.

Elbe River Campaign

From my point of view, the last campaign of World War II, brainchild of the British, was not only brilliant but mandatory in order to win the war. In light of the Soviet boast to "rule the world," the prescient English realized there could be a war with the Soviet Union. And if so, the Brits planned to have Hamburg as a German port of entry, thus controlling a sizable foothold along the Elbe. Crossing the river itself was a secondary goal aimed at thwarting the advance of the Russian Army toward Denmark.

Commanding this whole effort was one of Britain's best: Field Marshal Montgomery, who had requested that the 82nd Airborne lead the Elbe crossing with the Fighting 505th spearheading the attack. It would take place on April 30, the day after our arrival, with the English furnishing the boats to get across this wide expanse of water flanked by flat exposed land.

With movement set to begin at 1:00 a.m., I was determined to say Mass for anyone who could show up. And a lot did, veterans eager to get it over with, but anxious about what awaited. Finally, at 1:00 a.m. as promised, the boats arrived, the men boarded, and the attack began. Refusing to be stopped, the 505th dodged persistent German fire to finally climb ashore on the other side. This first victory lap, however, was not without casualties, thanks to the magnetic sea mines, blowing one jeep twenty feet in the air, that had been planted for protection by the Germans.

The crossing completed, troopers now faced an even more dramatic dilemma: how to end this "useless" fighting and defuse a situation ripe to wind up in disastrous hand-to-hand combat. The Germans, secure in trenches facing across "no man's land," had both time and material to post a protracted, effective defense against American forces, equally prepared to take on anything the Germans threw at them. But at this stage of the war, was that what either side really wanted? To keep on blowing out each other's brains? To continue, in the case of the Germans, risking their lives for a cowardly leader, a cause already lost?

The question hung in the air. But who would step up and make real what soldiers on both sides were thinking: enough bloodshed is enough? A split moment later, in a spontaneously heroic action, a German-speaking American officer, gun in hand, began rushing toward the middle of no man's land — every eye glued on his every move. Skidding to a stop, he lifted his rifle over his head in a neutral position and, yelling forcefully to the Germans in their own tongue, made the call himself. "The war is over! The war is over! There is no sense in fighting. We don't want to wound or kill you. Stop fighting. Surrender to us, and I assure you, as an officer with the American Army, that you will be given fair and good treatment. I swear on my honor that I will walk with you to the section for prisoners of war, stay with you to guarantee you receive good treatment. Surrender! Surrender! No American will shoot you, but surrender now!"

His hands over his head, the officer stood there, utterly alone, completely helpless, nakedly vulnerable. Nobody talked, moved, or fired a shot, each person no doubt trying to decide his own next action in the face of one so big, brave, loving. Finally, this brief silence, lasting an eternity, was pierced by the sound of two German soldiers jumping up, throwing down their rifles, and marching out to join the American officer. Their courage jump-started it in others, as one by one, the entire German army stepped forward and surrendered to their enemy, to us.

It is a vision that I shall never forget: this brave, hopeful soldier, hands over his head, hope in his heart, prayers no doubt on his lips, standing solo, completely undefended, shouting in German: "Surrender!" Surrender!" Even today I do not know his name; nor, sadly, does the world. All I was told was that he came from North Dakota. This young, selfless gambler who prevented such immense bloodshed, was never given a Purple Heart, a White House dinner, a standing ovation. But in heaven his reward is great.

The captured German soldiers brought with them the rumor that a close-by German army was approaching to surrender. Adding to the confusion, a German general was desperately trying to find General Gavin to proffer a surrender on behalf of his commanding officer. Finally, on May 2, Lieutenant General Kurt von Tippelskirch officially laid down Germany's arms, setting in motion the movement of a primitive nation composed of over one hundred fifty thousand German troops and countless refugees, fleeing as much from the Russians as surrendering to us.

The surrender engulfed our troops, whose duty it was to confiscate weapons and direct the masses into hastily erected, compound prisoner-of-war camps. Numbering one hundred fifty thousand men, the German Army, twenty-five miles long, required three days of constant work (by our soldiers) to disarm then stack the weapons in a huge pile later deposited with the British Army. Though German soldiers had a few rations, the plight of this unexpected horde fantastically eclipsed the division's resources. Immediately, horses, cows, sheep, every edible animal, every morsel of food from every store's existing stock was commandeered. Eventually, with typical American ingenuity, a makeshift, if efficient, system of feeding people began to shape up.

The German Army, I soon learned, was largely composed of Bavarian men, nearly half of whom were Catholics. Being in Prussia, with no Catholic center to turn to, we ended up caring for nearly seventy-five thousand Catholic German soldiers and refugees. To ensure security, German soldiers were assigned to eight different camps; while the Hungarian cavalry, by necessity, assisted troopers patrolling the prisoner camps. Visiting the camps, I sought out Catholic priests to serve as assistant chaplains but found just eleven — only one of whom owned a Mass kit which he'd left in the home of a German Protestant family, the Ihdes, in a village in Russian-occupied territory. With no time to ask the Colonel's permission, I told Jacques, who insisted on bringing a rifle, that we were going to get it.

Finally we located the town, whereupon I asked a woman where the Ihde family lived. "Everybody here is named Ihde," she said. "Which one do you mean?" "The one who has a Catholic Mass kit given by a Catholic German soldier." She took us to the house where I tortured the lady of the house trying to speak German. Suddenly, a neighbor appeared. The Protestant pastor who had turned his parsonage into a clinic, desperately wished to see me. Carrying my Mass kit, I walked into a completely heart-wrenching drama. In tears, the pastor explained that he had twenty-three women in his home, all suffering various stages of injury from the Russian soldiers who had beaten and raped them. Barely had I digested that horrible information, when a doctor appeared. "Can you get us penicillin?" he asked. "They need it terribly." Never had I felt so inadequate. "I'm very sorry," I said, "but we don't have enough for our own needs. I can't help you."

Concentration Camp Horror

As soul disturbing as that experience had been, it was merely a prelude to what came next. A day later, I received word that, near Ludwigslust, a concentration camp had been discovered whose prisoners included two Catholic priests. Immediately, Jacques and I set out for Wöbbelin, where the camp was located. Walking into the barracks, we were immediately assailed by a suffocating stench, leading to the shocking panorama of hundreds of half-alive, emaciated prisoners, dressed in tattered, utterly soiled uniforms, shuffling amongst clumps of corpses as if they were not there. Some, too weak to be on their feet, gazed through glassy eyes from cramped positions on four levels of multi-tiered, rudely made bunks of pine timber and branches. Everywhere, the living were interspersed with the dead, who had died in human excrement.

Due to starvation and disease, many of the deceased were victims of dysentery and diarrhea, their excrement splashed on the bunks below them. Never in my life had I experienced — nor will I ever again — such an incomprehensibly barbaric insult to the human spirit.

I helped carry victims of the concentration camp in Wöbbelin, a village near Ludwigslust, Germany

Inquiring about the priests, the prisoners indicated their bunks. One, a Belgian, too weak to walk, wanly but cordially greeted me, explaining that the other priest, also Belgian, revered by all for his heroism in helping fellow prisoners, had died the day before. When we assured him that we would do our best to continue his friend's mission, he urged us to aid those around him, adamantly refusing any personal attention,

The extent of what had transpired in these evil walls became clear when a tall, recently imprisoned young man in good condition, a member he said of the French Secret Service, informed me that of the camp's four thousand prisoners — French, Dutch, Belgian, Jews, Russians, all nationalities and religions — approximately eight hundred were still alive. Those who were alive gathered according to ethnic groups, as did the Dutch contingent, made it

A French Secret Service officer and I at the concentration camp in Wöbbelin, Germany, where the bodies of victims had been laid out in rows

quite clear they wanted to remain, and be evacuated, as a group. And they did, huddling together until escorted out the next afternoon.

Part of their distrust, quite possibly was derived from the Americans who preceded us. Other Yankees, Jacques and I learned, had come to the camp but, revolted by the sights and odors, left after a short time, declaring, in essence, that "this is too big a job for me." As with the Belgian priest, Jacques and I continually assured prisoners that he and I would stay and try to help. Later, when an American Major drove into camp and saw us, he pointed out a nearby German civilian hospital, offering to send a German truck to give us a hand.

A few hours later, in a burst of wheezes and groans, the truck, complete with a flatbed, useful for loading sick prisoners, pulled into camp complete with a German driver who agreed to pitch in. Due to their emaciated state — the first man I picked up couldn't have weighed more than seventy-five or eighty pounds — lifting the prisoners onto the flat bed was relatively easy. Many of course lacked energy to talk, much less comment on their brutal treatment; one formerly barrel-chested man, ribs sticking out like spokes, pointed to his withering upper body, saying: *"Dieses ist Deutsch Kultur"* ("This is German culture"). The truck finally loaded, I gave general absolution (the majority being Catholic), asking them, in my broken German, to say a prayer of thanks and contrition.

After that first truck, loading the disabled took on almost assembly-line routine: fill the truck, give general absolution, start the truck, pray it made it to the hospital. In between, we toured the camp, discovering a Dutch naval captain whose ship was captured in the South Pacific who, having taken care of the camp's records, was in rather good shape. "I always made certain," he said, "that my job would never be finished." In accord with general military policy of naming the ranking officer as the commanding officer, I declared him the commanding officer of the camp. Nobody questioned my authority.

In the afternoon, a GI from a nearby service unit brought large quantities of food and medical supplies which he, unable to speak German, deposited with the Dutch captain, who took over distribution. As his guard dropped, he began to explain the camp's brutal routine. "Life was terrible," he said. "They beat us often with rubber truncheons or hoses. We were constantly in fear of the guards who constantly feuded among themselves. After one treated us humanely, a bad guard, who tried to frame him, was grabbed and beaten to death by several prisoners."

One of our biggest problems turned out to be stopping people from over-eating at their first meal (in this case venison) since, doing so, could cause a heart attack brought on by severe cramps. Sitting down next to the naval captain now in charge of the camp, I warned him to eat very sparingly, launching into a blessing to buy time for him to gain control. Finally, offering him a piece of venison with a boiled potato, he wolfed it down, apologized, and promptly got sick, proving my point.

When told there was a second concentration camp nearby for Polish women, we went right over to investigate. Amazingly, all the female prisoners, though extremely thin, appeared to be in relatively good physical shape. Meeting with the first group, I asked why they seemed to be, well, healthy. Everyone pointed to a woman around thirty. "We lived on our faith and our hope," she answered, carefully drawing a tattered, homemade rosary out of her pocket. Her story was staggering. In Poland, when one was taken prisoner by the Nazis, religious articles and personal effects were confiscated. However, at her first "meal" — a bowl of watery soup and a piece of black bread — instead of eating the bread, she saved it. Fashioning small bread pellets into beads and finding a string, she attached enough to make the decades of the rosary. Twisting a pen she found in the shape of a cross, she affixed it to the end of her rosary. Late at night, the guards gone, she and fellow inmates surreptitiously recited the rosary, imploring the Blessed Mother to help them and their fellow prisoners.

Finishing, she extended her rosary toward me: "My rosary has never been blessed. Please bless it."

Frankly, I was taken aback. "I'm sure that the good Lord to whom you appealed for so long," I stammered, "already has blessed it."

Frowning, her voice grew firmly insistent. "You are a priest. You're supposed to bless rosaries. Bless my rosary."

And I did, truthfully feeling unworthy to be blessing such a reverent, "proven" article of devotion. For a moment, I thought about securing it, but rejected the idea. She treasured it too much. Talking further with her as well as her companions, it became evident that none among them was either bedridden or desperately ill. Their faith and prayer had literally saved them. When I walked out the door of that prison camp, I felt as though I was leaving a shrine.

The next morning after Mass, I went to Colonel Ekman, asking if he could assign men to help at the prison camp. He was sympathetic but firm. "My orders are to keep the troops combat-ready," he said. "I can't afford to let them go there and catch typhus or another disease. Your assistant and you can help, but not the others." I couldn't argue with him. The demands placed on the colonel were staggering, starting with amassing a guard duty to police over one hundred fifty thousand POWs. I returned to camp alone. Later that morning, American medics from the 8th Division did show up to help but left, to Jacques' unrestrained disgust, at the end of the day.

We, meanwhile, were beginning to run very low on fuel. Our medics had their hands full taking care of those wounded crossing the Elbe. Moreover, as Ekman pointed out, we couldn't risk the spread of infection from prisoners to soldiers. As dire as the concentration camp situation was, our officers were always conscious that our presence at the Elbe was to prevent/cope with an attack, predicted by Field Marshal Montgomery, by the Russian Army. In the midst of all this chaos, I understood the disgusted ruminations of our soldiers: "So this is the glorious day of surrender ending the war. Some day of glory!"

Given what they endured, the survivors' anger toward anything — anyone — German was completely understandable. It was not, however, permitted. Visiting the hospital for the weakest survivors, I arrived in time to mediate a volatile argument between a German nurse and a hostile prisoner who had cursed and struck her. "I understand your anger at the Germans," I firmly admonished him. "But bad language and violence against hospital personnel — of any nationality — will not be tolerated." He got the message.

The next day, Jacques and I were moved to see a long line of the mobile prisoners, filing quietly, solemnly into the nearby woods. Asking around, I was told that it was the funeral procession for the burial of the Belgian priest who had died the day before the camp was liberated. Arranged by the surviving priest and fellow countryman, it was a simple affair: his ravaged body, lying atop a pine wood plank stretcher, carried by other survivors, all of whom were, regardless of ethnic and religious differences, walking in respectfully mute testimony for the man who, in helping them, had sacrificed himself. His fellow priest had decided that the most appropriate place for his burial was a spot in the woods within the camp, the scene of his apostolate. They had not asked me or anyone else to participate. Only those sharing their bitter if bonding fraternity were included. Watching in admiration, I prayed for the repose of the soul of the deceased as well as all the other prisoners.

On Sunday I said Mass for the American troops before hitting as many prisoner camps as possible to do the same. At a camp for German soldiers, an officer came up to me: "I bring a special request not to forget to go to the camp of S.S. soldiers," he said. This was quite a surprise. Since the S.S. were known to be the most ruthlessly, fanatical of Hitler's troops, it never dawned on me that they would care about Mass. But if they did, I would celebrate it, I assured him, if, that is, I had the time.

The sun was beginning to set when I finally made it to the S.S. camp where, to my astonishment, the commanding officer stood at the entrance, greeting me with a snappy salute before escorting me to the site of the Mass where at least a hundred soldiers surrounded the carefully constructed altar. As I vested for Mass, an S.S. noncom appeared, saying, in perfect English, "Please remember that not all of us were volunteers for the S.S. I was a seminarian in Metz when the Germans took me and any other seminarian with a German name. It was not our fault. We were forced."

In view of these revelations, I decided that the Mass could use a little something extra. "We need some music," I said. "Is there a former choir conductor here?" Sure enough, a hand shot up and took over. "Once a choir director," I thought, "always a choir director. Not even the S.S. can erase that identity." Giving my usual brief pep talk, I led the congregation in an act of contrition and gave general absolution. The choir director ordered a hymn. Hesitantly, they began, voices growing stronger as their memories reawakened. The Mass, meanwhile, proceeded as usual until I got to the distribution of Holy Communion. Offering Communion to a soldier wearing the S.S. insignia on his collar, I instinctively recoiled. Though I was a priest first, I was also an American soldier. At the end, when our newly minted choirmaster led us in: "Holy God We Praise Thy Name," the music rang out like a trumpet blast. There wasn't a dry eye in the place.

Walking back to my jeep with the S.S. colonel, I said, "I'm surprised at the number and vigor of the soldiers at the Mass."

"Why should you be?" he replied somewhat incredulously. "This is Pentecost" — which I shall never forget.

Contrary to gossip that the Russians were coming, nothing happened. And despite V-E Day (Victory in Europe Day) being declared on May 8, nothing changed in the tedious daily guard duties. Copies of *Stars and Stripes*, blaring front-page pictures of soldiers and sailors kissing girls in Times Square, engendered more than one profane remark from American soldiers still thousands of miles from home. "Those bums haven't seen a day of war," as one trooper griped to me, "and they get all the kissing and cheering!"

It was decided that the 82nd would stage one final event to impress on the German inhabitants the gravity of the atrocities committed on the concentration camp victims. Chaplain Wood, the division chaplain, prepared a carefully researched address, translated into German, for the occasion. Unfortunately, he couldn't read the language, so I was given the task of delivering his blistering monologue. In the courtyard of the famous castle in Ludwigslust, bodies of victims of the Wöbbelin concentration camp were laid out in rows, while its German citizens, duly ordered, walked through to behold the dastardly work of the Nazis. As they did so, I read the proclamation. Though some wept, many protested that they had "no idea what was happening in Wöbbelin." We shook our heads in disbelief!

Eventually, the division was informed that we were being sent to a camp in eastern France, Epinal, to prepare for occupation duty in Berlin. For the veteran paratroopers of the 82nd, our last official review marked a climax. Since one thousand one hundred men had sufficient "points" to return home, the regiment was divided into two groups: departing veterans and remaining troopers. With Colonel Ekman in the lead, those remaining marched in review before veterans who, returning the compliment, did the same for those who were staying. It was an unforgettable moment of high emotion, a bittersweet experience that transcended a mere farewell. The departing 1,100 were the courageous survivors of the only-known regiment to fight through four combat jumps and three land campaigns. Trained in Africa, they executed the first U.S. Army regimental combat jump in Sicily, repeating it to rescue the beachhead at Anzio. Jumping in Normandy, they captured the strategic town of Sainte Mere l'Eglise, overcoming Nazi resistance, to hold it for advancing American troops. In Holland, they landed at noon, saving, together with the 504th Regiment and despite fire, the bridges across the Rhine. In the sub-zero degree temperatures of the Ardennes, they met Hitler's Panzer divisions whom they, despite heavy losses, successfully counter-attacked, helping to stem the Nazi offensive. Finally, they had guarded the Rhine where, by forcing passage of the Elbe River, they accepted the surrender of a whole German army.

This review was the end of an epic odyssey. For these jaunty, brave, lucky band of brothers were the remaining legion of a kind of fighting man never to be matched, or repeated, again. And everyone knew it. Even the toughest felt a swell of pride and profound emotion. As they marched off the parade ground into history, I, for one, had tears in my eyes.

Ever the pragmatist, however, Colonel Ekman lost no time in addressing the new troopers filling their combat boots. Promising to never again address us as "new" paratroopers, he urged us to build on the achievements of the Regiment. He also warned about the dangers of venereal disease. We were, after all, going into Berlin. Meanwhile, Jacques and I, bone- and heart-tired after four days of caring for prisoners from dawn to midnight, were completely whipped.

On to Berlin

We left Epinal bound for Berlin in the first week of August 1945 — just as the atomic bombs were being dropped on Hiroshima (August 6) and Nagasaki (August 9) thus ending the war in the Pacific. The first, over Hiroshima, rather than called an atom bomb, was simply described as a new, destructive bomb. Consequently, my immediate reaction was the hope that it would force the Japanese emperor to capitulate (as he did on August 15). The 82nd at that time was scheduled to be deployed in January 1946 to the Pacific Theater — a prospect no one favored since the military estimated two million casualties if that conflict continued. Moreover, with the Air Force not announcing specifics about the number killed and everyone thrilled the war was over, no one even questioned the morality of President Truman's decision. (My brother Tom was actually in the trenches at Los Alamos when the atom bomb was initially field-tested and measured. When it exploded, his trench collapsed. Nobody was ready for its force. Later, during the 1960s when the Second Vatican Council took up the discussion of the morality of nuclear weapons, I was one of few Catholic bishops who raised the unpopular argument that mere possession of nuclear weapons was not, in and of itself, immoral; in fact, it provides a deterrent effect to any countries threatening the world's freedom. I believe the same thing now.)

Having returned from France to Germany, the 82nd made its way to Helmsted, boundary of the Russian Zone, where red flags bearing the hammer and sickle were slapped on everything like a perpetual May Day celebration. Russian soldiers, stolid, impassive, saluting everything that moved, were stationed everywhere. Labor gangs of German women, under the supervision of Russian soldiers, cleared the streets of endless mounds of rubble. In fact, most of the backbreaking work of German recovery was done by their women. At the fringe of every pile of rocks and metal, once a village or town, women in worn-out, dusty clothes, large, dirty kerchiefs covering their hair, pulled bricks from rubble, neatly stacking them for future construction as small children, oblivious to the tragedy of war, played games in the dirt. Occasionally, upon seeing an American soldier, German civilians waved in delight, making us feel like saviors not conquerors.

As ordered, we came in Class A uniforms eager to compete with the "best in the world." The first Russians we saw, however, were in convoys of horse-drawn wagons, loaded with loot and trailed by cows requisitioned from the Germans. We were agape. This crack division was our competition? These disheveled, unshaven Russian soldiers sporting worn-out uniforms splattered with large, clanking medals?

The Russians, meanwhile, wanted nothing more than to look like us. Anything "Americanski" was worth buying, at an exorbitant price. With Russians not allowed to take any "script money" used in Berlin, they were always eager to trade; music to the ears of entrepreneurial troopers who, grasping this new market, turned it into cash. In top demand were Mickey Mouse watches, which enterprising Russian soldiers and officers had strapped from wrist to elbow. One shrewd soldier sold a roll of toilet paper for $200 to a Russian soldier who thought it was American cigarette paper; individual cigarettes went for ten bucks a piece in script with coffee beans fetching equally astronomical paydays. As Winston Churchill so prophetically put it: "As a result of the war, the Russians saw the West and the West saw the Russians." And the West, as it turned out, was the fulfillment of Russian dreams. Finally, we marched into Berlin, where the first sign I saw, planted atop wreckage, read: "*Dafur brauchte er funf Jahre*" — "For this he needed five years?" — a cynical reference to Hitler's boast that he would take a mere five years to build a new Germany.

Berlin was a spectacle of destruction. Miles of debris, punctuated by deep craters, the skeletons of buildings, tiger tanks, and antitank guns spelled out the Russian course of attack as well as the effect of Allied bombing. A spattering of Germans, mostly elderly women, furtively picked through the ruins for small household articles. On the occasional lawn, a burial spot for a Russian soldier was recognizable by a red star with hammer and sickle. Strangely, the Russians were slow to gather their dead into a cemetery, many shrugging, as if to say, "What's the use?"

While battalions of our regiment were assigned to various sections of the American zone, I was billeted in the Zehlendorf section which, not in the path of the attacking Russians, was somewhat less devastated. There, I was stationed in the partially destroyed home of the Matulat family. Because Herr Matulat was an engineer with a knowledge of Russian, having studied in St. Petersburg, he had been able to protect his wife and family from marauding soldiers. I was given a room on the second floor, kept immaculate by Frau Matulat, which I greatly appreciated, especially given the sanitary conditions in Berlin, which were frightful. The water supply, for instance, was hopelessly contaminated by the flow of sewage water into cracked water mains, the pipes of both systems ruptured by the bombing. Though we were issued halazone tablets to decontaminate the water, the chemicals gave it a terrible taste. (The Russians' heavy artillery tactics had caused enormous destruction throughout the city. After training their big artillery pieces on one section of Berlin, they moved their machinery a few paces forward, mowing down the next. It was ruthless but effective.)

When I was assigned an "office" in a home, my efficient assistant, George Melahn, scrounged up a typewriter and put us into business. Army regulations allowed me to hire a civilian assistant for desk work, and I found Annelie

Diehl, who, though only eighteen, had seen horrors of war I could only imagine. Annelie, desperately thin, lived with her mentally unbalanced mother in their heavily damaged home. Trying to save her daughter from being raped by a Russian soldier, her mother, placing her under the bed sheets, said she was only a little girl. But the soldier ripped off her nightgown anyway. When Annelie resisted, he shot her in the neck, leaving her for dead. Miraculously, she recovered, luckier than most of her girlfriends who had also been raped. I hoped that my job offer would help Annie and her family get back on their feet.

Though the laws of fraternization forbade German and American soldiers to attend the same religious services, German civilians often came to Masses celebrated for our soldiers. Those who spoke fluent English, gradually began revealing terror stories of the "Stalin days." After a victory, Russian officers permitted three days of vengeance on the German population. But in Berlin the victory period had been extended — with horrible results, many of which came to light when Germans came to Confession — invariably a grueling but rewarding experience. Their utter lack of food and clothing, as well as the absence of an effective central authority, allowed for an urban reign of terror. Murder, rape, attempted suicide, the entire gamut of vice spawned by the defeat and subsequent atrocities of the Russians, provided a flood of material for the confessional as every horror of war and survival came into review and judgment. The relief of those finally able to confess was inspirational.

It didn't take long to realize that this situation demanded a great religious renewal; accordingly, I launched a mission, assisted by Father Power, a religious priest attached to another American unit in Berlin and no stranger to parish crusades. Since Father Power had a reputation as a dynamic speaker, we agreed that I would hear confessions as he spoke, assuring everyone that as a paratroop chaplain, having heard "every kind of sin committed," they should fear no repercussions by baring their souls. And when he finished, he would also hear confessions. Sticking my paratroop boots under the confessional curtain to indicate my location, I settled in as Father Power, warming to his subject, spoke for nearly an hour! By the time he finished, I'd heard the confessions of everyone in the church.

The greatest temptation that people faced, not surprisingly, was rooted in despair. An elderly man, having lost his family, was tormented by the idea of suicide, gassing himself to death. "Late in life," he lamented, "I made one great mistake, not joining the S.S. troops. You Americans feed them in the stockade while we, the innocent, starve on seven hundred calories a day rations." Another man, a doctor, wanted to talk about his life. "What worries me are the experiments I performed under orders from the Nazis," he told me, "especially abortions. Now I know how wrong it was." "You mean you didn't know that it was a grievous, a mortal sin?" "No, not completely," he replied. "At only seven,

I was a Hitler Youth. For years I was brainwashed and believed them. You don't know what it was like."

Post-war Berlin wasn't just tough on Germans, it also affected many of the 82nd. Worn out by the drudgery of guard duty, troopers were getting restive. It was time, I decided, for a pep talk about their duties and the fine line that needed to be trod on behalf of their country: "On the one hand, if we show the Germans we are weak and ill-disciplined, they will deride us, saying we aren't worthy to be imitated — fit to direct the world. On the other, if we act stupid and overbearing, they'll say we are mere Nazis in American uniforms, that the occupation by the Allies is just the changing of the guard — the same kind of guard. But if we can deliver a firm but fair military rule, that of a conquering nation which, though rightly punishing a criminal nation, does not oppress or terrorize it, we won't need to worry about their falling for another dictator. The example of how we rule, can cause a bloodless revolution in government. The way Americans conducted the Revolutionary War made governments change all over Europe. Fate seems to have put our country in the position of being Europe's teacher. Remember that if we do not accept that responsibility, they will get another teacher. And look at those they have selected thus far!"

The Russians, of course, had their own ideas about imposing their will on an occupied people. Call it vigilante justice. The U.S. Provost Marshal relayed a story of two Russian soldiers who had been apprehended by U.S. troopers for entering a German house, raping a woman, shooting her husband when he came to her defense before knocking out her father with the butt of a gun. Following protocol, the United States turned the soldiers over to the Russian officer, who upon hearing the story, apologized to the Americans and immediately had the men shot. Later, a young Russian interpreter, Lieutenant Igor Bevs, approached me at our mess to discuss penalties for soldier misconduct. In short, he saw no point in a stockade or jail. "What good does it do to have a soldier put in a stockade?" he asked. "If what he's done isn't too serious, have a sergeant beat him up. If it's an officer, take away his privileges for awhile. If the matter is very serious, simply shoot him."

One of my duties was to see if I could be of assistance to the local bishop, in this case Berlin Archbishop Konrad Graf von Preysing, a celebrated foe of Hitler and cousin of Bishop von Galen of Munster, who once said of the Nazi regime: "We have fallen into the hands of criminals and fools." Having not heard from the Archbishop for a long time, Monsignor Carroll, assistant to the Secretary of State of the Vatican, wrote, asking for information about his health and safety.

I located Archbishop von Preysing in a Catholic hospital in the Russian zone. A cultivated and holy man, worn down by years of Nazi pressure, he greeted me cordially. "Your Excellency," I asked, "why not come to the American sector where we could help you communicate with your priests and people so much better than here?" "I appreciate that," he replied, "but I cannot leave this hospital. I am trying to guard the nurses and Sisters from further attacks by Russian soldiers. Already, three Sisters and a few lay nurses are pregnant. I must stay." Continuing, his candor was impressive. Hitler, pinpointing him as a particular target, often summoned him for meetings. Invariably a protracted, stormy lecture ensued, often lasting forty-five minutes, on the stupidity of the Catholic Church and the Archbishop. The dictator even tried to convince him that his cousin, Bishop von Galen, had joined the Nazis, but von Preysing wasn't fooled.

"Was Hitler so insane that he was not responsible?" I asked.

"Oh, no. He was definitely responsible," Archbishop von Preysing replied.

Having been an ambassador before becoming a priest, the Archbishop had a keen perspective on history. He realized that while the collapse of Nazism gave Germany an epochal opportunity to rid itself of militarism, it also provided the Church the opportunity to lead the German people to a Christian attitude. I heartily agreed, prompting him, perhaps, to later ask if I would stay in Berlin as a priest of the Archdiocese of Berlin. "I've thought about it." "How is your German?" he asked. "Not good," I replied. "I studied in college for a year but the only phrases I know are things like: *'Ihre lage ist hofenlos'* — 'Your position is hopeless,' used to persuade German troops to surrender." The Archbishop laughed, pushing his request no further.

One group that I desperately tried to assist was the Jews. A number of Jewish families lived in our neighborhood, and one day I received word that a forlorn band of three hundred Polish Jews in dire need were arriving in Berlin, having walked all the way from Poland. "Why did you come here?" I asked, finding them near the railroad station totally exhausted. "There was no other place to go," they replied. "Warsaw is totally gone. We thought maybe the Russians would help us." Unfortunately, they bitterly learned that the Russians couldn't care less about them. That night, however, appealing to a driver known for his diversity of talents, we did some "midnight requisitioning," providing the group with badly needed food.

Furlough

By this time I had qualified for my one and only furlough of the war and decided to travel to Nice, France, for a few days on the Mediterranean. While there, I bumped into two pilots carrying messages to Rome, one of whom offered to let me tag along if I promised to get a rosary blessed by the Pope for his mother. I couldn't pass up the offer! As an Army chaplain I was eligible to join other priests and nuns for a small audience with Pope Pius XII. As I was kneeling next to a group of nuns from Sicily, the Pope came down the line, bestowing his blessings. "Oh, Holy Father," one nun said in Italian, "we are dying to die for you." "Good Lord," I thought, "what can I say to match that?" But the Pope saved me. Spying my paratroop outfit, he took one look at my boots and asked where I was from. I told him I was an American chaplain. "A paratroop chaplain?" the Pope replied. "That's a very, very dangerous job." I didn't have to say a thing. "Let me give you a special blessing," he then said, "and here's another special blessing for the rosaries, too." Mission accomplished!

At the Brandenburg Gate, this former proud landmark, now a monument of defeat, was the scene of a thriving black market. While the Germans sold every conceivable item, especially jewelry, craftily concealed from the Russians, the Americans bartered with cigarettes, coffee, chocolate, butter, margarine, and liquor. (Each American officer received a monthly quota of cigarettes and, according to its availability, liquor, usually two bottles of cognac.) Since I didn't smoke and had no use for two bottles of liquor, my monthly "booty" enabled me to secure food for the poor and religious groups, including the Archbishop. In trade, a nickel Hershey's chocolate bar commanded $5; a bottle of cognac and a pound of coffee beans at least $100; and depending on demand, a pack of cigarettes had a sliding value. (Thanks to one pack, I secured the cleanup of a Protestant church for our troopers.) At one point I was offered a new Opel car (some had been hidden) for five kilos of butter (around twelve pounds). But with no gas available, there were no takers. Writing to one of my brothers, I prevailed upon him to send more coffee, chocolate, and cigarettes, but he simply refused to believe me.

After taking care of my favorite charities, I personally bartered for ignored oil paintings that I saw in a shop, owned by the Gehrlovs which, easily removed from their frames, could be rolled up and sent to the United States in an artillery shell case. (Younger troops were largely interested in Nazi souvenirs — lugers and insignias.) Years later, my friendship with the Gehrlovs turned out to be useful to the U.S. government. When I was serving as chancellor of the archdiocese, in Washington, D.C., the federal government became concerned about reports that German families in Berlin were becoming sympathetic to the Communists. Consequently, I was asked to go to Berlin with a member of the State Department to survey attitudes of the typical German family. Our first visit was with the Gehrlovs, who cordially welcomed me. Following pleasantries, I casually asked Mrs. Gehrlov, "How often have you visited East Berlin?" She looked at me as though I had gone insane. "I'll never go there," she said vehemently. "Even the air is poisoned." All my German friends turned out to feel the same way, telling the State Department official everything he needed to know.

In 1945, the Russian Communists did everything in their power to win the hearts of the German people. One day, an elderly German woman, who had lost all of her belongings, came to ask what I could do for her as the Russians in her sector were giving people — even former Nazi sympathizers — a zentner (100 pounds) of coal. I said I'd try to help her, checking out her story with the Matulats. "Yes, that's right, the Russians are going to give large amounts of food and fuel to their people," they explained, "until they get firm control, then nothing. Tell her to stay with the Americans, who won't lie and will guard her freedom." Delivering the message, I also gave the old lady food, far more acceptable than my promises. (Such experiences only served to highlight my certainty of the horrendous mistake made by President Roosevelt in his famous February 1945 "Big Three" meeting at Yalta with British Prime Minister Winston Churchill and Soviet Premier Joseph Stalin, who left Yalta with the promise that he could seize Poland and other Eastern European countries.)

As summer faded, tensions between the American and Russian soldiers worsened, as our soldiers, walking in pairs during daylight, avoiding the Russian zone at night, maintained a strict discipline protecting our sector. The Russians did not. Though building an imposing war memorial to themselves in their sector, nothing was being done to restore the economy. Rumors, meanwhile, were rife that another infantry division would replace the 82nd Airborne, the Russians finding General Gavin and our troopers too intransigent. In November, rumor became fact when we were ordered to leave Berlin, a decision pleasing no one. By now, the division's "new" men had melded with the older; we were a solid unit.

Every trooper's last item of business was getting rid of his money. Trading having continued apace during our stay, every trooper had a wad of German marks as well as script money used in Berlin. Not surprisingly, frantic buying of almost anything ensued. Why not, I thought, take advantage and stage a real "drive for charity." Immediately, I informed everyone that I'd happily deliver whatever money of whatever variety they could donate to the Church in Berlin. Instantaneously, my office turned into an international bank as I filled huge duffle bags with money, passing them onto the Church for their various charities.

Aboard the *Queen Mary*

Within a few days we were shipped out to England, the English Channel lived up to its terrible reputation as our boat pitched every direction but down. Everyone got seasick; I escaped by heading to the center of the boat, remaining the whole trip. After staying in a transit camp for a couple of days, the entire division boarded the *Queen Mary*, jammed with thousands of other returning GIs. I shared a room with several doctors, eight people living in a room for two singles. There was little food but no complaints even when, hit by a storm of gargantuan proportions, the railings ripped off the deck.

During our trip, several chaplains gathered to share our hopes for the future. Dogmatically, I said that once out of the Army, I hoped never to have a desk job. God must have been smiling. Since then, I've had nothing but "desk jobs" in the Church. Nevertheless, I can honestly say that I have never in my ministry been closer to God than I was in Berlin, where we took care of

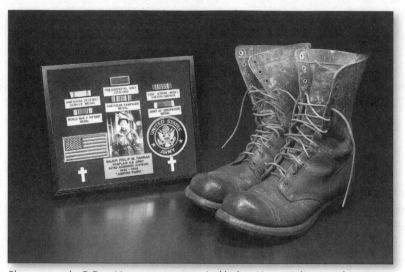

Showcase at the D-Day Museum containing Archbishop Hannan's boots and mementos of military campaigns of the 82nd Airborne Division

After WWII, I visited the New York home of the parents of twins Joe and George Melahn, members of the 82nd Airborne, one of the few outfits that allowed twins to serve in combat together. Joe was killed while trying to repair a communications line, and I, the chaplain, had to break the news to George that his brother had been killed. Mr. Joseph Melahn was a WWI vet. Mrs. Josephine Melahn thanked me for assuring her that her son had been spiritually cared for before he died.

My discharge document from the service

everyone, including refugees from Nazism, who needed help. Moreover, God had granted me the opportunity to anoint hundreds of the dead and dying on the battlefield.

Looking back on the war, then and now, I admire the wisdom of Pope Pius XII for urging the embattled Allies not to demand an unconditional surrender, having seen how such a threat had been used by the Nazis, and later the Japanese, to justify extreme measures, whipping their soldiers and civilians into massacres and last-ditch defenses, causing further death and destruction.

As the *Queen Mary* majestically pulled into the dock in New York, a noisy display of sound and water spray filled the harbor as boats, tugboats, and pleasure craft gave the *Queen Mary* a royal and boisterous reception. Slim Jim Gavin, who had preceded us in returning to the United States, came aboard for a formal greeting with New York Mayor Fiorello La Guardia. As I stood along the rail trying to locate my family members, the officer next to me leaned over. "Padre, you don't have to worry about me anymore. I see my fiancée out there. She'll take care of my religion." Suddenly, I was filled with a profound feeling of relief. We chaplains had done our best, and now civilian clergy and families would resume their duties. During my years in the military, my most important job was convincing soldiers not leading good Catholic lives that their behavior was a disservice to the men who had given theirs for their freedom. To honor those who sacrificed their lives, they needed to amend theirs.

As we docked, my first act was a quick prayer of thanksgiving for the gift of life. My second was to look around: "My Lord. Everybody in New York is fat!" The physical well-being of New Yorkers versus Berliners was startling indeed. Finally, I found my father and mother, who had come to New York for a joyous reunion with our Manhattan cousins, the Fitzpatricks. "You don't know how much we suffered during the war," one of the Fitzpatricks said in mock anger. "One time we even had to use substitute sugar!"

Shortly thereafter, I had to report to Camp Shanks, where the 82nd was quartered in preparation for January's victory parade. Having not been paid in

In 1962, I had a chance to drop in at Fort Bragg, North Carolina, to watch an impressive air drop by the 82nd Airborne, my old WWII outfit. I served in Belgium, France, and Germany in 1944 and 1945. In North Carolina I was able to celebrate Mass at the drop zone for more than 3,000 troopers and their families. More than 800 Catholic airborne soldiers at Fort Bragg were members of the St. Michael's Society for Catholic Paratroopers.

months in Berlin, one of my first chores was to collect my pay at the Finance Office where I was helped by a young, pretty, Irish-looking woman. When I asked for my full back pay, she hesitated. "I don't think that's a good idea," she said. "You should only get one month's pay."

"No, I want my full pay," I said. "I think I'm owed for about six months."

"You shouldn't take it all at one time," she countered. "Being just back from the war, you may go to a bar to celebrate and get rolled."

"I intend to put the money in the bank," I replied. "Please give me all my back pay." Reluctantly, she left to check my name and pay record. A few minutes later she returned, head-bowed and red-faced. "Your name is Hannan, and you're a chaplain," she exclaimed, "a priest! Oh, Lord, here's your pay."

I thanked her both for the money and sweet advice.

The parade for the 82nd down Fifth Avenue was bittersweet. Though the frenetic enthusiasm and blizzard of paper swirling around us was a big thrill, it was tempered when we marched past the special, reserved-seating section for wounded paratroopers, many in wheelchairs and recliners. Next to them, the reserved section for Gold Star mothers, unable to cheer their own sons, wept as they waved to us. By the time the parade finished, everyone's tears, including ours, were a matter of course.

That night there was another family gathering with the Fitzpatricks and McDonalds, our other New York cousins. Mom and Dad were in great spirits. My other brothers, Denny and Frank, both in the Army, had made it home, despite many campaigns, in perfect health. Denny, serving in the 3rd Division for thirty-four months, including one hundred eighty-five consecutive days in combat, had been through seven campaigns, including the fierce battle for Monte Cassino. Frank, a doctor who

An old soldier wearing my uniform in the rectory of St. Louis Cathedral, many years after the war

had been in the Army for the duration with an antitank unit in Patton's Army, received the Bronze Star for his action at Normandy. Despite endless dangerous campaigns, none of us had been wounded. The Hannan family had much reason to celebrate as well as give thanks to God. And we did.

A couple of days later, I took a train to Fort Bragg, North Carolina, permanent camp for the 82nd. All that was left now was leaving the Army, which involved a physical exam far more than routine from my perspective. The medical officer, informing me that I had a severe sinus condition which was "service induced" and entitled me to a claim for partial disability, produced a real conundrum. If I accepted the claim, I could never re-enter the Army, and I didn't want to give this option up because Europe was still unsettled due to the Communist threat. Baltimore-Washington Archbishop Michael Curley, feeling strongly there could be a war against Communism, suggested I stay in the Army active reserve. I didn't disagree. If a war broke out, I wanted to be part of our country's defense — and that of the free world — no matter how small my contribution. Furthermore, if it did, and I was still fairly young, I certainly wanted to, again, be a chaplain for the paratroopers.

(Ultimately, I left the Army with no claim for physical disability but with a profound respect and affection for the units in which I had served.)

Following our smash of a victory parade in New York, another soon followed in Washington, D.C. Though far less glamorous than its New York counterpart, marching down Pennsylvania Avenue filled me with a mass of competing emotions. As a high school cadet at St. John's College High School, I had marched in the inaugural parade of President Herbert Hoover. Now, eons later in terms of life experience, here I was again, marching in the parade marking the successful conclusion of a war (with the Nazis) which I believed to have been inevitable. As we strode proudly down Pennsylvania Avenue, I sensed that this victory parade, ushering in a new era in the life of our country, was monumental to me as well, indeed, a true defining moment in my life. What, I wondered, did God have in mind for me next?

Pope Pius XII

From my point of view, Pope Pius XII was greatly misunderstood, an unfair target of accusations of partiality toward the Axis powers as well as aiding Nazis and Fascists. Having served as Apostolic Delegate to Germany in the 1920s, he was intimately familiar with the German psyche in the aftermath of World War I, long before Hitler came on the scene. Though absolutely opposed to Hitler's reign of terror, his policy of avoiding provocative condemnations of the Nazis, at the behest of Jewish groups, actually waylaid further persecution. In Berlin, my limited experience in helping Jewish survivors confirmed the wisdom of his policy. Those I encountered were unanimous in owing their escape to the silence of those around them.

I believe that the magnitude of aid given to refugees from Nazism — from every national and ethnic group — was never recorded. For many Italian priests and laity, it was a near daily occurrence to give Nazi refugees asylum in their homes or Catholic institutions, especially in Italy. One priest in Washington's Apostolic Delegate's office told me that to save him from a concentration camp, he'd been "sent into a career of diplomacy in the Church." "The Nazis," he said wryly, "found out how many I was hiding."

CHAPTER 8

Back in Washington, D.C.

After returning to Washington, D.C., from Fort Bragg in 1945, I did not have a clear sense of what my first postwar assignment might be. I easily could have been assigned to a parish — Monsignor McGraw would have loved to have me back at St. Thomas Aquinas — but Archbishop Michael Curley and Father Joseph Nelligan, the chancellor of the Baltimore Archdiocese, felt it was best for me to take advantage of the new G.I. Bill that would defray the entire cost of my graduate-school tuition at Catholic University of America for my pursuit of a degree in canon law, beginning in September 1946.

Looking back from the perspective of today's strict and counterproductive limitations on church-state collaboration, it's hard to imagine the good will and common sense that marked church-state relations in the immediate post-WWII era. The federal government actually paid for me to attend graduate school to earn a degree in church law! Today we have an almost impossible time convincing legislators to support scholarships or vouchers that would give needy families a chance to provide a quality education for their children, who frequently are trapped in woeful public schools. The G.I. Bill changed the lives of thousands of veterans and their families in the 1940s and 1950s. A "Junior" G.I. Bill for children would do the same today.

My tuition was paid for, but first I had to maneuver through the bureaucracy that exists at most colleges. The professor in charge of the canon law program took a look at my background and gave me the shock of my life. "Because you've been away from your studies for three years, you'll have to start all over again as a freshman," he said. "You need to catch up with the events of the day."

Well, I thought that was weird. I immediately called the archdiocesan chancellor and told him I had absolutely no intention of becoming a freshman again, and he agreed with me. Catholic University quickly agreed to update its requirements for candidates returning from the Army.

I always had been interested in studying canon law, and I was excited that in three years I would have my doctorate. All the doctoral candidates — about one hundred were chaplains returning from the war — lived at Catholic

University and were under the strict control of Sulpician Father Louie Ahrens. He had his own ideas about what priests ought to do. We attended Morning Prayer together in the chapel, and then Father Louie made arrangements for us to celebrate Mass at the side altars in the crypt church of the Shrine, which was not yet completed. Father Louie was so strict he wouldn't let us fill in for a Mass at a parish when a priest got sick or needed a break. "Look, you were sent here to study," he'd say. That was that. No one could leave the campus.

A large group of guys from Philadelphia came to Catholic University to study canon law. Many of them already had earned advanced degrees, but their bishop sent them to Catholic U. anyway because they wouldn't be paying for the tuition! The G.I. Bill was amazing.

Because of our experiences in the war, we weren't afraid to speak up, but we didn't always win the admiration of our professors. On my first day of class, one of my professors introduced himself as Father Jerome Hannan from Pittsburgh. After class I sidled up to him to say hello and test his sense of humor: "I'm taking it for granted that it would be a terrible oddity if Professor Hannan flunked Father Hannan!" He didn't even crack a smile. I eventually passed the course, and the stern-faced Professor Hannan later went on to become the Bishop of Scranton, Pennsylvania. He and I renewed our acquaintance many years later at the Second Vatican Council. He died tragically of a heart attack in Rome in 1965 during the final session.

We had some wonderful professors. One priest, whose name I've forgotten, had a real love for the poor, and every time he got his check, he would buy groceries at the store and then distribute the food to the impoverished families in the neighborhood. He told us real-life stories you couldn't get from any textbook. One time a tearful wife, who wanted her marriage annulled, came to him because she couldn't get any of her relatives or friends to testify on her behalf before the Metropolitan Tribunal about her husband's aberrant behavior. My professor agreed to make a house call to speak to a man who might be willing to give testimony that favored her case. After talking awhile at the kitchen table, the man finally said to the priest, "Hey, you're an all right guy. I can trust you." And then he reached into his waistband, pulled out a pistol and laid it on the table. I guess that was a sure sign he'd earned the man's trust!

As a bow to the growing importance of Washington, D.C., as a world capital, Pope Pius XII had separated Washington and the five southern counties of Maryland from the Archdiocese of Baltimore in 1939 and created the joint Archdiocese of Baltimore-Washington. For about eight years until his death in May 1947, Archbishop Curley headed up both archdioceses. New York Auxiliary Bishop Patrick A. O'Boyle became archbishop of Washington on November 27, 1947.

Even during Archbishop Curley's tenure, the Baltimore chancery really didn't have anyone who knew Washington well enough to offer counsel in the buying of real estate for future expansion and in establishing sensible parish boundaries. In one case, the dividing line between two parishes in Washington directly bisected a large apartment house. It was comical: A person could sleep in his bedroom and be an official member of one parish in the morning, and then when he ate dinner on the other side of the apartment at night, he was a member of another parish.

The Baltimore chancellor, who didn't have the world's most agreeable disposition, certainly could think of things to keep me busy. During my three years of canon law study, by default I became the point person for evaluating and acquiring property in the Washington area. One day I was preparing to walk into class to take a final oral exam when I received a telephone call from Archbishop Curley, who asked me to eyeball a tract of land for the archdiocese. I told my professor: "I hope this exam doesn't last too long. The Archbishop wants me to go buy some more property." He couldn't get over it.

I became vice chancellor of the Archdiocese of Washington the day I got my doctorate in canon law in 1949. I prayed I would be able to use my abilities to help the mission of the Church.

Coming from New York, where he had run Catholic Charities and established one of the biggest orphanages in the United States that cared for one thousand kids, Archbishop O'Boyle had virtually no experience running a parish, much less an archdiocese. In fact, he didn't even know how to fill out the proper paperwork for a marriage dispensation. His lack of pastoral experience led to a prickly relationship with his chancellor, Monsignor James Cowhig. All three of us lived at St. Patrick's rectory, and at dinner each night there was such an awkward silence between them that I would always try to spark the conversation. Our first "chancery" was actually a big house, owned by the pastor of St. Matthew's Cathedral, which we turned into a quasi-office. The entire chancery was in one big room: Monsignor Cowhig and I each had a desk and a secretary, and Monsignor Robert Arthur, who was on the Tribunal, had a desk on the other side of the room, until he finally moved upstairs.

Archbishop O'Boyle decided to keep his office at St. Patrick's, so anybody who needed to see him would have to go to St. Patrick's rectory. It was a very poor way to run a brand new and incredibly important archdiocese.

In addition to my work at the chancery, I was helping out on weekends at St. Matthew's Cathedral, my home parish, by celebrating Mass. That lasted until the Archbishop decided in the summer of 1950 that Father Boehmer, the pastor of St. Mary Mother of God Parish at 5th and G Streets near the White House, needed some help, and I was assigned there as associate pastor.

I got along really well with Father Boehmer, but that assignment nearly wore me out. St. Mary Mother of God Parish specialized in all-day novenas, which meant on Mondays there were fifteen Masses and fifteen recitations of the novena prayers. I was in good physical shape, but when the pastor and another priest got sick on the same day during the summer, I had to do all fifteen services by myself. I blessed anything and everything that moved, and it was as hot as the devil!

Father Boehmer was a real character. We had vigil lights all over the church, and he had such a scrupulous conscience that if a vigil light went out before its wax had been exhausted, he threw the unused wax into a huge barrel in the basement of the church and lit a big wick so that every part of every candle was used up. "We owe it to the people to have these candles burn through completely," he told me.

I will never forget a classic disagreement Archbishop O'Boyle had with Father Boehmer. St. Mary Mother of God Church was situated in a prime real estate location, and the federal General Accounting Office was looking seriously at the area to construct its massive new office building. Father Boehmer, of course, had a personal interest in his church remaining untouched. The GAO put on the full-court press: it already had bought up most of the surrounding blocks for its new state-of-the-art structure, and it wanted to purchase St. Mary Church and School so that its huge building would be one contiguous unit.

When the GAO officials came to see Father Boehmer about selling the property, he played hard to get — very, very hard to get. Without consulting the chancery, Father Boehmer did some quick math, analyzed the weekly offertory collections, and gave the feds a purchase price that at that time could have choked a horse. In order for the GAO to expropriate his church and school, it would cost the U.S. government $27 million, a fantasy price that was a certain deal-breaker! Of course, Father Boehmer had never mentioned a word to Archbishop O'Boyle about his Donald Trump-style wheeling and dealing. The Archbishop had been very interested in negotiating with the GAO because he hoped to use the potential proceeds of a large sale to launch a Catholic foundation to fund the archdiocese's long-term needs.

Needless to say, when the Archbishop found out what had happened and why the government had ended negotiations, he called Father Boehmer into his office. The Archbishop ordered me to sit in on their conversation, and that's when I knew it was going to be bad. The Archbishop grabbed a piece of paper from the top of his desk — it was Father Boehmer's letter to him explaining his misguided $27 million foray into real estate — crumpled it up before the pastor's eyes and dropped it on his desk.

If you look at an overhead picture today of the GAO building at 441 G Street NW, you will see an enormous, six-story edifice, capable of hosting more than 3,000 employees, snaking around the Church of St. Mary Mother of God, still standing defiantly on the northwest quadrant. At least Father Boehmer kept his dream alive! The church is going strong.

Finally, Archbishop O'Boyle became convinced that my novena schedule and parish duties at St. Mary along with my chancery duties were conflicting too often. I came back to live at St. Patrick and devote my full attention to the chancery. By this time, the relationship between Archbishop O'Boyle and Monsignor Cowhig, the chancellor, was extremely tense. Word had gotten back to the Archbishop that Monsignor Cowhig had been criticizing him to fellow priests. Eventually the Archbishop appointed him pastor of St. Jerome Parish in Hyattsville, Maryland, and in 1951 he appointed me chancellor and pastor of St. Patrick's.

By that time I was heavily involved in acquiring real estate for the archdiocese. I attribute Archbishop O'Boyle's reluctance to get involved in buying property to his background as head of Catholic Charities under New York Cardinal Patrick Hayes. The Cardinal never had a high regard for acquiring property because he had the peculiar idea that the church should not be in the real estate business. "We're in the business of forming souls," Cardinal Hayes told Archbishop O'Boyle. At some point I finally laid it out directly to Archbishop O'Boyle: "I know that Cardinal Hayes is dead wrong. The only time he could be right is when we could support a rectory, a school, and a convent by skyhooks. When we can do that, then I won't have any interest in acquiring property." Washington was fast becoming the world's capital, and we should have been buying property twenty years earlier.

I knew New Hampshire Avenue was quickly developing, and we needed property in that area for a future parish. I approached a Jewish developer who owned a large parcel and told him we were interested in buying seven or eight acres for a church and school. He turned me down. Two months later, he died of a heart attack. I went to the next developer and repeated my offer. "I think I should tell you I tried to buy property from your neighbor and he turned me down, and in two months he was dead," I said. We made a deal immediately. That property became St. Camillus Parish in Silver Spring, Maryland.

I always made this pitch to developers: Putting a church and eventually a school on a piece of property leads directly to increased property values for the entire area. I've always had the dream of buying one hundred acres and putting ten acres aside for a church and school. That's enough space for parish operations. The other ninety acres automatically increase in value, enough to pay for the construction of one of the two major buildings needed for the parish — the rectory and the church.

Archdiocesan Newspaper

Archbishop O'Boyle subscribed to the theory of giving a busy person something else to do in order to get something done. In 1951, just a month before I became chancellor, he put me in charge of starting the *Catholic Standard*, the new archdiocesan newspaper. The archdiocese did have an existing paper, but it was not well done, for a number of reasons. When Archbishop O'Boyle first took over in 1947, he asked the *Catholic Review* in Baltimore to put out a separate Washington edition, but they bungled the project. The Archbishop knew it was a flop. Then he asked *Our Sunday Visitor* in Indiana — a national Catholic newspaper — to publish an edition that had a set number of national and international pages and a few pages for local news from Washington. But the early deadlines and transportation problems created a nightmare for getting timely news published. Stories and photographs on local events had to be airmailed to Indiana, galleys had to be produced, and then the newspaper had to be printed and shipped back to Washington. By that time the Second Coming could have taken place and our readers would not have known about it. It just wasn't very well done.

The Archbishop wanted a quality, locally produced newspaper, but he also told me he didn't have a dime for start-up costs. We would have to figure out not only how to start the paper but also how to keep it financially sustainable. I began at square one, hiring a very sharp business manager, Father Schellenberg. Our first editor, Clancy Zens, was a top-notch journalist who, unfortunately, did not get along well with the business manager in later years.

First things first. Father Schellenberg and I sat down and tried to project how many subscriptions we could sell. We figured that with a good circulation program, using the school kids to help sell the paper, we might be able to sell twenty thousand, and on that basis Father Schellenberg figured out how much money we could borrow to begin the paper. We signed a $125,000 printing contract with a printer on Thomas Circle, and we didn't have a dime.

Our initial subscription drive exceeded our expectations. We had sweetened the rewards for the students who were selling subscriptions for the paper. The top prize was a complete, four-year, tuition-free scholarship to Georgetown University, and the kids knocked themselves out for a chance at that. Father Schellenberg was a good man, but he didn't like to take risks, and I didn't blame him. But I knew nothing would happen unless we did gamble every now and then. Zens was a great editor, and I was kept extremely busy writing all the editorials and supervising the whole operation.

On the cover of the first issue in November 1951, we had a photo by Johnny DiJoseph of Archbishop O'Boyle addressing tens of thousands of people at the Washington Monument during the Family Rosary Crusade. We began to take off. We sold so many subscriptions we turned an $80,000 profit in the first year, which was astounding when you consider other Catholic newspapers around the country were operating in the red year after year. I made the mistake of telling Archbishop O'Boyle about our rosy financial health, and he decided to put his public relations man, who didn't do a thing for us, on the newspaper payroll. After that, I kept my mouth shut about our finances.

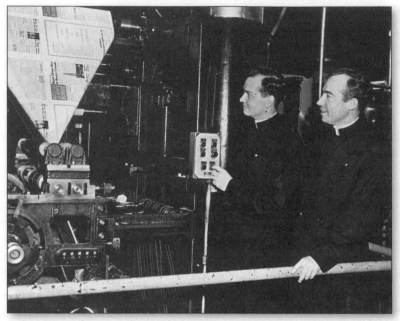

At the opening of the *Catholic Standard* newspaper in Washington, D.C., with Monsignor Schellenberg, the business manager

The paper turned into a great advertising vehicle for local businesses, especially for banks. Our pitch was simple and direct: The *Catholic Standard* is the newspaper in which every business should advertise because it is a family newspaper and stays in the home for an entire week. It isn't thrown out every night with the fish. That proved to be our best selling point. Advertising revenue was so good that when a relative of a woman I knew died, we were able to pay $20,000 for her house at 1711 N Street — a fantastic price — which became our first real offices. When we got into our new house, which was only one block from the chancery, we were overjoyed.

Even before the launch of the *Catholic Standard*, I was doing some writing for the previous Washington paper. In 1950, a jubilee year was proclaimed by Pope Pius XII. The Washington Archdiocese led a pilgrimage for two hundred twenty-five pilgrims to Bavaria, Holland, Lourdes, and Rome. In Konnersreuth, Bavaria, a small group of women and I got a special interview with Thérèse Neumann, a stigmatist who as a teenager in 1918 had been paralyzed in a fire at a neighbor's house. A month after Thérèse of Lisieux was beatified in 1923, Thérèse Neumann regained her sight, and then a few days later, she was able to get up and walk. After receiving the stigmata during Lent in 1926, she was said to have subsisted daily on only water or tea and Holy Communion. Her pastor was totally convinced that her stigmata were genuine and that she lived on nothing but the Host. At the end of our meeting, one of the women in our group held out a rosary for her to bless, and she said, "No, I'm not a priest. I cannot bless it."

I wrote chatty dispatches about almost every place we visited — in the style of a spiritual travelogue. Holland really intrigued me. I wrote about the windmills and the intriguing distinctions between Catholics and Protestants. If the owner of the windmill was Catholic, the windmill would stop after the day's work in the orientation of the cross; if the owner was Protestant, he would do everything he could to prevent it from looking like a cross. People seemed to enjoy the articles as much as I enjoyed writing them.

The 1950 jubilee pilgrimage in honor of the Blessed Sacrament was especially poignant because all of Europe was still in the throes of reconstruction after World War II. Any tourist business was greatly appreciated. As much as we warned our pilgrims to be careful, one of our women slipped in the bath made by the waters of the spring begun by the prayers of Bernadette, and she broke her hip. We also had to keep a special eye on the pickpockets. We told our people we would form a tight phalanx and walk together as a group, not allowing any outsiders to wander in where they might be able to grab a wallet or purse. Still, we had four passports stolen during the trip. Germany was in such terrible shape that people were willing to put their whole life's savings into buying an American passport. It was their only way out. I heard of a Catholic tourist being offered more than $100,000 for a passport.

Talented pickpockets made taking the crowded public buses particularly hazardous. One bishop had all of his money in his back pocket, and after he got off the bus, he felt a trickle running down the back of his leg. It was his own blood. A thief with either a very sharp knife or a razor had cut out his pants pocket to remove his wallet and sliced a little bit of flesh as well. I always carried my money and important papers next to my chest in an inside pocket, because that's the hardest place for a thief to get to. I also told people to watch out for children, because they often were used as a distraction while the thief plied his trade.

St. Patrick's Masses

In one of my other jobs — as pastor of St. Patrick — I was busy attending to the spiritual needs of parishioners and the thousands of government workers who daily passed through our doors. I likened St. Patrick's to a downtown monastery. Two of the city's biggest and busiest department stores were right across the street from us, and on Holy Days we had as many as twenty-two Masses and accommodated about one hundred thirty thousand worshipers. We even used the high school auditorium for Masses. We scheduled a Mass at every hour in the church and in the school auditorium to accommodate the congregation. Once we had so many people packed into the aisles of the church and spilling out into the vestibule that a rookie police officer came by and threatened to close the church.

"This is all illegal, Father," the young officer told me. "You're not allowed to have people standing in a pack like that. This has got to be stopped."

"Wait a minute," I replied. "You're the law officer. You go up there and tell the people that they must leave because it's against the law."

The officer walked up to one man standing in the vestibule and told him to leave. The man told the cop, "Go to hell!" I'm not saying that was a Christian response in the middle of Mass, but at least it was honest.

St. Patrick's wasn't just popular with shoppers and federal workers. It became the unofficial faith community for many prominent Catholic senators and congressmen from both sides of the aisle. The lead member was House Speaker John McCormack, an ardent Catholic Democrat from Boston. Archbishop O'Boyle was a real Irishman, and he frequently invited McCormack and his wife Harriet to dinner at the rectory. Every Sunday after Mass McCormack would position himself in front of church to shake hands with people as they left, almost as if he were the pastor himself. People who needed a minute or two with the Speaker knew he would be there, his shiny congressional limousine with the special insignia on the side was parked right in front. No one hesitated in the least to approach McCormack to describe a problem or plead for his support. Believe me. Those people were not talking about the weather or the homily.

Every Sunday outside St. Patrick's was almost like a Catholic congressional caucus. That's how I got to meet a future candidate for Speaker of the House, Hale Boggs, from Louisiana. His wife Lindy, who later became one of my dearest friends, a great congressional leader in her own right, and a future Vatican ambassador, did not attend Mass at St. Patrick's because the informal Catholic caucus, at that time, was an all-male affair. Those were the rules, and in Washington politics at that time, everyone followed the rules.

I always believed in shaking hands with people after Mass. I didn't place many obligations on my associate pastors, but one rule I always insisted on was for them to stand outside of church after every Mass. You pick up things from people that otherwise you never would have known about, and it means a lot to people that you are present and really listening to them. And I know McCormack liked the adulation he received. For him it was simply good business. McCormack used his Sunday morning time to great advantage because he scheduled absolutely no evening appointments. He spent every night of his married life with his wife Harriet at their private apartment at the Washington Hotel. She was regarded as a singer and concert pianist, and the Speaker absolutely fawned over her. In fact, when they came to dinner at the rectory, he occasionally would reach over and cut the meat in her plate!

I had some embarrassing experiences outside of church. A woman who was very pregnant came out of church one day, and I took one look at her face and could tell she was extremely sick. Before I could even say, "Look, I think it's time for you to get some medical attention," she threw up all over my cassock. My associate priests got a kick out of that and never let me forget about it.

Because we were right downtown, we had a number of drug addicts who came into church every now and then to rest, and sometimes they were so mired in withdrawal pains they screamed during Mass and created a disturbance. One year on the Feast of the Immaculate Conception, we had to call the ambulance eight times to take away drug addicts for help. At one Mass a goody-goody woman berated me for having a rail-thin, shaking addict

THE WHITE HOUSE
WASHINGTON

October 29, 1958.

Dear Bishop Hannan:

I just read your "Freedom in the East" editorial in the October twenty-fourth issue of The Catholic Standard.

It is encouraging to me to know of your endorsement of a policy the Administration believes to be right. It is heartening too to know that the views of your readers reflect an understanding of that policy and an agreement with the way we are implementing it. I particularly like your editorial comment that those who defend the rights of men should first understand the difference between right and wrong.

My thanks to you and your associates for this clear and articulate support. I particularly appreciate remembrance in your prayers.

With best wishes,

Sincerely,

Dwight Eisenhower

The Most Reverend Philip M. Hannan,
619 10th Street, N.W.,
Washington, D. C.

Thank you note from President Dwight Eisenhower for my editorial in *The Catholic Standard*

removed from the church. "You don't have any right to take away this man's freedom," she shouted at me. It takes a priest to handle that kind of situation.

We heard thousands of confessions at St. Patrick's, especially during Lent and Advent and on all Holy Days. We constantly got a number of French-speaking people in the confessional, and, of course, I had difficulty fully understanding what they were saying. One time a man who I knew spoke very good English came in and started confessing in French, and I asked him, "Why don't you confess your sins in English?" He replied: "Because when I do it in French it doesn't sound so bad!"

Because of the number of the faithful attending regular services, I tried to bring in inspiring priests to preach during special parish missions. Invariably that involved preaching a triduum — three consecutive Mondays. Somehow I was able to get New York Auxiliary Bishop Fulton Sheen to do the honors one year, and he packed St. Patrick's to the rafters. On the first Monday night, he gave an excellent sermon, as might be expected, but at dinner afterwards he told me, "I had just one minor difficulty. The microphone was not loud enough." I assured him I would take care of that problem by the following Monday, but the week passed and his request totally slipped my mind. As we were setting up for that night's talk, I asked my assistant in a panic, "Do we have another mike?" He said the only microphone we had was a big one that had a chord but didn't work. I told him to place the second microphone next to the first.

Bishop Sheen gave a wonderful talk, and at dinner afterwards I congratulated him and asked him how the microphone was. "It was much, much better," he said.

Believe me, Bishop Sheen was one priest who never needed a microphone for a relatively small audience.

CHAPTER 9

Episcopacy

In the spring of 1956, Archbishop O'Boyle told me that the Apostolic Delegate wished to see me. Not infrequently the Delegate, Archbishop Amleto Giovanni Cicognani, had asked me to perform small tasks, and so I thought this was just another such matter. To my complete surprise he informed me that my name had been submitted as a candidate for the episcopacy, to serve as an auxiliary bishop of the Archdiocese of Washington.

I didn't know what to say but I thought I should give such a serious matter some thought. The Delegate quietly told me there was no reason to hesitate so, to gain some time, I replied, "I have many relatives, and although they are all good Catholics, perhaps one of them may get into trouble, which might be a reflection on the dignity of a bishop."

He had a very ready answer. "That's no reason at all," he said. "Pope Leo XIII had a brother who was always borrowing money, and the Pope put a notice in the newspaper stating that no one should give him any money." I still wanted some time to consider the matter, so I lamely thanked the delegate for the honor he had helped bestow on me but also said I would talk with the Archbishop about it.

During the short ride from the Apostolic Delegate's office to St. Patrick's rectory I couldn't think of any substantial reason for delaying a response. I told the Archbishop I was stunned by the message of the Delegate, and although I would have liked to have some time to think about it, I couldn't find a reason for delaying a response. So I accepted the appointment with very deep gratitude. Archbishop O'Boyle hugged me, the only time he showed such affection.

Of course, my family was surprised and delighted by the news.

The Delegate wished to perform the episcopal ordination, to which the Archbishop graciously agreed. The Delegate asked me to give him my picture for inclusion in his album of bishops he had ordained — I was number 50. He also wished to deliver the homily at the ordination and told me, "I would like to speak about Abercius, the first bishop to leave a description of his visit to the Pope." What could I say... but yes?

I immediately made plans to have a retreat at the Jesuit retreat house, the Shrine of Our Lady of Martyrs, in Auriesville, New York. It was a splendid preparation for receiving the awesome office of a bishop. The "Decree on the Bishops' Pastoral Office in the Church" describes that office: "For their part, the bishops too have been appointed by the Holy Spirit and are successors of the Apostles as the pastor of souls. Together with the Supreme Pontiff and under his authority they have been sent to continue throughout the ages the work of Christ.... They should be especially concerned about those parts of the world where the Word of God has not been proclaimed.... Finally, in proportion to their means, bishops should give attention to relieving the disasters which afflict other dioceses and regions." What a prospect!

I prayed as fervently as I could, including petitions to the Jesuit Martyrs enshrined there. I always had a great devotion to these courageous and holy French priests who sought martyrdom from Indians. A person can never say he is completely prepared to be a bishop, but he can say he is sufficiently prepared to respond to an appointment to be bishop. I was ready to respond to the appointment.

Episcopal Motto

I chose as my episcopal motto "*Caritas Vinculum Perfectionis*" — "Charity Is the Bond of Perfection" (see Colossians 3:14). That statement of St. Paul

had always resonated with me, and I thought it was appropriate. As a matter of fact, the only person I checked it with was my sister Mary, who told me, "Yes, Phil, that sounds good." If Mary liked it, the issue was settled.

The date for the ordination was the feast of St. Augustine, August 28, 1956. That day was extremely hot and humid. One of our only concerns was that my brother Denis's wife Margaret was eight and a half months pregnant, and there was a question about whether or not she should go to the church because it wasn't air-conditioned. We had at least one ambulance parked right outside the cathedral, just in case. Margaret made it through without any difficulties. The only flaw in the ceremony was when Auxiliary Bishop

My original crest. "Caritas Vinculum Perfectionis" (Charity is the bond of perfection). The quote is taken from Colossians 3:14. The statement always resonated with me, and I checked with only one person – my sister Mary – when I decided on making it my episcopal motto in 1956.

John McNamara of Washington, the third co-consecrator, slipped and almost fell down the altar steps.

The sermon on Abercius mystified everyone. My mother expressed the general reaction, "Philip, what in the world was he talking about?"

Of course, upon receiving a bishop's miter I was promptly assigned a list of Confirmations. At that time it was customary to ask questions of those to be confirmed about our faith, always including a question on the definition of Confirmation. After the Second Vatican Council, to my regret, we no longer asked the candidates to define anything, following the general attitude of the people.

Not long after my episcopal ordination I was given a real test. The Archbishop had arranged to have all the adult converts confirmed in St. Matthew's Cathedral on the Feast of Pentecost. The idea was to make the converts feel they were a part of the family of the

My coat of arms for New Orleans

Church. The Archbishop and I did the Confirmations. One year the Archbishop got the flu on the feast of Pentecost, and I had to confirm more than four hundred converts. The first man I confirmed was sickly, so I confirmed him in his pew. At the end of the ceremony I returned to his pew — this time to anoint him. He had suffered a heart attack!

I appreciated the opportunity offered by the Confirmation liturgies to challenge the youth, especially those who were in high school or near it. "You'll hear it said that you've got to become a member of the common group," I would tell them. "That means that you must let the prevailing group do your thinking. God did not create you to be a shadow of somebody else. God made you to be His man or His woman. You'll be satisfied with yourself if you make yourself what God intended."

I often quoted the phrase that Pope John Paul II used later in his ministry to young people: "You are unrepeatable. You are unique. There is nobody else in the world exactly like you. Your distinctive fingerprints are given to you before you were born as well as your own DNA. Develop yourself as God intends."

In the 1950s many Catholic families believed in having more than one or two children. I remember that the first parish Confirmation I had numbered more than two hundred. Confirming was a very inspiring, if also a tiring, experience. After the Confirmation there was always the picture taking. Today I am frequently presented with a Confirmation picture, and the person will remark: "Look at me. I sure have changed." To which I generally reply, "Yes, you look much better now. I must have done a good job on you!"

Confirmations gave me the chance to visit every area of the archdiocese. I conferred Confirmation in a Maryland parish with a number of Native Americans and came away very impressed with their social life. There was a definite and proud feeling of separateness, even in the language they used to describe themselves. They were the "We Sorts" — a distinction used by the Indians to distinguish between themselves and the English-descent people ("You Sorts"). Their "chief" — sometimes called the emperor — was esteemed and served as a kind of revered social worker, settling differences among them. Like the rest, he was a tobacco farmer. The Indians had become Catholics in colonial times, through the influence of the early Maryland "pilgrims." The local Indians — the Potomacs — had been protected by the pilgrims from the predatory Indians living farther north who raided them using the Chesapeake Bay and the Potomac River to attack them.

The Sacrament of Confirmation was an excellent occasion for meeting the young folks. It gave me an opportunity to really challenge them in a very friendly atmosphere. I always felt I should take advantage of it, and I told

Archbishop Patrick A. O'Boyle, Apostolic Delegate Amleto Cicognani, Washington Auxiliary Bishop John McNamara, and me at my episcopal ordination at St. Matthew's Cathedral in 1956

families to take as many pictures as they wanted. I shook as many hands as I could reach.

Confirmation was only one of the many sacramental faculties I received through my episcopal ordination. The power to confer the priesthood was, in my opinion, the most awesome of those special faculties. The words of St. Paul to the Ephesians, which apply to all Christians, are particularly applicable to the episcopacy: "According to the riches of his glory he may grant you to be strengthened with might through his Spirit in the inner man.... Now to him who by the power at work within us is able to do far more abundantly than all that we ask or think, to him be glory in the church and in Christ Jesus to all generations, for ever and ever" (Eph 3:16, 20).

That power was not only in the realm of the Spirit. The status of a bishop conferred a prestige even in civil life and in society in general. An old bishop told me shortly after my episcopal ordination that there was another side of the coin. "Being a bishop means every Catholic has a right to push you around," he said. Frankly, that has not been my experience.

An outstanding lawyer, a Presbyterian, gave me another bit of good advice when we were in a discussion about the position of the Church in society. "You're too young to know the influence and the power of the Catholic Church." I was forty-three at the time. I thought a great deal about his remark — as an inverted compliment to the Church and as good advice for me.

Of course, all religious denominations and our whole society participate in activities for the common good. I thought it might be possible to have a very public celebration of Christmas, not far from the official White House Christmas tree. I worked with a devoted and wealthy Protestant businessman to promote a live Nativity scene with Christmas caroling by local church choirs of all denominations. The live Nativity included two reindeer on loan from the zoo — no, it wasn't historically accurate, but the kids loved the reindeer — and rotating choirs came in to sing carols. Of course, they brought their parents with them, who loved to snap pictures. The government provided some stands for spectators and for the performing choirs. Some enterprising tourist companies began to include the crib performances as part of their visit to Washington. The usual complaints were lodged about church-state relations, always from unnamed sources. Then the Christmas celebration became a "Peace" celebration, and a few years later it simply died off. The Christmas crib became an unrecorded piece of history.

Archbishop O'Boyle believed in public demonstrations of the faith. The most successful rally was the Lourdes Centennial Rally in 1958. Bishop Fulton Sheen was the speaker, and Monsignor John Roeder, the vice chancellor, was in charge of the arrangements. Monsignor Roeder really promoted the appearance of the now-famous Bishop Sheen, with the result that about 125,000 people attended the rally held on the Washington Mall. The Archbishop graciously invited the Apostolic Delegate, Archbishop Cicognani, to celebrate the Mass.

My assignment was to escort Bishop Sheen through the crowd to the altar, no easy task. He refused to have a police escort through the crowd, which left me as the blocking fullback to clear a path through 125,000 of his fans. Everybody wished to touch him, get a blessing, congratulate him, or give him a message. After about fifteen minutes of pushing and squeezing, we arrived at the altar. The address by Bishop Sheen on the Blessed Mother was superb. He had an intense devotion to Mary, and he was at the height of his extraordinary ability. He enraptured the crowd.

When the rally was over, my task was even more difficult. People were passionate to receive his personal blessing, touch his cassock, take his picture, get his autograph, or give him a personal message. I must have been doing a creditable job of elbowing a path for him because at one point he said, "Don't be too hasty."

THE WHITE HOUSE
WASHINGTON

July 19, 1956

Dear Bishop-elect Hannan:

At the time I was in the hospital, I read in the newspaper of your appointment as Auxiliary Bishop of Washington.   It was difficult for me to write you then, much as I wanted to, but even at this late date I want you to know how delighted I am that you have received this honor.   It is, I know, richly deserved.

With my congratulations and warm regard,

Sincerely,

Dwight Eisenhauer

The Most Reverend
    Philip M. Hannan
Auxiliary Bishop-elect of Washington
1719 Rhode Island Avenue, N. W.
Washington, D. C.

Congratulatory message from President Dwight Eisenhauer

Auxiliary Bishop Hannan and Secretary of State John Foster Dulles and his wife Janet in front of St. Matthew's Cathedral in Washington, D.C.

Joining me for my 1956 ordination to the episcopate are my parents, Patrick and Lilian Hannan, and my sister, Mary, and brother-in-law Robert Mahoney

I didn't realize sufficiently that he, as any normal person, relished this popularity. Well, we finally arrived at his car, which was guarded by the police.

As I approached Archbishop O'Boyle, he had a bemused expression on his face. He had watched the pandemonium surrounding Bishop Sheen, but no one had approached him. Pointing to a ten-year-old child nearby, he said with a smile, "See that little girl? She's the only one who asked for my autograph. She saved my reputation. God bless her."

The John Carroll Society

Even before I became a bishop I had noticed that Catholics in the White House, in Congress, in the judiciary, and in the higher echelons of the federal bureaucracy had felt somewhat isolated in Washington, D.C. Most of them were newcomers to Washington. Although "home" to them was where they were elected or had been born, they wished to make a second home in Washington, and knowing other Catholics was a part of that second home.

There was a definite need for Catholics in official Washington to know their Catholic peers. Likewise there was a need for the Church in Washington, which had become a separate archdiocese in 1947, to know its members in official Washington on a more personal level. Native D.C. Catholics also were eager to know the Catholics in official Washington. I remember hearing the wife of a Cabinet member remark at a Catholic gathering, "Isn't it nice to meet a group of Catholics here in Washington?" I thought if such a charming couple needed Catholic friends, other Catholic office holders needed them even more.

I spoke to several persons of different rank and position in official Washington about this need. They included U.S. District Judge Matthew F. McGuire, Navy Secretary John L. Sullivan, and William E. Leahy, a famous trial lawyer. In 1950 I asked them to attend a meeting at the chancery at 1719 Rhode Island Avenue, which long ago had been the home of Senator Underwood of Alabama, who at one time was a presidential candidate.

They were desperately eager to establish a society for prominent Catholics in official and unofficial Washington. We easily agreed that the sole purpose of the society was spiritual and fraternal — to know each other as members of the Church. We decided we should resist stoutly any effort to make it a lobbying or "fund-raising" organization. We wanted the members to become stronger in their faith and become more active in their professions, which would benefit the Church and the country.

Of course, I was asked to broach this matter with Archbishop O'Boyle, who was also a newcomer to Washington, although he had dealt extensively with official Washington in his position as head of the National Catholic Relief Services.

The chief elements of the society were easily agreed on: members were to be Catholic men. My question about whether we should invite women was soundly and decisively trounced. We were to have four meetings a year, consisting of attendance at Mass at St. Matthew's Cathedral and a Communion breakfast afterward at the Mayflower Hotel. We were to invite distinguished speakers — alternating between lay and clergy — to address the breakfast meeting. I feared the process of writing the constitution and bylaws because all three members of the group were lawyers, and this could have been another classic example of the saying, "God so loved the world that he did not send a committee."

The group quickly decided to leave the writing of the constitution and bylaws to Judge McGuire. We also decided that annual dues were to be $50, which would pay for the breakfasts (which originally cost only $2.50 each) and the fee for the speaker. I was to suggest the name of the speaker and invite him. There was a solid opinion against inviting any member of Congress to speak. The society was to be named in honor of Archbishop John Carroll, the first Catholic bishop in the United States. We finally decided also to host an annual banquet to which wives would be admitted, a compromise that pleased everyone.

I reported to Archbishop O'Boyle about the meeting. "What's the program for the society?" he asked. "*Esprit de corps* among the Catholics," I said, feeling that French phrase gave it added dignity. The Archbishop agreed on the name of the society but said he would like to see the group. So a meeting was held, and the Archbishop, who normally debated awhile before making a decision, gladly gave his permission within a few days.

Lists of the invitees were developed by the group, which met again and agreed upon Judge McGuire as the first president of the society. Attorney William B. Jones was made the secretary, mainly because he was a very exacting man and could be trusted to keep all lists complete.

Judge McGuire and Jones, his assistant, sweated over the list of invitees. McGuire was determined to cull all the outstanding laymen of the archdiocese and to make a special effort to secure a number of the outstanding black Catholics. Of course, I assisted him in this matter because of my friendship with so many of them.

We finally arrived at a very impressive list, including a large number of Catholic senators and members of the House of Representatives. The question was whether or not they would accept the invitations. The initial reaction came from the elderly Catholics who immediately compared the John Carroll Society to a defunct society called the Calvert Society, which, according to them, had lasted a few months and had died a very quiet and unheralded death. The common remark was, "We give the John Carroll Society six months of existence, and no more."

Nevertheless, there was a very surprising reaction to the invitations, and we felt at least two hundred would come to the Mass to be celebrated at St. Matthew's Cathedral and then attend the breakfast at the Mayflower Hotel. The speaker at the first breakfast was to be a convert, the editor of the *Reader's Digest*, Fulton Oursler, who wrote "The Greatest Story Ever Told."

By any standard, our first meeting was memorable. On the Friday before the Sunday Mass and breakfast, Oursler caught the flu and called to say he didn't know if he could fulfill the engagement. Judge McGuire called me, utterly demoralized. We agreed not to try to get a replacement but to pray that Oursler could appear. This did not quite satisfy the judge, who thought he should prepare an address in case the worst scenario occurred.

All the invitees showed up for the Mass and presented a very striking appearance along the pews of the main aisle of the Cathedral. After the Mass, I almost ran to the Mayflower to see if Oursler had arrived. I found him, standing next to Judge McGuire, who had spent the whole previous night writing a speech. Actually, Oursler looked much better than the judge!

Oursler did not eat or drink a drop of water during the meal. He sat tentatively at the table, and I had mapped out the fastest route to "you-know-where." Despite his illness, he gave a splendid address with the right mixture of humor and substance. The inaugural meeting was such a success that I decided to send a telegram to Archbishop O'Boyle, who was out of town, telling him how well everything had gone.

The society grew enormously, thanks to the efforts of the officers. There were no racial, ethnic, or political barriers and no "quotas" of any kind, and there was no "process" at the breakfast to introduce each other. As expected, there were some efforts from various crusaders to make the society an engine for carrying out their cherished agendas, but we held firm.

The speakers were my main concern. The primary rule that no member of Congress should be invited to speak at a breakfast was confronted when Senator John F. Kennedy became a candidate for the presidency. Clearly, it was time to consider a dispensation from the rule. All the officers — Matt McGuire, John L. Sullivan, and Bill Leahy — decided, surprisingly, to dispense from the rule. JFK gave an excellent speech, even in the opinion of the Republicans.

Perhaps the most interesting speech was given by William F. Buckley. He excoriated the Truman administration, especially Truman, with his full panoply of wit and sarcasm. At the same time, President Truman was in a meeting room next to our breakfast room in the Mayflower, receiving an honor. When it was over, I asked Judge McGuire what he thought of it. McGuire, an unvarnished Democrat, replied, "He mesmerized me. I have never heard such language."

Perhaps the most popular speaker, the only one who was an encore by demand, was Pittsburgh Bishop John Wright, an alumnus of the Boston Latin

School. He knew not only the Boston Irish jokes but also all the Slovak, Hungarian, and Polish jokes from Pittsburgh. He so convulsed the audience with his jokes at the beginning that McGuire whispered to me, "How is he ever going to get this crowd to stop laughing?" The subject of one of his talks was "fear." He spoke about using fear to guide us, even in our purchases of services. He quoted the slogan of the Baltimore and Ohio Railroad that one could sleep like a kitten on its trains, safe and comfortable. A search for security is at the heart of all human endeavors. I have often wondered what kind of a talk Bishop Wright could give today on fear in Washington, D.C.

The most disappointing speaker was Ambassador Jefferson Caffery, the dean of the U.S. diplomatic corps. He was a very scholarly man and was credited with convincing King Farouk of Egypt to resign — really, to abdicate — to defuse a very explosive situation in Egypt. I thought it was a good idea to invite him because Caffery had great prestige, was a convert, and had been in the center of a very troublesome spot in the world. Of course, I asked him to speak on the political situation in the Middle East, which, as ever, was in great turmoil.

Meanwhile, Ambassador Caffery had gotten into archeology in Egypt and had become acquainted with a team of diggers who had discovered a "moon ship" in one of the pyramids. He mentioned to me he would like to speak about it, and I politely told him I thought our members would be more interested in his achievements in the diplomatic field, especially in Egypt. I should have been put on guard by Caffery's offhand remark, but I was too well disposed toward him. He had come to see me after the conclusion of the Second Vatican Council to congratulate me on my paper defending the use of nuclear weapons as a deterrent. Archbishop George Beck of England had spoken in favor of my position, but the tide was running strongly in the opposite direction. So I was very pleased that the dean of the diplomatic corps had thought enough of my efforts to come to the Chancery on Rhode Island Avenue to tell me that "diplomacy would be dead if we do not have something to bargain with — a deterrent."

Well, Caffery spoke very briefly about his diplomatic achievements in Egypt, taking no credit for himself, and not taking us into any explanation of how he dealt with King Farouk, a very strong-willed man. Then Caffery quickly shifted into the search for and discovery of this "moon ship." I could see the glazed looks on the faces of the members. Amazement turned to disbelief and then to boredom. I thought it best to state at the end of the meeting, "We intend to invite Bishop Wright to speak at the next meeting!"

Dr. Thomas A. Dooley, the physician who was such a successful missionary doctor in Indochina, was a very impressive and effective speaker. He made some very important friends after the breakfast who benefited his cause remarkably.

Another doctor who made an excellent presentation was cardiologist William B. Walsh, who founded Project HOPE (Health Opportunities for People Everywhere). He raised the money to retrofit an old Navy ship into a 15,000-ton floating hospital, which treated thousands of people in medically underserved countries. Two of his three colleagues were members of the society. Dr. Walsh spoke about how the Communists tried to discredit the HOPE Hospital ship with their poor people by planting rumors denigrating the expertise of his doctors. Dr. Walsh's revelations spurred our members to help him financially.

One of the most unusual speakers was a young English politician, a convert, Lord Pakenham, a descendant of the Lord Pakenham who lost the Battle of New Orleans and whose body was sent back to England in a barrel of rum, later to be placed in Westminster Abbey. He was a member of the Labor Party, which made him a political convert, and was considered to be a rising political star in England. His very mediocre talk, however, convinced us he had no future in politics, which assessment was later realized.

One of the most critical speakers we had was the Jesuit who at one time was in charge of the Pontifical Russicum College in Rome, which trained volunteer priests to sneak into Communist Russia. He was very caustic about "you members of the Latin Rite who can't tolerate a priest unless he uses *'Dominus vobiscum'* in the Mass." Later we had another Jesuit who had been tortured in Russia, and he was a very inspiring speaker.

The women's evening banquet was a grand success, in large part due to a terrific speech by famous economist and writer Lady Barbara Ward Jackson of England, who berated the United States for not contributing more of its income to foreign relief. Charming and scholarly, I thought she would be pleased to meet members of Congress who might be able to do something for her cause of foreign relief. But claiming fatigue she excused herself, leaving lobbying chores to me, proving once again what I learned long ago: to get anything accomplished, you have to be willing to go the extra mile.

The Red Mass

The Society spent a great deal of energy arranging for the Red Mass, an annual celebration for members of the judiciary and government. We were so strict about the seating, strictly arranged according to seniority and status, that I insisted on having a dress rehearsal for the ushers. Working from huge charts of the cathedral, I assigned ushers to the various aisles, making them memorize every seat number so as to be able to direct any guest to his or her section.

There was always a tug of war between Cardinal O'Boyle and the ushers. As you know, there is no law requiring official guests to arrive on time or even to arrive. The higher the position of the guests, the less responsible he or she is about promptness. Therefore, there were always many vacancies in the seats near the front of the church. Archbishop O'Boyle had a particularly long-standing aversion to half inhabited front sections, explaining with gusto that for some charity events in New York he had frequently issued two tickets for each seat. The Cardinal of New York beamed when he arrived and found every seat occupied.

At the beginning of the Red Mass, he would glower at the ushers and pass the word down to them, "Fill up the front seats," which meant putting strange guests in pews with ambassadors and members of the cabinet and Supreme Court. Anticipating the Archbishop's mandate, the ushers did the only sensible thing — ducked out rather than offend some highly-placed personage — a strategy I soon adopted myself. Sometimes flight is better than fight.

Of course, the Red Mass was especially important because President Kennedy was scheduled to attend. Because there were still remnants of the antipathy toward a Catholic president, I checked with Archbishop O'Boyle and called Pierre Salinger at the White House. "We have decided that Archbishop O'Boyle will not greet the President at the sidewalk," I said. "Instead, he will be greeted by the president of the John Carroll Society, Dr. Charles Hufnagel, who will escort the President to his pew. There will be no pictures permitted during the Mass inside the Cathedral, and afterward Archbishop O'Boyle will escort the President to the front door of the church with Dr. Hufnagel escorting him from the door to the limousine." Pierre was more than happy with our plan.

Of course, the newspaper photographers tried to take pictures inside the church, but the ushers were delighted to be able to order the cameramen out. To make sure they left, we put a special guard for the sanctuary, Father William Awalt. Built like a linebacker, his order to desist was always obeyed.

There was one aspect of the Red Mass that was always unpleasant for me. With the support of the Archbishop, I demanded to see a copy of the homily at least a week before the Mass. Though the official reason was to make copies for the press, what I really wanted to do was check the text in case the homilist was taking the occasion to lambaste the government, as sometimes happened. It was my duty to explain that although we didn't want him to make any changes, perhaps his ideas, given our captive audience, could be expressed more politely. Using a worst-case scenario, I always told the story about President Truman, who, attending a Baptist church service in Washington, had to sit through the pastor's bitter condemnation of his efforts to appoint an ambassador to the Vatican. Truman never again returned to the church.

Our speakers continued to be high-level and interesting officials. When I invited General Alfred Gruenther, the Supreme Allied Commander in Europe from 1953 to 1956, to speak, he gave a splendid talk on "We Must Promote Our Faith." Thomas E. Murray, the chair of the Atomic Energy Commission, got rapt attention for his talk. The level of the speakers maintained a high attendance at our meetings. The camaraderie and attendance at the Masses, with the interesting talks afterward, stirred a number of lukewarm Catholics into active participation and renewal of their faith. Many asked for the names of books that might increase their knowledge of the faith.

National Shrine

One of the significant moments in the history of the Archdiocese of Washington came on November 20, 1959, when the National Shrine of the Immaculate Conception was dedicated, largely through the efforts of Archbishop O'Boyle. Thirty-nine years earlier my brother Bill and I were present at the groundbreaking ceremonies with Cardinal Gibbons, and now I was an auxiliary bishop participating in the dedication ceremony of this awe-inspiring edifice first dreamed up by Bishop Shahan, former rector of The Catholic University. My own love for the shrine grew out of my post-graduate experiences following the war at Catholic University, which used part of the shrine as its church (featuring the sparkling homilies of Father Fulton Sheen, then at the beginning of his great career).

The Shrine's construction had been dragging on for years. Finally, Archbishop O'Boyle, a member of the shrine's building committee which was inactive, decided it needed reinvigorating. Aided by four U.S. cardinals, he secured approbation from the National Catholic Welfare Conference for an annual financial drive benefitting the Shrine in each diocese. Its success, along with the Archbishop's soliciting a million dollar donationfrom the Knights of Columbus and $700,000 from the Catholic Daughters of America, enabled him to sign a contract to get the Shrine going. (His partner in keeping the dream alive was Fort Wayne Bishop John Noll, publisher of *Our Sunday Visitor* newspaper.)

The principal architect was Eugene F. Kennedy of the Boston firm of Maginnis & Walsh, while the contractor was John McShain, whose portfolio included the Pentagon, the Government Accounting Office building, and renovations to the White House. McShain, who had never built a cathedral nor any other major Catholic building was so "ripe" for the opportunity that I told the Archbishop, "This guy's so eager to build the shrine I think he'd pay for it himself if he had to."

And he almost did, submitting a bid so low that no contractor could match it, completing the building in record time. "If the men weren't working hard enough or the architect didn't complete the 'specs' on time," a friend told me, "McShain would yell and jump up and down, bawling them out." Finishing the Shrine, however, almost finished his nervous system. Finally, his doctor forced him to take a rest and develop a hobby. Going to Ireland, he bought some racehorses and in the first year won over $1 million in prize money.

The dedication of the shrine extended from Friday, November 20, 1959, until Sunday, November 22. The Archbishop nobly ceded to the U.S. cardinals the privilege of celebrating the first official Masses, the first celebrant being New York Cardinal Francis Spellman, with St. Louis Archbishop Joseph E. Ritter as the homilist (to please the Midwest, according to Archbishop O'Boyle).

It was my privilege, with Archbishop O'Boyle, to dedicate the altars. Pre-Vatican II liturgy, relics of saints were imbedded in each altar, requiring a lengthy set of blessings and holy water swabbed over the surface of the beautiful marble. Following that, everything was cleansed with wine. The Italian marble workers, their faces anything but devout, were instructed to stand by if needed and watch as their beautiful marble altars were being "spoiled." With thirty altars to dedicate, most of which were done by me, the blessings required a day and a half. When I finished, the workers, delighted to see me leave, murmured not a single "*grazie.*"

Experts in church art, meanwhile, expected it would take a generation to secure enough sponsorship to finish the side altars. "That's appropriate," the Archbishop said. "It's good to have more than one generation completing the Shrine." The devotion of American Catholics to the Blessed Mother torpedoed the need for any participation by future generations.

The shrine is, quite simply, my beloved second home. No visit to Washington, especially at Christmas, is complete without a visit to the shrine and celebrating Mass there. The awesome beauty of the marble walls and the *baldachino* over the main altar notwithstanding, I cherish most the commanding view of the great mosaic of "Christ the Pantocrator" in the apse, a view unobstructed from the back door (before the raw, brick walls were decorated), where its lack of adornment allowed your undivided attention in relishing this great source of devotion. It is always hard to leave.

Fortunately, Monsignor John O'Grady of Chicago was the first rector or administrator of the shrine. He was totally dedicated and fully competent. I had the pleasure of suggesting the first lay director of the shrine, Mr. Eduard Fusek, who was a Czech engineer and the former head of the Catholic Party in the Czech nation. A staunch anti-Communist, he was a refugee who gave up his chain of factories for the sake of his family's freedom. He knew every inch of the building.

He and his family lived in St. Patrick's Parish on G Place. Once, when Fusek was having trouble communicating with Monsignor O'Grady because of his Czech accent, he asked his adult daughter Vera to help. Monsignor O'Grady was skeptical until Vera came with her beautiful English-accented voice to interpret. Thereafter the Monsignor never doubted a suggestion by Eduard Fusek. Incidentally, Fusek purchased the former home of Mary Surratt (alleged friend of Lincoln's assassin John Wilkes Booth) and renovated it in one year into several apartments by himself. He refused any offer of assistance and ate only oatmeal for months to enable him to stretch his cash to complete his project.

The shrine now is the site of many wonderful events, richly deserving of its title as the National Shrine. Every November the U.S. bishops gather in Washington for their annual meeting and celebrate an inspiring Mass at the shrine. The administrators of the shrine have been excellent and dynamic. Two of them have become bishops — Bishop Thomas J. Grady of Orlando and Bishop Michael J. Bransfield of Wheeling-Charleston, West Virginia.

Incidentally, I think that there should be a statue of Archbishop O'Boyle in the crypt, next to the statue of Bishop Shahan, who suggested the building of the shrine. If you haven't visited the shrine, you have missed a great spiritual experience. If you haven't visited the shrine at Christmas, you have not had a complete Christmas.

Refugees

The Cold War of the late 1950s affected not only the politics of Washington, D.C., but also the work of the Church. Washington, D.C., became a haven for many refugee groups who looked to the Church for assistance, and we had to respond.

The anti-Communist revolt in Hungary in 1956 sparked the immigration of thousands of Hungarians to the United States. The Hungarian group in Washington amounted to about four hundred former students as well as a couple of hundred older persons. They were disappointed and angry because President Eisenhower had urged them to revolt but then provided no support when they did what he had asked.

Nevertheless, they were very glad to be in America and referred to the ambassador of Finland as a friend. They remembered their history: the original tribe of Hungarians, on leaving their ancestral homes in Asia, decided as they entered Europe to split up, one section going north to Finland and the other going south to the Danube River Valley, present-day Hungary. There was a similarity in the Finnish and Hungarian languages. To my surprise, the Finnish ambassador was friendly and helpful, despite his supposedly Communist convictions. We also discovered that ambassadors of other Communist countries would be helpful if they were quietly and sensitively approached.

The Hungarians had an intense devotion to Cardinal József Mindszenty, the Hungarian primate who had bitterly opposed the Communist regime. On their national Independence Day they attended Mass at St. Patrick's Church, always ending with a robust and tearful singing of their national anthem. After the Mass, they gathered in our high school cafeteria for dining, singing, and dancing, justifying the saying, "Where there's singing and dancing, look for the Hungarians."

Over the years they never softened their opposition to the Communists, protesting loudly the 1978 action of President Jimmy Carter to return to the Communist regime in Hungary the revered relic of the crown of St. Stephen, who had brought the Catholic faith to them. For them the relic signified their national identity. One Hungarian patriot showed his opposition in a striking way. When the Communist government in Russia sent Mikoyan, a member of their Politburo, on a goodwill tour to the United States, I read in the newspaper that an egg thrown by an immigrant in California had hit him. I knew immediately that it was thrown by Miklos Tottossy. He was the nephew of the vicar general of a diocese in Hungary, and Miklos had been imprisoned in one of their worst camps in a cell with no light. Sure enough, the night of the egg throwing, I received a telephone call from Miklos.

"I am sure that you threw the egg," I said. "Yes," Miklos replied, "and I hit him squarely. Now I need some help. The Americans arrested me, but the judge is very friendly. He fined me $50." I gladly paid the fine.

It was my duty to get the Hungarian students scholarships for the colleges and universities in Washington, and I had reasonable success. Gradually, the Hungarians began to trust each other and cultivate friends in their group. Their distrust of the Communists was so visceral they told me that during the train trip from Budapest to freedom in the West, they were afraid to speak to each other because they feared there were Communist agents among them. The only safe course was not to speak to anyone and not to admit that they were fleeing Hungary. They had a very strong survival instinct.

In addition to college scholarships, we secured unusual jobs for them. Many Hungarians were gifted athletes, especially in kayaking and canoeing. The Potomac Canoe Club was looking for athletes to fill their entries in regattas, and the Hungarians supplied their needs. They also filled our need for a housekeeper at St. Patrick's after our longtime housekeeper, Mrs. Russell, returned to her home in Baltimore. We hired a Hungarian mother and her daughter. We taught them everything about American cooking, and they taught us Hungarian cooking. Eventually both women left for very lucrative positions in California. There also were many scientists among the Hungarians, who received a warm welcome from their fellow scientists in the Washington area. John Leonard, a Catholic University alumnus, had a whole Hungarian family as guests in his home in Chevy Chase for several years. A neighbor of the Leonards even gave the visitors his own car.

A group of refugees from Czechoslovakia, headed by the former mayor of Prague, also made St. Patrick's their church in Washington. They were very devout. We had similar groups, especially from Poland and Lithuania. The son of the ambassador of Lithuania fell in love with a Catholic girl, an American, to the great distress of the ambassador. He wanted his son to be completely "Lithuanian" and marry a Lithuanian. I politely refused to become involved in that problem.

Supplying jobs for these refugees was not a great problem. The constant need for polite and hard-working men and women took care of the need. I remember especially the head of the waiters' union. "Bishop, I can't get enough good people to serve as waiters," he said. "I don't care how many there are. Send them to me." I very gladly did so.

The Ruthenian Eastern Rite Catholics needed special assistance. They not only had to have the auditorium for Mass in their Rite (a Mass lasting over two hours) but they also needed to use the refectory. They came from such a distance that the children needed to eat right after the Mass. They numbered about ninety families, and their pastor, Father Rosak, was very pious and had a very good singing voice. Their singing attracted persons of other rites, including the Latin Rite. They sang every part of the Mass, and their rich voices were a great attraction. Occasionally I would greet Father Rosak and his congregation, and each time I would see a number of black Catholics in the back of the hall quietly following the melody of the Mass.

When Father Rosak's congregation began to notably increase, he asked my help in purchasing a church building. He had found an excellent church on 16th Street whose Protestant congregation had moved to the suburbs. A few years later he was assigned to a parish near Pittsburgh, and on his twenty-fifth anniversary of ordination, he insisted that I attend the Mass. It was inspiring. After the Mass, Father Rosak said, "We'll have dinner at our country club." I said, "Our country club?" "Yes," he explained. "When our folks came to this country they promptly formed an insurance society. It developed so well that we bought a country club for our celebrations." The Slavic people, realizing that no group in the United States would be supportive of them, decided to take care of their own people. What a wonderful example of the realization of the American dream!

U.S. Government

The presence of the U.S. government in our archdiocese presented a delicate and special relationship between the priests and the members of the government. A case in point was Archbishop O'Boyle's policy that no priest was to approach the government with a proposal unless it was approved by him. The priests understood and completely cooperated with the policy. There was only one known instance of a violation of the policy — a priest invited President Truman to join his parish for a novena!

Of course, every priest and religious, as citizens of the United States, had the right to write or approach any person and any official at every level of the government. They also recognized that as special members of the Church they had an obligation to recognize the right of the Church to regulate to some extent their lives for the good order of the Church.

My only regret about Archbishop O'Boyle's leadership style was that he did not utilize more fully the unusual opportunities he had to provide information and advice, when requested or needed, to governmental officials. The Archbishop had been the head of Catholic Relief Services during World War II and had impressive experience in charitable matters in New York. Frequently he had made trips to Washington to government agencies on official business. As the Archbishop of Washington he received many requests from charitable organizations for advice, and on one occasion the whole group of charitable concerns in Washington asked him to head their appeal to the President. The meeting was held in the White House. Naturally, his appeal was televised, and he spoke from a lectern, which had the seal of the President on it. This disturbed him. He felt very queasy about a TV shot showing him using the podium of the President.

On another occasion in the 1950s, U.S. Supreme Court Chief Justice Earl Warren attended the annual Pan American Mass and Dinner at St. Patrick's that we put on for all the ambassadors of the Pan American union. Justice Warren was seated next to Archbishop O'Boyle at the meal, and I heard him compliment the Archdiocese for the way we had engineered the integration of our Catholic schools with no open opposition. Rather than take the cue, the Archbishop just let the subject drop. After the dinner I politely bawled out the Archbishop for not being more forceful in providing advice for officials who requested it. It was almost as if political figures to him were ten feet tall and he had nothing special to offer. That was the maddening element — these public officials wanted to know what the Church thought. The Archbishop took my constructive criticism in stride. He was very tolerant.

An unusual fact about the Washington Archdiocese was that the Jesuits, from 1634 on, controlled the ministry in a large part of the territory in southern Maryland. For more than three hundred years they ministered to the parishes in St. Mary's and Charles counties as well as sections of Calvert County. From time to time the Jesuits mentioned they might not be able to supply the priests for all the parishes they had in southern Maryland. Their system was unique: For mutual support, the pastors of several nearby parishes would live in a common rectory. The people loved them and their system. Unfortunately, they were not getting enough priestly vocations.

The inevitable happened. The Jesuit Provincial informed the Archbishop he could no longer supply enough priests to minister to all the parishes, and he requested that the archdiocese assume responsibility for that ministry. The Archbishop delayed. The Jesuits' record was very impressive. In more than 300 years of service, they had never had a recorded defection of a priest, and their reputation with the people was unequalled.

The Provincial persisted, and the Archbishop finally had to consent. The problem was formidable. It was not simply a matter of supplying the number of priests needed, but it also meant completely changing the system of parish ministry. Individual rectories had to be built at each parish, but, above all, the people had to accept the changes. With painstaking care the Archbishop chose the priests, and in a surprisingly short time the people adjusted very well to the new system — a single priest in each rectory. A principal reason was that the diocesan priests were then easily available to all the parishioners.

The Jesuits also made the transition easy because of their friendliness with the people. At one Maryland parish with a significant number of Native Americans, I witnessed a return visit by their former Jesuit pastor. He was mobbed and hugged by the people, especially the few natives (Indians) who remained.

Naturally, there were some problems in the transition. For instance, one pastor would never tell his fellow Jesuits how much money the parish had, so there was no real accounting. "My people have no money," he told the Archbishop. "They have only nickels and dimes to give." But with only nickels and dimes he had half-finished a new parish building with a number of rooms for catechetical classes and had complete plans for all the auxiliary rooms.

In addition to his secrecy about finances, he had not allowed any Jesuits to see his plans. Obviously, this was a case for the Chancellor. It comes with the duties of being an auxiliary bishop. I met the pastor at the site of the CCD building and introduced myself. "My father was a plumbing contractor," I told him. "I congratulate you very heartily for the progress you have made on the building. Will you please show me the pipes for the water supply and heating?"

"I will, but you must do a lot of climbing," he replied. I answered, "That's okay, I like climbing."

The pastor gave me a meticulous inspection of everything. Without the help of ladders, we climbed all over the building. At the end of the tour, I congratulated him again and then posed the dreaded question, assuring him that only the Archbishop would get the information. Miracles do happen. He went to his safe and pulled out his deposit books. Let's just say he had collected very many "nickels and dimes."

To avoid any questions from his fellow Jesuits, I did not go to the rectory. I went back to Washington and astounded Archbishop O'Boyle with the news and the exact amount in the parish bank account. I had earned my keep that afternoon, for sure.

A keen regret during my time as vicar general was my failure to develop a better arrangement for the use of the commercial property controlled by St. Patrick's Church. Through the foresight and generosity of the first pastor as well as other events, the parish owned valuable rental properties on F Street. The pastor controlled the management of the property, and the income was used to pay for the parish and for archdiocesan needs.

The care and repair of the rental properties was a constant burden, and I thought we could reap much greater benefits if we built a large, modern office building with stores on the first three floors on the site. The realtors I consulted were enthusiastic about the project. We developed a sketch of the proposed building so that we could make a proposal to the national Knights of Columbus organization to provide a loan for the construction. They made a very attractive offer. The loan was to be repaid in annual installments of 8 percent, 5 percent of which was interest and 3 percent for the payment of the principal.

Enthused, I submitted the proposal to the Archbishop. After some discussion, he turned it down. He did not wish the Church to be engaged in a commercial venture of such a scale. I did not have an opportunity to make a more modest proposal before I was appointed archbishop of New Orleans.

Archbishop O'Boyle's reluctance to sign off on such an ambitious proposal probably had a lot to do with his background. In conducting charity programs in New York, he had not dealt extensively with real estate matters, and this was a problem even in selecting a suitable home for him in Washington. Fortunately for me, he decided to ask Monsignor Cartwright to establish a small committee to find a suitable residence. Monsignor Cartwright came up with almost thirty possibilities, but the Archbishop didn't accept any.

Fortunately, a wonderful offer from a friend and businessman solved the problem. Charles Maloney offered to sell his home at a "give-away" price. His home was in an attractive residential section on Warren Street, very close to St. Ann's Parish. The home had a spacious lawn, and the interior was very suitable for the Archbishop's use. He acquired a wonderful home with a large room that was made into a very attractive chapel.

A similar problem occurred when a group of Eastern Rite Catholics asked the Archbishop to select a piece of property for the establishment of a seminary for their Rite. To complicate the matter, the men were not very precise in describing the kind of property they wanted. Negotiations went on for months with no results. The committee came to see the Archbishop once when he was away. They asked for my help.

"Fortunately, I have a friend," I told them. "She's a widow, who wishes to sell her home, which is very large, has a lawn of about an acre. She is very devout, and if we promise her that part of her home will be used for a chapel, she will practically give you her home. This is the best possible opportunity. If you don't accept the offer, please do not come back to see me." They bought the house the next day. The Archbishop was mystified by their quick decision. Today it serves as a seminary for that rite.

The Archbishop was a very solid and committed supporter of unions, but he was always conscious of costs. There was a limit to their demands. The cost demands of a union company in Washington to make repairs in a church in St. Mary's County, with working hours from "portal to portal" (at least three hours daily for travel), was promptly turned down. A local company did the work.

NCWC

Appointment as a U.S. bishop also meant election to the national organization of the bishops, which in 1956 was called the National Catholic Welfare Conference. During World War I the bishops organized a national group primarily to help the American soldiers engaged in the war. The organization was so successful the bishops decided to retain it after the war. It was called a "welfare" conference to indicate its extent and also to denote that it was not engaged in doctrinal matters. The Holy See was eager to avoid a national organization of bishops that would be engaged in discussing or proposing changes to doctrine. But a conference about welfare was perfectly acceptable. In fact, the NCWC (National Catholic Welfare Conference) was so successful it served as a model in the Second Vatican Council for the establishment of national conferences of bishops throughout the world.

Archbishop Joseph Schrembs of Cleveland was a leader in securing the Vatican's approval of the conference, and my distant cousin, Bishop William Turner of Buffalo, was a leader in preventing any name indicating any activity by the bishops in doctrinal matters. The word "conference" was acceptable to Rome.

I was duly elected to the NCWC and attended my first bishops' meeting in November 1956. The meeting was held in two conjoined classrooms in Caldwell Hall in Catholic University. Nothing could have been less pretentious. The seats were those used by the students. This made it very easy for a newcomer, and so I was very pleased with the "arrangements."

I purposely did not sit near Archbishop O'Boyle. Very shortly I learned from the discussion that Cardinal Edward Mooney of Detroit and Cardinal Samuel Stritch of Chicago were the most respected members. Whenever they forcefully supported a motion it was accepted by the whole body.

Archbishop Joseph Rummel of New Orleans passionately introduced the cause of integrating the Catholic schools, and he made a wonderful presentation. Almost before he finished, Archbishop O'Boyle jumped to his feet and spoke strongly in support of the cause. We had already integrated our schools in Washington, as had a number of other dioceses such as St. Louis. I don't remember any of the bishops in the Province of New Orleans speaking in support of the cause, but I heard Bishop Richard Gerow of Natchez say to a neighbor, "We'll support him, and we know that we'll take our lumps." He was right.

Archbishop O'Boyle was such a champion of Archbishop Rummel that he dispatched me to New Orleans a few months later to discuss what the Washington Archdiocese had done to integrate its schools peacefully. When I got to Archbishop Rummel's residence, just to the right of Notre Dame Seminary, I saw immediately why he was in such a predicament — a burning cross, the ultimate symbol of "segregation yesterday, segregation today, segregation forever," was squarely planted on his front lawn.

As soon as I entered his residence, I told him, "You don't have to explain to me what your troubles are. I can see it for myself."

The major difference between the integration of schools in Washington and New Orleans was obvious — we had the federal government supporting us all the time, and New Orleans had local and state governments that were staunchly opposed to any integration and did everything they could to block federal intervention. Archbishop Rummel wanted to move more quickly on integrating the New Orleans schools, but he also feared that moving too quickly would drive thousands of people away from the church. It was a real spiritual concern for him.

In Washington, we began integrating the schools in the first and second grades and then added a grade every year. Archbishop O'Boyle also confronted the issue head on. He made me his point person to the parishes in southern Maryland — where slavery had been an institution for hundreds of years — and my job was to attend open meetings to explain why integration was a supreme moral issue. Then I let people vent their feelings for three hours, which provided a very useful emotional release. They could say anything they wanted.

Judge Leander Perez, a staunch segregationist who ruled Plaquemines Parish in south Louisiana as though it were his fiefdom, and who later was excommunicated by Archbishop Rummel for refusing to stop his efforts rallying Catholics to oppose church teaching on integration, thought he could hold out and get the church to back down. He couldn't. Perez also forgot about the feds. There's a famous quote from Louisiana Gov. Earl Long, which might even be true: "Hey, Leander, what are you going to do now that the feds have the A-bomb?"

Archbishop Rummel had announced his intention to integrate Catholic schools as early as 1956, but most of the parish school boards wanted him to delay until the public schools were integrated. Archbishop Rummel's health also was seriously declining. The Sisters of the Holy Family, who cared for him at his residence, told me after I became archbishop of New Orleans that they had found him unconscious several times but waited for him to revive himself. They didn't report his blackouts because they feared he would be forced to retire. He also had serious glaucoma and was almost blind. Twin concerns about Archbishop Rummel's health and the plodding pace of desegregation obviously led the Vatican to appoint John Patrick Cody in August 1961 as coadjutor archbishop. Archbishop Cody was a no-nonsense bulldozer who came to New Orleans with the tacit understanding he would implement integration without delay.

Archbishop Cody had absolutely no problem telling people what the church wanted. He simply said: "That's it. You either line up with us or you're done." The archdiocese announced on March 27, 1962, that its schools would be integrated for the upcoming academic year. Perez and another public protestor, Mrs. B.J. Gaillot, were excommunicated by Archbishop Rummel on April 16, 1962. Integration began for the 1962-63 term.

I learned a few things in my early years as an auxiliary bishop. I was very much impressed with the candor and simplicity of the national bishops' meetings, which lasted only two full days. Those meetings left me with a clear impression, "If you get up to speak in this group, you'd better know completely what you're talking about."

One aspect of the meetings I did not like was the secrecy. No reporters were allowed — no press, radio, or TV. The result was predictable. The exclusion of reporters nurtured a feeling of suspicion and distrust about the accuracy of the press releases submitted by the NCWC. Ultimately, the matters discussed in the meetings became entirely known.

Having known many of the reporters through my position as editor of *Catholic Standard*, I received a barrage of complaints, especially from the *New York Times*. I told them frankly that if the press were allowed in, they would be disappointed by the discussion. "You'll find most of the discussion boring," I said. "At the end of the daily sessions you will find that you learned just as much from the regular press meeting as you did from your day-long attendance." That is exactly the result when the meetings were opened to reporters.

Meanwhile the press expended extraordinary energy to get the "inside dope" on the meetings. I received a message from a reporter I scarcely knew who offered me a substantial reward for information, with the assurance that my actions would be kept absolutely secret. The fleeting thought came that I could easily double-cross him, but I rejected the offer. I wondered, however, how many bishops received the same offer.

Archbishop O'Boyle was an unusual guy in this respect. If he trusted you, he would load you down with jobs. In the early 1960s, I had about twelve different jobs. I was auxiliary bishop, chancellor of the archdiocese, pastor of St. Patrick's Church, editor of the archdiocesan newspaper, director of vocations, chaplain of several organizations, and involved with property transactions. I made up a list one day to show him, and when he read it he said, "But you don't have to do all of these things at the same time!" He never took away any of my jobs.

Actually, toward the end of the Second Vatican Council, he wanted me to become his coadjutor, which was a supreme compliment. But I thought it over, and I just didn't think it would work. I always felt he was a little too timid, and if I were his coadjutor, we might have a lot of arguments and it might not be in the best interest of the archdiocese. In retrospect, I regret that I did not accept his offer. He was always very loyal to me.

When Archbishop O'Boyle retired in 1973, he tried to get me appointed as his successor, but he had a long and checkered history with Cardinal Amleto Giovanni Cicognani, who had served as the Apostolic Delegate to the United States from 1933 to 1959. Washington had a number of Italian-descent priests who would make end runs to the then-Archbishop Cicognani, a fellow Italian, whenever they needed a special favor, and he would grant the favor without checking with Archbishop O'Boyle. A group of Italian Sisters bought property to run a residence for the elderly in the archdiocese, but they bypassed Archbishop O'Boyle completely and got Archbishop Cicognani's approval. That really puts the local ordinary in a tough position. Archbishop O'Boyle didn't approve of that method at all and had a very heated discussion with Archbishop Cicognani, but Cicognani simply disregarded his contentions. Cicognani later become the Vatican Secretary of State and Dean of the College of Cardinals, so I'm sure he wasn't going to do Archbishop O'Boyle any special favors.

Really, had it not been for Hurricane Betsy in 1965, I think I probably would have remained in Washington as an auxiliary bishop for a very long time. And when I got the word to go to New Orleans in September 1965 — while I was attending the Second Vatican Council — believe me, it was an emergency situation. They wanted me to get to New Orleans as fast as I could.

CHAPTER 10

The Kennedy Years

One afternoon, shortly after the presidential and congressional elections of 1948, I received a telephone call from a friendly Catholic congresswoman. "We have a new, young Catholic congressman from Massachusetts named John Kennedy," she said. "He's got a complaint about the Church you might like to hear."

"Sure," I replied. "Hope I can help. What is it?"

Apparently, she continued, a priest whom Kennedy didn't know had walked into his office sans appointment and proceeded to give a forty-five-minute lecture on Mexican politics, the government persecution of the Church, and what the Massachusetts representative should do about it. "Kennedy," she added, "felt almost insulted."

"I'm glad you called," I said. "I've heard about this Father Thorning," I said. "He's an educator specializing in Latin America, but just because he knows a lot about Mexico doesn't mean we approve of him barging into a congressman's office to conduct a policy lecture." (Any formal contact by a priest to a member of Congress, per the National Conference of Catholic Bishops, had to have prior approval of either Archbishop O'Boyle or his local bishop. Even individual bishops were obligated to check with the NCCB before privately addressing a congressman.) "Until now, however, I've only heard stories secondhand. Please tell Kennedy I'd appreciate him calling and telling me everything directly. That way I can act on it more easily." Not long after, my telephone rang, and a young man with a distinctively nasal Boston accent authoritatively announced: "I'm John Kennedy. I was told to call you about a complaint."

"Thanks for calling, Congressman," I replied. "I'd appreciate hearing exactly what happened." Recounting the incident, Kennedy didn't seem that disturbed. Nevertheless, his call was a significant indication that the Church was important to him. Moreover, despite the misguided crusader having knocked on the doors of many Catholic legislators, Kennedy was the only one to ever contact me about his tactics — a clear sign that he felt important. This young legislator wanted to state for the record that he would not tolerate such cavalier treatment from a priest. "Obviously," I thought, "this guy has big plans for the future." Assuring Kennedy that Father Thorning had acted completely on his own, I promised that henceforth the guy would be forbidden to engage in any informational activities unless speifically requested by someone on the Hill.

"Look," I said. "Archbishop O'Boyle doesn't believe in harassing Congress. I'm confident this priest will understand his position and not bother you again. I certainly hope you like living here and can move beyond this incident." With that, Kennedy's voice grew noticeably friendlier for the remainder of our twenty-minute conversation. Hanging up, I had the feeling that Kennedy, now trusting that I gave straight answers, would call back when faced with a problem stalled at the intersection of political strategy and Church teaching.

And, indeed, he did. The next time we spoke it was as though we were longtime friends. Still, I could never have imagined that my first conversation with then-congressman Jack Kennedy was the beginning of a collaborative, mutually respectful friendship that would last until his death. It would also remain a virtual secret. I could not — never did — publicize our relationship. (Consequently, no picture of us together exists nor did I ever, consciously, ask him for anything, even an autographed photograph.) I wanted nothing from Jack — and he knew it.

For his part, Kennedy, above all else, was a savvy politician. To become America's first Roman Catholic president, John Fitzgerald Kennedy had to overcome centuries of religious prejudice — which victory didn't end. Assuming the presidency, Jack realized that every association or interaction with a member of the Catholic Church would be scrutinized by opponents waiting for him to install a Vatican hot line in the Oval Office. I, meanwhile, was delighted to keep my Church friends out of the loop. The last thing I wanted was to be seen as a go-between for personal favors (like getting an audience with the president), much less be held accountable for anything he said or proposed.

Jack's desire for secrecy surfaced during one of our early phone conversations. The moment he hinted about a gentleman's agreement, I ran with it. "I want to assure you," I said, "that I do not wish to be known as your consultant. Our conversations should be kept secret by you and your staff" (a promise I honored even after he was gone). Following the assassination, Kennedy speech writer Ted Sorenson sent over a preliminary version of the book he was writing about his former boss in which I was mentioned several times. Calling immediately, I thanked Ted for the advance look, asking that he take out my name. "Please remember that Jack and I agreed to secrecy." When Sorensen asked what to use in its place, I paused. "Just say 'a priest.'" "All right," he demurred, "but it'll hurt the book." (Though my usual contact with Jack was by phone, his enquiries sometimes came via a staff member, frequently the very bright Sorensen. Interested in how Kennedy's Catholicism could be "overcome" among the general populace, Ted liked testing ideas on me. He also correctly understood that his boss needed the solid support of Catholic priests who could influence without speaking a word from the pulpit.)

Though our confidentiality agreement was mutually beneficial, it was especially important for Kennedy, allowing him to figure out — minus public debate and knowledge of the source — "the Catholic viewpoint" on any subject. For me, however, it involved an awkward arrangement with Archbishop O'Boyle, who as president of the National Conference of Catholic Bishops (1961 to 1966) would normally be entitled to know everything involving my official duties. However, the Archbishop understood perfectly that an up-and-coming, Catholic presidential candidate should not be perceived as being subservient to a Catholic bishop or superior. As a result, he agreed to disclaim any knowledge of my clandestine exchange of ideas and information with Kennedy — a promise tested during JFK's 1952 Massachusetts senatorial race against Henry Cabot Lodge. Hearing rumors of Kennedy's kinship with a clergyman, Congressman John McCormack confronted the Archbishop: "I hear Kennedy is confiding in a priest and following his advice. Do you know who he is?" True to our pact, the Archbishop said no — but it gnawed at him. "I don't like this arrangement," he dejectedly informed me.

"I don't either. But doesn't the probable presidential candidate have the right to receive information anonymously for the common good?" Our agreement stood firm.

Following my initial phone conversation with Kennedy, his name didn't come up again until the night that Archbishop O'Boyle invited future House Speaker John McCormack to dinner at St. Patrick's rectory. A vintage, scrappy, self-made, Irish-Catholic Bostonian, McCormack, always blunt and entertaining, was a favorite of the Archbishop, who relished his colorfully candid stories and unvarnished evaluations of new Catholic congressmen. Asked about Kennedy, McCormack begrudgingly rated him "satisfactory," though overly endowed with "free spirit — judging each piece of proposed legislation through his personal, not party, prism." Moreover, Kennedy had a bad habit of not showing up for every congressional session. Nevertheless, like Kennedy, McCormack, a World War I machine gun runner, admired the novice politician for serving in WWII, where he had sustained a back injury that still caused considerable pain. Coming from the take-no-prisoners McCormack, his evaluation of Jack was practically a home run.

As I learned more about my new friend, it became apparent that a bad back wasn't his only health problem — a fact echoed by another Massachusetts native, Father Pat Nagle, an assistant priest at St. Patrick's who seemed to know everything about Jack. Kennedy's physical issues, especially his

Addison's Disease, affecting the immune system, were far more serious than McCormack reported. "His back injury was so bad he developed complications," Nagle revealed. "Before they took him to the hospital for an operation, I hear he got the Last Rites." (In fact, Kennedy allegedly received the Last Rites three or four times in the course of his life.)

Though Jack made no effort to deny his obstreperous back, his fragile health receded from public view as Kennedy's political and social careers revved up. Dubbed Washington's "Most Eligible Bachelor," Kennedy graduated from the Society to the Front page in 1952 when he decided to challenge Massachusetts' incumbent Republican senator, Henry Cabot Lodge. It was a contest made in Media Heaven: the conservative, old-line senator, descendant of one of the state's first families versus the young, untried but attractive, Catholic Irishman, son of the brash, aggressive, newly rich, Wall Street banker, Joseph P. Kennedy.

(I first met Joe Sr., then-U.S. ambassador to Great Britain, in the 1930s in Rome, when I was a seminarian at the North American College. In town with wife Rose and second son Jack for an audience with Pope Pius XII, Joe and Rose also met with the College's faculty and seminarians, which I covered as a reporter for *Roman Echoes*, the seminary publication. Though the ambassador and I shook hands, it was the vivacious Rose Kennedy who caught everyone's attention. "Rome is a wonderful place to understand our faith," she told me. "I believe in not only teaching our children Catholicism, but showing them where things happened. Instead of simply talking about the martyrdom of St. Peter and those killed in the Coliseum, we ought to go see it.")

It was during this campaign that a conversation involving John McCormack, curiously enough, again put me in touch with Kennedy. His campaign against Cabot Lodge was at a standstill due to division in the ranks of the state's Democratic Party, whose undivided support Jack desperately needed to win. Prominent among the uncommitted was McCormack, who favored a more experienced candidate from a family distinguished for its knowledge and practice of Catholicism. (As a young man, McCormack had also refused to support the first Catholic, Democratic presidential candidate, Al Smith, whose down-to-earth, cigar-chomping manners McCormack, a self-educated high school dropout, deemed too pedestrian.) During a casual conversation with one of Kennedy's Washington supporters, I was asked how Jack could get McCormack on board. "Well, John McCormack is crazy about his wife, Harriet," I threw out, off the top of my head, "If there's an occasion where he can give her a big compliment, I'm sure it'll help." (I had witnessed McCormack's legendary devotion to his wife every Sunday at the 10:00 a.m. Mass where, always together, they sat on a side aisle in the same seats. Moreover, insisting the couple spend every evening together, McCormack refused to attend any night functions, regardless of political importance.)

Shortly thereafter, presumably heeding my advice, Kennedy made a point of singling out — and, of course, charming — Harriet McCormack. The following week, at dinner with the Archbishop, Mrs. McCormack turned glowingly to her host, saying: "That nice, young John Kennedy said some of the loveliest things about John and me at a banquet in Boston. He's very attractive." When told of her remarks, I laughed. On such profound grounds are political alliances forged!

Meeting Jack Kennedy

When I finally met Jack Kennedy in person, he looked so frail that I feared health, not religion, would be the real obstacle in a competition for the White House. Though over six feet tall, his baggy suit hanging on his bones, he couldn't have weighed more than 160. Once he opened his mouth, however, all sickliness vanished. Jack was a natural. He had the charm of the Irish — with no limitations. From Harvard bluebloods to the abjectly poor, philosophy to Hollywood gossip, his interests were universal. Moreover, his privileged childhood, traveling the world from England to China, had ignited a keen interest in international affairs. Whereas, his father's isolationism — opposing America's engagement in World War II as Roosevelt's ambassador to Great Britain — had ruined Joe Kennedy's own dream of becoming America's first Catholic president, his second son emerged from the patriarch's disgrace a true citizen of the world. And now, following the tragic WWII plane crash death of twenty-nine-year-old Joe Jr., his father's original designated presidential hitter, Jack (whether he liked it or not) was the Kennedy male up to bat. The political firm of Kennedy and Sons was poised to make its move and triumph. No matter what the game, Joe Kennedy played to win, expecting his children to do the same. In his world, second place was no place at all.

The degree of his competitiveness was driven home years later when I got a call from Jack who was with his father in the Oval Office. "My father's here with me," he explained. "We want to talk to you about a matter on which we disagree. Tell us what you think." Though the "matter" is lost to memory, the dynamics aren't. After listening to the President's explanation, I wholly agreed, freeing him, as it turned out, to stand up to the old man. "That's what I think, too," he crowed triumphantly, "so that's my decision." It was definitely not the right one for his father, who was livid with me for siding with Jack and with his son for exerting his independence. Joe Kennedy couldn't stomach losing, even to the President of the United States.

When Kennedy beat Lodge, I wasn't surprised. Based on personality, background, political wisdom, and charisma, I'd always figured he had it in the bag. From my position in the chancery, I had watched scores of politicians — those comfortable with their position and those who wanted more. And Kennedy definitely wanted more. Ever since 1928, when the first Catholic presidential candidate, Alfred E. Smith was defeated, despite an outstanding record as the governor of New York, it was common political wisdom that a Catholic couldn't get elected to the White House. During our subsequent conversations, however, it became clear that Jack was determined to break through the "stained-glass ceiling." Acknowledging that a Catholic had yet to achieve even Chief of Staff of the Armed Forces, much less Secretary of State, he truly believed that a member of the faith could become President of the United States. And if so, why not him?

That question was more fully answered — and realized — when he met and married Jacqueline Bouvier in September of 1953. Jackie's beauty, refinement, intelligence, taste, and mastery of languages put the perfect patina on Jack's raw, political ambition. She was also Catholic, thanks to her Catholic father, Jack Bouvier, who, even after he and Jackie's mother, Janet, divorced, insisted that his daughters be raised Catholic. When Janet subsequently married Hugh Auchincloss, she and daughters Jackie and Lee moved to Middleburg, Virginia, where the girls were raised. In that wealthy milieu of horses, fox hunts, old money, and Protestants, Jackie's Catholic education had been limited, though in deference to her great love for her father, she remained Catholic. Following a two-year courtship, during which Joe Kennedy became Jacqueline's biggest booster, the twenty-four-year-old married thirty-six-year-old John Kennedy. Though they were definitely in love — and remained so throughout their lives together — the marriage was also exactly what Jack needed (as his father realized) to complete the perfect political ticket, even though the rough-and-tumble of campaigning would definitely be an acquired taste for his new wife.

By nature, Jack was neither particularly tender, nor affectionate, at least publicly. However, I never doubted that, despite their differences, Jack and Jackie's relationship was based on a deep, if complicated, love — made more so by Kennedy's reported philandering. Let me say up front that I, like the vast majority of Americans, knew nothing about Jack Kennedy's infidelities, which, sinful and reprehensible, caused his wife enormous embarrassment and pain. In those days the mainstream media never reported on the personal life of the President; and though it's unimaginable now, no one ever told me about the rumors. When criticized for not upbraiding him on the subject, I can only respond honestly that, under the circumstances, I was the last person to learn about it. No responsible report about his actions was ever given to me.

The ideal place for dealing with this problem, of course, would have been the confessional, but Jack never asked me to hear his confession. If he had, and had he confessed infidelity, I would have counseled him to immediately amend his life. If his excuse (as I imagine it might have been) was that he had a compulsion, I simply would not have accepted it — which is perhaps why he didn't come to me. Jack did not really want to hear what I would have had to say to him on the subject.

Unfortunately, Jack and his brothers had grown up watching their father flaunt his own relationships outside marriage, though by the time he was elected to office Jack, presumably, was a grown man, independent of his father — except in their shared ambition to make him president. Though the Kennedy boys respected and loved Joe Sr., it was an affection tempered by the knowledge of his unfaithfulness to their mother, a destructive pattern of womanizing, sadly, passed on to his sons. Except, perhaps, for Joe Kennedy, Jr. According to Father Maurice Sheehy, an Army chaplain and later vice president of Catholic University, Joe Jr., whom he met as a young pilot in England, was more like his mother in his devotion to his faith. Though her children loved and appreciated Rose — formidable, tough, charming, and political in her own right — her apparent decision to overlook Joe's infidelity for the sake of the children, and appearances, was a catastrophic misjudgment. Not laying down the law to her husband about his numerous, public dalliances with other women ended up having painful consequences — especially for Jacqueline Kennedy.

In truth, whenever John Kennedy and I spoke, it was strictly business. He would ask questions about the faith: "Why does the Church do this?" or "The Pope says *that*?" And I would answer. Like me, Jack was deeply interested in questions of social justice, one reason he supported Pope John XXIII, whose April 1963 encyclical, *Pacem in Terris* ("Peace on Earth") — dealing with universal peace in truth, charity, justice, and liberty — greatly affected him. "As a Catholic, I admire what the Pope says and writes," he told me, "and as a president I can use his suggestions."

Fifty-some-odd years later, people forget how tricky it was to be a Roman Catholic running for the office of President of the United States in 1960. In those days, Catholicism was shrouded in the same misunderstanding and mythical fear as, perhaps, Islam is today. The ignorant believed that to elect a Catholic was to elect the Pope to whom Kennedy, as a Catholic, would owe his first allegiance. From their uninformed perspective, Jack would be obligated to consult Rome on policy decisions.

Given the plethora of erroneous intentions, unfairly credited to the Catholic Church, John Fitzgerald Kennedy turned out to be the right Catholic at the right time. Though he carried a St. Christopher money clip in his pocket, Jack was what I would call, in language of the time, a cultural Catholic. (Brother Bobby, on the other hand, popped into St. Patrick's noon Mass a couple of times a week.) Though Jack wanted to practice his faith, he also liked keeping it at a distance, thus avoiding blame if he didn't show up at Mass every single Sunday. Jackie was also criticized for much the same reason, especially by women who after Mass, would flock to me, complaining that both Kennedys simply were not sufficiently fervent. Countering that sentiment, of course, were those who recognized that John Kennedy, mindful of voters who resented his Catholicism, had to walk a fine spiritual line indeed.

(In general, the Kennedys seemed at ease in the company of bishops and priests. During a state visit to Italy in July 1963, the President naturally arranged to have an audience with the newly elected Holy Father, Pope Paul VI. Concerned about the protocol, "professional Catholic" Ralph Dugan called to ask what gestures the President should make in the Holy Father's presence. Smiling to myself, I assured him that the Pope knew the score. "Being in the diplomatic service of the Church, I'm certain the Pope realizes that any pictures taken of the President, kneeling and kissing the Pope's ring, would be very badly received by many Americans. Protestants would put a real spin on it." Subsequently, the meeting, though personally joyful and inspiring for Jack, was more a family visit than formal reception. Still, the gravity and symbolism of their encounter was extraordinarily significant: the head of the Catholic Church, the world's largest religion, talking to the first Catholic president of the most important nation in the world.)

Though, politically, Jack and I generally agreed, there were exceptions. Kennedy felt that colonial African territories (and others) should immediately obtain freedom from their former European rulers, but I believed that long-colonized countries, shackled for years, first needed to become experienced in a representative form of government. Americans, after all, spent nearly fifty years in colonial status before inaugurating our successful democratic form of government. Another point of disagreement was the hot-button item of the sixties: public funding for private schools. Though Kennedy pushed, as a young Congressman, for federal aid to private schools, he changed his mind, calculating that a Catholic advocating that position could never win a national election. Nevertheless, he completely understood why I carried the banner. Disagreeing with Jack never injured the friendship — one of his stellar qualities.

The Catholic Balance

My job, as I saw it, was to help Jack maintain, in any way possible, the proper, if workable, Catholic balance in that often explosive equation of church versus state — even when it came to preaching to the choir. In February 1958, Kennedy, one eye on his Senate re-election, the other on the White House (and looking for an opportunity to strengthen his ties with Catholic voters), decided that speaking to Washington's John Carroll Society would be just the ticket. (The society of prominent lay Catholics met four times a year, attending Mass at St. Matthew's Cathedral, followed by a breakfast and address from a high-profile Catholic.) He gave me a call. Would I contact the John Carroll Society and ask if they might be willing to waive the bylaws prohibiting a politician as a speaker?

Immediately, I consulted the Society's founding group, Judge Matthew McGuire, former Navy Secretary John L. Sullivan, and trial lawyer William Leahy, all of whom agreed that a special exception should be made. Subsequently, the Senator was invited to address a powerhouse group of three hundred prominent Catholics, including congressmen from both sides of the aisle. The morning of the breakfast I felt so tense that I couldn't get my eggs down. I needn't have worried. Jack knocked 'em dead, outlining his social and economic programs, including the abolition of racial — and any other — segregation in the workplace and elsewhere. Halfway through his remarks, my relief turned to exultation. Winding up by enunciating his plan for church-state relations, my friend got a standing ovation. I raised my eyes to heaven. That son of a gun could charm friend and foe alike! Not only had we rearranged the rules of the John Carroll Society, we also had delivered a timely, valuable exposition of Kennedy's thinking and programs.

But could he also capture the imagination of those not so predisposed to a Catholic in the White House? Shortly thereafter, the philanthropic Jewish women's organization Hadassah, holding a gala dinner in Washington, invited Senator Kennedy to be the main speaker. Thoughtfully asking that I give the invocation, they sat me next to Jack. Condemning the massacre of Jews by the Nazis, Kennedy made an eloquent plea for worldwide recognition of human and civil rights as a means of rectifying America's own economic obstacles to women. As he spoke, the growing enthusiasm was palpable. In my experience, women are far more responsive to speeches than men, and these ladies didn't hold back. By the time he wound up, Jack had made them believers. The noisy, prolonged ovation convinced me that John Kennedy could one day well be president. If the guy could transform a room of Jewish females into something akin to a Catholic sodality, anything was possible.

We would soon find out. When it came to capturing the Democratic nomination for the presidency, John Fitzgerald Kennedy flashed all of his peerless political skills, not to mention those of his highly attractive, energetic family, who galvanized for an all-out campaign. Still, when it came to combating the ongoing anti-Catholic rancor, Jack, confident, cool, matter-of-fact, was invariably his own best advocate. A case in point was the May 10, 1960, West Virginia Democratic primary battle against Hubert Humphrey. Ninety-five percent Protestant, the state was a crucial litmus test for the Catholic candidate. And when he won, by an astounding 60 percent, it was a shot across the bow that perhaps a Catholic could get elected president — if, that is, the Catholic press would leave him alone.

The West Virginia victory was clouded when Robert Hoyt, editor of the Diocese of Kansas City's *Catholic Reporter* (precursor to *The National Catholic Reporter*), sent a long telegram threatening to publish a front-page editorial accusing Kennedy of being an unfit Catholic candidate due to his stand on birth control. In addition, he demanded an immediate apology. (No theologian, Kennedy, during one of hundreds of campaign stops, most likely made an inadvertent statement contrary to the Church teachings about contraception.) Caught off guard, Jack instantly sent me a copy of the telegram.

I immediately called Bishop John P. Cody, the Bishop of Kansas City. Assuring him that Kennedy did not support contraception, I asked that he restrain Hoyt from going ahead with his threatened denunciation until we could formulate a reasonable reply. But the bishop's hands were tied, having given Hoyt, as a symbol of his confidence in the Catholic laity, complete control of the paper. Desperately, I turned to Boston Cardinal Richard Cushing, who didn't let me down. Beating Hoyt to the draw, he closed the rift between the candidate and Catholic voters by issuing an unswerving statement assuring Catholics that Kennedy supported the teaching of the Church.

Chalk it up to my paratrooper training in the 82nd Airborne, but when it came to the Catholic question, my advice to Jack was always: the best defense is an offense. He heeded that counsel on September 12, 1960, when he addressed the Greater Houston Ministerial Association, three hundred Protestant ministers, at Houston's Rice Hotel. The topic: "How can a faithful Catholic discharge the duties of a President of the United States?" His decision to meet the question head-on was vintage Kennedy: courageous and politically expedient. And Houston was the perfect forum. While refuting bigoted assertions about Catholics in public office, he could also reaffirm his freedom from religious influences in the official performance of his presidential duties. His first attempt to publicly make the point, a 1959 *Look* magazine interview, had drawn the ire of both Catholics and Protestants. "Whatever one's religion in his private life," he told the reporter, "for the officeholder nothing takes precedence over his oath to uphold the Constitution and all its parts — including the First Amendment and the strict separation of church and state."

To ensure the Houston speech wouldn't boomerang among faithful Catholics, Kennedy speechwriter Ted Sorensen consulted me, in general terms, about the planned remarks. I, in turn, suggested he run them by Maryland's Jesuit Father John Courtney Murray in Maryland, an expert on church-state relations (the leading U.S. theologian at the Second Vatican Council, he would be principal author of the Declaration on Religious Freedom). My aim was two-fold: assure that the content reflected proper interpretation of theological positions; and introduce Murray to Kennedy's team as their theological point man. Unfortunately, personalities didn't mesh. And, up against a deadline, Kennedy's staff (also advising the candidate) was forced to read the speech over the phone to Father Murray as well as Pittsburgh Bishop John Wright, another preeminent U.S. theologian. Though both gave guarded thumbs-ups, I instantly regretted not insisting that each be sent copies of the actual address. Vetting a speech this important over the phone definitely wasn't smart politics.

Moreover, when I was told that John Cogley, editor of *Commonweal*, had also been coaching Kennedy on Catholic doctrine, my Irish really got up. Too many conflicting views make for too many problems.

In Houston, Jack began by asking the three hundred Protestant ministers "to judge me on the basis of my record of fourteen years in Congress, on my declared stands against an ambassador to the Vatican... unconstitutional aid to parochial schools... any boycott of the public schools which I, myself, attended." He then reiterated the evolution of his thinking, leading him to oppose, as "unconstitutional," vouchers for children in private schools — a position loudly supported by Boston Cardinal Richard Cushing. "I won't take a nickel," the Cardinal liked to proclaim, "from the government for our schools." Given Boston's supportive Catholic population and plethora of Sisters and religious Brothers eager to staff classrooms at low salaries, it was an easy stand for Cushing to take.

Though Kennedy claimed that his change of mind was the result of an intellectual evolution, the truth was far more straightforward: Jack believed that championing the idea would cost him the election. (The Church argued that Catholic parents, as U.S. citizens, deserved, as a service to the nation, state aid for their children's education. My own position turned more on principle than priority: even a nickel or dime from the government would establish that parochial schools, serving the common good, saved taxpayers money. Complicating the issue, Texas Senator Lyndon Johnson, equally hell-bent on the White House, having decided to back the legislation, pulled out when Kennedy did not.)

In the end, Jack promised the Houston ministers — and nation — that his duties as president would transcend his religious beliefs, adding the tactically appealing caveat that if a political decision ever conflicted with his Catholic beliefs, he would resign. From my perspective, Kennedy went overboard in emphasizing his independence from the Catholic Church, essentially promising an arm's-length manifesto as well as a wall of separation between himself and the Church — starting with aid to private schools. Despite my personal misgivings, Kennedy's speech was a box-office hit — especially among fair-minded Protestants — across the country. As for the Houston ministers, former House Speaker (and Baptist) Sam Rayburn summed it up best: "He ate 'em blood raw!" Most importantly, Kennedy made his views on church-state relations perfectly, publicly clear: "I believe in an America that is officially neither Catholic, Protestant, nor Jewish," he had said, "where no public official either requests or accepts instruction on public policy from the Pope, the National Council of Churches, or any other ecclesiastical source." Upon finishing, he turned the tables on his unsuspecting audience, asking how they felt about school integration. Not one minister responded.

Meetings Kept Secret

I never gave up on the idea of the federal government supporting private schools, discovering a few months after Jack took office that I had an ally in Abraham Ribicoff, the Secretary of the Department of Health, Education, and Welfare. Though Jack felt handcuffed, he allowed members of his inner circle, behind the scenes, to investigate the feasibility of public funding behind the scenes. Secretary Ribicoff, eager to understand my position, came to see me at the chancery. We hit it off immediately. "Your name is Hannan," Ribicoff said. "In Hartford, I have a very good friend whose name is Mrs. Mary Hannan Mahoney. I asked her to be my secretary of state but she turned me down. As president of the National Conference of Catholic Women, Mary wanted to avoid any conflict of interest. Are you related?"

"Very closely," I replied with a smile. "She's my only sister."

"Well, if you're like your sister," Ribicoff said, "you're all right."

To ensure secrecy, Kennedy's special advisor, Ted Sorensen, and I held our first meeting at Ribicoff's Georgetown home. Surprisingly, Ribicoff, harboring a deep personal interest in the matter, favored government support for public and private schools. The son of a father who attended synagogue daily, Ribicoff naturally wanted Jewish Yeshiva schools to equally benefit from federal money. Sorensen, meanwhile, open-minded but acutely conscious of the widespread opposition, was interested in exploring novel approaches to make vouchers politically palatable. After a lengthy discussion of possible initiatives, I got the impression that Kennedy might eventually launch a massive educational campaign, aimed especially at the poor, including poor Catholics. Though Ribicoff subsequently briefed the President — as he swam in the White House pool — nothing of substance, alas, came from that or subsequent meetings. (My relationship with Ribicoff, however, paid huge dividends when, as Archbishop of New Orleans, I sought federal money for badly needed senior housing.)

When it came to Ted Sorensen and the rest of Kennedy's fabled cabinet and advisors, writer David Halberstam's description of the lot as "the best and the brightest" was not an exaggeration. Because Jack demanded so much from himself, he expected the same from those around him. Sorenson, whom I always liked, was Kennedy's main sounding board, his alter ego, if you like. In fact he took up so much of Kennedy's time that Jackie, once in the White House, began to resent — even dislike — Ted. In her mind, Sorensen was the quintessence of politics, which, when it came to her husband's attention, was always her biggest rival. Though she might not be able to control Jack's time during the day, the nights were her call. When the First Lady was in Washington, the small, exclusive dinner parties that she hosted upstairs in the White House family residence for family and the couple's closest pals, like *Newsweek* editor Ben Bradlee and his wife Toni, were the most sought-after invitation in town — albeit one that apparently never showed up in Ted's mailbox. Jackie got even with her "rival" by never including Sorenson at even one of her chic, after-work soirees. Following Kennedy's death, however, she showed up at a reception for Ted at the Department of State where she was particularly gracious to Sorensen.

Aside from Sorenson, I particularly admired and enjoyed writer and special assistant Arthur Schlesinger as well as the quick, practical, witty mind of press secretary Pierre Salinger. Perhaps my personal favorite in the "Kennedy Army," however, was Sargent Shriver who, in charge of the first Peace Corps initiative, turned it into a smashing success. Choosing the Philippines as the Peace Corps' first project in 1961, Sarge personally traveled to the country to enlist the active help of local Catholic priests. Even before the first Peace Corps volunteer arrived, he had a strong, dependable substructure in place. From that hands-on start, a great organization was born which, within two years, was thriving. At one point, expressing my admiration for his achievements, I asked Sarge why it took the U.S. Army four years to develop the skills and spirit of underprivileged soldiers, while he took only two. "Why can you do in two years with less money," I asked, "what it takes the Army four years to do with more?" "I'll tell you why," he laughed. "We have a deadline. Congress only gives us (the Peace Corps) two years in appropriations."

As Kennedy's seemingly unstoppable presidential campaign accelerated, so did our conversations about the impact of Catholic issues on politics — civil rights for African-Americans, economic rights for women — the list grew weekly except now, with Kennedy always out of Washington, the questions also came via staff members. Presuming, naturally, that it was still Jack, personally, requesting information, I was stunned, deplaning in Dallas, to be accosted by three staffers, spitting enquiries. And I didn't like it a bit. "No one is supposed to know about my agreement with him," I lectured, "Our conversations are supposed to be confidential."

The climax of the 1960 campaign was a series of four television debates between Kennedy and Nixon beginning in late September. Having answered so many questions for JFK's staff, I listened with a keen ear for the topics that we had covered. What I saw, however, trumped anything that was said. Kennedy, cool, relaxed, and tan, looked like he'd just stepped off a sailboat in Hyannis. Confident, charming, sufficiently aggressive, Jack was made for television, while Nixon, pale and sweaty, obviously wanted to be anywhere but on camera. "Why in the name of God," I thought, "didn't any of Nixon's people check with TV experts to make sure he looked good?"

Actually, I liked Nixon. During the 1950s, transparently interested in someday running for president, he made a point of stopping by the chancery to say hello. And he was always unfailingly polite. Though subliminally hopeful, I'm sure, that he might snag a new supporter, I sensed that what really drew him was an interest in religion, which he liked to discuss. And his wife, Patricia Ryan Nixon, whose father was Catholic, provided just the opener for this guarded man to muse about God with a priest. Like many things pertaining to Nixon, his own beliefs were paradoxical: though raised a Quaker and pacifist, he loved boasting about his naval service during World War II. Despite a strong Quaker presence in nearby Montgomery County, Maryland, I believe that Nixon was conflicted over whether or not to attend Quaker services. In fact, I've always felt that the reason Nixon never made an issue of Kennedy's religion during the presidential campaign was because of his own — fearing if he did that the press might unearth some of his own faith's controversial beliefs. However, no amount of prayer could save Dick Nixon during that first debate. Initial impressions are paramount, and Kennedy's panache, quick intelligence, and wit left the brooding, stern, professorial Richard Nixon in need of a charisma implant.

In my world, meanwhile, the campaign "in the pews" was completely straightforward. Politically, the Church always remains neutral. In D.C., Archbishop O'Boyle forbade pastors to put anything in parish bulletins that directly supported the Catholic candidate, a stance echoed by Cardinal Spellman in New York. As editor of the *Catholic Standard*, I wrote nothing that favored — or criticized — either candidate, despite the urgings of Catholic Democrats: "Why don't you come out for him?" (Even colleagues, Catholic bishops, priests, and laity weren't above — especially after Jack was elected — making requests and offering opinions on the President's programs, always with the implication that I should do something about them.) "I suggest," I invariably replied, "that you speak to your congressman about it." One volunteered observation, however, left me feeling inadequate. Monsignor Robert Peters of Peoria (later to become the president of the Catholic Press Association) sought me out to discuss the possibility — based on some of the President's programs — of a "rift" between the hierarchy and young priests, not to mention the laity. Thanking him, I pointed out that he was talking to the wrong man. "You're completely overestimating my influence," I said. "You and other members of the Catholic press are the ones with influence. What do you expect me to do?"

"Stay friendly with the Kennedys," he replied. And I did — though far more out of genuine affection than religious politics.

In the end, Jack could not ask Catholics to vote for him simply because they were Catholic, since doing so would contradict what he had stated in Houston. Nor could he expect Catholic congressmen to make his case to voters. JFK's challenge was to portray himself not only as Catholic, but favorable in every dimension: a capable, forward-looking president who would improve the lives of all citizens.

By Tuesday, November 9, 1960, Election Day, I was convinced that John Kennedy would prevail. Voting early at St. Patrick's School, I dashed to the chancery to avoid phone calls. The night that the Kennedy family came to power, I was at home with my own: my mother, father, and brother (Bill). Each week, one Hannan boy spent a designated evening with our parents, and election night was mine — though Bill showed up hoping to celebrate history-in-the-making. He wasn't disappointed. Even though it was an extremely close race in terms of the popular vote — a difference of fewer than 120,000 votes out of 68 million cast — it looked like Illinois, with a mighty assist from heavily pro-Kennedy Cook County (Chicago), would go to Kennedy, giving a clear Electoral College victory. As soon as the election results flashed on the TV screen, everyone let out a loud whoop. Suddenly, Bill stopped us mid-cheer. "We ought to say a prayer together," he said. "Will you lead us, Phil?" I very willingly did so.

For my parents, especially my father who had suffered discrimination and bias because he was Catholic, the historic news rendered relief more than euphoria. Finally, an American could not be denied the presidency because he was a Catholic — or a Jew. Kennedy's election had settled that issue forever. (Nixon, meanwhile, did his own favor for the country — for which I praised him — by not contesting the lopsided Cook County vote, feeling that a long, drawn-out fight would damage the nation.)

In every way, God seemed to be blessing John and Jacqueline Kennedy. On November 25, 1960, sixteen days after the presidential election, John F. Kennedy, Jr., joined his older sister, Caroline Bouvier Kennedy, born in 1957. His successful arrival in the world was a great relief to Jackie who, before Caroline, had suffered the painful loss of two other babies: a miscarriage in 1955, followed by a stillborn daughter, delivered via Caesarean section, the following year — the same time that Jack came close to becoming the Democratic vice presidential candidate on a ticket with Adlai Stevenson. Happily, the glamorous couple had kept trying — though the outcome of their final pregnancy broke both of their hearts, when a second son, Patrick Bouvier Kennedy, born in August of 1963, lived only thirty-nine hours, dying less than four months before his father the following November. Following Patrick's death, I sent a note of condolence to the couple. In response, the President wrote a brief letter, expressing his disappointment and grief over the loss of their baby.

August 15, 1963

Dear Bishop Hannan:
    You were kind indeed to think of us at this very difficult time. Your message was a comfort to me and my family and we are very grateful to you.

Sincerely,
John Kennedy

THE WHITE HOUSE
WASHINGTON

August 15, 1963

Dear Bishop Hannan:

You were kind indeed to think of us at
this very difficult time. Your message was
a comfort to me and my family and we are
very grateful to you.

Sincerely,

The Most Reverend Philip M. Hannan
Auxiliary Bishop of Washington
1721 Rhode Island Avenue, NW.
Washington 36, D. C.

Letter from President Kennedy in thanks for consolation after the
loss of their newborn baby

With the presidency won, attention turned to the inauguration. When it came to the religious component, Kennedy faced a ticklish test. Determined not to slight any religious group, he nevertheless fell heir to a sticky situation created by Eisenhower. When Ike was elected, Greece was being assailed by a Communist rebellion. Showing his support, the new president invited a Greek Orthodox bishop — in addition to a rabbi and a Protestant and Catholic clergyman — to give an inaugural invocation. By 1960, however, with the Greek crisis having subsided, most felt it unnecessary to include a Greek Orthodox bishop. The final decision fell to the subcommittee of the Committee for the Inauguration, where because of my familiarity with Kennedy's campaign staff, I served. Aiming for clarity, we went straight to the source. "Follow Eisenhower's precedent," Kennedy judiciously decreed, adding that each of the four were to observe a strict, two-minute prayer limit.

It was my touchy task to tell Cardinal Richard Cushing, who had married Jack and Jackie in 1953, that these politico-liturgical rules included him. Though fervently making my case, it didn't sink in. (Our personal friendship, frankly, made it even harder to exert serious influence on what and how much the Cardinal could say about a Kennedy. To him, they were family. When Jack was president, Cushing checked in with me once a week. "How's John doing?" Naturally, I always reported that he was very popular. "Good, good. Glad to hear it.")

In the final analysis, Cardinal Cushing was simply irrepressible. When the Kennedys heard I had a recalcitrant high priest on my hands, the alarmed president-elect sent two further requests emphasizing that I make certain that Cushing understood the family's desired time limitation. Passing along both messages, I could only pray.

The other thing that neither a Kennedy nor anyone else could control was Mother Nature. The morning before the inaugural, I woke up to sheets of snow and a slew of problems; namely, getting Cardinal Cushing from Boston to Washington where he would stay with the Archbishop. With trains off schedule and radio and TV reports useless, no one could give me an ETA for my distinguished guests. Moreover, hotels were a mess. Alarmed, Archbishop O'Boyle ordered Monsignor Thomas Lyons, the Archdiocese's Superintendent of Education, and me to his house to plot a course of action. Setting out in my car, I quickly abandoned it in favor of walking through the rapidly piling snow. By the time I stomped through the Archbishop's front door to find Monsignor Lyons, my face was frozen red. When a round of phone calls convinced us that Cushing's train was probably in New York, we called Cardinal Spellman to rally him to our cause. But no go. Undaunted, we enlisted Manhattan Police Commissioner Stephen Kennedy, whose squad cars arrived at the train station just in time to watch the Cardinal's train pull out for Washington.

A man of action, Archbishop O'Boyle decided to go to Union Station and simply wait for his close friend to show. Piling into the car, we made it a block before skidding to a halt. Taking up the snowy slack, Monsignor Lyons ushered us into his four-wheel-drive vehicle and, turning sidewalks into roads, masterfully maneuvered the five blocks to Union Station. Once there, we sat down and waited... and waited... and waited. Finally, at 5:00 a.m. the train bearing the Cardinal, along with a close friend's four, young, unexpected daughters, pulled in. The Cardinal, scant hours from playing a lead role in the high drama of his life, was totally whipped. Though determined to present the special prayer that he had composed for Kennedy, attending the inaugural parade afterwards he declared would be out of the question. Thrusting his gold presidential box ticket into my palm, he insisted I go. Though I happily agreed, the parade felt eons away. First, we had to find the girls a place to sleep. Deciding that the good Sisters of Georgetown Visitation Academy might offer accommodations, I was assigned to make it happen. Astounded to get a call with a request from the Cardinal himself, the Sisters sprang into action, insisting I drop off my charges on the way to the rectory. By the time I walked in my own door, it was after eight.

Like millions, I watched the inaugural ceremony on television — watched, that is, as everything that could go wrong, almost did. The podium caught fire (an errant electrical cord)... sun-blinded, poet laureate Carl Sandberg couldn't read his poem... and Cardinal Richard Cushing, ignoring not only me but the President of the United States, threw caution, and time, to the wind. His prayer, this decades-long culmination of dreaming, planning, and prayerful labor, wasn't about to get short shrift. And so, the good Cardinal, leadoff hitter, took his place at the plate and started swinging in excruciatingly slow motion.

"In this year ... of Our Lord," he began deliberately, his acutely nasal, Boston tone even scratchier than usual ... "nineteen hundred ... and sixty-one," he continued, wringing every iota of drama from every syllable, letter... "we ask Thee, Almighty God, to enlighten us." He paused. "That we may know, as men"... pause... "our personal responsibilities"... pause... "that we may know, as Americans"... pause... "our political"... pause... "social"... pause... "and humanitarian responsibilities"... pause... "that we may know, as citizens of the world, our global responsibilities to ourselves and our fellow men; that we may know, as children of God, our responsibilities to mankind...."

Though Cardinal Cushing's six hundred twenty-nine-word invocation contained fewer than half those of the Inaugural Address, he spoke twice as long, repeating, at least four times, syllable by deadly syllable ... "On this ... the twentieth day of January"... pause... "one thousand"... pause... "nine hundred"... pause... "and sixty-one years after the birth of Christ...."

Sitting in the rectory, I stared helplessly at the television screen as each of my suggestions, instructions, and warnings washed down the drain. "Mission not accomplished, Hannan," I thought. "Jack must be seething." (The next day, the *Washington Post* excused his performance with uncharacteristic benevolence: "Richard Cardinal Cushing, Catholic Archbishop of Boston, pronounced the invocation, one of extraordinary length." In retrospect, Cushing's stentorian proclivities may well have been the main reason why Jackie chose me to deliver the eulogy at Jack's funeral. She wanted control and, as the inaugural ceremony made clear, no one could rein in the Cardinal.)

Inaugural Address

In contrast, Kennedy's Inaugural address was an oratorical masterpiece, the equal of anything ever written by Jefferson or Lincoln. His staff would tell me later that Kennedy resented speculation that Ted Sorensen had written it for him. Though Sorenson undoubtedly contributed several resonant phrases to the finished work, the thoughts and expressions were pure Kennedy, a past master at oratorical magic. He deserved full credit. Consider, for instance, the phrase: "Let the word go forth from this time and place." Would any other American president have dared to employ such imperialistic words, matching those of the Declaration of Independence? And even years later, I wonder what the reaction of today's courts would be to the speech's pronounced spiritual language to quietly, but effectively, speak for all mankind. Kennedy couldn't have been more emphatic about the need for religious convictions in the work of government: "Knowing that, here on earth, God's work must truly be our own." (He once let slip that, post-White House, he might look to be involved with the European Union.)

The ceremony over, I quickly walked to the Presidential reviewing stand on Pennsylvania Avenue, cleared of ice and snow by Army flamethrowers, presenting my ticket to a security officer. Apparently, I was the only guest to arrive on foot since my presence, as I threaded past others to my seat, was greeted with loud whispers: "Who is he?" Their collective curiosity further peaked when, spotting my face, the new president of the United States waved me over to shake hands. The presidential section, epitomizing the excitement of the new administration, rocked with energy as noisy, exuberant Kennedys and their friends yelled to pals in the parade. When veterans from the fabled PT 109 (boat), commanded by Kennedy during World War II, marched by, the cheers, led by Sargent Shriver really exploded. In the eye of this joyous storm, a happy, serene, Jackie Kennedy, wearing the elegant, daring sand-colored dress and pillbox hat that would change the course of American fashion, sat piquant and unforgettable — apparently to everyone. Stopping afterwards to cheer up an ill, elderly nun, I started describing the parade. "Forget that," she interrupted. "What did Jackie wear?" "A 'pillbox' hat," I offered. "What color?" "Umm, a light one," I fumbled. "Sorry, Bishop, but you're no help."

Before the inauguration, Kennedy had wryly announced that, symbolic of his dedication to the office of the president, he would be at his desk "by the crack of nine" the morning after taking the oath. And he was. I can vouch for it because his first call from the Oval Office — as I later discovered — was to me.

"Well, we certainly got prayed on enough," he greeted, cutting to the Cardinal Cushing chase.

Defending the Cardinal was useless. "Mr. President, by the way, I certainly like the sound of that title," I said, laughing, "no one will ever recall that long-winded prayer; while everyone in the world will remember your magnificent address. No inaugural address can match it. We'd have to go back to the Gettysburg Address to find something comparable. We — I — am so very proud of you. People will be quoting those words for generations." (Little did I know I'd be doing exactly that at his funeral less than three years later.) My praise, apparently, caught Kennedy off-guard. He seemed both genuinely

surprised and touched by my sincere words of appreciation. Thanking me
profusely, he repeated again and again how much my observations and glowing review meant to him. (Though the President didn't bring up Cardinal
Cushing again, others didn't hesitate. For weeks afterwards, I was cornered
by people asking if the Cardinal's repetitiveness resulted from having lost his
place. Everyone, it seems, had something to say — most of it not good. Only
his staunchest friends tried to applaud his effort.) Two weeks later, the President sent a short, handwritten note.

February 7, 1961

Your Excellency:
    I was especially grateful for the generous message you sent me after
my inauguration.
    It means a great deal to me to have your thoughtful response to the
themes that I attempted to convey in my inaugural address. Your advice
and counsel during the past years have been unfailingly helpful to me.

With every good wish,

Sincerely,
John Kennedy

Once in the Oval Office, security arrangements had to be instituted to
ensure that America's first Catholic president could worship in safety. And
when it came to practicing his faith as president, Kennedy always struck a
careful balance. For starters, any church that he and the First Lady attended
had to be integrated. Going to Sunday Mass, however, posed a problem for
the Secret Service. Though only six blocks from the White House, St. Matthew's Cathedral was too large and always full; resulting in the Secret Service's
preference for St. Stephen Martyr Church at 25th and Pennsylvania Avenue, a
smaller structure far easier to guard and control. Eschewing the custom of previous Protestant presidents, it was not officially announced that St. Stephen's
would be "the President's church" — the Secret Service wanting to ward off
undue publicity as to his whereabouts on Sunday mornings. Their demands
were rigorously observed. Gone were the senatorial days of Jack and Jackie
casually showing up on Sunday at Holy Trinity in Georgetown where Jack,
helping take up the collection, endeared himself to many as a "a regular guy."
    For his part, Archbishop O'Boyle decreed that no pictures be taken of
the President with a "favorite" priest or bishop. The Church did not want to
be seen as taking advantage of the President for its own benefit. Moreover,
we wanted to avoid the implication that the President was being "controlled"
by the Church. Consequently, I informed the President's astute public relations man, Pierre Salinger, that when the President did come to St. Matthew's

THE WHITE HOUSE
WASHINGTON

February 7, 1961

Your Excellency:

I was especially grateful for the generous message which
you sent me after my inauguration.

It means a great deal to me to have your thoughtful
response to the themes which I attempted to convey in
my inaugural address. Your advice and counsel during
the past years have been unfailingly helpful to me.

With every good wish,

Sincerely,

The Most Reverend Philip M. Hannan
Archdiocese of Washington
Chancery Office
1721 Rhode Island Avenue, N.W.
Washington 6, D.C.

Letter of thanks to me after the presidential inauguration

Cathedral for the annual Red Mass (or any special occasion), the Archbishop would neither meet his limousine nor accompany him into the Cathedral. Instead, a layman would greet Kennedy at the curb and walk him into the Cathedral where — no cameras allowed — he would be greeted by the Archbishop. "Mr. Salinger," I said, "please tell Mr. Kennedy that these arrangements are the decision of the Archbishop, not the President." Salinger couldn't have been happier since our new protocol meshed perfectly with Kennedy's needs. (Until November 23, 1963, a day after the assassination, and two days before his funeral, a Mass had never been celebrated in the White House, since doing so would have stirred up a politically damaging ruckus.)

Less than three months into the exciting, new Kennedy administration, reality hit. The Bay of Pigs — an ill-fated, near-laughable attempt by CIA operatives to overthrow Fidel Castro in April 1961 — cast an early questionable cloud over the Kennedy presidency. A few weeks before the attempted invasion, a Cuban friend asked that I secure Mass kits for a handful of paratroop chaplains. Asking no questions, I complied, throwing in a couple of medals of St. Michael the Archangel, patron saint of the 82nd Airborne Division, and praying that he'd protect these chaplains just as he had the 82nd. The day before the invasion, my Cuban friend telephoned again, saying that plans were going ahead. "How do you know?" I asked in amazement, knowing our call was unguarded.

"A friend in Miami just called to tell me." Did everyone in the world know?

Details of a supposedly top secret attack being bandied about by people on the phone was not a good sign. And, alas, I was right. The mission was a miserable failure with the paratroop chaplains captured immediately upon landing. But, then, the whole operation was so poorly planned that I had a hard time believing the Army had been properly briefed on the situation. In fact, I was so personally disgusted with the failure of the Bay of Pigs that I didn't even ask the Kennedy staff what went so terribly wrong. They, meanwhile, never even mentioned it.

The Bay of Pigs nightmare could hardly have occurred at a worse time, calling into question the decision-making and prudence in military matters of the youngest commander-in-chief in American history. The fiasco led indirectly, seventeen months later, to the Cuban missile crisis — a ten-day face-off with Russia over the installation of nuclear missiles, aimed at the United States, on Cuban soil. Before then, however, Nikita Khrushchev would take his devastatingly public international swipe at our inexperienced president during the June 1961 summit in Vienna. Though the trip is best remembered for Kennedy's unsuccessful face-off with the Soviet premier, it stands out in my mind for quite another reason. Kennedy disdained corny showmanship, refusing, unlike most politicians, for instance, to wear any hats even when a Stetson might have garnered a few Texas votes. He was equally adamant when it came to religious trappings in public appearances.

So it was unfortunate indeed when Sunday Mass in Vienna turned into the ceremonial equivalent of popping a clown hat on Kennedy's head. Scheduled to attend Mass in Vienna's grand, historic Cathedral of St. Stephen, Jack and Jackie were met at the entrance by Cardinal Franz König, who, thrilled about having the President of the United States on his territory, showed up decked out in full regalia, trailed by a cross bearer and two acolytes with candles aflame. Given Jack's reluctance to call attention to his Catholicism, it couldn't have been a worse miscalculation. Already squirming over how this would play back home, an embarrassed Kennedy was then led up the Cathedral's main aisle by the proud Cardinal, who directed him to sit in a special chair in the sanctuary. Having no recourse, the President complied, sitting there like a window display during what may well have been the longest Mass of his life.

This ill-fated incident was squarely on the minds of Kennedy staffers in the summer of 1962 (June 28–July 1) as they planned the President's trip to Mexico. Even before takeoff, it was a journey fraught with church-state land mines due to the Mexican government's persecution of the Church and subsequent confiscation of property, actions that ignited widespread debate in the American media. Those contending that the Church didn't legally exist in Mexico felt the American presidential presence at Mass would be a grave breach of diplomacy, eviscerating the visit's entire purpose. Practicing Catholics, on the other hand, felt that a failure to attend, besides being a serious sin and grave renunciation of Kennedy's faith, would also be a rebuff to Mexican Catholics and an insult to the Blessed Virgin Mary. Deluged with calls, our chancery couldn't begin to satisfy everyone. Kennedy, meanwhile, while viewing the trip as an opportunity to stand up against religious oppression, had always planned to fulfill the expectations of the Mexican faithful by attending Sunday Mass at the Shrine honoring the Blessed Mother — as it happened, the wrong church. Though the President's office had requested Mass in the Mexico City Cathedral, plans were ultimately moved to the famous Shrine of Our Lady of Guadalupe, popular not only with Mexican Catholics but all of Latin America.

Determined to avoid the royal Catholic treatment foisted on him in Vienna, Jack asked Ralph Dungan, the Kennedy staffer in charge of "Catholic questions," to call me. "Do you have any friends in the Cardinal's office in Mexico City?" he asked. "The President would like to attend Mass at the Shrine, but definitely doesn't want a Vienna repeat." I got on the phone to Mexican Auxiliary Bishop Alonso Manuel Escalante, educated at the University of Notre Dame, making it clear that the President, wanting no special attention, preferred to sit in the front pew, not sanctuary, during Mass. Delighted that the President would be gracing their beloved Shrine, Bishop Escalante agreed to keep a secret.

The rest of the arrangements didn't go so smoothly. Though Kennedy had asked the Archbishop of Mexico City to take care of details concerning his attendance, there had been no response, prompting the President to ask that I send a follow-up. In a letter to Bishop Escalante, I came very much to the point:

June 4, 1962

His Excellency
Most Reverend Alonso Manuel Escalante, M.M.
Superior General
Misioneros de Guadalupe
Balderos 32/610
Mexico 1, D.F.

Your Excellency:

I have been asked to convey a message in the hope that you can possibly find an opportunity to enforce the request, made by the White House, concerning arrangements for the Mass that President Kennedy will attend at the Cathedral of Mexico City during his forthcoming visit to Mexico (June 28 – July 1).

The White House has informed the Archbishop of Mexico City, through the embassy, that the President wishes no arrangements be made to receive him at the doors of the cathedral. He simply wishes to attend a Low Mass (in the cathedral), occupying the first pew. He absolutely does not want any special place be allotted him in the sanctuary. The President would like to attend Mass in the Cathedral of Mexico City just as he attends Mass here in Washington, D.C. — that is, like any other parishioner, sitting in a pew.

I know it will be very difficult for the Church authorities to understand the President's wishes in this matter. However, I feel that you are in a unique position to explain to everyone that they must be carried out. To be precise, he wants to avoid what happened in the Cathedral of St. Stephen in Vienna — the Cardinal meeting him at the cathedral's front door and the President, flanked by two acolytes, being escorted to his place of honor. President Kennedy absolutely does not wish a repetition of this, nor any, special ceremony.

I know that you realize how much it will mean to the Church in Mexico to have our President attend Mass. And since this will not be his last visit to Latin America, we are most anxious that his attendance at Mass be in accordance with his wishes.

With assurances of my gratitude for your kindness in this matter, I remain

Sincerely yours in Christ,
Most Reverend Philip M. Hannan, Chancellor

On the appointed Sunday, Kennedy, accompanied by Jackie (though not the President of Mexico), rode to the Shrine for Mass. To his utter surprise, the crowds lining the route were far larger and more enthusiastic than those who greeted him and Mexico's President upon his arrival. Contrary to negative predictions, the populace heartily endorsed his effort to worship alongside them. His instructions, happily, were followed to the letter, with one hitch. Though I'd made it clear to the Cardinal's office that Kennedy wanted no special attention for the processional, I neglected to mention the recessional. Leaping to take advantage of my lapse, the Cardinal staged a full-flourish-and-retinue recession to accompany Kennedy out of the Shrine — which I

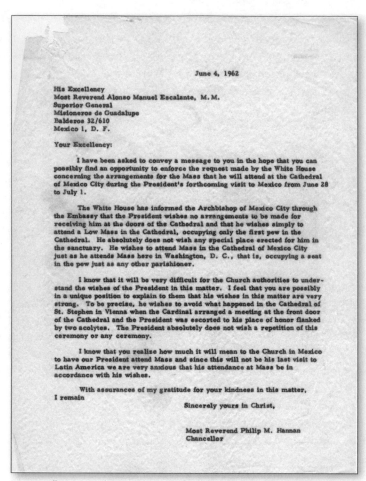

June 4, 1962

His Excellency
Most Reverend Alonso Manuel Escalante, M.M.
Superior General
Misioneros de Guadalupe
Balderos 32/610
Mexico 1, D. F.

Your Excellency:

I have been asked to convey a message to you in the hope that you can possibly find an opportunity to enforce the request made by the White House concerning the arrangements for the Mass that he will attend at the Cathedral of Mexico City during the President's forthcoming visit to Mexico from June 28 to July 1.

The White House has informed the Archbishop of Mexico City through the Embassy that the President wishes no arrangements to be made for receiving him at the doors of the Cathedral and that he wishes simply to attend a Low Mass in the Cathedral, occupying only the first pew in the Cathedral. He absolutely does not wish any special place erected for him in the sanctuary. He wishes to attend Mass in the Cathedral of Mexico City just as he attends Mass here in Washington, D. C., that is, occupying a seat in the pew just as any other parishioner.

I know that it will be very difficult for the Church authorities to understand the wishes of the President in this matter. I feel that you are possibly in a unique position to explain to them that his wishes in this matter are very strong. To be precise, he wishes to avoid what happened in the Cathedral of St. Stephen in Vienna when the Cardinal arranged a meeting at the front door of the Cathedral and the President was escorted to his place of honor flanked by two acolytes. The President absolutely does not wish a repetition of this ceremony or any ceremony.

I know that you realize how much it will mean to the Church in Mexico to have our President attend Mass and since this will not be his last visit to Latin America we are very anxious that his attendance at Mass be in accordance with his wishes.

With assurances of my gratitude for your kindness in this matter, I remain

Sincerely yours in Christ,

Most Reverend Philip M. Hannan
Chancellor

I personally arranged a trip to Mexico for President and Mrs. Kennedy to show solidarity with Catholics there.

never lived down, especially with Ralph Dungan, who delighted in reminding me of my mistake, using the President's own words: "What happened, Ralph," he'd say, mimicking his boss's iconic twang, "to, uh, the ... Plan? The Plan, Ralph?" For my part, I learned the hard way that anything not specifically prohibited, could specifically happen. Bishop Escalante's follow-up note, especially the last paragraph, told the tale:

July 3, 1962

Most Rev. Philip M. Hannan
Chancellor
Chancery Office
1721 Rhode Island Ave., N.W.

Washington, D.C.
USA

Your Excellency:

I arrived here the very day that the President of the United States and Mrs. Kennedy came.

I attended several of the ceremonies and especially the one at the Basilica, where the President heard Mass.

His wishes were followed to the letter, and he was received without ecclesiastical ostentation.

He heard a Low Mass in which the Archbishop spoke a few words and afterwards, together with the Apostolic Delegate, I was able to meet the Kennedys to express my thanks to them for the material and spiritual help that they have given.

Needless to say, they took Mexico by storm. Everybody speaks so nicely of them, of the manner of their talks and of their example, and it is hard to imagine who could have done a better job.

I am enclosing one of the pictures that came out in the newspapers where the Archbishop says goodbye to the Kennedys after Mass at the Basilica.

Sincerely yours in Christ,
+ A. Escalante
Alonso M. Escalante,
Titular Bishop of Sora
Superior General

Four months later, in October 1962, Kennedy was thrust into the most important test of his presidency to date: the Cuban Missile crisis. In a secret agreement, Soviet Premier Nikita Khrushchev and Cuban dictator Fidel Castro conjured up a plan to plant medium-range missiles and intermediate-range ballistic missiles, aimed directly at the United States, on Cuban soil. Though Khrushchev claimed they were solely for the protection of Cuba, American U2 spy planes, flying over the island, reported increasing construction of missile sites as well as the arrival of Soviet specialists. Within the Kennedy Administration, alarm grew to the point where 100,000 troops, including the 82nd and 101st Airborne Divisions and a contingent of Marines, were sent to Florida. This time there would be no repetition of the Bay of Pigs. On October 14, when a U2 plane garnered conclusive pictures of a missile, buildings, and launch pad, the rubber, as they say, met the road. The President and his exhausted staff had to make a decision. Even good Christians praying for peace felt testy: "I'm wearing out my rosary beads," remarked a weary woman exiting St. Patrick's.

COPY

Misioneros de Guadalupe - Seminario de Misiones
                        Balderas 32-610 - Mexico 1, D. F.

                                    July 3rd, 1962

Most Rev. Philip M. Hannan
Chancellor
Chancery Office
1721 Rhode Island Ave. N. W.
Washington 6, D. C.
U. S. A.

Your Excellency:

        I arrived here the very day that the President of the United
States and Mrs. Kennedy came.

        I attended several of the ceremonies and specially the one
at the Basilica, where the President heard Mass.

        His wishes were followed to the letter and he was receiv-
ed without ecclesiastical ostentation.

        He heard a low Mass in which the Archbishop spoke a few
words and afterwards, together with the Apostolic Delegate, I was
able to meet the Kennedys to express my thanks to them for the material and spiritual help that they have given.

        Needless to say, they took Mexico by storm. Everybody
speaks so nicely of them, of the manner of their talks and of their
example, and it is hard to imagine who could have done a better job.

        I am enclosing one of the pictures that came out in the news-
papers where the Archbishop says good-bye to the Kennedys after
Mass at the Basilica.

        Sincerely yours in Christ,

                                    + A. Escalante

                                    Alonso M. Escalante,
                                    Titular Bishop of Sora,
                                    Superior General

Letter from Mexico referencing the trip there by President and Mrs. Kennedy

As well she should have. Ultimately, the Soviet scheme, audacious, reckless, and destructive, placed weapons into Cuban hands capable of obliterating great portions of the United States. As it, strangely, turned out, St. Patrick's Church, school, and rectory, located near the White House, were directly in the epicenter of such a threat; enough so, that one afternoon I got a call from the pastor of Sacred Heart Church, Monsignor John Spence. Never one to pass up a chance to fret, his voice was urgent. "I've got to see you." When he arrived, the Monsignor was a cat on a hot tin roof. "I'm really concerned about a possible atomic bomb attack," he began, "especially since there's no official decision by the President. A fellow who claims to be a bomb expert spoke in our parish hall and said an atomic bomb would wipe out the whole of Washington, especially our area around 16th Street."

"Wait a minute," I said, frantically conjuring up a font of knowledge that I did not possess. "My brother, Tom, an engineer who was at Los Alamos for the first atomic bomb tests as well as those on Bikini Island, told me all about these bomb blasts. And I can assure you," I continued, speculatively, "that you have nothing to worry about."

"How's that?"

"Your church, at 16th and Park Road, is at least three hundred feet higher than the White House, where the bombs, of course, will be aimed. And since the blast goes up and out, the bomb's outward force will hit that long hill separating you from the White House. Did this speaker explain the importance of the bomb blast direction?"

"He didn't say a word about it."

"Well, my advice is to let the President worry about the bomb blast. It will affect neither you nor Sacred Heart." It worked. Calming the man was crucial since, as Superintendent of Education, he was strategically positioned to contaminate teachers and students with his misgivings. Monsignor Spence wasn't alone in his fears. House speaker John McCormack, third in the order of presidential succession, was extremely worried about the Capitol — as well as St. Patrick's, six blocks from the White House, on the same level — being attacked. Were we, he demanded, prepared?

We were indeed. In fact, the Sisters of the Daughters of Charity and their students were as unperturbed as the Rock of Gibraltar. Though discussing bombs and any changes to normal curriculum weren't permitted, every available space in our granite buildings — designated and marked as an official shelter — were piled high with government supplies provided by the government. Every day, literally, tons of medical supplies, canned foods, and enough fresh water to fill a swimming pool were examined and renewed. As I quickly learned, when facing an international crisis, you want the Daughters of Charity in charge and on your side. My pride in them was such that I had to restrain myself from hugging each of these irrepressible daughters of Christ.

Finally, with tensions mounting to a dangerous level, Kennedy decided to talk to the nation — an address I watched with Archbishop O'Boyle and the priests at St. Patrick's. "The purpose of these bases can be none other than to provide a nuclear strike capability against the Western Hemisphere," Kennedy said, condemning the Soviet action as a "deliberate and provocative change in the status quo which cannot be accepted by this country if our courage and commitment are ever to be trusted again by friend or foe." Setting out the conditions for a solution — in essence, "removal of all the missiles forever" — he ended with a dramatic declaration of purpose, "Our goal is not the victory of might, but the vindication of right, not peace at the cost of freedom, but both peace and freedom, here in this hemisphere and around the world. God willing, that goal will be achieved."

The more we heard, the more our enthusiasm mounted. At the end of Kennedy's remarks, the Archbishop jumped up from his chair: "God bless him. That was a historic speech. Let's say some prayers for peace." And we did.

The next day, Khrushchev ordered that the missiles be dismantled and shipped back to Russia. At St. Patrick's, meanwhile, all five Masses were flush with jubilant, relieved, grateful Catholics, many of whom worked for the government. That afternoon, in three hours of Eucharistic Adoration, a culmination of daily prayers, we again gave thanks for the peaceful ending to the crisis. Later, attending the first session of the Second Vatican Council in Rome, I met briefly with Pope John XXIII, who immediately expressed his own thankfulness for the peaceful resolution of the missile crisis. After doing so, he walked me over to his office window, overlooking the Vatican gardens, where a telescope, a gift, sat poised on its tripod. "Look through it," he exclaimed, like a kid with a new toy, "and you can see everyone walking in the garden!"

General J. Lawton (Joe) Collins and Archbishop Hannan

A possible war with Russia, meantime, wasn't the only worrisome conflict on Kennedy's international screen. Also causing sleepless nights was the success of Communist insurgents in Vietnam, then under control of the French. In fact, Kennedy became so concerned that he asked for a demonstration of Army firepower by the 82nd Airborne Division, my former Army unit, in Fort Bragg, North Carolina, more famous for pine woods than jungle. Undaunted, the 82nd pulled off such a thundering display of fireworks that even the Commander in Chief was stunned.

Nevertheless, the Army feared getting the United States involved in a jungle war. General Joseph "Lightning Joe" Collins, head of the Chiefs of Staff and a native of New Orleans who led the breakout from Normandy during World War II, was especially adamant about America staying out of Southeast Asia. After a personal inspection of the situation in Vietnam, Collins invited me to his home to hear the message that he, along with other top military brass present, hoped that I would, privately, convey to New York Cardinal Francis Spellman. A staunch anti-Communist, Spellman was also head of the Military Ordinariate, a position he coveted after being turned down — he was too short — as a Navy Chaplain during World War II. He was also a huge supporter of South Vietnamese President Ngo Dinh Diem, a Catholic whose government, unraveling in 1963, led to a U.S.-backed coup and, ultimately, his assassination. The message that night was clear: Collins and his military colleagues were completely against fighting a jungle war in Vietnam. In the end, however, Collins was ignored. Instead, Kennedy, in the name of protecting the Philippines from falling to the Communists, increased our presence in that part of the world. Joe, meanwhile, ever loyal to his government, never made public his disagreement with President Kennedy.

Bobby Kennedy

Dealing with the President usually meant dealing with Bobby. And Jack's younger sibling — bullheaded, tough as nails, lacking Jack's *savoir faire* and charisma — was his brother's polar opposite. Whereas JFK's enemies frequently viewed his religion as more cultural than religious, the same could not be said for Bobby, who devoutly practiced his Catholic faith, which I credited, in large part, to his wife, Ethel, who never missed Mass. (I liked and admired Ethel, whom I found maternal, charitable, and sensitive to the needs of other members of the Kennedy clan. Once, following a meeting of the Board of Directors of the Kennedy Center, she pulled me aside to privately ask that I "spend some time" with Joan Kennedy, Ted's wife. "The life in Washington is all very new to her," Ethel said. "She'll need some help.")

Bobby Kennedy's religious fervor apparently manifested in prep school. When his roommate, verbally disparaging the Catholic faith, covered up a crucifix in their room, Bobby took everything the kid owned and tossed it out the window. Unlike Jack's even-tempered disposition, Bobby's feelings were lived in the open as he questioned the wisdom of clerical, academic, or administrative decisions on every level. When Bobby finally declared his own presidential candidacy, I wasn't at all certain how his temperament, inevitably compared with Jack's, would play with the public.

As I discovered firsthand, Bobby demanded the same energy back that he gave — and as fast. Having given the Knights of Columbus leadership team the names of several high-ticket donors to solicit, Bobby Kennedy flew into a fury when his people weren't contacted as quickly as he thought they should have been. As the group's spiritual advisor, in charge of securing donors' final cooperation, he called and laid me out: "You mean I gave the Knights all those names," he roared, "and no one has contacted anybody yet?" The Knights got the message — as did I.

Since his office in the FBI building was close to St. Patrick's, I often took matters of minor importance to Bobby instead of the President. He, meanwhile, used me as a sounding board, especially when it concerned questionable religious leaders — and there were plenty — trying to get to the President. In one case, for instance, the patriarch of a small Eastern Rite wrote to the Attorney General, requesting a private meeting with the President. One glance at the letter and I laughed aloud. "Bobby, this 'rite' hasn't been in communion with the pope for centuries! He's a *fakir*."

Some matters, of course, were not so inconsequential. In fact, the only time I ever heard anything pertaining to Jack's supposed extramarital activities (about which I knew nothing), I took it to Bobby. The genesis of the rumor was Jackie Kennedy's famous television tour of the White House in 1962. After completing a much-needed renovation of the interior of 1600 Pennsylva-

THE ATTORNEY GENERAL
WASHINGTON
July 16, 1963

Your Excellency:

Many thanks for your kind letter about the baby. Your prophecy has been duly noted and passed along to the proud mother.

Both Ethel and I are most grateful for your great interest in our family.

Best,

Robert F. Kennedy

His Excellency
The Most Reverend
Philip M. Hannan
Vicar General
Archdiocese of Washington
1721 Rhode Island Avenue N. W.
Washington 36, D. C.

Thank you note from Ethel and Bobby Kennedy relating to the birth of their son Christopher, the eighth of their eleven children

nia Avenue, funded by a private foundation, the First Lady had hosted a highly rated television program, walking viewers through the many improvements, historical and otherwise, that she had made to individual rooms in the White House. Though the President, in a brief appearance, announced that their goal was to double the 1.3 million annual visitors to the mansion, he certainly didn't go overboard in praising his wife for her accomplishments — a *faux pas* noticed even by Archbishop O'Boyle with whom I watched the program. "Jack," he remarked aloud to no one in particular, "you ought to show yourself more supportive of Jackie."

Several months after the TV show, I got an urgent call from the highly respected chancellor of the Archdiocese of Baltimore, Monsignor Joseph Nelligan. "Phil, we have a bad situation at one of our hospitals, Union Memorial," he explained. "A nurse is spreading the word that she had an affair with President Kennedy in the White House, proving it with a detailed description of every piece of furniture in the room she says they used. Can you do something about it?" The following morning I was sitting in the office of the Attorney General, located in the FBI Office Building, telling him the story. Writing down the nurse's name, Bobby stared at it momentarily. "I don't recognize the name at all," he said, "but I can assure you that the family neither employed — nor knows — her. I'll investigate immediately."

The next day, Bobby called. "This woman never even met the President," he reported. "The FBI investigation discovered that she memorized all the furniture in the White House by watching Jackie's White House TV tour. They have no relationship. Rest assured, we gave her a stern lecture about her actions." Immediately, I passed the news on to the Monsignor, who was palpably relieved. I, meanwhile, with no reason to believe otherwise, didn't give it another thought. Could Bobby have been protecting, covering for his brother? Frankly, it never even occurred to me. Why would he risk telling a story that could be so easily checked by me (or the press)? Whatever may have happened between Kennedy and this woman, the President's moral flaws, which I discovered after his death, proved injurious collectively, to public morality, and privately, to Jackie Kennedy.

Bobby and Ethel were always generous about volunteering their Hickory Hill estate in Vienna, Virginia, for charitable events, like the fund-raisers for their "adopted" parish, Our Lady of Victory on MacArthur Boulevard in Washington, D.C. Besides opening up the house and spacious lawn, guests could count on mingling with the healthy assortment of donkeys, dogs, cats, and hamsters roaming the six-acre property strewn with footballs, baseballs, basketballs, and gloves. Walking into one typical benefit, I was confronted with the normal bedlam: a little boy, clinging to a donkey's bridle, being chased by a frantic mother who didn't know the animal's front from back; a gaggle of enthusiastic women, desperately trying to organize games; a lone, wandering maid, baffled as to who needed the most help first. In the midst of this happy chaos stood Ethel Kennedy, calm as a praying saint. "I'm delighted you came," she greeted. "You're probably wondering where all of this stuff comes from. Every time Bobby takes a trip he comes back with a special gift for all of us. As you can see, he makes many trips."

The British would have euphemistically called Bobby's kids "unusually lively." And, in fact, he was very indulgent with them. Any normal rules, like picking up after themselves, seemed suspended for Bobby's brood, who left such duties to the overburdened maids who were constantly quitting. At one point, Bobby and Ethel decided their children would attend Our Lady of Victory School in Washington, D.C. As parents, of course, they expected the school to provide all the services that their kids required, including adequate space for recreation, which the church sorely lacked. Consequently, there was a lot of head-butting between Bobby and the pastor, Monsignor Hess, who, also from a wealthy family, wasn't about to throw around money to please a high-profile family — or anyone for that matter. According to his assistant, Monsignor Edward Hermann, the Monsignor, even on the hottest days, refused to turn on the air conditioner. Personally, I thought the pastor did as much as he could to satisfy Bobby's demands for extra recreation space, but he wasn't about to buy extra land at the drop of, well, a parent. As a result, Bobby and Ethel sent at least one child to St. Alban's, an Episcopal school, which boasted better recreational opportunities. That experiment lasted only a year before one Kennedy boy, having expanded his vocabulary with a handful of vulgar words, was returned forthwith to Our Lady of Victory.

Nevertheless, Bobby's hands-on, often overbearing, attitude continued to vex Monsignor Hess. If one of their children was sick (as David, in particular, often was), perhaps missing First Communion with his class, the Kennedys would call asking that we provide a First Communion ceremony specifically for them. And we did. The whole family would attend Mass at St. Patrick's where, afterwards, they'd be served breakfast in the rectory. Was it a special privilege? Certainly. But Monsignor Herrmann, the associate who later became Bishop of Columbus, always assured us that the Church was striving to meet the needs of all its parishioners. And since he was my go-between with the pastor (Monsignor Hess), we simply handled whatever arose.

The flip side of Bobby's sometimes aggressive coin was his genuine concern and compassion for the underdog, like the students at St. Patrick's Girls Academy, a commercial high school for young women not planning to attend college. Where many of his stature might have ignored these students, Bobby exhibited a keen interest in all their student activities. One Christmas, to lift community spirit, we erected a beautiful crèche on St. Patrick's church lawn, where our girls' choir would sing Christmas carols in front of the crib following noon Mass. Ever polite, Bobby always stayed a while to listen and applaud, including even one gruesomely cold and snowy day, when, as the sole audience member, he stayed for the entire performance, shaking hands with each afterward. He also stepped up to the plate when St. Patrick's poor boxes were being burglarized. As a busy downtown church, with eighteen receptacles for charitable cash donations, we were an easy mark. After a week of particularly brazen thefts, Bobby sent over FBI agents who sat in the back pews nearest the doors. Needless to say, our thieves were apprehended. Though others were too often critical of Bobby, my own experience with him was first rate. Whenever I needed him, he was there. I hope he felt the same.

Caroline's Catechesis

One thing that the Kennedy brothers did share — regardless of their demanding obligations — was an interest in family, particularly their kids. In the fall of 1963, as Caroline was about to turn six, Jackie had her secretary call to inquire about the two-year religious education necessary for Caroline to make her First Holy Communion. Picking up the phone, I was immediately put through to the First Lady whom I'd never actually met. In fact, the only information that I'd gleaned about her came via the press who, primarily, reported on her social life. Her voice, quiet and unassuming, was much gentler than that of the President. She came directly to the point.

"Caroline is at the age when she should begin preparing to receive Holy Communion."

I was surprised and delighted. "Thank God," I thought, "she sounds like a good Catholic mother properly interested in the religious education of her daughter." After discussing the kind of teacher she wanted for Caroline, I assured her that we could provide someone first rate, either a lay person or a religious Sister.

Her reply was instant and positive. "I want a Sister. Having never had the opportunity myself to know a Sister, I think I missed a great deal. I'd be delighted if Caroline could have that chance."

"Very good," I said, as several highly competent nuns at Catholic University popped to mind. Hanging up, I immediately called the University's Director of Catechetics to pick his brain about the best candidate for this wonderful opportunity. His most extravagant recommendation was Sister Joanne Frey, Mission Helper of the Sacred Heart, currently in a graduate-level teaching class at Catholic University. Shortly thereafter, when she and I met, it was abundantly clear that Sister Joanne had all the right stuff to tutor the First Daughter: intelligence, warmth, patience, and an appreciative wit. Inwardly, I gave her the nod, completely jubilant about so much progress, sans complications, in so short a time. "The Lord is certainly the director," I thought, "in this event."

What did surprise and disappoint me, however, was Jack's lack of partici-pation in Caroline's initial classes. When it came to the religious education of his daughter, I felt that the President's more traditional Catholic upbringing, might, perhaps, have given him more insight into the process than his wife. Raised in Middleburg, Virginia, where horse-crazy residents were known to spend more time at the hunt than church, Jackie's Catholic education had been sparse. In fact, under the circumstances, I always thought it remarkable that she had remained Catholic, thanks in part to the great love she felt for her Catholic father. However, when conversations about Caroline's progress continued to be exclusively between Jackie and me, I was puzzled. Eventually, I concluded that Jack somehow felt inadequate on the subject and that Jackie would be more effective anyway. In fairness to the President, he had grown up in a family where his mother, like Jackie now, was in charge of the children's religious studies. So it was what he knew. Moreover, being the leader of the Free World could keep a man awfully busy!

When I told Jackie about Sister Joanne she was very pleased, especially when I suggested that, to avoid publicity, the two of us deal directly with her. Classes, we next decided, would be held at the Georgetown Visitation School where my distant cousin, Visitation Sister Mary Berchmans Hannan, was an assistant principal. In order "to prevent gawking by the other Academy stu-dents," as Jackie put it, I also suggested that none but those being instructed attend the class.

Jackie, however, quickly interposed. "I wish to attend all the classes." "Fine," I said. Whether or not she should was best dealt with later. "No argu-ments now, Hannan," I thought. "You're getting along too well." As for the size of the group, Jackie, obviously, had devoted a lot of thought to which chil-dren would be invited. Ultimately, we agreed to start with six or seven, and, if more were needed later, we could include children of the staff. Among those on her initial list were Dario Duke, son of Angier Biddle Duke, the President's chief of protocol (and the only father present at the first class) and Christopher Walsh, son of Dr. John W. Walsh, Jackie's obstetrician.

To assure that preparations were in place, I kept in constant touch with the First Lady. One big problem involved the logistics of getting mother and daughter to the Academy — enough to give James Bond a run for his money, as it turned out. Though neither of us, not to mention the principal, Mother Cecilia, wanted Jackie and Caroline to face a throng of staring students every time they arrived, Mother Cecilia couldn't guarantee that wouldn't happen. Though the scheduled start date in September was delayed, alas, by Jackie's recuperation following the heartbreaking loss of infant son, Patrick, the fateful day finally arrived. Jackie and Caroline in the official limousine arrived at the Academy first, followed by private autos carrying the other students. Every-thing was going exactly as planned until I looked up and, to my horror, saw every window in the school crammed with enraptured students peering down at their famous visitors. I clearly couldn't control everything. Once inside, Jackie was seated in the Visitation School's private living room where she could see and hear all discussions.

If anyone was ever born to guide little minds in the engagement with their faith, it was Sister Joanne who knew exactly how to get the attention of her energetic, wiggly charges. The first thing she did was give them a subject whereupon, after some reflection, they would draw a picture representing what it meant to them, how they saw it. Following that, she continued, cautioning students to neither race ahead nor draw pictures of subjects not yet described, the class would move onto workbooks where, after being told or read a story, they would again render a defining image.

Starting at the very beginning, as it were, she told her class the story of creation from Genesis. Caroline's artwork on the subject, Sister Joanne later recalled, "was mostly black with a large blue crescent and some white marks." As Caroline explained it, the black was the darkness covering the earth, while the crescent and dots were the moon and stars that appeared when God said, "Let there be light." On the back of the paper she proudly wrote in large letters: Caroline Bouvier Kennedy. Next, the good Sister instructed her charges to offer up their pictures as a gift to the Sacred Heart, an image of which hung near Jackie in the living room. When Sister Joanne praised Caroline's offering, it elicited a negotiating tactic from the curly-headed little blonde. "Instead of leaving my drawing in front of the picture of the Sacred Heart," asked Caroline, "can I take it home and show it to Daddy?" Needless to say, that night Caroline's father clucked over his daughter's burgeoning art career.

When I telephoned Jackie the next day, she was delighted. Not only had their arrival and departure been efficiently low-key, the methods that Sister Joanne used to explain Church doctrine were inspired. "If I had a teacher like her when I was being instructed," she repeated several times, "I would have learned much more about the faith."

As classes continued, expanding upon her theory that a picture is worth a thousand words to young, impressionable minds, Sister Joanne took her students to visit some of the archdiocese's principal churches (like Catholic University's Shrine of the Immaculate Conception). During one such outing, the children were asked to join in the Church procession. Upon learning that singing was hardly Caroline's strong suit, Sister Joanne took her aside, assuring the neophyte songstress that she needn't be embarrassed about not joining in with the others. Their chat clearly worked miracles as Caroline, overcame her hesitation to parade up the aisle, enthusiastically warbling away with the rest of her friends. Rushing over to compliment the little girl for giving it her best, Caroline set the record straight. "Oh, I wasn't singing," she informed Sister Joanne. "I told Mommy about it and she said, 'Well, just mouth it.' So I did."

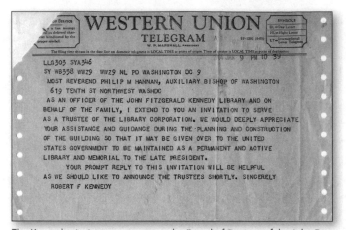

The Kennedys invite me to serve on the Board of Trustees of the John F. Kennedy Library.

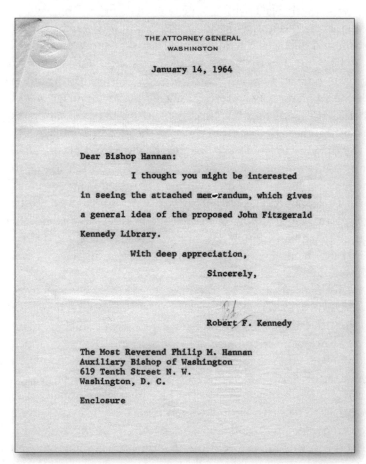

Letter and memo from Robert Kennedy relative to the mission of the John F. Kennedy Library

THE JOHN FITZGERALD KENNEDY LIBRARY

The John Fitzgerald Kennedy Library will be erected in Boston, Massachusetts, at a site along the Charles River donated by Harvard University. President Kennedy personally chose this site both because he wished the Library to be close to the scenes of his own youth and because he wanted it to be part of a living educational community. The location will not only permit a close relationship with Harvard University but will be within easy access of other colleges and universities in the Boston area.

The Library will be a memorial to President Kennedy. It will seek to express in architecture the spirit and style of the 35th President. But it will be much more than a monument; for an appropriate memorial must also express President Kennedy's vivid concern for the unfinished business of his country and the world. The Library will therefore include, in addition to an austere and beautiful memorial room, several working components: a Museum; an Archive; and an Institute. The challenge to the architect will be to combine these elements in a single harmonious design which will both contain the various functions of the Library and celebrate the memory of President Kennedy.

The Museum will display memorabilia of President Kennedy and his times -- photographs, panoramas, scientific objects, and artifacts of all sorts arranged to portray and convey the issues, the achievements and the atmosphere of the Kennedy years. The Museum will not be simply a static exhibition of items in glass cases. It will employ the modern resources of electronics and design to engage the spectator in active participation and to give the exhibits a living impact. Thus there might be a room where individuals can enter a booth, select a Kennedy speech or a significant episode of his times, and then see a film or hear a tape of the actual event. The goal of the Museum will be to make the experience of recent history as direct and intense as possible for the visitor, and especially for students and young people.

The Archive will house the personal papers of President Kennedy, his family and his associates, as well as copies of the public records necessary to an understanding of the issues and actions of his administration, and transcripts of interviews with his colleagues and contemporaries. In addition, there will be a collection of books, magazines, newspapers and printed documents bearing upon President Kennedy and his times. The Archive will hopefully become a center for the study of mid-century America, its basic problems in domestic and foreign policy, its conception of itself and of its destiny. It will contain the necessary facilities for scholarly research, including study rooms and the most advanced equipment for a continuing oral history project, for documentary reproduction, for the use of microfilm and for the full exploitation of audio-visual materials.

The Institute will seek to further one of President Kennedy's deepest concerns -- his continuing attempt to bring together the world of ideas and the world of

**Goals of the
John F. Kennedy Library**

2.

affairs, the world of scholarship and the world of decision, as, for example, these worlds existed together in the early days of the American Republic. No purpose more consistently animated his life, and no cause could better serve his memory. The Institute will be under the direction of a man who combines scholarly eminence with practical experience in public affairs. Its object will be to enlist young Americans and young people everywhere in the understanding and practice of democratic political life and public service. It will be a living institution, responsive to the needs of the times, and its resources and programs will therefore not be rigidly committed in advance; but it can be assumed that it will strive to bring intellectual and public affairs closer together in a diversity of ways -- through lectures and seminars by professors, politicians and public servants of all parties and from foreign countries as well as from the United States; through professorial chairs, perhaps in joint appointment with Harvard and neighboring universities; through meeting rooms for undergraduates interested in politics and public affairs; through fellowships for students and scholars, American and foreign; through visitors-in-residence; through organization of study groups and conferences bringing together scholars and practitioners to consider vital issues; through a publication program; through literary and public service awards; and through a variety of other means. The Institute will be committed to no program or policy but only to President Kennedy's own spirit of free and rational inquiry.

****

Under the law of 1955 authorizing the establishment of presidential libraries, the libraries themselves are to be built by public subscription and then transferred to the United States Government. The General Services Administration (National Archives) will thereafter assume responsibility for the maintenance of the physical plant as well as for the operation of the Memorial, the Museum and the Archive. The legislation makes no provision for an Institute, however, and this project, which is the most distinctive part of the conception, will require a substantial endowment.

It is estimated that a sum of $10 million will be required to build the Kennedy Library with the Memorial, Museum and Archive and to establish the Institute.

THE ATTORNEY GENERAL
WASHINGTON

July 7, 1964

Your Excellency:

Many thanks for all your help in arranging the
taping of "The House on the Potomac". You
were particularly forbearing about the many
cancellations and delays. I now hear that the
tape is to be shown in cities other than
Washington. I hope it spurs more interest in
the Center but, of course, whatever success we
have is really due to you. Again, my thanks.

Sincerely,

Robert F. Kennedy

His Excellency
The Most Reverend
Philip M. Hannan
Vicar General
Archdiocese of Washington
1721 Rhode Island Avenue, N. W.
Washington 36, D. C.

Thank you note from Robert
Kennedy for taping of "The
House on the Potomac"

THE ATTORNEY GENERAL
WASHINGTON

January 29, 1964

Dear Bishop Hannan:

Your thoughtfulness in sending the
framed copy of your wonderful editorial
about my brother is greatly appreciated.
It was most gracious of you to have this
especially prepared for our family and we
shall always be grateful for another of
your many kindnesses.

Best,

Robert F. Kennedy

His Excellency
The Most Reverend
Philip M. Hannan
Auxiliary Bishop of Washington
1721 Rhode Island Ave. N. W.
Washington 36, D. C.

Letter from Robert Kennedy regarding editorial about John F.
Kennedy

ROBERT F. KENNEDY
NEW YORK

United States Senate
WASHINGTON, D.C.

January 28, 1965

Your Excellency:

    I am sorry to be so late in writing but
I just wanted to express my deep appreciation
of your presence at the recent Ground-Breaking
Ceremony for the John F. Kennedy Center.

    I know how hard you are working for the
success of this project and I wish to convey the
personal thanks of my family.

    With kindest personal regards,

                        Respectfully yours,

                        Robert F. Kennedy

Most Rev. Philip M. Hannan, D.D.
Archdiocese of Washington
1721 Rhode Island Avenue
Washington, D.C.

Letter of thanks from Robert
Kennedy regarding ground-
breaking ceremony for the
John F. Kennedy Center

Edward M. Kennedy
Massachusetts

United States Senate

January 14, 1964

Most Reverend Philip M. Hannan
1721 Rhode Island Avenue, N.W.
Washington 6, D. C.

Dear Bishop Hannan:

    Please accept my heartfelt thanks for your
note and for the framed copy of your editorial in the
Catholic Standard.

    I am pleased to have this in my personal
collection of momentoes and appreciate your thoughtfulness in sending it to me.

    With every good wish.

                        Sincerely,

                        Edward M. Kennedy

EMK:MJD

Thank you note from Senator Edward Kennedy for copy of
editorial

Note from Ethel Kennedy upon the death of their son Michael

Thank you message from Joan Kennedy after plane crash

Note of thanks from Joan Kennedy

Letter of thanks from Ethel Kennedy for her son David's first Holy Communion

Sweet note of thanks from Ethel
Kennedy

HICKORY HILL
4700 CHAIN BRIDGE ROAD
McLEAN, VIRGINIA

June 22, 1962

The Most Reverend
Philip M. Hannan, D. D.
Auxiliary Bishop
Archdiocese of Washington
1721 Rhode Island Avenue N. W.
Washington 6, D. C.

Your Excellency:

    You have probably already heard
what a glorious time the children had at
the special performance of "Brigadoon."
They enjoyed themselves thoroughly (and
the hot dogs and cokes). Everyone was
in a gay, holiday spirit that afternoon
and Dorothy Collins was especially gracious
to the children.

    Bobby and I both deeply appreciate
your kindness in seeing that not only
the children from Catholic institutions
but those from Junior Village as well
arrived. I am sure all of these children
would like to join us in expressing our
thanks to you.

        From

        Your loving child,

        Ethel Kennedy
        Mrs. Robert F. Kennedy

EDWARD M. KENNEDY

April 1, 1980

The Most Rev. Philip Hannan
Archbishop of New Orleans
7887 Walmsly Avenue
New Orleans, Louisiana 70125

Dear Archbishop Hannan:

    Please accept my most sincere thanks
for your kindness in seeing my daugther
Kara and neice Kerry during their visit
this week to New Orleans.

    I know how much they enjoyed meeting
you, and how delighted they were to receive
the thoughtful Mardi Gras remembrances.

    Again, thank you for the gracious
courtesies extended to Kerry and Kara,
and with my respectful regards,

        Sincerely,

Note of thanks from Senator Edward Kennedy

SARGENT SHRIVER
1325 G STREET, N.W., SUITE 500
WASHINGTON, D.C. 20005

September 2, 2003

RECEIVED SEP 0 9 2003

His Excellency Archbishop Philip M. Hannan
President
FOCUS Worldwide Network
Retired Archbishop of New Orleans
106 Metairie Lawn Drive
Metairie, Louisiana 70001

Your Excellency:

With deep respects to Your Excellency, Archbishop Hannan, I am happy to continue my endorsement of what you have already written and my hopes that you will continue to write to anyone qualified to enlarge or simply add useful facts to everything you write about the Kennedy years including, of course, suggested enlargements or additions to what Your Excellency has already encompassed in the 30 pages you covered concerning the various elements and facts about the Kennedy family history.

Almost needless to say, I am sorry that your appointment as Archbishop of New Orleans in September 1965 terminated your active presence in the meetings of the Boards of The Kennedy Center and the John F. Kennedy Library. May I add just one thought, namely that even though you may not be able to participate actively in the meetings of those boards and organizations, I hope and I am sure I am correct in saying that the Kennedy Family would be grateful for any thoughts, any suggestions, any requests you might be able and willing to give to that family and its work.

And, although you are retired as Archbishop of New Orleans, I am sure you are continuing to contribute profoundly to the Church in New Orleans and throughout our country. I am certain, therefore, that everyone would be interested to know not only about your insights about "the Kennedy years" but also about the most recent years in your life. All of us, I am sure, would be grateful to receive from you any suggestions or recommendations regardless of subject and regardless of length which you could supply to those of us who would benefit deeply from your thinking and experience.

Respectfully,

Sargent Shriver

Sargent Shriver

Very nice letter from Sargent Shriver on book

By this time, the President was so impressed by Caroline's growing religious aptitude — not to mention Sister Joanne's catechetical system — that he glowingly bragged both to me and, I daresay, anyone who would listen. Jack adored Caroline, who returned his unconditional admiration. Finally, in November, he gave me a call. "I'd like to sit in on one of Caroline's classes," he said. "Fine," I replied, "we'd be delighted. When would you like to come?" Checking his schedule, he made a tentative date to attend the following week after returning from a campaign trip.

"Where are you going?" I asked.

"Dallas."

The catechism class that the President would have attended was earmarked for November 26, the day after his funeral. Assuming it was cancelled, Sister Joanne was surprised to receive a call from the White House, suggesting that she go ahead, albeit without Caroline. However, when she walked into the classroom, Caroline was already there, accompanied by the Secret Service and her nanny, Mrs. Shaw. "I know I'm early," Caroline explained to Sister Joanne, "but we were just riding around in the car, and I thought I'd rather be in school."

Recognizing the spiritual significance of this moment for the only daughter of the suddenly slain President, Sister Joanne sat down next to the little girl. Taking her hands, she gently explained, as no doubt many already had, that her father had gone to heaven to be with her little brother, Patrick. Fortunately, the class had discussed the Catholic view of death only weeks before, that to earn entrance into heaven we must live according to the teachings of Christ. For her presentation on the subject, Caroline brought to class pictures of her whole family, including one of little brother Patrick, who had died three days after his birth in 1963. "Patrick is no longer with us," she, earnestly, explained to her classmates. "He's in heaven." And so, now, was her father.

In the inexplicably tragic days following the assassination, Sister Joanne, having developed such a close bond with mother and daughter, regularly visited both in the White House. As the minutes, hours, and days of their terrible test passed, it seemed providential that she had entered their lives to bring consolation and application of the faith in their crisis. (At one point, in fact, Caroline so missed Sister Joanne that she begged her mother to take her to visit the nun's convent.) The friendship with Sister Joanne was central in helping Caroline and Jackie understand and accept, in a Christian manner, the death of JFK. Once, spotting a crucifix, Caroline asked why Jesus let men put him to death. "We do very difficult things for those we deeply love," Sister Joanne replied. "Christ so loved us that he allowed himself to be crucified to save us."

As Sister Joanne had discovered, Jackie was a dutiful mother, determined to raise a thoughtful, gracious, young woman. For her part, Caroline, not only intelligent, possessed an appreciation (well beyond her years) of the pain of those around her. During one class following the assassination, Sister Joanne introduced her students to the story of the woman who washed the feet of Jesus with her tears — triggering a profound emotional response from Caroline. "My mommy cries all the time," she told Sister Joanne. "In the morning I get up and go visit Mommy when she's still in bed. And she's always crying."

Though Jackie intended to have John-John begin religion classes with Sister Joanne the following fall, the crush of curiosity seekers constantly surrounding the Georgetown house (where Jackie moved after leaving the White House) was becoming unbearable. Her home felt like a fishbowl. Determined that she and her children have their privacy, she decided to leave Washington and move to New York City. Her departure, of course, ended Caroline's official classes with Sister Joanne who, the following year, was thrilled to receive a letter from Jackie saying that Caroline wanted her to attend her First Communion ceremony in New York. Of course, Sister Joanne went, along with a handful of other guests: Bobby Kennedy; Caroline's grandmother, Mrs. Hugh D. Auchincloss; Evelyn Lincoln, President Kennedy's former secretary; and Jackie's sister, Lee Radziwill. After the Mass, she joined the Kennedys for a private reception at Jackie's Manhattan apartment. A few months later, Sister Joanne received from Jackie a photograph, taken before the assassination, of the First Family coming out of a church in Florida. On it she had inscribed: "Caroline has received all that her father would have wanted." (Sister Joanne, who remained in touch with both women, is still in contact with Caroline.)

Bobby Kennedy's Assassination

In June 1968, when Bobby Kennedy was gunned down in Los Angeles, I was the Archbishop of New Orleans. (By a strange coincidence, James Mundell, the priest who gave Bobby absolution as he lay dying on the kitchen floor of the Ambassador Hotel in Los Angeles, was a fellow Washingtonian and member of St. Matthew's parish. As a missionary priest in Chile, he had sought and received dispensation from his vows by the Vatican, but could, as a priest, still administer the Last Rites of the Church to a stricken Catholic.) Since Bobby's Funeral Mass, celebrated by Cardinal Terence Cooke, was scheduled to be held on June 8 in New York's St. Patrick's Cathedral, Archbishop O'Boyle and I decided to attend together. When the Kennedy family found out that we were coming, they asked for the name of my hotel. Checking in, I was given a message from one of Bobby's staffers, asking that I be available the evening before the funeral.

That night, Adam Walinsky, an attorney and adviser to Bobby, knocked on my door. After introducing himself as writer for the eulogy that Ted would be delivering the following day, he candidly admitted that he was having "a hard time writing the speech." In the event that his efforts failed, he asked, would I write one as well — just in case? Of course. Furthermore, he continued, the family had a second, somewhat unusual request. If Ted were unable to complete his remarks, would I cover for him? I would be seated in the sanctuary within eyeshot of the Senator so, if he crumpled, I could hurry forward and take his place. I gladly said yes, praying fervently that Ted would hold up. And he did. Despite a cracking voice and the odd tear, he managed to deliver a splendid, perfect eulogy: "My brother need not be idealized, or enlarged in death beyond what he was in life, to be remembered simply as a good and decent man who saw wrong and tried to right it, saw suffering and tried to heal it, saw war and tried to stop it."

On the train ride to Washington, Ted, already assuming his role as family patriarch, endlessly waved in gratitude to the swelling throngs on either side of the tracks who, town by town, spontaneously broke out singing "The Battle Hymn of the Republic" as the train passed. In fact, "Glory, glory halleluiah, His truth is marching on" could be heard throughout the sad, surreal trip, made even more so by the death of a man, who, accidentally slipping under the train's wheels, was crushed to death.

When we finally arrived at the burial site in Arlington, Ethel and her children paid me the great compliment of asking that I perform the Rite of Interment. Including a few words from the eulogy that I wrote the previous night,

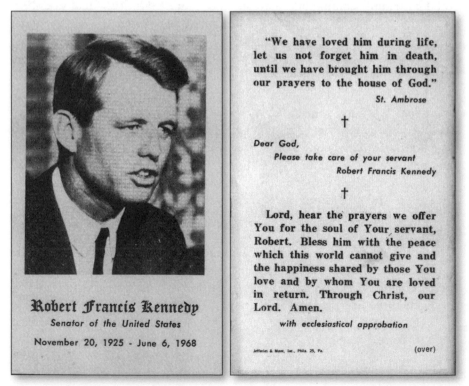

Prayer card for Robert Francis Kennedy

I, nonetheless, kept it brief, in deference to all the Kennedys, especially Ethel, who had endured such a taxing, exhaustive ordeal which, like sister-in-law Jackie, she bore with remarkable nobility. At the end of the service, I offered the prayer of committal: "O God, the author of the unbought grace of life, you are our promised home. Lead your servant Robert to that home bright with the presence of your everlasting life and love, there to join the other members of the family. Console also those who have suffered the loss of his mortal presence. Give them the grace that will strengthen the bonds of the family and of the national community. May we bear your peace to others until the day we join you and all the saints in your life of endless love and light. We ask this through Christ our Lord. Amen."

Forty years after the fact, I am still asked about the circumstances of John Kennedy's assassination. In short, do I believe that Lee Harvey Oswald acted alone? I do not. The "single-gunman" theory simply isn't plausible. I do not believe that one person was able to get off — in hair-trigger sequence — the three shots that killed the President. After the assassination, the Marines did their own test. Placing their most skilled rifleman in the exact same position as Oswald, the soldier could barely, in the required time, shoot three shots — much less with perfect aim. From my point of view, Oswald had to have help. As for who was behind the killing of the President, there were plenty of candidates. The mafia — seeking revenge for Bobby's official efforts to put them behind bars — certainly had a motive to kill Jack. (Interestingly enough, Oswald's wife, Marina, called one day, asking to see me at the chancery in Washington. And though we met, Marina, a peculiar woman, added nothing of substance to the existing saga.) I simply do not believe that the entire story of the assassination of John F. Kennedy — our President and my friend — has ever been told.

In the final analysis, it was my privilege and honor to play even a small part in the lives of three such extraordinary human beings; Jack, Jackie, Bobby... May you rest in peace.

CHAPTER 11

The Second Vatican Council

I t was a bombshell.

When Pope John XXIII announced during the Church Unity Octave on January 25, 1959, in the Basilica of St. Paul's Outside the Walls that he would convene the Second Vatican Council, his blockbuster announcement came out of the blue. Normally, Vatican rumors spread at the speed of light, but there had been neither intimation nor rumor about such an historic convocation.

Pope John XXIII acknowledged the mysterious genesis of the Council in his opening address at St. Peter's Basilica on October 11, 1962. He told the thousands of assembled cardinals, archbishops, and bishops that the idea was completely unexpected. It came, he said, "like a flash of heavenly light, shedding sweetness in eyes and hearts."

Little did I realize that Vatican II would become another defining moment in my life as a priest and bishop. Over the course of four historic fall sessions, I helped coordinate the Vatican press panels which explained the inner workings of the Council to English-speaking media representatives from around the world. And as one of the few bishops who had served in World War II and personally witnessed the tyranny of Communism and Fascism, I spoke passionately about the morality of nuclear deterrence, a position that at first isolated me from my brother bishops but eventually was adopted by the full Council. That remains, to this day, one of my most cherished achievements.

As soon as I heard the news of Pope John's call to convene the Council, I rushed into Archbishop O'Boyle's office and relayed the news dispatch. He was sitting at his desk, and after I told him what I knew, he didn't say a word, he didn't even move. Pausing for what seemed like an eternity, he finally asked, "What does that mean? What are we expected to do?"

When the Pope told us exactly what it meant, it was even more stunning than the announcement. In his Apostolic Constitution convoking the Council on Christmas, December 25, 1961, he said the Council would examine "the doctrinal and practical programs which correspond more to the requirements of perfect conformity with Christian teaching, for the edification and in the service of the mystical body and its supernatural mission, and therefore, the sacred books, venerable tradition, the sacraments, prayer, ecclesiastical discipline, charitable and relief activities, the lay apostolate, and mission horizons . . . to the international organizations, and to the working out of its social doctrine regarding the family, education, civil society, and all related problems."

What an agenda!

In his opening speech to the Council in 1962, Pope John gave some clues about the nature of this "Pastoral" Council. In the past, the Church condemned errors with the greatest severity, but this Council was to be different. "Nowadays, however, the spouse of Christ prefers to make use of the medicine of mercy rather than that of severity," he said. "She considers that she meets the needs of the present day by demonstrating the validity of her teaching rather than by condemnations."

The single Italian word that captured the spirit of the Second Vatican Council was "*aggiornamento*" — an updating of the whole teaching of the Church, an opening of the Church's stained-glass windows to let in the fresh wind of the Spirit.

Pope John also cautioned us that progress should be made "little by little." This mystified me. As a pastor I began to wonder how such a gigantic amount of instruction could be taught to the people in a short time frame. Much later, I realized that no time was allocated to actually teaching the Council's ambitious body of work, something that has had repercussions even to the present day.

The massive scope of Pope John's agenda intrigued me, but I did not feel there was an overpowering need for extensive changes. The United States bishops had talked about many desirable changes — such as racial integration, a new emphasis on social justice, use of the vernacular in the Mass, better training for the priesthood, changes in the medieval garb of religious sisters, improvement in Catholic education, and freedom of religion. In the United States, there was a deeply established, constitutional principle establishing religious freedom. Because we had so successfully practiced freedom of religion in our country, I thought we could make a real contribution in sharing our experience with the universal Church. We had no thought about changing the discipline of celibacy for priests, ordaining women, or radically changing seminary training and popular devotions, such as the Forty Hours Devotion and Benediction of the Blessed Sacrament.

After receiving additional information from the Vatican, Archbishop O'Boyle asked me to canvas the ecclesiastical faculties at Catholic University about any ideas that might be submitted to the Council. I started immediately with the faculty of the School of Canon Law, with whom I was very friendly. They had a few ideas, but the rector of Catholic University thought some of the ideas were too open-minded and edited out several suggestions before sending them on to Rome. The other faculties supported the demand to celebrate Mass in the vernacular and their perennial ideas about social justice. Eventually, we coalesced on the idea of freedom of religion, an unpopular idea for many in the Roman Curia. Jesuit Father John Courtney Murray, an esteemed professor at Woodstock College in Maryland and author of *We Hold These Truths*, became the chief U.S. proponent of religious freedom.

From my reading of history, I had always thought the Church called a general council only to confront a heresy or to define clearly a doctrine, as, for instance, in the First Vatican Council, which ended in 1870, when the Church defined the infallibility of the pope when speaking on matters of faith and morals. Pope John XXIII had a different idea for this General Council.

In convoking the Second Vatican Council on December 25, 1961, the Pope cited the need for the Church to confront a massive world crisis. This crisis included the danger of nuclear war, the corruption of moral values induced by atheistic Communism (with no explicit condemnation of Communist regimes), excesses in consumption by the wealthy, and a reorganization of the world's economy for the benefit of the world's poor. It was to be a pastoral council aimed at the renewal of faith of people across the globe. The Pope stressed — and he repeated this several times — that updating the Church did not mean changing in any way the accepted doctrines of the Church.

In preparation for the Council, the world's bishops were invited to submit suggestions for topics to be discussed. I sent in several suggestions: a greater explanation of the doctrine that there is no salvation outside the Church (*extra ecclesiam, nulla salus*); the historicity of the sacred Scriptures; conditions for a just war; the purpose or ends of matrimony; and the use of the vernacular in liturgical ceremonies.

I had a peculiar experience with the Pope a few weeks before the first session of the Council. He gave me an audience in one of his private rooms, and he expressed his hopes that the United States and the Soviet Union could peacefully resolve the Cuban missile crisis. He was very friendly and immediately asked me which suggestions I had sent in for possible consideration during the Council. As he said this, he walked over to a huge set of volumes on a special table, containing all the suggestions. Completely startled, I forgot what I had sent in! Very politely, he simply "forgot" his question and started discussing other matters. He told me he really didn't care for the food in Rome because he was convinced his native Northern Italian cuisine was superior. Occasionally he would get someone from the Lombardi region to come down to Rome to cook for him. Then he immediately began to talk about some of the presents he had received recently. He was especially intrigued with a short telescope, and he walked me over to his window overlooking the Vatican gardens. "Look through it and you can see everyone walking in the garden!" he exclaimed. Naturally, I praised the telescope and everything in the garden. We chatted for almost forty minutes; at the end of the conversation, he said,

"That's one of my faults. I am a chatterbox." "And," I thought, "a very polite Pope," as I asked for his blessing and left.

Later during the Council itself, I submitted a paper or "intervention" on the conditions for a just war in regard to the possession of nuclear weapons or the doctrine of deterrence, the duties of the laity, the nature of our democratic form of government, and the discontinuation of some vestments used in non-liturgical and liturgical services.

I was also struck by the announcement that the Pope was very interested in changing our relationship with the Orthodox Church. I wrongly concluded that the Pope would be interested in securing names of the Orthodox clergy who might serve as observers. Relying on my friendship with the pastor of the Greek Orthodox Church on Massachusetts Avenue, I contacted him by phone to see if he was interested. His answer totally floored me. He informed me that the Orthodox did not consider the Second Vatican Council to be an authentic general council because they were not consulted. The Orthodox did not consider any general council to be authentic after the rupture of relations with Rome in 1054, after the condemnation of the Patriarch Michael Cerularius of Constantinople. He also said his feelings would be deeply hurt if he were to receive a letter of invitation to be an observer. I apologized. I thought, "I hope the Holy Father knows how to solve all this!"

I was more successful in another preparatory matter for the Council. I was the assistant to the chairman of the Committee on Communications of the National Conference of Catholic Bishops, Archbishop Thomas A. Connolly of Seattle. He had been asked to secure the services of a priest who could handle all the arrangements for meeting the needs of the English-speaking press at the Council, especially regarding the daily press conferences. Knowing I was the editor of the *Catholic Standard* and had a lot of press contacts, he telephoned me and said, "Phil, you're in Washington, and you can handle all this better than I can. Please get us a good priest for this job. You write the letters, and I'll sign them."

After a little thought, I was determined to secure the services of Holy Cross Father Edward L. Heston, the *economo* (bursar) for the Holy Cross Fathers in Rome. I had known Father Heston when he was a graduate student at Catholic University in Washington and had helped me out, along with some of his fellow Holy Cross Fathers, in hearing hundreds of confessions each week at St. Patrick's Church. He was a thoroughly competent, personable priest, and I also knew that any priest who could handle the financial affairs of a religious congregation in Rome had to have a lot on the ball. I told Archbishop Connolly that his superior probably would refuse to free him up for the press responsibilities, so we'd better think of some other candidates. But the Archbishop said, "Phil, we're not going to take any other names." As I suspected, Father Heston's superior initially refused to release Father Heston

Passport to the Vatican for the Vatican II Council

Left: With Archbishop Thomas Connolly of Seattle — we are both members of the Press Corps in Rome during Vatican Council II. *Right:* Seen with Cardinal O'Boyle and other bishops leaving St. Peter's at the end of a session of Vatican Council II

Speaking on nuclear deterrence at the Vatican II Council at St. Peter's in Rome

With Pope John XXIII in the Pope's office, where he showed me his new telescope

Pope Paul VI with Bishop Harold R. Perry and me in 1965

With Auxiliary Bishop Harold Perry on October 2, 1965, in Rome. I knew that Archbishop John Cody had some input into the decision to name me as his successor when he asked Bishop Perry and me to pose for a picture before the official announcement. "It was Cody's way of announcing that the first black bishop in the U.S. in modern times was his work," I said. "That was okay by me." When I was an auxiliary bishop in Washington, D.C., I arranged to have then-Father Perry, superior of the Society of Divine Word, give the invocation to an opening session of Congress, at the request of House Speaker John McCormack.

Bishops of the New Orleans Province gathered for a dinner on Monday, October 4, 1965, at the Rome residence of the Missionary Servants of the Most Blessed Trinity to honor me on my selection as Archbishop of New Orleans, and Auxiliary Bishop-Designate Harold Perry, the first African-American bishop in the southern U.S. in the twentieth century. Seated: Archbishops John P. Cody and myself. Standing, from left: Benedictine Abbot David Melancon of St. Joseph Abbey, St. Benedict, La.; Baton Rouge Bishop Robert E. Tracy; Alexandria Bishop Charles P. Greco; Little Rock Bishop Albert L. Fletcher; Bishop Perry; Lafayette Auxiliary Bishop Warren L. Boudreaux; and Natchez-Jackson Bishop Joseph B. Brunini.

My main job during the Second Vatican Council was to coordinate the afternoon press briefings for English-speaking reporters in a room just off St. Peter's Square. Sometimes the questions for the panel of bishops and periti (seated) went far afield, but I believe the patience they displayed in answering questions went a long way in fostering a favorable view of the Council's deliberations.

Archbishop Cody makes a point at a November 1966 meeting of the National Conference of Catholic Bishops. In a statement on peace, the bishops supported U.S. policy in Vietnam and commended the valor of men in the armed forces. But they said it was "the duty of everyone to search for other alternatives."

Chicago Archbishop John Cody, my immediate predecessor in New Orleans, at a 1965 session of the Second Vatican Council, a few days after my appointment to New Orleans

Five American bishops were named to a committee that was to assist reporters in their coverage of the Second Vatican Council. Shown standing in front of St. Peter's Basilica are, from left, Dallas Bishop Thomas H. Gorman; myself; Belleville Bishop Albert R. Zuroweste (chairman); New York Auxiliary Bishop James H. Griffith, and Pittsburgh Bishop John J. Wright. Wright was tremendously intelligent. I remember asking some eminent cardinal in Rome, "What do you think of Bishop Wright?" The guy said, "He's probably the most outstanding brain at the entire Council." All reporters were welcomed by the panel. It didn't make any difference if they were pro-Catholic or anti-Catholic, as long as they asked reasonable questions. We had estimated that fifty or so would show up. It turns out two hundred showed up regularly for the news conferences.

for the appointment, but when I wrote him back stressing the importance the bishops placed on this position, he finally acceded to my request.

Initially, we guessed that maybe forty or so English-speaking reporters would cover the Council. But before the end of the first session we had registered about two hundred reporters — we had forgotten that most of the Western European reporters spoke English. For example, in Germany, all the Reuters reporters spoke fluent English. The press corps grew to such an extent we needed to find a bigger room, so we eventually made a deal with the USO Club on the Via della Conciliazione — the wide thoroughfare that runs from St. Peter's Basilica all the way to the Tiber River — as the site for our daily 3:00 p.m. press conferences. The USO had a large basement room, and it was a very convenient place for both the bishops and media. We just took over the place.

Pope John organized an "Ante-preparatory Commission" to plan the coming Council. The Commission included the heads of the ten Congregations or Departments of the Roman Curia, which was the administrative body of the Church. This gave the appearance of lodging control of the Council in very conservative hands. Forestalling criticism, he named as the head of the Commission Cardinal Domenico Tardini, who was Secretary of State and also in charge of the Congregation for Extraordinary Ecclesiastical Affairs. A relatively unknown auditor of the Roman Rota, Archbishop Pericle Felici, was chosen as the general secretary for the Commission. From the viewpoint of conservatives, it was an awesome selection, but the Pope had avoided naming ultraconservative Cardinal Alfredo Ottaviani, the head of the Holy Office, the most prestigious and conservative Congregation, as the leading figure of the Commission.

The Commission's task was to gather the material for the Council. The knotty question was: Who would furnish the material? The Pope settled that — the bishops were promptly asked to suggest the questions and problems to be handled in the Council. In no time the Vatican was deluged with more than two thousand replies.

Preparatory Commission

Meanwhile, Pope John, as Bishop of Rome, set up a preparatory commission — consisting of eight subcommissions — for the synod he was to hold for the Diocese of Rome in advance of Vatican II. When the Rome synod lasted only one week — from January 24 to 31, 1960 — and discussed no major or groundbreaking questions, many Church-watchers got the impression the Council itself might be a rubber-stamp process, if the Curia had its way. In fact, Cardinal John Cody of Chicago told me he learned the Council would be finished in a few months. Pope John actually hoped the Council could be finished in at most two sessions — the fall of 1962 and spring of 1963.

The burden of determining the subjects or topics that would be treated in the Council was allocated to groups corresponding to the ten commissions of the Roman Curia. In addition, three secretariats were set up: for media communications, for economic and technical aspects, and for helping separated brethren to follow the Council. The Pope remained as the head of the central commission, which was to review and supervise the work of the preparatory commissions.

The Pope was intensely interested and dedicated to the work of the Council. In addition to his constant exhortations, he went on retreat on board the papal train to travel to Assisi and Loreto on October 4, 1962. This was the first time a Pope had used the Vatican railroad. He had already made a personal retreat at Torre San Giovanni, which ended on September 15, 1962. A few days later he submitted to a thorough physical examination, which revealed a very serious illness that in 1963 was to take his life. There was no public report of this development, but a premonition of this condition led him in August 1962 to make a *motu proprio* (a statement "on his own impulse"), specifying conditions during the *sede vacante* ("vacant seat") following his death. He instructed that no pictures were to be taken of him on his deathbed, that only those persons with a definite duty were to be permitted in the crypt where he was to be buried, and that no one, during this period, was to be allowed to live in the papal apartments.

Meanwhile the first seven *"schemata"* — documents on the material to be discussed at the Council — had been prepared and sent to the world's bishops, the "fathers" of the Council. The fathers were given only a short time to reply. Many bishops from France, Germany, Belgium, and Holland were disappointed by the tone and substance of the *schemata*, which seemed to lack the core idea that the Council was primarily a pastoral council. I would guess a majority of the fathers gave tacit approval to the *schemata*, but there were seeds of strong discord among the fathers before the Council met. The ultimate unanimity gained by the open discussion in the Council over a period of four years was one of the remarkable, if not "miraculous," achievements of the Council.

The bishops of the Northern European nations also communicated with each other in a series of strong national meetings, developing, as we discovered later, a general attitude of strong disappointment with the *schemata* submitted to us. This intercommunication strengthened the resolve of these fathers, especially the Belgian bishops, to demand a greater degree of pastoral care in the Council.

At first we Americans did not have meetings about the content of the *schemata*. One reason was that we had been holding national meetings for years and had welcomed a pastoral Council. Personally, I felt strongly that the *schemata* were too pedantic. The contributions to the *schemata* of Jesuit Father Sebastian Tromp, who taught dogmatic theology at the Gregorian University in Rome and helped write Pope Pius XII's 1943 encyclical *Mystici Corporis*, sounded a lot like his classes. He was more of a scholar than a pastor.

October 11, 1962 — the opening day of the Second Vatican Council — was a brilliant day that had the feeling of a gala. Scores of TV and press photographers scurried to get shots of the huge assemblage, especially of the resplendent, gorgeous, sacred dress of the patriarchs and prelates of the Eastern rites. We Latin-rite bishops, in our comparatively mundane robes, were virtually ignored.

Making a special plea for open-mindedness, the Holy Father told the 2,504 assembled bishops and heads of male religious orders that he was both a brother and a father. He was certainly committed to a "pastoral" Council.

The first general meeting, or congregation, was held on October 13, 1962. Secretary General Felici convoked the Council. After the opening Mass at St.

Peter's Basilica, the fathers were handed a list of those present at the Council, the rules of the Council, and the cards for electing members of the ten conciliar commissions. Each commission was to have sixteen elected members and eight appointed by the Pope. Each father was given a list of the names of those who had participated in the preparatory commissions — a convenient way of nudging us toward choosing these veterans and keeping the Curia happy.

To our astonishment, we were then told that we should vote immediately for the members of the ten commissions. In the ensuing uneasy moment, Cardinal Achille Liénart of Lille, France, arose at his place with the members of the Committee of Presidents in charge of the meeting and said, "We are not disposed to accept the list of candidates proposed to us until the Council meets again. We have had too little time to choose our own candidates. We ask for a delay." Cardinal Josef Frings of Cologne rose and seconded the motion, and there was an immediate burst of strong applause. The first meeting of the Council was adjourned after just fifteen minutes.

Frings was a powerful, liberal presence at Vatican II, and he frequently was cast in the antagonist's role opposite conservative Cardinal Ottaviani, the pro-secretary of the Holy Office. Ottaviani's motto was *semper idem* ("always the same") — and he favored an abbreviated Council that would short-circuit any reform movement. Ironically, Frings' *peritus* (theological adviser) was none other than Father Joseph Ratzinger — the future Pope Benedict XVI — who was known at the time to favor church reform. However, after the Council, Father Ratzinger began teaching dogmatic theology at the University of Tübingen, and he witnessed the increasingly radical nature and Marxist leanings of the student movement of the 1960s. Those experiences prompted him to become more conservative in his views. Ottaviani, meanwhile, believed that any reform of the Mass was anathema to the faith.

The Holy Father granted a delay of three days to enable the bishops to draw up their own lists of names. During this break there was a flurry of meetings, and eventually thirty-four lists were developed, mostly by national groups. The U.S. bishops offered a list of twenty-seven bishops for nine commissions.

Meanwhile, a group of younger American bishops, including myself, decided to hold a meeting to secure support for the change in the voting procedure. To garner support among the U.S. bishops, each of us was assigned a bishop to contact, with the goal of persuading him to accept the change and vote for a list of candidates. I was assigned Bishop Ignatius Strecker of Springfield-Cape Girardeau in Missouri. It was about 10:00 p.m. when I pounded on the door of his hotel room to solicit his support. To my amazement, he was very cordial and, dressed in his pajamas, thanked me for bringing the matter to his attention.

Finally, on October 20, the results of the voting were announced, and the Americans had placed a member on each of the ten commissions. Archbishop O'Boyle was voted membership on the education commission. Our actions had one goal — to guarantee that the Council would be definitely pastoral as well as theological. The new voting procedures increased the number of bishops from Central and Northern Europe on the commissions.

For centuries, Latin had served as the language of the Church, so the Pope decided it would be the official language in all proceedings of the Council. Later, Melkite Patriarch Maximos IV Saigh refused to speak Latin because he said it was the language only of the Western Church, and not, as many Romans kept claiming, the language of the universal Church. When he was allowed to speak in French, some of the Eastern Fathers who spoke Latin very fluently also decided to speak in French. Nobody ever asked to speak in English. Maximos was trying to remind people that the Eastern Rite churches were parts of the Church with as much right to their own traditions — and languages — as the Western.

The Council took up the liturgical reforms first — the major change being the use of the vernacular for the celebration of Mass — and the changes were passed 2,162 to 42 in November 1962.

The Council Begins

As the Council started, the members of the Communications Committee responsible for accommodating the English-speaking press had to deal immediately with numerous demands. The committee, which was different in membership from the press committee of the National Conference of Catholic Bishops, consisted of Pittsburgh Bishop John Wright, New York Auxiliary Bishop James A. Griffiths, Belleville Bishop Albert R. Zuroweste, Dallas Bishop Thomas K. Gorman, and me. Our task was to choose the bishop who would preside at the daily afternoon press meetings and the group of theological experts — *periti* — who would handle the questions. This meant that the membership of the panel would vary according to the discussions in the Council, not always an easy task.

Reporters covering Vatican II were as different as the newspapers they represented. By the end of the Council we had a rare collection — an official of Protestants and Other Americans United, who was speechless when I welcomed him to the conferences, and a truculent reporter stationed for years in Moscow, who admitted, "My boss has sent me here to ask the hard questions. But I don't know anything about a Council."

Serious trouble began with the press corps as soon as the Council began. The Vatican decided all the discussions would be secret, and so it would issue daily only a brief summary of the subjects discussed. The "CliffsNotes" version of Council discussions was not at all informative and frustrated the reporters. Father Heston, who was our point man with the press, said the reports were so uninteresting and lacking in substance that some journalists remarked they were written before the discussions even took place. By the end of the first session, the flood of protests against the "secrecy" forced the Vatican to provide more timely and useful information.

At the second session of the Council in 1963, Father Heston rescued everyone from this intolerable situation. He announced, "Every day I'll give you the summary of the speeches in the order in which they were delivered, and then I'll give you the names of the speakers in the order in which they spoke." The routine worked beautifully. Father Heston would tell the press: "Here are statements A, B, C, D." And then he would stipulate the order in which each bishop spoke: "Bishop A (Bishop Jones), spoke first, followed by Bishop B (Bishop Smith), C, D." That allowed Father Heston to get around the Vatican rule that no statement could be directly attributed to a bishop. It was a brilliant idea!

As the Council progressed with increasingly newsworthy material, the meetings with reporters grew in importance. A crucial assistant was Elmer von Feldt, head of the press department of NC News (now Catholic News Service). Elmer took over as moderator of the bishops' press panel and handled all the administrative details. He hired a very able employee, Mary F. Ingoldsby, who could speak three languages fluently.

I was placed in charge of the press conferences for the last session of the Council. Father Vincent Yzermans, the extremely knowledgeable and personable director of the bureau of information of the U.S. bishops, handled all the business occurring during the time of the general congregations of the Council.

Our first duty during the press conferences was to try to keep the questions germane to the material debated that day. Have you ever tried to rein in two hundred reporters? It really is like trying to herd cats. On September 25, 1964, the Council had a major discussion and a positive vote on the Declaration on Religious Freedom. This was huge, groundbreaking news. In fact, the final speaker of the day, Cardinal Giovanni Colombo of Milan, who was a theology adviser and close friend of Pope Paul VI, praised the document. His general endorsement was tantamount to the Holy Father's cautious endorsement. I had asked Father John Courtney Murray to be present for the press briefing to handle questions about religious freedom, because I naturally figured his expertise about the inner workings of the document would be extremely enlightening.

After one question on the religious freedom topic from reporter Michael Novak to Cincinnati Archbishop Karl Alter, the press corps turned on a dime and started peppering the panel on the Council's debate of a revised *schema* on the Jews and non-Christians. Many questions followed on the exegetics of passages from St. Paul's Letter to the Romans and why the second draft of the *schema* had been changed to drop the reference to the charge of deicide against the whole Jewish people. After we had consumed about fifty minutes of the hour, I finally declared: "The subject for discussion today is the Declaration on Religious Freedom. Father Murray is a well-recognized expert on this matter. We will not accept any questions except on that subject." After an awkward silence, a Catholic reporter proposed a question, and there was some desultory interest in the subject. After the conference was over, I tried to apologize and explain the situation to Father Murray. He just shook his head in recognition of the situation.

Listening for weeks in the Council and in the informal weekly meetings of the U.S. bishops encouraged me to express my convictions. I also learned that information delivered to the appropriate commission of the Council was just as effective as a speech from the floor of the Council. That led me to submit eventually twenty-three interventions during the four years of the Council. My contribution was very modest compared with the two thousand pages of script in the seventy *schemas* produced by the preparatory commissions. According to Father Ratzinger, that was "more than double the quantity of texts produced by all previous councils put together."

My Interventions

One of my first interventions, made in 1962 with sixty-one bishops concurring, was that we be allowed to discard some of the pompous, so-called "regular" vestments of bishops, including the huge *cappa magna* (an outer vestment with a long train), silk gloves, buskins, and colored shoes matching the color of the vestments. The intervention was a flop, although after the Council, most of the suggestions were included in the new regulations for vestments. I got a different perspective of how lay people were reacting when I took an airplane flight home and was seated next to a bank executive. "I read that some bishop wants to get rid of some of the vestments," the banker said. "He's dead wrong. I'm a Protestant, and I cover the Far East for the bank. They love vestments. The more the better." I made no comment and no admission of guilt!

The intervention I made on October 17, 1963, about laity in the document on the Church (*Lumen Gentium*) fared much better. I wrote that Catholic laymen "should be urged to be genuine witnesses to the faith in their domestic, business, social, and civic activities and to join organizations which can influence daily life: associations of parents interested in educational activities, organizations with professional, charitable, and civic aims not excluding participation in politics." It was well received in the Council and even by the *Washington Post*. Bishop Wright of Pittsburgh spoke in support of the idea, asking also for a deeper theological treatment of the position of the laity in the Church.

I also made a rather long plea for changes in the laws of the Church concerning participation in prayer, worship, and sacraments (*communicatio in sacris*). I cited that in many Protestant services there was no mention of opposition to or denial of the Catholic faith. I also stated we should encourage more precise thinking about our Catholic doctrine and help Protestants to do the same. Much of the bitterness expressed against the Church's doctrine has long been forgotten, and therefore the Church "in its charity and care for souls should help to bury the dead past." To encourage this development, I suggested that the bishop be empowered to establish a committee that would make timely decisions about this matter in his diocese.

I submitted a lengthy intervention on the subject that was at the heart of the Council — ecumenism. The document was called "The Restoration of Unity" (*Unitatis Redintegratio*). I was deeply interested in the subject for several reasons, including my Protestant relatives who certainly believed in charity and led good lives. I cited the good produced by Protestant communities, especially the works of charity they performed in the United States. In this respect I praised the good effects from the Instruction of the Holy Office in 1950 permitting the recitation of the Our Father, the Lord's Prayer, at discussions and meetings with Protestants. Another point was that the prohibition in Canon Law (now revoked) forbidding the attendance at Mass of Protestants prevented the spreading of Catholic doctrine as well as participation in a sacred ceremony.

Obviously, there was no possibility that a document on ecumenism would fail at a Council called largely for that purpose. The document was promulgated by Pope Paul VI on November 21, 1964, amid a chorus of proclamations by both Catholics and Protestants. Cardinal Ritter of St. Louis won the contest for the most appropriate description of a Council document when he said the ecumenical statement "rings the death knell of the Reformation."

Archbishop Maxim Hermaniuk of Winnipeg took the occasion to state that the Latin Church must make reparations for the wrongs it had committed against the Orthodox Church, citing that Cardinal Humbert of Silva Candida, the legate of Rome who had excommunicated the Patriarch of Constantinople in 1054, falsely attributed "every kind of heresy" to the Oriental Church in order to condemn it.

These discussions about the rights of various groups also produced a number of interesting events. Prominent among these groups were Catholic women. A petition had been made by Cardinal Léon Joseph Suenens of Belgium to have Mrs. Montini, the sister-in-law of the Pope, receive Holy Communion at one of the morning Masses of the Council. It was refused — a rigid application of the idea that the Council was only for bishops and other male members of the Church. This was remedied; she later attended Mass and received Holy Communion.

Then a demand was made by Monsignor George Higgins that a Catholic layman be permitted to address the Council; he suggested Patrick Keegan of England, the President of the World Movement of Christian Workers.

Eventually it was agreed to have James Norris, famous for his part in Catholic Relief Services and other charitable causes, make the address. No doubt it was Archbishop O'Boyle, past president of Catholic Relief Services, who influenced that decision. Norris jolted the Council by delivering his splendid address about world hunger in pristine Ciceronian Latin, demonstrating the superiority of the Catholic high school he attended in New York.

Paul VI became very active in these matters. He announced on September 8, 1964, that some women auditors would be invited to attend the Council — and a special coffee bar for the ladies was erected. Also, the Pope's visit to the Patriarch Athenagoras in Jerusalem in January 1964 resulted in the sending of a representative of the Patriarchate of Constantinople to the third session of the Council, the first time a representative of the Patriarchate attended a function of the Church in Rome. This action resulted also in an increase of observers, finally amounting to eighty-three. The increased attention of the Council by the world press also resulted in an increase in attendance at the Council of Bishops. The attendance grew from 2,466 bishops in 1962 to 2,488 in 1963.

Please see the Appendix for my role in persuading the Council fathers to accept the morality of nuclear deterrence and my brief recollections of the major documents of Vatican II.

CHAPTER 12

Appointment to New Orleans

The bishops attending the Second Vatican Council in the fall of 1965 knew this climactic session would conclude our historic four-year assembly. Both Pope John XXIII and Pope Paul VI did not want the Council to drag on indefinitely, and Paul VI had made sure he established a firm timetable to force us to concentrate on the work at hand and finish in a timely manner.

In late September 1965, I had just finished coordinating the routine afternoon media briefing for English-speaking reporters when a monsignor I had never seen before approached me. From his Italian accent and manner, I knew immediately he was from the Curia. Thinking he wanted to sit in on the press conference, I welcomed him warmly. Instead, he had a brief message: "I would like to talk to you after the press conference," he said, and I suggested that we meet afterwards at the Hotel Eden.

When he came to my room a few hours later, he was all business. I expected him to give me his background so that he might persuade me to use him as an expert on a future press panel, and we chatted cordially for a couple of minutes. But he quickly cut off the small talk.

"Look," he said, "I've come from the Curia, and I have a simple message for you — the Holy Father wants you to become the archbishop of New Orleans."

I was stunned — that was absolutely the last thing on my mind. I had read newspaper reports about the devastation wrought by Hurricane Betsy, which had struck New Orleans on September 9, 1965, and flooded large parts of the city, including one hundred sixty thousand homes, but I hadn't given the slightest thought I might be considered for that appointment.

"You've got to read this message from the Holy Father," the monsignor said, handing me a small slip of paper with the Latin words of my appointment.

"I'd like to have some time to think about it," I told him. "I'm certainly willing to do whatever the Holy Father wants, but I have some questions..."

The monsignor broke right in on my measured response. "Look, you don't even have to read this," he said. "The Holy Father wants you to do this, and nobody turns down the Holy Father! Please sign the paper right now."

I took his pen and signed the paper immediately. As soon as the monsignor secured my signature, he took off, and I never met him again. There was no formality to it whatsoever. The Vatican officially announced my appointment a couple of days later on September 29, 1965 — less than three weeks after Betsy.

One of the reasons I initially hesitated in accepting the appointment was that it meant, of course, that I'd have to relinquish the position of coordinating the daily press conference, and I wanted to make sure I had left that job in good hands. As the Council progressed toward its climax, the pace of the decisions and the news increased markedly, which in turn made the press conferences more active and demanding. Reporters made strident demands for interpretations of the approved documents, and that ramped up the workload and placed additional pressure on the members of the press panel.

After the announcement of my appointment as archbishop of New Orleans was made at the end of September, I received a flurry of questions about my plans for New Orleans, which I assiduously dodged, and suggestions about everything, including the status of Plaquemines Parish Judge Leander Perez, who had been excommunicated by Archbishop Rummel for his opposition to the Church's teaching on desegregation. I was also corrected on my pronunciation of New Orleans. I made the New "Or-LEENS" mistake only once!

The appointment changed my place of seating at the Council. As an auxiliary bishop I had been seated in the "bleacher" section of St. Peter's Basilica farthest from the main altar and presidential chair. As an archbishop I was escorted to the first section, just behind the cardinals. Naturally, somebody on the press panel dubbed me "Rookie of the Year."

Even though I had visited New Orleans once as a bishop to consult with Archbishop Rummel about his fierce and nearly insurmountable challenges in integrating Catholic schools, I really didn't know a soul in the Crescent City. Of course, I was acquainted with Archbishop John P. Cody, who had been appointed coadjutor archbishop of New Orleans in August 1961, became Apostolic administrator in June 1962, and then served as Archbishop Rummel's successor from November 1964 to June 1965, at which time he

Formal portrait with miter and crosier

was named archbishop of Chicago. Archbishop Cody was a few years ahead of me at the North American College in Rome, and despite his domineering leadership style and his tendency to pontificate and insert the words "as the Pope told me last week" into almost every conversation, he was well-regarded as a future leader of the U.S. Church.

I remember pulling out the National Catholic Directory to examine the statistics of the Archdiocese of New Orleans, and I was surprised at the relatively small number of diocesan priests (about two hundred), in comparison with Washington, D.C. (about three hundred fifty). I knew New Orleans was a great Catholic center and had a rich Catholic culture, so I had expected the archdiocese to have a few more priests. I also noted that most of the Catholic schools were parish-based, and there weren't a large number of schools operated by religious orders.

One of my first jobs was to get rid of my main duty in Rome — coordinating the daily press panel. I knew Father Edward Heston would do a great job with his expanded duties, and he did just that.

My September 29 appointment as archbishop of New Orleans was twinned with the appointment of Divine Word Father Harold Perry as the first African-American auxiliary bishop in the United States in the twentieth century. Bishop Perry, a native of Lake Charles, Louisiana, was the provincial of the Society of the Divine Word and national chaplain of the Knights of Peter Claver. His appointment to New Orleans made a very strong statement

Washington Archbishop Patrick A. O'Boyle congratulates his former auxiliary bishop, Archbishop Philip Hannan, as Archbishop Hannan takes leave of Washington, D.C., on October 11, 1965.

that racial integration was not simply window dressing. Actually, Cardinal Cody, in Chicago for just two months, had steered both of our appointments through the Vatican. Cody never told me this directly, but a few days before the appointments were publicly announced, he asked Bishop Perry and me to pose together for a photograph. The purpose of the photo became obvious when the simultaneous announcements were made. It also proved to me that Cody had been totally clued in on the Vatican's decision.

I had known Father Perry from my days in Washington, D.C. House Speaker John McCormack was tired of having the House of Representatives open its session with a Protestant minister delivering the annual invocation. McCormack wanted a Catholic priest to break the unwritten protocol — and he wanted an African-American priest to show how serious the country and the Church were about integration. "I want you to get me a black priest," McCormack told me bluntly on the telephone. "And I don't want any of these black people who look white. I want a black priest."

I called the Society of the Divine Word because I knew they were one of the few religious orders that was warmly welcoming black seminarians. Father Perry, the provincial, immediately accepted the Speaker's offer to deliver the opening prayer, and he did a great job. McCormack treated Perry royally, so it was a real home run.

Bishop Perry was perfect for New Orleans, especially with its large percentage of African-American Catholics. He simply brushed aside the few times he was publicly insulted by white parishioners. I remember the outstanding instance when he went to one parish to confer Confirmation, and as the children were lining up to go into church, a white mother who suddenly realized Bishop Perry was going to be the confirming prelate yanked her child out of line. Bishop Perry did exactly the right thing — he never said a word to the woman — and the other people who witnessed this horrible incident gave him great credit for his forgiving heart. Bishop Perry was not only liked but loved. He had a very good sense of humor. I cannot conceive of a better bishop to handle the situation in New Orleans.

When he came to New Orleans, Bishop-designate Perry told the *Clarion Herald*: "Many white persons in the South now feel that integration is inevitable, but they face this dilemma: How can we accept defeat without losing face? How can we salvage our self-respect after disrespecting such a large percentage of the people for so long?" Bishop Perry was a spirit-filled man whose life was cut short by Alzheimer's Disease. I think the priests and the people who knew him recognize the great service and witness he provided in their midst during a very tumultuous time in our history.

Within a few hours of the announcement of my appointment in late September, I received an urgent telegram from New Orleans Auxiliary Bishop Louis Caillouet, who had been named administrator of the archdiocese after

Archbishop Cody had left for Chicago. His telegram didn't pull any punches: "Hurricane Betsy has been extremely destructive, and we need you to get to New Orleans as quickly as possible." I placed an immediate call to Bishop Caillouet, and I never talked to anyone who was so eager to get rid of an office in my life. He reiterated several times his request that I get to New Orleans immediately, and by the tone in his voice, I knew he meant every word.

I dictated a statement on September 29 to Monsignor Elmo Romagosa, director of the archdiocesan Bureau of Information:

> "I wish to express my heartfelt gratitude to his Holiness for the confidence placed in me by the appointment as Archbishop of the Archdiocese of New Orleans. I pledge my utmost efforts in serving the cause of Christ in this office, and I humbly request the Holy Father's apostolic blessing upon me and all the people of God in the Archdiocese of New Orleans.
>
> "I eagerly look forward to serving them as their shepherd in God, especially in this hour of trial by nature in which they have shown such magnificent courage and charity under the excellent leadership of Bishop Louis Abel Caillouet, the administrator. I salute very cordially my fellow citizens of all faiths in the Archdiocese.
>
> "I pledge to continue according to my ability the splendid work of Archbishop John P. Cody and my other illustrious predecessors.
>
> "May I ask the prayers of all in the Archdiocese of New Orleans, as well as those of the Archbishop, clergy, and people of Washington, whose wonderful goodness has benefited me so much and to whom I shall be eternally grateful."

The difficulty in getting quickly to New Orleans was compounded by the fact that I was also the pastor of St. Patrick's Church in Washington, D.C., as well as editor of the newspaper and chief person in charge of buying real estate for the archdiocese, so that put Archbishop O'Boyle in a bind. A few days after the announcement was made, the local New Orleans TV stations dispatched reporters to Rome to interview me. I took them to the roof of the North American College, which has a great view of the dome of St. Peter's, and they interviewed me about my background as a paratroop chaplain, my connection with President Kennedy, and my hopes for New Orleans.

A few days later I caught a flight to Washington, D.C., and within a week I celebrated farewell Masses at St. Patrick's Church and at the National Shrine of the Immaculate Conception, where I had dedicated many of the side altars as an auxiliary bishop. Both Masses were very crowded, and I was able to offer my heartfelt good-byes to so many close friends.

Arrival in New Orleans

When I arrived at Moisant International Airport in New Orleans in early October, I didn't exactly know what to expect. In a sense, I was coming to New Orleans blind. I figured I would start my fact-finding tour with Bishop Caillouet, who greeted me at the airport. The pilot and co-pilot got off the plane, and I heard them talking about me within earshot of several reporters. The pilot said to his co-pilot, "How did a young fellow (I was fifty-two years old) like this get such a big job?" The pressmen overheard the question and playfully repeated it to me. "If you ever find out," I replied, "please tell me because I surely don't know!"

Bishop Caillouet took me in his car to the archbishop's residence on Carrollton Avenue next to Notre Dame Seminary, and as I walked into the house, I saw a few people gathered for a reception. To my great surprise, my mother was in the parlor and came out to give me a big kiss. Of course, the news reporters naturally got a few pictures of me standing next to my Mom, and they suggested to her, "This must be the proudest day of your life." In typical Hannan fashion, Mom replied, "No, it isn't. The proudest day of my life was the day I married my husband!"

A reporter then said: "Well, you must be very proud of your son." To that, my Mom replied, "Which one?" As the mother of seven boys, Mom was not a very demonstrative person, but she could handle any situation with diplomatic flair.

Talking with kids upon arrival at New Orleans International Airport in 1965

I realized one of my first responsibilities was to offer sympathy to the people who had lost so much in Betsy. I asked Bishop Caillouet if he could take me to any nearby parishes that had been heavily damaged by the storm. "Oh, yeah," he said ominously. "There's a pile of them."

I went to one parish in the Lower 9th Ward where virtually every home had taken in eight feet of water. As I greeted the family, I naturally told them how sorry I was for their suffering, but then their little boy blurted out to me: "I found a big fish in the parlor!" That was all Betsy had meant to him. That little boy had no trouble at all recovering from Betsy.

The next day we started to visit the areas outside of New Orleans, and that sobering misery tour revealed the widespread devastation. We drove down to lower Plaquemines Parish and went as far as the road would take us, dead-ending at a swollen bayou. One of the local fishermen said, "In order to go any farther you have to go by boat. You ever been in a pirogue?"

"No," I replied, "but there's a first time for everything."

"Before you try to step into the pirogue," the fisherman said with an air of caution, "do you know how to swim?"

"Yeah, I can take care of that," I told him.

It was a bouncy ride over to the other side of the bayou. Arriving on the opposite shore, a woman was there to greet our party. The eerie silence and the teeming wilderness we encountered couldn't have been much different than the setting Sieur de La Salle experienced while exploring the Mississippi River basin in the 1680s. But there was a key difference — the woman had a car. "I know who you are and what you're trying to do," she said, handing us the keys to her sedan so that we could make a further inspection of the area. We were able to continue our visit and met dozens of families who had lost everything.

I was tremendously impressed by the attitude of the people. They realized that they had suffered tremendous damage, but they had absolutely no intention of giving up. They all said they simply were going to repair their homes and camps and move forward. I remember especially one family with a little baby. They had lost everything in their home, and I told the mother I'd like to give her and her infant a blessing.

"I'm so sorry," I said. "This must be such a great burden on you."

"It's not so bad," the mother told me. "The only thing we saved was a pillow, so we have a pillow for the baby to rest on. As far as sleeping goes, the rest of us sleep on the floor." They were so unfazed by the desolation and destruction around them. I said to myself, "These are good, tough people."

One of the priests who accompanied me on this tour — Father Allen Roy — is still serving today as a pastor in New Orleans. I remem-

Auxiliary Bishop Louis Caillouet and I looking at a church damaged by Hurricane Betsy

Helping to block a break-through in a dike due to Hurricane Juan in 1985

I, along with other priests, survey the damage done to buildings in lower St. Bernard Parish by Hurricane Betsy.

ber how he and the other priests took the destruction in stride. There was no wailing or whining. They were sorry it had occurred, of course, but there was absolutely no doubt they would rebuild and persevere. In the subsequent months — after I returned from the final session of Vatican II in December 1965 — we had to discuss the rebuilding in terms of the limitations of our current budget. Because of Archbishop Cody's ambitious plan to establish new parishes in the suburbs and build new elementary and high schools — a plan I came to agree with because the Catholic population was expanding and needed to be served — the Archdiocese was significantly in debt by late 1965.

Several high schools that Cody had started in 1962 were unfinished, and now the question was whether or not, in the face of Betsy, we could afford to complete them. In Thibodaux, Betsy had severely damaged Mount Carmel Academy and Thibodaux College, and that forced us to move the students into a new Catholic high school — at first called Thibodaux Central Catholic High School — that was still under construction. But everyone pitched in, and it worked. A year later, I asked the school to change its name to Edward Douglas White Catholic High in honor of the Catholic Supreme Court chief justice, a Thibodaux native. As an eight-year-old in 1921, I had served at White's funeral Mass at St. Matthew's Cathedral. I vividly remember his horse-drawn caisson approaching the church, along with another horse that had neither a bridle nor a saddle.

Capital expansion and Betsy's damage had plunged the Archdiocese of New Orleans deeply into debt and, of course, we didn't have any money to pay it back immediately. Reflecting on my one-on-one conversations with residents after Betsy, I knew the archdiocese had an abundance of good Catholics who were devoted to the development of the Church, so I tried not to push them into making extraordinary financial contributions. The debt didn't bother me at all because I knew the caliber of the people I was dealing with. Certainly, Hurricane Betsy had wrecked a great deal of the city, and at a time like that there's always a doubt about whether or not we could recover completely and move forward. My job was to be a spiritual director, making sure the Archdiocese, through its own efforts, inspired people that we could, indeed, make it all the way back.

I got that can-do feeling from the start. I was installed as archbishop of New Orleans on October 13, 1965, at St. Louis Cathedral, and my lasting impression of the occasion was how thoroughly the Catholic culture had permeated New Orleans in the city's two hundred fifty years of existence. After all, where else in the United States does a cathedral serve as the icon of a city? I kept wondering, how in the name of God did they build this massive cathedral in the epicenter of a city that is surrounded by water and bedeviled by sinking soil? Whatever Frenchman made the decision to plant the flag here — and erect the cathedral as its focal point — certainly knew what he was doing. Despite Betsy, the cathedral building was in remarkably good shape. I expected it to have a few more aches and pains. As I walked through Jackson Square, I also felt an emotional tug on my Washington, D.C., heartstrings — the statue of Andrew Jackson astride his horse is one of three crafted by American sculptor Clark Mills in the 1850s. The same Jackson statue is the centerpiece of Lafayette Park directly across the street from the White House! Yes, I felt very much at home.

I quickly had to make difficult decisions on whether or not we would rebuild some of the small churches in lower St. Bernard and Plaquemines civil parishes that were destroyed in Betsy. One church in Reggio in lower St. Bernard had floated a half-mile away from its original location. We decided to combine two churches by building one church in Florissant — San Pedro Pescador — that could withstand hurricane-force winds, and that would better serve the people.

The day after Christmas in 1965, I went to my office in the chancery, and Bishop Caillouet told me: "I think it's time for you to know the whole picture about our indebtedness. We have a $1 million payment to make on Monday, and we don't have one cent to pay it." I decided right there that we would have to form a syndicate of banks to help us navigate through the financial shoals. I promptly called a number of local banks and said, "Look, we're in a difficult financial position. If you lend me enough money just to pay the interest on these loans, then I know we can make out just fine when we get back on our feet." The banks stepped up to the plate, for which I was eternally grateful.

The local bankers could have mistrusted me, an outsider, from the start. Archbishop Cody had not catered to them at all, instead preferring to take the Archdiocese's financial affairs to New York banks. By ways known only to him, Cody had obtained loans at fantastically low interest rates in New York. He was paying only 5 percent interest on loans, and I don't know of anybody in America who had a better deal than that. But I thought it was imperative to use our local banks, and they helped us out of a very difficult situation.

I felt at home analyzing the Betsy damage because of my childhood background — I had learned a few things from my father, who was a master plumber and also knew everything about construction. I also had been in charge of buying real estate and monitoring construction in Washington. The new St. Frances Cabrini Church in Gentilly, a massive, 1,600-seat church with sweeping rooflines and an imposing spire that was dedicated in 1963, had made it through Betsy intact. But the first time Monsignor Gerald Frey showed me the "Cathedral by the Lake," I had some bad premonitions. Every time a breeze would blow, the spire would wiggle and shake part of the curved roof loose, leading to continuous leaks. Cabrini's design may have won some national architectural awards, but that leaky roof was flawed and a maintenance nightmare.

I was on the scene early enough to head off another potential mistake. Monsignor Fatty Bourgeois was planning renovations to Our Lady of the Rosary Church on Esplanade Avenue, and the architect got the idea that the downspouts for the copper gutters would look ugly attached to the outside of the building. His "ingenious" plan was to hide the downspouts inside the walls of the church. When I saw the blueprints I changed that immediately. Sometime architects sacrifice functionality and common sense for beauty, and that's a very expensive mistake in the long run.

Establishing Priorities

In addition to getting our financial house in order, I had two pressing priorities as I entered my first year as archbishop of New Orleans: our elderly needed decent, affordable, safe places in which to live; and our children needed more educational and recreational opportunities, especially during the oppressively hot summers typical of New Orleans.

I never could fathom the approach taken by some bishops to restrict the work of the Catholic Church to Catholics only. Christ commissioned his Apostles to make disciples of all nations. The only way to make the kingdom of God more than a spiritual platitude is to take concrete steps to improve the wider community. The Church does that not by turning inward and hoping some good gets accomplished; rather, the Church uses the gifts of the Holy Spirit to touch people where they are. The Second Vatican Council clearly articulated the importance of interfaith outreach, not only to Christian denominations but to all the people, including our Jewish friends. I know that the bishops felt burdened with trying to support their Catholic schools and institutions and they realized that they must maintain their focus on preaching the Gospel. But, there are many community problems that the Catholic Church, because of its prophetic witness and sheer size, is uniquely positioned to address.

As archbishop, I relished the chance to work with people who could enhance our mission of serving the common good. I'll never forget the first time I met New Orleans Mayor Vic Schiro. During the chaos of Hurricane Betsy, so the story goes, he had appealed for calm among the citizenry by pleading on live TV: "Don't believe any false rumors unless they come from your mayor!" I went to Schiro's office one day to formally introduce myself, and all I had to do was look at his walls to see what made him tick. Every tribute, every award, every photo ever given to him by any citizens' group was hanging on the wall. It was Vic Schiro-motif wallpaper! Even though Schiro had a limited knowledge of construction projects, he was always very cordial and even helpful in our determination to provide affordable housing to the elderly poor and to offer constructive outlets for youths during the summer.

Our new Office of the Social Apostolate grew out of the first, ten-week Summer Witness program in the summer of 1966. It began with a simple premise — poor kids, especially African-Americans, needed a place to balance fun and academic enrichment during the three, broiling months of summer vacation. I vividly had seen the need for such a project during a walk through

the Desire Housing Project in late 1965. I decided to visit the area unan-
nounced in the middle of the week so that I could see things as they really
were. A resident walked up to me and asked, "Are you one of those people who
will promise us things and leave?" I replied, "I will not leave." The Catholic
Church was the only entity that could speak to all groups, and I wanted us
desperately to be involved in solving community problems. Many of the residents couldn't read or write.

One Desire apartment complex resident told me everything I needed to
know. The city had passed an ordinance that no tenants could be evicted for
nonpayment of rent unless they were two months in arrears. Even then, the
process simply started, and then it dragged on without much urgency. When
it looked as though the eviction finally would be enforced, very often the tenant would rent a truck and cart off the refrigerator and other major appliances
from the apartment. That vicious cycle increased the number of apartments
that couldn't be put back quickly into commerce and also created a sense of
despair and abandonment among the remaining residents. We had a heroic
Sister from Samoa who actually lived in an extra Desire apartment and worked
with the women residents to learn carpentry and plumbing skills so that they
could fix the crumbling infrastructure on their own rather than wait for the
city to get around to it. She also started a little school for the kids and taught
the women how to sew and repair clothes. She was always cheerful and optimistic. She finally organized groups of women who could make any repairs
needed in the whole project!

It didn't take long to draw an accurate assessment of the recreational
opportunities available to black children — they simply didn't exist. There was
one tiny, decrepit playground at Desire for thousands of kids. I approached the
railroad company that owned lots of green space near Desire and asked if we
could use some of its excess property for recreational space — with the promise that we would return the land if the railroad ever needed it — and that's
how we began the Summer Witness program at Desire in 1966. Incidentally,
I'd love to meet the person who got rich selling the property on which the
Desire Project was built. That soil was so porous that it probably couldn't support a multi-story apartment building. Some of the multi-story buildings were
supposed to be used exclusively for the elderly, but there were so many rob-
beries in the elevators that the elderly chose not to live there, and the housing
authority opened up the building to everyone. The elderly were, once again,
lost in the shuffle.

Even though Congress had passed several Civil Rights bills, the reality
facing black children in New Orleans at the time was that most public recreational facilities — including the largest and best public swimming pools
maintained by the New Orleans Recreation Department — were essentially
off limits to them. Whenever a group of black children wanted to swim at a

Top: Bishop Caillouet and the Patriarch from the East and me at the Greek Cathedral. *Middle:* At residence with Sister Guadalupe and Sister Aurelia of the Sisters of the Holy Family. *Bottom:* With singer Bing Crosby upon his arrival in New Orleans for the Archdiocesan Charities Ball on September 10, 1976.

1966 photo

Serving meals at Ozanam Inn

With Lindy Boggs at a groundbreaking ceremony for a senior residence

Visiting a home for the elderly

Left: Shown blessing the new senior residence, Chateau de Notre Dame, which opened on December 8, 1977. My concern for the elderly and the needy was the catalyst for the focused building program I established and funded.

Seen flanked by New Orleans Mayor Vic Schiro on the right reviewing personnel from the New Orleans police and fire departments in Jackson Square after a May 5, 1968, Mass at St. Louis Cathedral

NORD facility, suddenly — magically — the pool developed "pump problems" or confounding "leaks" that made them inoperable.

I didn't have to look far to find a swimming pool for the inaugural Summer Witness program in 1966 — it was in my backyard! Notre Dame Seminary had a pristine, Olympic-size swimming pool that was barely used from June through August because the seminarians were mostly away from the seminary working in parishes. My brainstorm wasn't wholeheartedly embraced, even within the seminary community. Several people came up with objections: Who would provide the lifeguards? Who would take care of the extra maintenance for the pool? Who would organize things to make sure the kids didn't damage the pool?

It almost sounded like an official NORD press release.

I determined that providing a swimming pool for these children was not a luxury but a necessity because it would give them an incentive to perform their academic work diligently. Those who tried their best would be rewarded with one or two hours of pool time each week. I didn't think that was too much of a burden on the seminary. The swimming program was incredibly successful, even though I heard the grumbling from white Catholics that I was going "overboard" in helping out non-Catholic black kids. I had been through all kinds of racial tensions in Washington, D.C., so those sentiments were nothing new to me. I completely expected it — and I completely ignored it.

We did, however, have a major tragedy at the pool. Even with several lifeguards on duty, one child jumped into the deep end and was not spotted when he got into trouble, and he drowned. A few years later, another child drowned after being caught in an undertow while swimming in Lake Pontchartrain. I went to the Protestant church that was conducting his funeral service, and I explained to the entire congregation everything that had happened. I also called a meeting of Protestant ministers in the area, and more than twenty attended. They were understanding and even appreciative of everything the Catholic Church was trying to do for their children. "If you have any programs for our children, just tell us about it, and we'll follow your lead," one pastor told me. The Protestant ministers were always cooperative. No one even thought of filing a lawsuit. How times have changed!

The Summer Witness program — which in its early years enrolled two thousand four hundred children ages five to twelve and assisted another five thousand six hundred children with its summer feeding program and swimming program — also had a powerful effect on the seminarians, religious, and other Catholics who helped direct its enrichment programs. Realizing in advance that I would need to recruit seminarians to serve as teachers and moderators, I went to Boston, where I knew the rector of St. John's Seminary, Monsignor Lawrence J. Riley, because he had been a student with me at the North American College in Rome.

When I arrived to give my pitch to the seminarians about spending their summer in New Orleans, Monsignor Riley nervously informed me that the seminarians were almost in a state of revolt over changes they wanted to see incorporated into the seminary curriculum. They were even holding demonstrations to get Cardinal Cushing to accede to their demands for change. I knew then I wouldn't be able to speak to the entire seminary, but I was able to address a few men to see if they had any interest in helping out with our inner-city program. In the end, we got about seventy seminarians to come down from several dioceses. I knew the young men wouldn't cause any problems in New Orleans because we were going to work them so hard they would only have time to pray, eat, and sleep. Most of them lived at Notre Dame Seminary.

One of the men who came down to New Orleans from Boston was Roger Morin, who later entered Notre Dame Seminary, was ordained a priest for New Orleans, headed our Department of Community Services for many years, and later became auxiliary bishop of New Orleans and in 2009 became the third bishop of Biloxi. Roger always had a passion for social justice, and the Summer Witness program lit a spark in his vocation.

Unfortunately, there was another seminarian who didn't have Roger's wisdom or passion. He got off the bus in New Orleans, found his way to the chancery, and walked into the building barefoot. The first person to greet him was Sister Barbara Ashey, who ran our summer program, and she rushed over to my office to give me a firsthand report. "We can't use this volunteer," she told me. "We're trying to get the kids to dress properly, and here he is with no shoes." I immediately gave "Shoeless Joe Jackson" a one-way bus ticket home.

We told all of the seminarians exactly what we expected of them in teaching, and if they didn't feel they could do it, they could find their way back home. Without question, the 1960s ranks as the craziest decade of the twentieth century. The cultural revolution culminated in 1969 with the Woodstock "love-in," where thousands of young people broke just about every drug and sex law on the books with impunity. The police apparently were told by their superiors not to enforce any laws. Nobody expected to get arrested for any crime, and nobody did. That kind of revolt found its way into our colleges and our youth throughout the nation.

I was interested in attacking our community's social problems from the perspective of the Gospel imperative. In the Matthew 25:35–36, Jesus clearly states: "For I was hungry and you gave me food, I was thirsty and you gave me drink, I was a stranger and you welcomed me, I was naked and you clothed me, I was sick and you visited me, I was in prison and you came to me." That was the kind of revolution I was interested in. At one point I even broached the idea of the archdiocese taking over management of one of the city's housing projects to serve as a model of what lasting improvements could be made. We would have hired people from within the community to do first-rate repairs, and we could have monitored safety, educational, and recreational matters. But we never went forward with the plan because such an idea, I admitted upon reflection, probably was too ambitious. You can't do everything.

But, I also knew we could do more than we had been doing for our poor and frail elderly. On my walks through Desire and on my visits throughout the archdiocese, I spoke to people about their most pressing problems, and one thing that came up consistently was the lack of good housing at fair prices for senior citizens, and also a need for more nursing facilities to care for our aging population. As a stand-alone entity, the Archdiocese of New Orleans could not possibly take on such a building campaign because it would have been prohibitively expensive. However, not many people knew that in the mid-1960s, the federal government was practically hyperventilating to provide almost limitless funds through grants and other tax breaks to nonprofits to build affordable housing for low- and middle-income families. The federal agency dispensing the money was the Department of Health, Education, and Welfare, and that was run by my old Kennedy friend Abraham Ribicoff. Congressman Hale Boggs and his wife, Lindy, were instrumental in seeing that our proposals to HUD were approved. They secured approval for every plan we submitted, and I was determined to use the federal funds to build housing that would improve the quality of life for our entire community.

Christopher Homes

That was the beginning of our archdiocesan housing agency called Christopher Homes. We used our track record as a successful charitable organization to successfully seek zoning changes to allow for the construction of "scattered site" housing for families. Mayor Schiro, and later Mayors Moon Landrieu and Ernest "Dutch" Morial, were extremely helpful in pushing for zoning relief to make these developments work.

Whenever I met politicians for the first time, the very first thing I did was to ask them about the challenges and difficulties of their office. Their replies would reveal the kind of administrator they were and tell me where they stood. I also knew I needed to have a relationship with the governor and members of the Louisiana congressional delegation. The first time I met Louisiana Governor John McKeithen, I could tell immediately he was at the end of his rope with Schiro. McKeithen told me, "I don't know what to do with him. He'll come to me and say his people want such and such. I'll write that down and take it into consideration. And then a different group will come to me the next week and say they want the opposite. So I'll call Schiro back and tell him there were two different groups coming to see me with two completely different agendas — so which one did he favor? Schiro will always tell me, 'Both of them.'"

In 1965, the archdiocese of New Orleans had only three Catholic-sponsored facilities for the elderly — the Lafon Home of the Holy Family Sisters, the Little Sisters of the Poor Home, and the St. Margaret Daughters Home. The Sisters of the Holy Family, founded by Mother Henriette Delille, a free woman of color, were pioneers in the care of the elderly, having begun their mission to educate and care for slaves as far back as 1842. The Little Sisters of the Poor had served the elderly in New Orleans since 1868. But those three homes accommodated a total of only two hundred sixty persons.

The person who most convinced me of the need for housing for the elderly and families was Sybil Morial, Dutch's wife. She knew it was a dire problem, and I knew it as soon as I toured the Lafon Home shortly after arriving in New Orleans. The dear Sisters of the Holy Family were doing everything they could to care for their elderly residents, but their old wooden building was a complete tinderbox — there was no sprinkler system. If a fire had broken out in that facility, it would have been an unmitigated disaster. Even with Sybil's support, I had a difficult time convincing some of our skeptical priests, who couldn't see the point of building homes for the elderly. "Why should we be getting into this when we've been able to handle our elderly just fine?" one priest asked me. "Also, black families take care of their elderly quite well." To me, the evidence was quite to the contrary. I asked Sybil Morial her opinion, and she replied, "Of course, we badly need these facilities, but nobody asked our opinion!" I believed Sybil and acted accordingly.

I knew in order for Christopher Homes to succeed, I had to hire a cracker-jack manager who was above reproach, someone who could handle the intricacies and tedium of dealing with the federal government and also be a servant leader to his staff and the residents. I wanted an African-American director because this would signal our intent to serve the wider community. Josephite Father Eugene McManus, the principal of St. Augustine High School which served black males, was the first Chairman of the Board of our New Orleans Archdiocesan Commission on Housing, and he suggested the perfect candidate for the job: St. Augustine's humble but passionate English and industrial arts teacher Tom Perkins. The Holy Spirit truly must have inspired Father McManus because I can say, without a doubt, I have never made a decision that turned out better than my decision to have Tom Perkins lead Christopher Homes.

Tom was the one of the most self-effacing gentlemen I ever knew. He had a Pied Piper's ability to get kids off the street and into school. He told me once about how he handled an unruly class. "When they get louder, I speak softer," Tom said. "Eventually, they quiet down because they're curious about what I'm saying." That was Tom, always the perfect gentleman and the consummate psychologist. He never had a cross word for anyone. At the end of his thirty-year tenure, Christopher Homes was managing thirty-four housing sites with more than three thousand five hundred apartments for the elderly and families — the largest housing operation of any U.S. diocese. Tom used to tell me, "Housing is not mortar and brick. It's people." How true.

I just wish I could have convinced more U.S. Catholic bishops to join hands with the federal government in responding to the desperate need for affordable housing. The head of the Department of Housing and Urban Development asked me to do some back-channel work with several bishops to promote the affordable housing program. I traveled to Chicago to speak to Cardinal Cody and endeavored to sell him on the idea. "You've got such a big archdiocese and so many Catholics," I told Cody. "Certainly there must be a huge need for this kind of housing." But Cody wouldn't bite. "Phil," he said, "I've got my own plans."

I even gave several other bishops our blueprints for the apartments we had constructed in New Orleans, and I told them all they had to do was write to HUD and request the funding and the project would be fast-tracked. Eventually several dioceses accepted our offer and constructed excellent homes for the elderly. In the Archdiocese of New Orleans, we were receiving far more requests for elderly housing than we could handle.

Our first housing development was Christopher Inn on Royal Street on the fringe of the French Quarter, the former site of Holy Redeemer Church, which had been badly damaged by Hurricane Betsy. Against a wave of public opposition, we brokered a deal with the city to purchase the adjacent former public library that had sustained severe wind damage and was planned to be mothballed. The combined properties gave us the footprint we needed to make Christopher Inn work. The peculiar result was that it was built so well and so fast that we were swamped with applications from whites, who were parishioners of the nearby parishes and were very eager to live in their former neighborhood. I sought the help of some Josephite priests to convince some blacks to move into Christopher Inn, and our intention was to provide a large percentage of units to elderly blacks. We had to make sure those applications were balanced.

On reflection, the reason I got so heavily into providing housing for seniors was the wonderful experience of my own family life. My parents worked hard for a living and did well. We never had to struggle for anything — be it material goods or good education at some of the country's finest universities. My dad had always looked out for his workers and wanted them to have a decent place to call home. I think providing quality housing is the least we can do for our elders who may not have been as fortunate as I was.

The success of Christopher Inn and the Wynhoven Apartments on the Westbank led, in 1973, to our most ambitious project — providing low-cost residential units and nursing home beds for the elderly. We launched the $4.4 million HORIZONS capital campaign in both our churches and the business community to provide seed money for five senior residences and nursing homes. The total project was estimated to cost $21.7 million and would provide nine hundred forty five additional nursing home beds and apartments for seniors. One year later, we had surpassed the campaign goal. Our early success led to even more projects because the federal government now could analyze our track record and was willing to look at any new project we proposed.

I did have to overcome a few political and racial hurdles in furthering the mission of Christopher Homes. In 1980, when the archdiocese was interested in building a 150-unit senior housing facility in St. Bernard Parish, I ran directly into lingering racial animosity. Some St. Bernard residents were against the project because they feared it would mean African-Americans, a tiny percentage of the parish's population, would be moving into their "neighborhood." In fact, one of the Council members even stated that he wanted the archdiocese to state explicitly that no black residents from the 9th Ward would be allowed to rent any of the St. Bernard units. He apparently wasn't listening when he was told the archdiocese was already in the process of building two new apartment complexes for seniors in the heavily African-American 9th Ward — right next to Annunciation and St. Maurice churches.

I answered every objection the Council raised. *There would be increased traffic*: "Unfortunately, the old folks are not visited very often by their relatives." *The project would overburden the parish's sewer system*: "There is a hospital going up right next to the apartments, and perhaps we could tap into that. If not, we'll build our own sewage disposal system." *It's going to increase our garbage disposal costs*: "No, we've taken care of that at all of our other facilities." *This will require extra security on the part of the sheriff's department*: "No, we provide our own security."

The barrage of objections was petty and — at its core — racially motivated. These apartments were going to be a boon to the parish because they would provide affordable housing for the elderly relatives and friends of the Council members. Even though the parish had not provided a single housing facility for seniors, the Council displayed almost no shred of Christian charity. In the face of such nonsense, I was determined not to stop my efforts. By the hardest work, we finally got the project approved, and it was a fantastic success story.

When I blessed Metairie Manor in Jefferson Parish in 1980, a number of seniors came up to me at the reception to thank me for remaining so steadfast in providing them with a safe place to live. It struck me just how many residents were there out of fear, which was a sad commentary on our times. One woman told me, "Now we can go to bed at night without worrying whether or not someone is going to break in the front door, whether we're going to get stabbed or mugged or burglarized." Those comments reflected the signs of the times, and we as Church must respond to those signs. It was great to serve the old folks who now had a tangible reason to believe the Church was truly doing something just for them.

The housing program was a perfect example of how the church and state could work together on programs for the common good. I remember in 1988, just before submitting my resignation as archbishop of New Orleans, I attended a Christopher Homes banquet at the New Orleans Hilton Riverside Hotel. About 800 of the 1,325 attendees were residents of Christopher Homes facilities. One resident, Mrs. Elvire Drufner, gave tributes that summarized the contribution of Christopher Homes, one of the nicest tributes I've ever received: "God saved the best thing for the last years of our lives."

I'll never forget another story Tom Perkins told me about an elderly man who had resisted for weeks when his family wanted him to move to a nice apartment at Wynhoven, which is on the West Bank. He was from the other side of the river, and he resisted the idea of making such a major move. After a few days, the man fell in love with his new home. With Thanksgiving Day approaching, his kids invited him to join them for a fabulous meal at their home in New Orleans. "When are you having dinner?" the man asked. His son replied: "As usual — about noon." The man answered: "Okay, if you promise to bring me back across the river in time for me to attend the party we're having at two thirty in the afternoon."

The Social Apostolate

We began the Social Apostolate in 1966 with ten programs, and two years later we expanded by opening six year-round community centers, the idea being that people's needs extended far beyond ten weeks during the summer. We based everything on the philosophy of self-help and giving people what they needed to better their lives.

Of course, any initiative worth doing well carries with it a basic fact of life — finding the money to sustain the year-to-year operations. I've often joked that, for me, one of the nicest rewards of heaven will be the peace of mind from not having to raise another dime. I know Jesus will not ask us to launch another capital campaign to build more apartments or schools. But as archbishop, finding the money to accomplish the Church's mission is critically important, because it's hard to care for your priests and teach the faith if you don't have a framework in place to pay for your efforts. Laypersons are eager to be partners in these projects.

That's where lay Catholics come in, because they want to do everything they can to participate in that mission. Quite often, all an archbishop has to do is ask for help. Doc Laborde, a tireless, brilliant engineer who made an enormous contribution to offshore oil drilling, came to the chancery one day in early 1966 on some other business, and I met him in the hallway. I explained I was trying to launch the Social Apostolate's Summer Witness program because I thought it was vital for the city and its children. "How much are you talking about?" Doc asked. I replied, "Well, I need a good gift to get it started. We're trying to raise $150,000." Without pausing for a second, Doc smiled and said, "I'll give you $25,000" — and he wrote out a check on the spot! That's how the annual Archbishop's Community Appeal started — we needed the funds to operate these critical community centers.

I've always found that people who are blessed with a lot of money and are favorably disposed to the Church find it a supreme compliment to be asked to help financially with special projects. Invariably, the ones who are the most successful will give you a hair-trigger response — they don't hem and haw and tell you they'll "think about it." There is a trust factor, of course, but these individuals can size you up pretty quickly and see if you're real or phony. I thank God every day for the lay people who have come into my life and wanted to support our mission. They are truly living out their Gospel call. Doc Laborde, by the way, is just a couple of years younger than I, and he's still actively pursuing his business interests. I tell most people who are facing retirement that if they feel good and are doing well in their jobs, keep on going. I've seen so many people retire only to experience crushing boredom. Well, Doc retired at age ninety-three, and about four or five weeks after he retired he called me up and said he was going back into business. At age ninety-four, he

In the 1980s, I visited children served by the Summer Witness program, which I started in 1966 as a way to serve needy children of all faiths. The boldest move I made in 1966 was to open the Notre Dame Seminary swimming pool to African-American children at a time when, despite civil rights laws to the contrary, segregation kept whites and blacks from mingling in public facilities.

bought a company in Texas that produces special boats for offshore drilling, which he had designed.

We started Summer Witness with the basics. We found out many of the children who came to us didn't have enough food to eat — many were coming into the program without having eaten breakfast or even dinner the night before. We also discovered that so many of their families lacked the resources to buy nutritious food. After checking with the American Academy of Pediatrics, we went up to Capitol Hill to tell Congress that the milk products the federal government was providing for infants through its commodities program — Pet milk and Karo syrup — were unacceptably high on calories and low on nutrition. We demanded real infant formula. Practically the entire Louisiana delegation attended the meeting, even Congressman F. Edward Hébert, who normally was not a champion of poor, single mothers. We found out from Louisiana Senator Russell Long and Congresswoman Lindy Boggs that the federal government already was supplying the Navajo Nation with authentic baby formula in its food packets, so there was a precedent already established. When I got back to New Orleans, I wrote a letter to the head of the supplemental food program requesting the change, and we got it done. It was nice to have friends in high places so that we could do the right thing for

Looking out over St. Louis Cathedral from the Pontalba Apartments in 1981

our children. It made absolutely no difference that most of these children were not Catholic. Each child has human dignity.

The community centers cost a lot of money to run, but they were absolutely essential to our mission. We had a cadre of women religious run the centers, and most were former teachers or principals who knew how to organize their small staffs effectively. We were able to get permission from the Orleans Parish Public School system to use some of the public schools as Witness sites during the summer. One summer we had to overcome a problem with the school janitors, who weren't too excited about having students in their schools during what normally would have been the slow summer months. We took action by demanding that the students pick up after themselves and keep the classrooms and bathrooms spotless. I followed up by speaking directly to the janitors at a hastily called meeting. I praised them effusively for giving up part of their summer for the purpose of helping out needy children. It was amazing how a little validation of their efforts removed any obstacle to our having access to the schools during the summer.

The Summer Witness program, which developed into the far-reaching Social Apostolate, was so successful and addressed such crying community needs that I wrote on my tenth anniversary as archbishop of New Orleans in 1975: "I think we're winning!" All I was doing was getting out of the way and letting the Holy Spirit create the tailwind.

1999 picture for the Archdiocese of New Orleans pictorial directory

Leading a pilgrimage to Rome in the 1980s for Catholics associated with The Catholic University of America and the Archdiocese of New Orleans, I arranged a special audience with Pope John Paul II. The woman in white next to the Pope had lost her husband six months earlier. The Pope embraced her and kissed her on the cheek. "I can't believe the Pope kissed me," she said. "You can believe it," the Pope replied. The group agreed that the number one thing they saw in Rome, among all the art and ancient churches, was the catacombs.

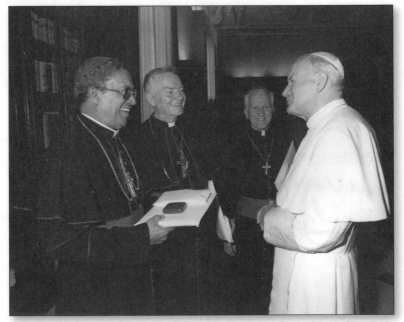

An ad limina visit in the 1980s with Pope John Paul II. From left, Auxiliary Bishop Harold Perry, S.V.D., me, and Bishop Nicholas D'Antonio, O.F.M.

APOSTOLIC NUNCIATURE
UNITED STATES OF AMERICA

3339 MASSACHUSETTS AVENUE, N.W.
WASHINGTON, D. C. 20008-3687

No. 2307/89/5
This No. Should Be Prefixed to the Answer

May 23, 1989

Dear Archbishop Hannan:

    With joy have I heard of the celebrations in your honor in the Archdiocese of New Orleans this May 28th, and was pleased to receive an invitation. Regrettably, my presence in Rome will keep me from being with you. However, I did want to convey to you an assurance of my prayerful solidarity, as well as unite with the distinguished citizens of your grand city in paying tribute to a truly outstanding religious and civic leader.

    To hundreds of thousands of your fellow citizens, you are a symbol of wisdom, charity, and faith. As a brother bishop, I have come to admire the attractive blend of natural talent and supernatural virtue that has come together in your person.

    It is my distinct privilege to convey to you the prayerful good wishes of His Holiness Pope John Paul II. To the people of New Orleans he sends his affectionate greetings, gratefully mindful of his joyful visit to you almost two years ago. The Holy Father desires to unite with your legion of friends in expressing esteem for the leadership and example you have given during your years as Archbishop of New Orleans.

Sincerely and Fraternally in Christ,

Pio Laghi
Apostolic Pro-Nuncio

Most Reverend Philip M. Hannan
Archbishop Emeritus of New Orleans
New Orleans, Louisiana

Letter of appreciation from Papal Nuncio upon my retirement

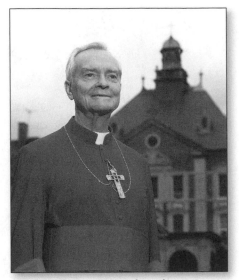

Retirement photo in 1989 in front of Notre Dame
Seminary

With the 2009 appointment of Archbishop Gregory M. Aymond, far right, as the
fourteenth archbishop of New Orleans, the New Orleans Archdiocese lays claim to an
unprecedented distinction, according to records kept by the United States Conference
of Catholic Bishops: four living archbishops. The archbishops and their respective
dates of tenure are: Philip M. Hannan, (1965-89), second from right; Francis B.
Schulte, (1989-2002), third from right; Alfred C. Hughes, (2002-09), far left; and
Gregory M. Aymond. Archbishop Schulte said with a laugh, "We're going to have to
go through this again for the fifth one." Archbishop Aymond, referring to me, said, "He'll
probably bury all of us — hopefully, not at the same time."

170 GRESCENT ROAD
TORONTO, ONTARIO
CANADA M4W 1V2

May 25, 1989

Dear Archbishop Hannon—

Happy birthday!

I am just one among countless numbers who are mighty grateful you were born.

Your loving guidance and keen judgement were an invaluable support to me and mine during our mutual "tour of duty" in Washington.

I have no doubt that you have rendered the people of Louisiana a pastorial wisdom of unique value during what I know has been a mighty trying time.

In hours of need God often lights the way through one wise and loving person. Thank you for being such a beacon of hope for me.

With birthday love always—
Luci Baines Johnson

Wonderful letter from Lucy Baines Johnson for my birthday

CHAPTER 13

Race Relations and Politics
in New Orleans

Because of the dark, centuries-long history of slavery in the Deep South and New Orleans' pre-eminent position as the waterway to America's cotton and sugar trade, race relations in New Orleans have played a pivotal role in the political, economic, cultural, and spiritual life of our region. Even before the Civil War, the presence of free persons of color, some of whom owned slaves, as in the Melville area of Louisiana, provided another layer of mystery and intrigue in perpetuating an intolerable institution.

For years the Catholic Church in New Orleans had separate churches for blacks and whites, and many African-American Catholics in New Orleans today still can recall being told to sit in the side pews or in the back of the church by a white usher or even being denied the Eucharist at Mass. Their depth of faith in the face of harsh discrimination by a Church that vowed to no longer distinguish between Jew or Greek, slave or free, is amazing to me.

I made my first trip to New Orleans in the early 1960s when Archbishop O'Boyle asked me to visit Archbishop Rummel on my way back from a Dallas meeting to share with him our experiences in the archdiocese of Washington regarding the desegregation of Catholic schools.

Archbishop Rummel had written and spoken out forcefully about the sin of racism and segregation — he wrote a pastoral letter on the immorality of racial segregation in 1956 — but he was butting heads with an entrenched state legislature and a city power structure that wanted not only to dig in their heels but also to seek any opportunity to punish the Church for moving ahead with its integration plans. In addition, there were some pastors who refused to read Archbishop Rummel's pastoral letter from the pulpit because they considered it a radioactive teaching that would drive white parishioners out of the church. Archbishop Rummel's failing health also made it difficult for him to summon the physical and emotional energy to complete the struggle, and he worried that moving too quickly on integration without the support of a large majority of the laity would split the archdiocese asunder and damage it spiritually.

There's no question that the Vatican decided to appoint a strong-willed, young bishop, John Patrick Cody, as coadjutor archbishop of New Orleans on August 14, 1961, so that he could carry out, without any further delay, the integration of Catholic schools. Rummel was the elderly grandfather, painting the vision and pointing the way to the truth; Cody was the steely-eyed enforcer, the cop with the nightstick. And, that's exactly the way it had to be done.

Cody had a direct way of speaking that absolutely brooked no opposition. His leadership style would never work today, of course, but in the early 1960s, his autocratic manner was accepted in part because the Church had an abundant supply of priests. It's not that priests of that era were more pliable — people are people, no matter what the generation — but because vocations were flourishing, a bishop could use fear as his ultimate motivator. A priest who refused to toe the ecclesiastical line or who seemed reluctant to support the bishop's decisions could be dispatched quickly and easily to a smaller, less prosperous parish. Cody used elemental human fear to further his aggressive agenda.

Cody was fearless in doing what he thought was right for the Church — regardless of the ultimate effect on his popularity. That explains why he did not hesitate to pull the trigger on integration. Obviously, Cody's style angered many pastors, and some of them criticized him to me after my arrival in 1965 for going on a capital spending spree that resulted in dozens of new parishes and schools being built — leaving the archdiocese with a sizable deficit. However, when it came to Cody's building program, I totally agreed with the decisions he had made. I certainly didn't think the debt he had incurred was an unbearable burden. In fact, that building boom was absolutely necessary to serve the growing needs of the archdiocese. I think most of the criticism of Cody's extravagant spending was based on people's distaste for his stance on integration. I felt I owed Cody support for his tough stance on race relations because it was absolutely the right thing to do.

Cody's reputation as a taskmaster was well-earned. One of his classic idiosyncrasies was insisting that every question posed by a priest to the chancery be answered the same day it came in — even if it meant the administrative staff stayed in their offices until midnight to get their work done. Monsignor Clinton Doskey spent many late nights in his office, carrying letters to the main post office at midnight so that the Archbishop's answer would be in the next day's mail. That was an efficient way of doing things, but it put a notable strain on his staff.

There were weighty situations that needed handling in the early 1960s. Archbishop Cody was the key person who sealed the official excommunications of Plaquemines Parish boss Leander H. Perez, Sr., and two other lay persons — Jackson G. Ricau, secretary of the Citizens Council of South Louisiana, and Mrs. B.J. Gaillot Jr., president of Save Our Nation — for challenging Archbishop Rummel's authority on the issue of integration. While the archdiocese continued to insist on integrating its schools, Perez advocated publicly for white parishioners angered by integration to stop making financial contributions to the Church. "Shut their water off and you'll see them turn about-face," Perez told parishioners in Plaquemines. Archbishops Rummel and Cody sent out personal letters to many individuals warning them they would incur excommunication if they continued their public opposition to Church teaching, and most agreed to cease their verbal attacks. However, when Perez, Ricau, and Gaillot refused to capitulate, Archbishops Rummel and Cody officially excommunicated them on April 16, 1962.

Because Perez, the main subject of the excommunication decree, was a national figure — and because the decree figured to be challenged on canon law grounds — it was carefully written and executed. The decree was read publicly by archdiocesan Chancellor Monsignor Charles Plauche. Perez, Ricau, and Gaillot were being excommunicated for continuing "to hinder (the archbishop's)

It's hard to believe now, but when I was installed in October 1965 as Archbishop of New Orleans, I had to walk through a phalanx of women picketing against the integration of churches and schools and the appointment of Bishop Harold Perry as the first African-American bishop in the modern-day South. At left is Msgr. John B. Roeder, chancellor of the Washington Archdiocese. The woman picketing in the background is Mrs. J.B. Gaillot, an avowed segregationist who was one of three persons excommunicated by Archbishops Rummel and Cody in 1962 for defiantly opposing parochial school integration. Leading the procession is then-Father Earl Woods, who became guardian of the Old Ursuline Convent and restored it beautifully.

orders or provoke the devoted people of this venerable archdiocese to disobedience or rebellion in the matter of opening our schools to all Catholic children." The decree said the three had exhibited "flagrant disregard" for the "fatherly counsel" of the Archbishop. The three were barred from attending Mass and receiving the sacraments, including the right to receive a Catholic burial. Catholic schools were officially desegregated in the fall of 1962.

Perez and Ricau eventually were reinstated into the Church following public retractions of their previous positions. I met Perez personally, only on a few occasions, but I certainly was involved in his formal reconciliation with the Church. In 1965 at the final session of Vatican II, there was intense discussion about how canon law should treat individuals who had been excommunicated but desired to return to the Church. I remember Bishop Fulton Sheen, in a crowd of bishops, bringing up Perez and his flagrant actions and telling me, "Phil, I think you should just forget about the whole thing and not even pay any attention to it."

"Wait a minute," I replied. "A lot of people down there backed the bishop when he excommunicated Perez, and I certainly cannot just disregard what he did."

What complicated the issue was the advice Perez was receiving from a local priest, who suggested that the decree of excommunication was invalid according to canon law. But Monsignor Plauche, chancellor of the archdiocese and an excellent authority on canon law, said the letter of the law had been followed: it was signed by both archbishops and the announcement was made over television. Cody, by the way, was an expert in canon law and made sure everything was exactly right.

If Perez were to reconcile with the Church, I was determined to make him publicly recant his position. In 1967, Perez's son Chalin came to see me, at the urging of his mother, who was a very good Catholic and was urging Leander to come back to the Church before it was too late. I told Chalin, "Excommunication is a public act, and I need to have a public statement from your father disavowing what he has done and stating that he now follows the dictates of the church. I'm not going to write the statement for him. Your father has to read his statement at a public event."

"But we don't have any really big public events on our schedule in Plaquemines," Chalin told me.

"Well, you're the head of Plaquemines Parish, and you can certainly schedule something," I replied.

Leander Perez decided to do his official recanting at the dedication of an incinerator in Fort Jackson — not exactly riveting material for the ten o'clock news! I sent a priest down to Fort Jackson to hear the speech and give me a firsthand report on the substance of his declaration. While there were only a few people there, Perez retracted his statements challenging the authority of

Archbishop Rummel. I lifted his excommunication, and a year and a half later Perez was buried from Holy Name of Jesus Church in New Orleans when he died at the age of seventy-seven. Perez's New Orleans residence was on Audubon Place, which was in Holy Name Parish. There was some grumbling among Catholics about his elaborate funeral, but he had been reinstated to communion with the Church.

Mrs. Gaillot called me a couple of times to request that I lift her excommunication as well. I think she believed Cody or someone else had forged Rummel's name on her decree of excommunication. But she never recanted her original statements, and she said she wanted to preach the same thing — that integration was morally wrong. That sounded crazy to me, and when she told me her position had not changed, there was nothing I could do for her.

Perez thought he could bring the archdiocese to its knees by having white parishioners withhold their financial contributions, and he got only a very few people to go along. Some people dropped chocolate candy and licorice into the collection basket. A number of white parishioners wound up taking their children out of Catholic schools and stopped giving to the Church, but their actions didn't make a significant impact on our operations. There weren't enough people to follow through on Leander's brazen threats.

I received a few telephone threats from angry whites at night, but none of that bothered me. The only things that did bother me were the actions of a small number of priests who actually supported Perez and criticized Cody for his actions. I knew how to handle those priests from my days in Washington. Some of the Jesuits in Maryland who objected to integration in the Archdiocese of Washington loved to quote St. Thomas Aquinas, who said that under certain circumstances slavery was permissible, provided the human and spiritual needs of the slaves were met. The hell that people in New Orleans raised about integration was nothing compared to the conflagrations I had to deal with in Maryland.

For the most part, our priests went along admirably with integration. We had a couple of very conservative but well-respected priests, Anthony and Raymond Wegmann, who did not like Cody's style and the forceful manner in which he enforced integration. Monsignor Anthony Wegmann was head of the Priests' Council and was pastor of St. Matthias Parish, which had a thriving school. He wasn't crazy about quickly integrating the schools because he thought a lot of white parents would pull their kids out of school and maybe even leave the Church, but he was loyal to the archbishop. Both Wegmanns saw that they had to get over their own misgivings about integration, and they were able to influence many people.

Anthony Wegmann told me that at a Priests' Council meeting, Archbishop Cody had complained that some pastors were not doing everything in their power to promote integration among their parishioners. At the end of the meeting, Monsignor Wegmann stood up and looked at the priests and said, "We're all going to support what the archbishop wants. Answer me by saying, 'Aye!'" Everybody had to say "Aye." I know this for sure: Monsignor Wegmann didn't ask for a roll-call vote. I think some of the priests in the room held that against Monsignor Wegmann for a long time.

Moving integration beyond platitudes was one of my major tasks in the late 1960s. By 1968, there were about six thousand students in eleven new schools that the archdiocese had built in that decade — most of them in the fast-growing suburbs on the east and west banks of Jefferson Parish — but very few black students attended those schools. The reality was that many white parents whose children had attended public schools in Jefferson Parish began to transfer their children to Catholic schools. A very few white parents were deliberately fleeing integration. I told pastors not to accept students whose parents were motivated simply by wanting to avoid integration.

In the final analysis, the integration process went more smoothly than most would have expected. In the first few years, some schools lost close to half their enrollment, but the numbers shot back up again when white parents realized they had made a mistake in pulling their children out of school. At Annunciation School in Bogalusa — a town that had the smallest Catholic population in the entire archdiocese — the white parents who removed their children from the school got a big surprise. The school had such a good reputation that Protestant children filled all the spots relinquished by the Catholic families, and when the Catholic parents wanted to put their children back into the school, there was no room to take them. They had to wait their turn. The Benedictine pastor Father Hugh Bauman — rightfully so — absolutely refused to ask the Protestant families to step aside. That pastor had a great deal of "pastoral" sense. I liked his style. When the white parents appealed to me to reverse the decision of the pastor, I refused. That sent a strong message throughout the archdiocese.

One of the big disappointments I encountered in the early years of integration was the fact that some of our established Sisters did not want to teach black students at all. That's the reason I worked so hard to recruit several congregations of Irish nuns — especially the Cabra Dominicans — who were so willing to teach in inner-city Catholic schools. They did a marvelous job. Of course, those Irish nuns have my eternal gratitude.

I also give great credit to the Josephite Fathers, who have a special ministry to African-American Catholics, for helping the Archdiocese of New Orleans negotiate the racial minefields of the 1960s. The Josephites agreed to open and operate St. Augustine High School for black males in 1951, and they staffed numerous black parishes throughout the city. I wanted them to continue their great work, but I also wanted them not to come across as "preachy" to other priests in the archdiocese on the issue of integration. I did not want a split among our priests, because that would have been deadly in the long run. The Josephites used great judgment in determining how far they could push the envelope without causing a counter-revolution.

Another champion during those trying times was Dr. Norman Francis, the first lay president of Xavier University of Louisiana, who assumed office in 1968 just after the assassination of Dr. Martin Luther King in Memphis. For forty years, Norman and his wife, Blanche, have been quiet heroes of racial integration and advancement, carrying on the legacy of Xavier foundress St. Katharine Drexel. By building Xavier University into an educational power-house — Xavier leads all U.S. colleges and universities each year in placing African-American graduates into medical school — Norman has done more to advance the cause of brotherhood in New Orleans over the last five decades than anyone else I know. He is a shining example of what Vatican II was all about — allowing lay Catholics to take their rightful position in the Church.

Norman could always be counted on to defuse any volatile situation. In May 1969, a group of Xavier students waving the black flag of liberation tried to lock the doors to the administration building. Norman agreed to meet the group and listen to their demands. They wanted more books by black authors in the school library, and they wanted a black priest to serve as chaplain. Norman was able to resolve the situation by getting Divine Word Father Jerome Ledoux to serve as chaplain in the fall.

No matter how well the archdiocese handled integration, race was an explosive issue in the 1960s in New Orleans. Dr. King was assassinated in April 1968, and Bobby Kennedy, who was viewed as the Democratic presidential candidate most attuned to black voters, was assassinated in Los Angeles in June. Major cities across the country experienced riots and searing racial tension.

Racial Conflicts

New Orleans and the archdiocese were not immune to the strife, and we had several racially charged confrontations that could have exploded into serious violence. In May 1968 — one month after Dr. King's assassination — black activist H. "Rap" Brown led a group of more than three hundred African-Americans to a rally at Shakespeare Park. Brown was the leader of a group called the Student Nonviolent Coordinating Committee, which wanted to use the church for a rally to decry the "appeasement" policies toward blacks that they claimed had been fostered for years by the Catholic Church and by Gov. John McKeithen. The meeting had not been authorized by the pastor — the church was simply suggested as a site by young members of the student group. Actually, Father Gorham Putnam, the pastor, and Father Clinton Doskey, his associate, fully supported integration, and the racially mixed church was a reflection of that.

Brown really knew how to work a crowd. Standing in Shakespeare Park at the corner of LaSalle Street and Washington Avenue — a few blocks away from St. Francis de Sales Church — Brown exhorted his listeners, calling them "chumps" if they did not react more forcefully to the oppression they had experienced from whites. A driving rain began to soak the outdoor assembly. "I'm not going to stand in the rain and talk to you," he shouted. "If you want to hear me and they won't let you in that church, which is in your community, then you should kick the door down."

The group then marched to the church. The New Orleans police in riot gear had stationed themselves on the perimeter of the church. The pastor, Father Putnam, was a quick thinker. Before the crowd reached the church, he pulled all the fuses that fed electrical power to the church and school, and he stationed a police officer inside the rectory to protect that building. The crowd pressed toward the front door of the rectory, but Putnam and Father Doskey met them and refused to let them in. Rap Brown actually stayed inside a car parked on the side of the church. His attorney, William Kuntsler, had enough knowledge of the law to know that a forcible entry into a church or rectory would be illegal and certainly hurt his cause. Still, Kuntsler kept poking Father Doskey in the chest and shouting, "If you don't let us use your church, there's going to be blood spilled all over the place." Doskey didn't know if the militants were going to shoot him. He was a much bigger guy in those days, and he stood resolutely in the door of the rectory and refused to step aside. The protestors knew they could attend Mass at St. Francis de Sales, but they wanted to use the church as a symbolic pulpit.

The crowd then decided to break into the school, but that tactic didn't work because Putnam had pulled the fuses. The marchers eventually dispersed down Dryades Street in the pouring rain. We were fortunate that no one was hurt that night, and I credit that positive outcome to the savvy of Father Putnam and Father Doskey and also to the police presence, which had been dispatched by New Orleans Police Superintendent Joe Giarrusso, a good friend who always was very sensitive to our needs in an emergency. The event had mushroomed into a nervous stare-down with police, but the final result was very positive. The crowd learned that the school and church were integrated, and they also understood that the parish would remain in control of its buildings.

The Desire Housing Project and the adjacent St. Philip the Apostle Church became the backdrop for another racially charged incident. Despite our efforts in establishing a Social Apostolate center in the Desire area to serve women and children, Desire was a racial powder keg in the late 1960s. I had assigned Clinton Doskey to serve as pastor of St. Philip the Apostle Church, located just a few blocks away from Desire. Clint was assisted by Father Jerry Prinz and Father Doug Doussan. In 1968, the King assassination, cultural unrest, and economic disparities in the United States created a perfect breeding ground for revolution, and the Black Panther movement grew in size and influence in major cities across the country, including New Orleans. One Sunday while Father Doskey was celebrating Mass, a group of militants marched into St. Philip Church and essentially took it over. They walked up to the ambo, grabbed the microphone and shouted down Clint in his attempts to continue the Mass. They were not going to leave until they had their say. They finally left, and Clint was able to finish the Mass.

The following week, a group of militants broke into the church and took all the statues, crucifixes, missals, and hymnals from the church. Clint and his parishioners were left with a totally bare building. When the militants left, they chained the front doors with a padlock, and Father Doskey needed a hacksaw to cut through the chains and get back into the church. On another occasion, someone posted a sign in front of the church that read: "For Sale: Consult Your Local Archbishop."

It got worse. In the middle of one night, a group of militants came to the St. Philip rectory and woke Father Doskey from his sleep. Father Joe Latino, the future bishop of Jackson, Mississippi, was also residing in the rectory, as was Father John Lauer of the Glenmary Fathers, who was working in the summer program. But the militants wanted to make a scapegoat of Father Doskey, and they demanded that he come with them for a kangaroo court trial. At that moment, Clint didn't know if his feet were being fitted for cement shoes. The militants drove Clint into the middle of Desire and ordered him to get out, and then he was escorted into another car. It was a scene right out of "The Godfather." The second car took Clint to the

Reverend Douglas Moore of the Black United Front presented demands for Black Reparations to the U.S. bishops through me at the November 1969 meeting of bishops. I was the communications director for the bishops' conference, so I was assigned to handle the delicate task. He wanted to get on the bishops' agenda, but I had to tell him we already had a full program. He got the press he wanted

nearby Florida Housing Project, where he was taken into the basement of one of the buildings there.

The militants read a list of demands, and they wanted Clint to agree that he would get the church and local authorities to accede to their demands. But, the Lord was with him, because they eventually released him, and he was allowed to return to his rectory at two o'clock in the morning.

These were harrowing times, but I knew I could not allow my priests to twist in the wind. Shortly after the militants broke into St. Philip Church and disrupted the Mass — an act of desecration according to canon law — I went to the church to reconsecrate it for proper liturgical use. I told Father Doskey, "They are not going to take over this whole place. I've faced Tiger tanks in Germany, and I can face this, too." You have to stand up to aggression and a clear evil, and this was evil. The parishioners at St. Philip were forever grateful for our resolute response.

During another of the Black Panther takeover episodes at Desire, the police, without my knowledge, decided they might be able to infiltrate the militant group by dressing a police officer in a priest's black cassock and having him gain access to the apartment. The ploy worked to the extent that the disguised "Father Cop" was able to identify the people in the room and determine their numbers, but I was totally upset about the tactics when I found out about it afterward. I warned the police that any future use of a priest's cassock to impersonate a priest would result in a long jail sentence for any culprit. We have never been able to find out who impersonated this priest.

I always was willing to help the police in any emergency situation. No one who was in New Orleans in January 1973 will ever forget the surreal sniper attack perpetrated by a former Navy sailor, Mark Essex, at the former Downtown Howard Johnson's Hotel — now the Holiday Inn Downtown — on Loyola Avenue across the street from City Hall.

Essex, a native of Kansas, had been discharged from the Navy in 1971 after a series of behavioral problems, and his hatred and psychological imbalance apparently pushed him to embrace radical violence. He moved to New Orleans and began targeting white police officers for murder. On New Year's Eve 1972, Essex killed police cadet Alfred Harrell and police officer Edwin Hosli, Sr., near police headquarters, but he somehow escaped an intense police dragnet.

On the morning of Sunday, January 7, 1973 — just about the time I was celebrating Mass at St. Louis Cathedral — Essex shot grocer Joe Perniciaro and then made his way to the Howard Johnson's Hotel. He shot and killed a white couple on the eighteenth floor and then went to the eleventh floor, where he set a series of fires. When firefighters and police arrived, Essex began firing at will, picking off firefighters on ladders and police officers. He eventually scampered up the stairwell to a cement, rooftop bunker, where he could shield himself from direct attack and still be able to fire.

This incredible drama played out live on national TV. The three major networks took live feeds from their local affiliates, so everyone across the country was gripped by the unfolding terror. After Mass I was able to contact Mayor Moon Landrieu, and I told him about my paratroop regiment, the 82nd Airborne, which had expertise in retaking a property that had been captured by an enemy force. The Army had the special weapons and the know-how to go room-to-room to secure a property.

A police officer picked me up at the cathedral and drove me to the three major New Orleans TV stations, where I was able to get on the air and offer a prayer for a peaceful resolution of the incident. Completing that task, I drove with the officer to the command post set up near the hotel, where Mayor Landrieu and the police department's top brass were directing the rescue operations. I kept asking the mayor and the police chief if they had the proper weaponry to face this unknown threat. From my Army experience, I believed the police were underprepared to respond, which is the reason I urged the mayor to call in the Army to handle the situation. This was in the days before most major metropolitan police departments had finely tuned SWAT teams to handle hostage situations and other unusual standoffs.

Unfortunately, my advice fell on deaf ears. I even offered to go to the hotel and talk personally to Essex if they could establish contact with him, but it never got that far. The police were determined to run the operation themselves. The long standoff ended in incredible carnage. Essex was pummeled with two hundred bullets from a helicopter gunship, but not before he had killed nine people and wounded thirteen others. As it turned out, some of the injured and killed police officers were hit by friendly fire in the stairwell leading up to the rooftop bunker. I made my way over to Charity Hospital to console the families of the dead and injured. The saddest reality was that it was a foolish situation that could have been handled so much better.

Race relations have been intertwined with New Orleans politics for centuries. I had very minor difficulties with Mayor Moon Landrieu over the years. As mayor, Moon was a lion among white politicians in the way he opened up city government to African-Americans. I will always give him credit for his progressive stance on race, which certainly did not endear him to the city's white power structure.

Moon didn't get enough credit for his bold actions of inclusion. I sympathized with him because even though he did more than any white politician in New Orleans history to advance the cause of racial justice, his efforts were not adequately acknowledged by Mayor Ernest N. "Dutch" Morial, the city's first black mayor and someone who was very successful in his office. The racial rancor was evident at the dedication of Louis Armstrong Park, right behind the Municipal Auditorium. The $9 million project had been conceived and started under the Moon Landrieu administration. Yet, of the eight speakers on the dais, three community leaders got up and blasted Moon, who was then secretary of the U.S. Department of Housing and Urban Development. After one particularly virulent attack, I leaned over to Moon and said, "I'm prepared to give you general absolution in case you get killed on the platform." I was surprised because Moon was laughing the entire time. When the speaker finished, he passed by Moon, and Moon was still laughing. "You've kept up your average, Jim," Moon said. "You haven't told the truth yet. There wasn't one person moved out of this area to make way for the park." And the fellow shook hands with Moon and said, loudly enough for me to hear, "You know, Moon, I have to say that in front of this crowd."

When it came time for Moon to speak, he got up and gave the "government" speech — praising the federal officials for ponying up the millions for its construction. Then he issued a point-by-point rebuttal of the attacks. "The original plan for the area, dating back to the 1950s, was for that area to be nothing more than a parking lot for the Municipal Auditorium and the Cultural Center," he said. "There was not one person moved. As a matter of fact, we preserved two buildings that were on this property. The people had been relocated, and one building was scheduled to be demolished, but as mayor I stepped in and kept it from being demolished. I had both of those homes moved to another section, and now they are being put to good use."

Moon was a big backer of our Summer Witness program because he knew it filled a huge void in city services. He recognized the Church's competence in providing an incredibly effective program that saved the city thousands of dollars and advanced the common good. I also made sure I kept him filled in on our plans for affordable housing for seniors. I knew I had to keep our relationship open and transparent. I did that by dropping by his office occasionally. I went to see him one day and told him, "We're projecting a big capital campaign that will help us build housing for the elderly, but I don't want to be running a program that might be useless if the city is going to get into that." Moon replied, "I don't have any plans to do that." He didn't really help us build affordable housing, but he certainly didn't get in the way, which sometimes is all that's needed from your local government.

The Church must stand up to politicians when its vital interests are at stake. In the late 1960s we had heard of plans by the city, supported by Mayor Victor Schiro, to use federal highway funds to construct an elevated Riverfront Expressway that would ring the city and carry thousands of fast-moving vehicles directly in front of Jackson Square and the cathedral. As soon as I heard of the plans I knew a highway of that type would be aesthetically awful, harm the ambience of the French Quarter, and impact the cathedral. No other American city has a cathedral as its icon, and building an elevated Riverfront Expressway would have been equivalent to defacing the Mona Lisa with a permanent marker.

I canvassed a few of the leading citizens in the New Orleans business community, and we decided to hire an expert who could conduct a study that would raise substantive issues about the harmful impact of an elevated expressway. The cost of the study — about $50,000 — was defrayed by an interested citizen, and it was well worth it. We made several points: the Interstate highway really did not match the size and scope of the French Quarter streets adjacent to it; it would permanently obstruct the views of the Mississippi River; and it would prevent any future development of that portion of the riverfront. The *Clarion Herald*, our archdiocesan newspaper, came out strongly in opposition to the expressway and really hammered the point home, and the tide eventually turned. The federal government thought it was doing us a favor by its willingness to finance 90 percent of the highway's construction costs, but building that monstrosity would have been a disaster. The senseless project died an ignominious death on August 22, 1969. When I walk over to Washington Artillery Park next to the Mississippi and gaze upon the postcard setting of General Jackson astride his horse — directly in front of the cathedral — I give thanks to God that that we were on the right side of history.

Although I admired Mayor Dutch Morial and appreciated his wife Sybil for her graciousness, intelligence, and willingness to help advance Catholic causes such as our elderly housing and summer programs, I must say I had many roller-coaster experiences with Dutch. Of Creole descent, Dutch was a proud but polarizing figure, a man of groundbreaking personal achievements but with a prickly temperament. He was the first black to receive a law degree from Louisiana State University in Baton Rouge (1954), the first black member of the Louisiana Legislature since Reconstruction (1967), the first black Juvenile Court judge in Louisiana (1970), the first black elected to the Louisiana Fourth Circuit Court of Appeal (1974), and New Orleans' first black mayor (1978).

From my interactions with Dutch, I learned a lot about class distinctions within the New Orleans black community. As a Creole, Morial was proud of his French heritage and was totally opposed to a trend popular in the African-American community in the 1970s to give African names to their children or to change their given names. "You ought to live with the name that your Momma gave you," he told an audience of African-Americans. He also didn't like the fact that I consulted with African-Americans of all backgrounds, especially non-Creoles. He certainly was conscious of class distinctions, and he didn't want me counseled by anyone in the black community of whom he did not approve. I felt the least I could do was to listen to groups who wanted my ear, but Morial didn't appreciate that at all. He wanted to be the ultimate gatekeeper.

Dutch also had an ax to grind against the Church over our willingness to welcome thousands of Vietnamese refugees into the Archdiocese of New Orleans beginning in 1975. He opposed our open-door policy because he felt the Vietnamese would take jobs away from the black community, which was his political power base. After a number of his public statements, I called and asked him to come to my residence for lunch. I told him, "Look, I have to be for everyone in this community, not just for the blacks. The Vietnamese are not going to take jobs away from blacks, but they are going to work hard, and I'm going to support them. I'm just not going to pay any attention to your complaint about the Vietnamese." He finally gave in and at least didn't cause me any more trouble.

I tried to help Dutch whenever I could be of service. In 1981 there was a huge stir within the African-American community about police brutality. There were many instances of blacks being taken into custody and being beaten by cops on the way to central lockup, and there were many shootings of blacks by police officers that were challenged by the black community as to whether or not they were justified. In July 1981 I met with a committee, headed by African-American leader Bill Rouselle, to look into the complaints of police brutality. We agreed at the meeting that the best course of action was to ask the mayor to set up a committee with wide representation in order to examine and possibly redraft the police manual. This was not intended to raise an accusatory finger at the police but simply to review the manual to get rid of any questionable practices that were being allowed. It was through these kinds of efforts that we were able to nurture racial harmony in New Orleans.

Vietnamese Catholics

After the Vietnam War ended in chaos in 1975, thousands of Vietnamese refugees who had managed to escape from Saigon by boat ended up in camps in the Philippines. From there, thousands were shipped to Fort Chaffee, Arkansas, and, at last to New Orleans. Their twentieth century exodus reflected the Gospel coming to life in brilliant Technicolor. They were sheep without a shepherd. Their abject living conditions were the ultimate shame: They had counted on the United States to protect them from Communists aggression and now, because we had failed in our mission, they were virtually prisoners in a foreign land.

Then I made one of those snap decisions that my old Christian Brother teacher had warned me against — except that this decision turned out to be a grand slam. I wanted to invite 6,500 Vietnamese refugees to the Archdiocese of New Orleans simply because it was the right thing to do. But in order to care for so many refugees, we needed Vietnamese priests.

Among the Vietnamese priests who came to the archdiocese by the grace of God was Father Dominic Luong, who had been serving in the Diocese of Buffalo until he went to Fort Chaffee to minister to the thousands of refugees as a chaplain. In 2003 Father Luong became the first Vietnamese-born bishop in the United States upon his appointment as auxiliary bishop of the Diocese of Orange in California.

Bishop Dominic is one of those rare leaders imbued with an abundance of intellectual, spiritual, and pastoral qualities. He is fluent in three languages — in addition to his native Vietnamese, he speaks English and French well — and he has a master's degree in biology. The first time I met him I could see he was a people magnet, and I asked him to come to New Orleans for at least two years to minister to our growing Vietnamese population. He wound up staying for more than twenty-five years! I had to plead with Bishop Edward Head of Buffalo to allow him to stay in New Orleans, and Bishop Head graciously granted my request because of the outstanding and vital work Father Luong was doing.

It didn't take me a long time after visiting Fort Chaffee to decide that the Archdiocese of New Orleans would throw out the welcome mat to the Vietnamese. Some dioceses across the country placed limits on the size of families they would accept, but I wanted to keep the large Vietnamese fishing families together. Counting aunts, uncles and grandparents, some fishing families had as many as twenty members. I think we did a tremendous favor to the archdiocese and to the Vietnamese, who were so industrious that they returned that favor a hundredfold. I also was very concerned that the single Vietnamese men — most of whom were military men — should be taken care of. Because we took so many Vietnamese refugees at one time, we had to find a place for them to live, and we found out that the old Claiborne Towers on Canal Street and Claiborne Avenue had plenty of vacancies to provide temporary lodging. It didn't take long for the Vietnamese to establish themselves and move into places of their own. From 1975 to 1979, we accepted about ten thousand refugees, and by 1986 the Vietnamese population had soared to twenty-thousand.

In short order, Father Luong became the undisputed spiritual leader of the Vietnamese community in the Archdiocese of New Orleans, and that immigrant community flourished and multiplied like a lovingly tended garden. And, it was easy to see why the Vietnamese blossomed despite the initial obstacle of their language barrier — they had drive, ingenuity, obedience, and industriousness, virtues that when combined with perseverance almost guaranteed success. Within a very few years of the Vietnamese community's arrival in New Orleans, many of their children, born knowing absolutely no English and having the additional obstacle of parents speaking no English in the home, were valedictorians and scholarship winners in their schools, public as well as Catholic.

Strong academic and spiritual education and a supportive, involved family are the keys to succeeding in life. Those attributes are universal and cross all ethnic and racial lines. I was asked to give the invocation at the graduation ceremony for one of our local colleges, and the president there was boasting about several of his high-achieving black graduates. Every one of them, I found out later, had been educated at a Catholic elementary or high school. I was asked one year to participate in a national panel on youth and education. After three days of tedious meetings in which there were representatives from all ethnic groups, my theory was confirmed. A young Latino asked me to come see his home, which was sparsely furnished but pristine and orderly. "My mother was the difference in my life," he told me. "The morality of my family was that we children could never turn to drugs. I turned down job after job when people wanted me to be a lookout for the cops. We could have used that money, but my mother wouldn't tolerate that. I knew that I had to go to school and get a good education." What practical wisdom from a teenager! I've always felt that sacrifice is the basis of the whole Christian life. If we don't learn that as children, we've been neglected and set up for failure.

I'll never forget when a television reporter asked former New Orleans Police Chief Joe Giarrusso following a multiple shooting in the city why he couldn't prevent such massacres from happening. "The police can't prevent murder," Giarrusso said. "We could have a police officer on every corner and still not be able to control it. The only way for it to change is for the family to change."

The drug culture has sucked the life from so many millions of people in this country that it is impossible to overestimate the damage. Somehow kids have to be convinced that selling drugs is like taking blood money. People objected strongly when I gave sermons chastising drug users. "Anybody who even smokes a marijuana cigarette is, in the long haul, responsible for murder

Nguyet Nguyen, mother of two young Vietnamese who were gunned down in the restaurant where they worked in New Orleans East in 1995, was emotionally distraught at their funeral Mass at Mary Queen of Vietnam Church. In 1994, the scourge of violence in New Orleans was so great that 421 people were killed (85.8 per 100,000 people), the highest murder rate of any major U.S. city. (Photo by Frank H. Methe III, *Clarion Herald*)

because there is so much murder produced by the drug trade," I said. "If you smoke marijuana, you are cooperating in evil."

As an archbishop, I have a unique platform from which to challenge people. I went to the St. Augustine High School graduation in May 1981, and I told the seniors two things: they had talent, but they were bound by God to use that talent to the best of their ability. I cited the case of author Alex Haley, how it took him eight years to write a short story that would even be accepted for publication, and how his novel, "Roots, The Saga of an American Family," was now an international best seller. I also told them about Pope John Paul II, who suffered enormously at the hands of the Nazis as a young man in Poland, but he recovered and became the spiritual leader of the human family. "If you simply develop your talents, as I know you can," I told them, "you will also be a great force for good in your immediate community. I also ask you to stay in New Orleans. New Orleans is a great city, and it's a great city because St. Augustine is a great high school!" That's all I had to say — that always brought down the house.

And New Orleans is a great city because of the contributions of so many diverse groups, including the Vietnamese, who enriched us immeasurably. Because of the rich spiritual life they practiced and the crucible of persecution through which they had emerged, the Vietnamese provided hundreds of vocations to the priesthood and religious life. At one point there were thirty-eight Vietnamese priests serving in the Archdiocese of New Orleans, many as pastors. God only knows how we would have been able to staff our parishes and provide the Eucharist to south Louisiana Catholics had it not been for the incredible faith witness of the Vietnamese. We were able to purchase a huge house on Bayou St. John for a community of religious women, and they wound up with forty Sisters residing there. I told the Superior, "You can't possibly have forty beds in that house." She replied with a laugh, "We don't need a bed for each person. They each sleep on a mat on the floor." They could take care of a whole lot of Sisters that way!

Father Luong eventually became a monsignor, and he came by to see me one day with a request that his parish be allowed to build a large, permanent church. I told him, "Of course, you can. But you're going to have to pay for it, so you'll have to start a capital campaign." To my utter surprise, Monsignor Luong replied, "We've already had the campaign. We have four hundred families, and the big church we want — without all the decorations — is going to cost about $400,000. We decided each family was responsible for $1,000, and every family made its donation." He showed me the check for the full amount. It probably was the quickest capital campaign in the history of the Archdiocese. True to his word, the exterior of the church was completed in record time.

The Vietnamese have a love of family and a deep respect for their elders. I attended a fair across the river at St. Agnes Le Thi Thanh Parish one year and a young man, probably eighteen years old, won the grand-prize raffle for a new automobile. As soon as the fair chairman handed him the keys to the car, the young man walked over and placed the keys in his father's hands. That was his father's car — no questions asked.

A Vietnamese girl presents a candle to me during a celebration on the feast day of Our Lady of Lavang. (Man-Pham Photography)

Not knowing the American rules of the water, the Vietnamese fishing community had many contentious meetings with American fishermen. They used gasoline instead of diesel to power their boats, and that led to a rash of boat fires. They overfished and poached in certain areas that did not belong to them. In Plaquemines Parish, one of the Vietnamese boats was firebombed. With Father Luong, I tried to mediate disputes between the Vietnamese and Anglo fishermen so that they could live in harmony. One of the secrets of the Vietnamese fishermen's success was their teamwork: they rented a boat in the beginning and pooled their money from family members to buy a bigger boat and then several boats.

A Cajun fisherman told me candidly that the reason the Vietnamese succeeded in fishing was that they worked longer hours than the Americans. "When we go out we fish long enough to take care of our immediate needs," the Cajun told me. "They stay out long enough to fill the boat. They also use all their relatives on the same boat, and they pool their resources and they've practically bought out all the boats." I guess to some that might seem like a recipe for confrontation; I call it good, old-fashioned American work ethic, Vietnamese style. Most of the most successful seafood restaurants in New Orleans today now buy their shrimp, oysters and redfish from Vietnamese crews. The Vietnamese cultural attitude of self-reliance was nowhere more clearly displayed than in New Orleans East after Hurricane Katrina, when the Vietnamese community did not wait for government assistance to renovate their homes and property to make them whole. They merely bailed out the water, threw out the trash, cleaned out their houses, and went on with life.

These are tough people — people who rely on faith, hope, and love and who are inured to difficulty — and many would do well to follow their inspirational example. My only concern for the future is what will happen now that the second and third generations of Vietnamese are born into a culture that is less Vietnamese and much more American and secularized. I pray they can retain the virtues that have made their culture thrive.

One of the powerful attributes of the Archdiocese of New Orleans has been its multiethnic and multicultural makeup — whites, blacks, Asians, Hispanics all worshipping and working together. Before the Diocese of Houma-Thibodaux was carved from the Archdiocese of New Orleans in 1977, I had made a personal visit to Ireland in order to recruit four congregations of Irish nuns, who were experiencing an abundance of vocations, to teach in our archdiocesan schools. The need was especially severe in Houma-Thibodaux, where we had built new schools but did not have any religious women to staff them. My recruiting trip paid immediate dividends, and one community of Irish nuns gratefully went down the bayou to teach. Naturally, I was concerned about how the Cajuns might accept these religious women with their unusual accents and customs! But one Thanksgiving, the Irish nuns invited me down to Raceland for a Mass and a reception. At the dinner, the Cajuns told me to get ready for some toe-tapping entertainment. Not knowing what to expect, I surmised we might be serenaded with Cajun zydeco music.

Well, the accordion started picking up steam, and out onto the stage came the Cajun students. But instead of performing a Cajun *fais-do-do*, the bayou kids did a spectacular Irish jig!

I also was able to recruit a fair number of Irish seminarians to come to New Orleans and study for the priesthood. I had started my recruiting trips when I was an auxiliary bishop in Washington, D.C., in the 1950s, so I knew many of the bishops and seminary rectors in Ireland. In the early 1960s, Ireland was flush with vocations — I remember one year, four hundred men were ordained to the priesthood in Ireland. Sadly, Ireland today has only one major seminary — St. Patrick's College in Maynooth — and it had only sixty-seven seminarians in 2006. In many ways, the flourishing Irish economy and the emergence of materialism have caused Irish vocations to sag.

In order to successfully recruit priests for Washington, D.C., in the early 1960s, I first had to secure the bishop's permission to visit the seminaries. Dublin Archbishop Charles McQuaid was a proper, demanding archbishop, and he wouldn't listen to you at all unless you told him your diocese was in terrible straits. I made sure I told him we were having a heck of a time with attacks by the Scotch Free Masons in the Washington, D.C., area, and as soon as I said that, he said, "My God, you *are* in desperate trouble."

Armed with a letter of recommendation from Archbishop McQuaid, I would then rent a car and visit the seminaries, whose rectors were unbelievably

cooperative. I was allowed to speak to those seminarians who were not incardinated in any diocese and invite them to come to the United States. The rectors
even gave me a scouting report on each seminarian: "He's a good student and
will become a good priest." ... "He's pious." ... "At times he argues too much
with his superiors." It stunned me that they were so candid in revealing to me
the young men's good and bad points.

Again, at that time in Ireland, vocations were abundant, and there was
a willingness on behalf of Irish bishops to have their men immigrate to the
United States. In a way, it took a financial burden off them because they no
longer had to pay for their studies at a time when there simply were too many
priests. Imagine that!

I always like to tell the story of one of my favorite Irish seminarians, Harry
Bugler, who is now a monsignor and one of our most respected priests in the
Archdiocese of New Orleans. Even Harry would admit that he has a thick
Irish brogue — and back when he was in his twenties, it was thicker than
pea soup fog. Harry came from a part of Ireland where there were very thick
brogues. After I ordained Harry in 1975, I assigned him to St. James Major
Parish in Gentilly. After preaching at his first Mass in his new parish, young
Father Harry was greeting people outside of church when one good lady came
up to him and shook his hand. "Father," she said, "isn't it great to have Latin
back in the Mass!"

CHAPTER 14

The Cajuns' "Joie de Vivre"

I came to New Orleans with little knowledge or understanding of the complex ethnic makeup of the area. South Louisiana was originally populated by a mixture of immigrants — first by the French during the early days of the colonization of the continent. It later came under the Spanish flag, already securely planted in Central and South America and the Caribbean Islands. The area reverted to French control during the Napoleonic era, then to the United States under the Louisiana Purchase of 1803.

The first settlers were mostly French, establishing the port of New Orleans on the banks of the Mississippi River as its trade and cultural center. They also established sugar cane plantations along the banks of the Mississippi and westward along the bayous of south Louisiana. The plantations were manned by slaves and thrived due largely to the rich alluvial soil, the warm climates, and the great worldwide market for sugar.

After Louisiana came under control of the United States, some Anglo-Saxons from New England moved in and established more plantations, similarly manned by slaves. Also, other nationalities moved into the area, mainly Germans, Italians, and Irish.

When the British defeated the French in the "French and Indian Wars" (1850-1860) and took over all of present-day Canada, the French colonists in Nova Scotia (Acadia) who refused to take the oath of allegiance to the British crown were expelled from the land — loaded onto ships and sent to various parts of the world. Some returned to France, others to the Caribbean Islands, mainly Haiti, and the majority of them were brought to south Louisiana, where they would join other Frenchmen there. They were mostly poor and illiterate and were not welcomed by the more aristocratic people of New Orleans. Thus most of them continued westward to the environs of Bayou Lafourche and farther west to the area around the Attakapas Post (St. Martinville), where they worked on the plantations or "*vacheries*" (cattle ranches), or else scratched out a living by trapping the marshes or fishing in the bayous.

This latter group of colonists were known as the "Acadians," and this appellation was soon shortened to "Cajuns." Over the years the name has come to be applied to other inhabitants of French ancestry all over south Louisiana, even though they were not part of the Acadian migration — "Le Grand Dérangement." Some of the more aristocratic Frenchmen still object to being included among the Cajuns.

There is also another group, fewer in number, who were and still are known as "Creoles," springing from a mix of French, Spanish, and African Americans, whose early route to Louisiana was through Haiti, where there existed a similar plantation culture. These plantations were operated by British or Spanish owners and manned by black slaves. In time, the races became intermixed, and some of them came to Louisiana. Thus the term "Creole" sometimes became erroneously applied to the Cajun, who did not like being confused with the Creoles.

Before I was appointed archbishop of New Orleans, I had heard in passing about the proud Cajun culture but knew virtually nothing of it. I thought Cajun was simply another segment of an exotic south Louisiana culture, with no real distinguishing characteristics. I was not aware of the cultural differences among the various segments of the society. That first impression changed after the first Mass I celebrated in the famous St. Louis Cathedral.

As I stood in the front of the cathedral shaking hands with the congregation, the second woman I greeted immediately addressed me.

"Do you know what a Creole is?" she asked in a tone that indicated to me I was definitely lacking some important knowledge.

"No, I am sorry, I don't," I replied.

She explained there was a lot of misinformation about Creoles. Then with an air of someone who is imparting world-shaking advice, she said, "A real Creole is one who is of French or Spanish blood or a combination of them. You'll hear other descriptions of Creoles, but the real definition is what I just gave you."

I thanked her for her genealogical lesson, and then turned to greet an African-American woman who was in line just behind her. She had heard the previous lady's comments, so she came right to the point. "I've got as much French blood in me as she has," she said.

After nearly fifty years of living in south Louisiana, I can attest that Cajuns are among the most joyful, warm-hearted and warm-blooded people I have ever known. They do not blush whenever they tell you what's on their mind, and they have a passion for life and for the Church that is unsurpassed.

It's often reported that the Cajun men in the 1800s and 1900s were spotty in the practice of their Catholic faith. The men didn't go to church every Sunday, but there is no denying the Cajuns were very generous in building churches, which was a tangible expression of their faith. In Opelousas, the Cajuns got together to build the magnificent St. Landry Church, which celebrated its first Mass in 1909 and compares favorably to any parish church in the world. St. Charles Borromeo Church in Grand Coteau, dedicated in 1880, is another outstanding church. The Cathedral of St. John the Evangelist in downtown Lafayette, dedicated in 1919, is as beautiful a church as I have ever been in. The financial sacrifices and generosity of spirit it took to build these worthy edifices should be taken into account in any discussion of the religious nature of the Cajuns.

Cajuns have a great deal of affection in greeting each other. They always kiss or embrace each other. If a priest was assigned to a Cajun parish and did not like such a tremendous show of affection, then that attitude probably doomed him from the start. The priest had to look inside himself and try to get comfortable dealing with an affectionate congregation.

I recall dinners in the small village and church parish of Kraemer in the heart of Cajun country. The meal included part of an alligator which Father Trahan, the pastor, had encountered that morning as he walked on the path between the rectory and the church. The gator, nine feet in length, was easily dispatched by Father Trahan using the gun he kept in the rectory for such events. The hide of the gator was worth at least $15 dollars a foot, in addition to the use of its flesh in the excellent dinner.

Cajun generosity knows no bounds. Whenever we launched a charity drive for the common good, the Cajuns were right there, contributing mightily to the success of the project. I've been given credit for my work with the poor and the elderly and for building affordable apartments, but I could not have done any of that without the support of the Cajuns. As soon as I gave them a rationale for the cause, they stood by me in total support. I point this out because I get pretty steamed when I hear people belittling the Cajuns. They are the salt of the earth.

Oil Discovery

In 1905, oil was first discovered in south Louisiana. Due to a number of successful wells, the industry became an important factor in the life and progress of the area. The early operations were carried out mainly by "wildcatters" from Texas and Oklahoma, who brought in the drilling rigs and the "roughnecks" (rig workers) and managers to operate them. These "oil people" were not too welcome and did not at first fit into the local culture. However, gradually, local Cajuns began working on the rigs, at first in the lowest capacities, and as time went on, they became an important part of the industry. In the 1930s, operations were expanded into the marshes and shallow water bottoms, where boats and tugs and barges were needed to service the rigs. This became a natural for the Cajuns, who were eager to supply the needs at fees much better than they were able to eke out in fishing and trapping.

Then, after World War II, in 1947, oil was struck in the open waters of the Gulf of Mexico, and a whole new opportunity was opened for the Cajuns. These offshore rigs needed to be supplied by crew boats, supply vessels, barges, and the like, and a whole new industry resulted. As offshore drilling moved to other parts of the world such as the North Sea, Nigeria, Indonesia, and the Persian Gulf, many Cajuns, on the rigs as well as with their marine equipment, followed the opportunity opened for them, and they became an important part of the industry.

This development of offshore operations also created excellent opportunities for local entrepreneurs to enter the business of oil field services. In my years as Archbishop of New Orleans, I came to know several successful entrepreneurs who had taken advantage of these opportunities created by the development of the offshore oil business. Two men with whom I became friendly were Alden J. "Doc" Laborde and Nolte Theriot, whose ingenuity and drive were catalysts in the growth of worldwide expansion of the offshore oil business.

Nolte, a fellow member of the 82nd Airborne Division, was in a group of thirty American troopers captured in the Battle of the Bulge in Belgium. In the early days of that atrocious campaign the Germans decided for a short time "not to take any prisoners." Nolte was seriously wounded in a mass slaughter, but the extremely cold weather prevented him from losing too much blood. Conscious that he was still alive, Nolte pretended to be dead. The place where the execution took place was strategically very valuable, which prompted the remaining elements of the 82nd to quickly recapture the area. When the troopers did so, they found Nolte barely alive and promptly resuscitated him. He was hospitalized and ultimately sent home.

After returning to Louisiana, Nolte decided to enlarge his one-engine boat used to deliver supplies to the oil rigs in the Gulf. Realizing that his father also had a one-engine boat, he decided to place both engines in the same boat, making it speedier than any other boat engaged in that service. The idea worked and, gradually, Nolte's boat became the most productive boat in the area, gaining him a leading position in that trade. His business grew so much that he established a satellite office in Scotland.

One day a powerful storm whipped into the North Sea, and a large ship was in serious danger of capsizing. No boat in the area attempted to save the crew until one of Nolte's captains decided to risk everything. Exhibiting great courage, the pilot drew close to the endangered ship and finally rescued the entire crew. After the storm one of the countries whose boat was saved insisted on granting an award to Nolte's boat. The pilot felt very uncomfortable in acknowledging the award before such a large audience, so Nolte went to his rescue, expressing his gratitude in good "French." Shortly afterwards, other nations whose boats had been rescued by Nolte's pilot also arranged to grant an award. This process only increased the embarrassment of Nolte's pilot until, finally, after six awards, he was thoroughly disgusted. The pilot grabbed the award and said to Nolte, "You tell them that if I must go through this process again, the next time a boat begins to sink I'm going to let the damn boat sink."

Another Cajun leader in the oil industry was Alden J. "Doc" Laborde, a native of Marksville, Louisiana. "Doc" was a graduate of the U.S. Naval Academy, served with distinction in World War II, first as captain of a destroyer-escort in the North Atlantic that escorted convoys from the United States to Europe and back, protecting them from attack by German submarines. A group of these escorts would guide a fleet of supply ships, numbering one hundred or more, delivering critical supplies of munitions, aviation fuel, personnel and supplies for the war in Europe. Hitler's submarines were determined to prevent these deliveries, and they were quite successful, particularly in the early days of the war. Many such convoys were devastated by the feared German "wolf packs" which took control of the Atlantic as soon as the United States entered the war. However, "Doc" said not one of the ships in convoys escorted by his group over a two-year period was lost. He attributes this to good fortune and prayers rather than to any particular advantage that they had over other groups.

Once during a sudden winter storm, not uncommon in the North Atlantic, thirty-foot waves and fifty-knot winds buffeted his relatively small ship. One huge wave broke over the bow of his vessel and washed overboard a gunner's mate who was on watch at his gun station some thirty feet above the waterline. Standard procedure for recovering a "man overboard" did not work because of the severe wind and seas. After several failed passes, Doc decided to attempt a rescue from the windward side, with the ship drifting rapidly toward the man, and the ship rolling some forty-five degrees. Luckily on a roll, a crewman was able to grab the man just before the ship would have drifted over and swamped him. Thereafter, Doc was considered to be a magician at ship handling, but he attributes it to his rosary, his constant companion at sea. Doc always carried and said his rosary, dangling it openly as he stood at his station on the boat.

Many years later when I interviewed Doc on his career for a TV show, I was very eager to show that rosary. When I asked him where the rosary was, Doc replied, "I have no idea. I guess I just left it in one of my discarded clothes." Whereupon I appealed to his very dutiful and resourceful wife Margaret, "Please search all of his clothes for that rosary." In two days Margaret found eight, well-worn and dusty rosaries in his discarded naval clothes. We selected the dirtiest rosary as possibly the right rosary. It certainly looked as though Doc had given it a mighty workout.

Doc eventually married his long-time, beautiful girlfriend — Margaret — and in the course of his long career in the Navy and oil business they lived in about twenty different places in the world. Doc had an epochal success in the oil industry, but he remained very quiet and humble about his work. At one time in Washington, D.C., I was invited with a number of religious leaders to attend a meeting at the White House with President George H.W. Bush. The President graciously invited each of us to be photographed with him. As I shook hands with the President, I said, "I think I know one of your good friends in New Orleans — 'Doc' Laborde." President Bush immediately grabbed my hand and said, "He taught me how to get started in the oil business! Please give him my fondest regards." As he was talking, he snapped off a pair of his cuff links and asked me to present them to Doc "with my deepest regards" — a task that I very willingly fulfilled.

Doc had taken courses in naval engineering at the Naval Academy, and he used his God-given talent and common sense to apply these basic principles to an extraordinary array of accomplishments. He designed and built "Mr. Charlie," the world's first offshore submersible and transportable drilling rig, which critics said would capsize on its maiden voyage but in reality performed so well that it drilled continuously for more than thirty years in the Gulf of Mexico. "Mr. Charlie," named after the father of Charles Murphy, Jr., of Murphy Oil Company, was based on the concept of a submersible barge that could support a drilling platform and a large house for its crew. It revolutionized offshore drilling.

But, as with anything new, it was a huge gamble. A major oil company had to be convinced it was worth the risk. Doc told me that an executive of the J. Ray McDermott Company dropped by the fabrication yard one day to get a close-up look at "Mr. Charlie." He told one of Doc's employees that he should weld some large *padeyes* on each side so that his crane could have something to grab when it was called on to salvage the capsized rig from the bottom of the Gulf! The McDermott executive didn't think the rig would submerge upright. Doc told me, "My rosary got a good workout every day, and I also attended daily Mass, which gave me a lot of comfort."

Because "Mr. Charlie" sat on the bottom of the ocean floor, it was limited in the water depth in which it could operate. It soon became apparent to Doc that a unit which could drill in greater depths than were practical for a bottom-sitting rig would be required by the industry. Doc's answer to this was to design and construct the "Ocean Driller," the world's first floating unit, which could operate in water depths of several thousand feet. This soon became the standard around the world.

The pay for work on the offshore rigs was high, but the odd work schedule caused a problem for marriages. Normally workers were allowed to work twelve hours a day. For the final four hours of work they were paid time and a half, giving them an excellent salary. The hefty pay gave teenagers an incentive to quit school and marry early, and I quietly instructed priests in the Houma-Thibodaux area not to allow any marriage for a person sixteen years of age or less.

The priests told me that the rule would be hard to enforce, and they asked me to explain the new rule when I came to the area for a Confirmation. It turned out that in the rectory there was a couple requesting marriage, and the prospective bride was under age according to the new rule.

The girl, it so happened, was only fourteen years old, but her mother wanted her to get married. She felt the new rule was driving her daughter out of the Church. I asked the mother, "How old were you when you were married?" "Fourteen" she answered. I explained to the daughter that life was different now. "It's necessary for you to finish high school so that you can get a job in case your husband gets sick or loses his job," I said. She said she intended to finish high school. Then I asked her how old her friends were when they got married. "Most of them now are seveteen," she said.

I did not relent. "If you will wait until you are seventeen," I said, "I'll give you a good wedding present. In fact, I'll consider being at your marriage." I did not prevail with her, but gradually the young people accepted the general rule of being seventeen years of age before being married. The priests in the area helped by being pastorally sensitive to the young couples and getting them to understand the wisdom behind it.

The Cajuns are unmatched in throwing parties, and that *joie de vivre* always was on fine display at parish fairs in the Cajun areas of the archdiocese. Parishes needed fairs to generate extra income, and some churches went to great lengths to add special attractions such as parachute jumps to bring in more customers. At one parish fair not far from Houma, a scheduled parachute jump was impeded by a heavy rainstorm, which prevented the airplane, mired in the mud, from taking off with its crew of jumpers. Seeing the crew's plight, I asked the pilot if I could offer any assistance. "You can help us if we can use part of this state road as a runway for taking off and then landing," the pilot told me. The fair had come to a miserable halt because of the rain. I spied a nearby state trooper.

"Officer, can you help us?" I asked. "We need to pull this plane to the road so it can take off and the crew can parachute for the crowd. And then the plane needs to land on the road."

"How much space do you need?" the trooper asked me. "And how much time do you need to let the plane land on the road?" I was surprised by his interest and cooperation. I figured we needed only about two hundred yards of space and a half-hour to complete the flight.

"Okay," he said, "you're lucky. Not too much traffic. Let's go." The crew was delightfully surprised. Like me, they thought the policeman would turn down the request. But I had learned a long time ago never to be bashful when making a request. The worst response someone might give is "no." But you'll never know unless you ask.

With the help of some men enjoying the fair, the crew dragged the plane to the roadbed, then quickly climbed aboard and took off. To the crowd's immense delight, the crew jumped with their parachutes, landing very safely, and the plane then landed on the road near the state policeman. Some months later, I discovered that the pilot was Pat Taylor, an "oil man" who later made history by developing the first oil drill to extend 30,000 feet deep in the Gulf of Mexico. He said, "I was not serious when I made that request. I made it as a joke. You really surprised me — and we both were surprised by that state policeman!"

Pat Taylor later became nationally famous as a public benefactor by devising the "Taylor Opportunity Program for Students" (TOPS), providing a means for every capable and serious student to get a college education. While in his teens, Taylor had secured a grant from the state of Louisiana to finish his engineering degree from Louisiana State University. To exhibit his gratitude, he inscribed in huge letters the words "Made In Louisiana" on the drill machinery, which bore his history-making oil well. Pat and his wife Phyllis and I remained friends, and they were generous toward many of our charities and other projects, especially our TV station.

Pat always insisted on hiring Americans, and that helped the Cajuns because it created jobs and wealth. We ought to remember that those people in the oil business have made tremendous contributions to the country and to the world, because they have gone across the globe to develop the oil business. The money every American pays for gas would be substantially higher today were it not for guys such as Pat Taylor and his Cajun workers. God bless them all.

Cajun Humor

One of the great qualities of Cajuns is their ability to poke fun at themselves. They are some of the best storytellers around, and I've always loved a good story. It seems a group of counterfeiters from New York came to Golden Meadow, Louisiana, one day, but they had made a big mistake by forging a number of twelve-dollar bills. Figuring they could pass them off in Golden Meadow, they drove up to a Cajun grocery store. The store owner greeted them warmly and accepted the twelve-dollar bill. Without blinking, the store owner asked, "How do you want the change? In three-dollar, four-dollar, or six-dollar bills?"

Another great story I heard on the bayou went like this: One day a Cajun mother brought her young son, who had not received his First Communion, to the parish priest. The pastor said to the mother, "I'll make it real easy for him to receive his First Communion, but he must pass an examination on his faith." So he asked the boy, "Pierre, what is the name of the day on which Our Lord died?" Pierre shook his head, *"Je ne sais pas."* The pastor persisted, "I know you know the answer, but I'll ask your mother to help you." So he directed the question to his mother. She replied, *"Mon pere,* we are real poor folks. We don't get the newspaper. We didn't even know that he was sick!"

Father Charles Palughi recounted a joke for me that he picked up from the Cajuns in Galliano in Lafourche Parish. It seems the town needed a new fire engine, so it went about raising the money, and sure enough, the town finally had enough funds to buy a brand new beautiful fire engine. Then the town council had a discussion about what it should do with the old fire engine. So the council offered it to other communities — to no avail. No town wanted it because it said the old fire engine wouldn't be effective. So finally, one person stood up at the council meeting and said he had the perfect solution. "Since we've got this second fire engine," he said, "we might as well keep it and use it for false alarms."

Bishop Louis Abel Caillouet, who was the administrator of the New Orleans Archdiocese before I took over just after Hurricane Betsy, also had a great sense of humor. He told me the story of Louisiana Governor Richard Leche, the first Louisiana governor to be sent to prison for enriching himself at the public's expense. After *New Orleans States'* reporter F. Edward Hébert, the future congressman, revealed the dubious practice of LSU employees doing millwork on Leche's home in New Orleans in 1939, Leche took umbrage with the report: "I deny the allegations, and I defy the alligators!" Louisiana politicians have a way with words.

No mention of Cajuns is complete without a mention of former governor Edwin Edwards, a very gifted and intelligent but flawed politician from Avoyelles Parish who was elected to a fourth term as governor in 1992 with the most unusual motto: "Vote for the crook. It's important."

A "vote for the crook" — Edwards — was critically important because his opponent was former Ku Klux Klan grand wizard David Duke, a proponent of vicious anti-Christian principles of the Klan. Duke was anti-black, anti-Catholic, and anti-Christian. In his three previous terms as governor, Edwards had pushed through some very important measures, particularly a new state constitution. The old constitution was impossibly complex because legislators often made a law a part of the Constitution, thus making it very different to expunge it because a two-thirds vote was required to cancel it.

Edwards was brilliant and possessed a great sense of humor. When confronted by a reporter after a visit to the gambling joints in Las Vegas, he was asked about reports that he had lost $8,000. Was that true? "No," Edwards replied. "I lost $10,000." It's not a coincidence that the law finally caught up with Edwards because he extorted money from a gambling interest that coveted a riverboat casino license in Louisiana. Edwards finally came up snake eyes.

Edwards was an inveterate lady's man. In meeting a couple, he invariably would ask the husband, "Would you please introduce me to your daughter?"

Although Edwards was baptized a Catholic, he had been a Protestant preacher for the Church of the Nazarene in his teenage years and then declared, after his election, that he was a Catholic and wished to have a solemn Mass in the Cathedral with his whole cabinet in the front pews, with him in their midst. I asked to see him and said, "I appreciate your wish to become a practicing Catholic, but I must tell you that I don't approve of your histrionics. You have never been seen in the Cathedral before. I strongly suggest that you practice your faith, be seen at Mass in the Cathedral before having such a public display of your faith."

"I wish to assure you that I am very serious about my faith," Edwards told me. "The family of my fiancée are strong Catholics and would not allow her to marry me unless I become a Catholic." We argued for a considerable amount of time, with his constant reiteration that he was a serious, practicing Catholic. Of course, his desire became publicly known, and I was portrayed as an unreasonable priest refusing to fulfill the desire of the Governor to be acknowledged as a good Catholic. I made some conditions before giving permission to him to have such a public display, and told him that I would give the homily at the Mass.

Edwards was very cooperative to the Archdiocese of New Orleans in many respects: the state paid for the salaries of the cafeteria workers who provided the meals to the students in our schools and covered the cost of textbooks. We also had a meeting with him to determine the payments by the state to our schools for state-required services.

Edwards was helpful in many ways, but a few months after he assumed his office he made a public statement containing a faulty explanation of the Resurrection — that it was to happen at a time other than the general judgment — and I was obliged to join with Baton Rouge Bishop Stanley Ott in correcting his statement. He made no further misstatements of the faith, but it was always worrisome to have the constant duty of monitoring his theological pronouncements. We would have annual meetings with Edwards at the governor's mansion, and all of a sudden he would bring up some question about Scripture just to prove that he knew something about it. Usually, it was a complete misuse of Scripture. I would always be frank in my discussions with the governor, but Bishop Ott was always more polite and restrained. Inevitably, Edwards had a quiet parting with the Church. Sadly, his political career ended when he landed in jail.

At times Edwards was very helpful. When Pope John Paul II arrived in New Orleans in 1987, Louisiana Attorney General Billy Guste, who was a prominent Catholic as well as an important politician, was standing far in the back of the welcoming delegation. Edwards yelled out: "Archbishop, you must put Billy Guste at the head of the line. He is a better Catholic than any of us here." So, I asked Billy to come to the front of the line to greet the Pope.

One of my all-time favorite quotes from Edwards came as we were preparing for the historic visit by John Paul II. In the midst of our preparations it became quite apparent that security concerns would be paramount, and that, of course, meant a lot of extra police protection for the Holy Father. The total budget for the trip — between the state police and city police — was estimated to be about $2 million. This was in the midst of the oil collapse and the state's massive fiscal woes. But ever the showman, Edwards insisted he wasn't worried in the least.

"If we have to," the governor promised, "we'll rob Peter to pay for John Paul."

CHAPTER 15

The New Orleans Saints

As a child, I was more of a baseball fan than a football fan — Washington Senators pitcher Walter "Big Train" Johnson was my hero. But I found out very shortly after coming to New Orleans in 1965 that football ranked just behind Catholicism as a religion.

On November 1, 1966 — ironically enough, All Saints Day — *The Times-Picayune* trumpeted the announcement that New Orleans had been awarded a National Football League expansion franchise with a banner headline worthy of the end of World War II: "N.O. GOES PRO!"

I had become good friends with Louisiana Governor John McKeithen, and a short time after the announcement was made about the expansion franchise, he called me on an urgent matter.

"You know, Archbishop," the governor began, "we were given permission to have a professional football team, and I'd like to name it after the people down there, but they're overruling me. They say they want to call it the 'Saints' because of the song, 'When the Saints Go Marching In.' Is that agreeable with you and the Church, or would that be sacrilegious?"

It didn't take long for me to reply. "There would be no objection at all to name the team the Saints," I told the governor, "but I have to tell you, from the viewpoint of the Church, most of the saints were martyrs."

I knew the Saints were going to need all the help they could get — and, actually, they did, for the better part of five decades! But I consider all those struggles to have been "the cross before the crown."

On February 6, 2010, the Saints became world champions by pulling off the most incredible victory of all, a 31-17 rout of the Indianapolis Colts in Super Bowl XLIV in Miami. As I watched the confetti cascade from the skies above Sun Life Stadium, all I could do was turn to Kent Bossier, my personal assistant, and say, "New Orleans will never be the same. This changes everything!"

The Super Bowl victory was an incredibly emotional experience for me because I was on the field at Tulane Stadium when the Saints played their first game in history on September 7, 1967, against the powerful Los Angeles

President George H. W. Bush and I in the suite of the Saints team owner Tom Benson for the first game played in the Superdome after Katrina. We beat the Atlanta Falcons.

Rams. I had been in Washington for a meeting in the days leading up to the inaugural game, and the Saints contacted me to ask if I would be willing to give the invocation before the kickoff. I wrote the prayer while flying back to New Orleans. I entitled it, "Prayer for the Saints":

> "God, we ask your blessing upon all who participate in this event, and all who have supported our Saints. Our Heavenly Father, who has instructed us that the 'saints by faith conquered kingdoms... and overcame lions,' grant our Saints an increase of faith and strength so that they will not only overcome the Lions, but also the Bears, the Rams, the Giants, and even those awesome people in Green Bay.
>
> "May they continue to tame the Redskins and fetter the Falcons as well as the Eagles. Give to our owners and coaches the continued ability to be as wise as serpents and simple as doves, so that no good talent will dodge our draft. Grant to our fans perseverance in their devotion and unlimited lungpower, tempered with a sense of charity to all, including the referees.
>
> "May our beloved 'Bedlam Bowl' be a source of good fellowship, and may the 'Saints Come Marching In' be a victory march for all, now and in eternity."

In front of 80,879 screaming fans at Tulane Stadium, my prayer went over very well. In fact, life as a Saints fan hardly could have started any better. Just a few seconds after the prayer, Saints' rookie wide receiver John Gilliam took the opening kickoff and raced ninety-four yards up the middle of the field — it was like Charlton Heston parting the Red Sea! — to give the Saints a 7-0 lead less than fifteen seconds into their first game in history. It's doubtful any expansion team in any professional sport will ever have that kind of explosive start.

I had to confer Confirmation at a parish later that day, so I couldn't stay to watch the game. The Saints wound up losing 27-13, but at least I could boast that as long as I was there watching, the Saints were winning.

Unlike my later close relationship with Saints owner Tom Benson, I never really got to know the original owner, John Mecom, Jr., a Houston oilman. Our paths simply didn't cross. But I was good friends with Dave Dixon, the man responsible for bringing pro football to New Orleans, and who followed up that feat a few years later by securing political backing for construction of the most advanced domed stadium in the world — the Louisiana Superdome.

Dixon is somewhat like me. He is relentless and irrepressible when he thinks he has an idea that is good for New Orleans. He knew this area was football-crazy, and he proved that to NFL executives by staging yearly exhibition games in Tulane Stadium that drew sellout crowds, previously unheard of in the NFL. More importantly, Dave knew how to work the political circuit, and he convinced U.S. Senator Russell Long, the powerful senator from Louisiana, to pressure the NFL by threatening that Congress might remove the league's sacred antitrust exemption unless it was willing to expand into New Orleans.

In the late 1960s, many people, especially in north Louisiana, dismissed as foolhardy and frivolous Dixon's idea to use state funds to build the world's

Army Four-Star General Ann E. Dunwoody and I at the 2010 National Football Conference Championship in New Orleans

greatest indoor stadium in New Orleans. The Superdome was planned to dwarf Houston's Astrodome, then touted as the "Eighth Wonder of the World." With the benefit of hindsight, try to imagine where New Orleans would be today had it not built the Superdome, which became the catalyst for an amazing downtown renaissance and an anchor for a highly profitable NFL team for four decades.

Not all the opposition to the Superdome came from north Louisiana. In fact, New Orleans supermarket magnate John Schwegmann, who touted himself as a man of the people for his ability to provide low-cost groceries, was Dixon's harshest critic. First, Dixon had to sell Gov. McKeithen, who came from Caldwell Parish in northeast Louisiana, on his wild dream. Dixon thought McKeithen might be a tough sell, but when Dixon arrived early for his appointment with the governor, he got to chat for fifteen minutes with the governor's secretary and pitched his proposal to her. She loved it! When McKeithen called Dixon into his office, it took Dixon only a few minutes to cement McKeithen's support. The logic was that if it was good for New Orleans, it would be good for the state of Louisiana.

Schwegmann's opposition, meanwhile, was one of the reasons the Superdome's price tag expanded from $35 million to $163 million by the time it was opened in 1975. Schwegmann was a Catholic, but he had a real ornery, negative streak. He used his full-page newspaper ads not only to describe the daily specials at his supermarkets around town but also to pontificate on social

Celebrating Mass with Archbishop Aymond the morning before Super Bowl XLIV

and political matters. Invariably, it seemed that if the Church was interested in some proposal, Schwegmann was against it.

The biggest example of Schwegmann's negativity manifested itself after I decided to come out publicly in favor of a half-cent sales tax increase in Orleans Parish that would go toward improving teacher salaries in the public school system. I felt it was the right thing to do, and I even said so in the *Clarion Herald*. Schwegmann took out a bunch of ads in *The Times-Picayune* in which he editorialized against the sales tax increase. He was so demonstrative in his opposition that I got loads of letters from angry Catholics saying I should keep my nose out of the public school system and simply take care of our Catholic school children. Of course, if anyone really analyzed the issue, more than half of our Catholic children were already attending public schools,

Archbishop Aymond, current archbishop of New Orleans, and me at Super Bowl XLIV

and this was going to help them. Even the New Orleans Chamber of Commerce came out against the sales tax increase, but in the end it passed, and I felt good about giving the idea moral impetus.

I got along well with Schwegmann and visited him in his final illness, but I never truly understood his politics. McKeithen was strong enough eventually to rally enough north Louisiana support to build the Superdome, and it was built over Schwegmann's objections. I don't think Schwegmann ever set foot in the Superdome, and he died in 1995.

The Superdome became the home not only to the Saints and to several Super Bowls, but in 1987 it also hosted the spectacular youth event during the visit of Pope John Paul II to New Orleans. I will never forget when Bing Crosby came to New Orleans in 1975 to sing at our annual Catholic Charities gala, he asked me to give him a quick tour of the Superdome because he had heard all about it. I got Lieutenant Governor Jimmy Fitzmorris to lead the tour, and we walked through the Poydras Street entrance and onto the massive floor. Standing in the Poydras Street end zone, Bing gazed across to the other side. The lights were very dim, but he got a sense of the Superdome's massive size. Jimmy told Bing, "We'll not only play football and baseball and basketball in here, but we can host the largest musical concerts in the world."

Bing shot back: "Not a chance. That would be impossible. I can't see how a person standing on this end of the stadium could ever feel as though he is in contact with someone on the other end. The distance is just too great. If anybody ever invited me to give a concert here, I wouldn't accept."

When Pope John Paul II came to New Orleans twelve years later, I never even hinted about my conversation with Bing Crosby when I discussed with

Dr. Condoleezza Rice and I in Saints' team owner Tom Benson's suite for Super Bowl XLIV

the Vatican officials where I wanted to hold the youth rally. I knew it had to be conducted at the Superdome. But you know what? The Pope created an intimacy with the eighty thousand young people in that stadium that defied the common wisdom. Pope John Paul II drew on his strengths as an actor and communicator — and he proved Bing Crosby dead wrong.

By the way, I wanted to make sure virtually all of the tickets for the youth event at the Superdome went to young people. My only exception was this: Dave Dixon, the father of the Saints and the father of the Superdome, had to be there. "You don't even have to ask me for tickets," I told Dave. "You are owed these tickets." We put him right in the center of the Superdome, which is where he belonged. No one will really ever know for sure, but the Pope might never have come to New Orleans had it not been for the Superdome — which for one day, at least, we turned into the world's biggest church!

I'm sure Dave's wonderful wife Mary, who is a devout Catholic, had an influence on her husband becoming a Catholic in 1979. Dave took instructions in the Catholic faith right around the time he was recovering from a heart surgery. We grew so close that I asked Dave to chair a capital campaign in 1986, which was a smashing success. He and Mary remain great friends of mine.

In 1985, Tom Benson bought the Saints, and I agreed to give the invocation at a preseason game in August. It went like this:

> "O God, who has ordained all things, including sports, to serve your purpose, we beg your blessing on all gathered here this evening — the spectators, the players, and especially Mr. Benson and the other new owners of the Saints.
>
> "Above all, give our reborn Saints perseverance in their commitment. Make them as wise as serpents and simple as doves so that they may over-

come the Giants and Vikings and outsoar the Falcons, Seahawks, and all other opponents.

"Be gracious to the spectators who have offered up for your sake years of anxiety and sorrow. By your help, this year may we 'serve the Lord with gladness' in a winning season.

"Keep all from harm in this contest and grant that we may at last with all the Saints 'go marching into your heavenly home.' Amen."

As usual, my prayer didn't stick. The Saints started out the season 3-2 but lost six games in a row to finish 5-11. A woman called the Chancery one day and asked me for which saints the Saints were named. "I don't know," I told her, "but it should have been St. Jude!"

I've had a close relationship with Saints' owner Tom Benson for nearly a quarter century, and he and his family have been tireless supporters of Catholic causes over the years. At his request, I try to attend every Saints home game, and I was able to do that during their magical Super Bowl season despite suffering a stroke on October 30, 2009.

When I sustained the stroke, I had a lot of friends really worried about my health. But, thanks be to God, I missed only one home game, and I was back at the Superdome in Mr. Benson's private suite when the Saints crushed the New England Patriots, 38-17, on national TV on November 30.

I kept coming back, and the Saints won their first thirteen games of the season before hitting a three-game losing streak. That tough patch didn't bother me at all. I knew this team had great leadership across the board —

Louisiana Governor Bobby Jindal and his wife Supriya with me at Super Bowl XLIV

My assistant and friend Kent Bossier and me at the 2010 NFC Championship Game in which the Saints defeated the Vikings

Rita Benson LeBlanc, Tom Benson, Gayle Benson, President George H.W. Bush, and I at the 2010 NFC Championship Game against the Minnesota Vikings

starting with Coach Sean Payton and quarterback Drew Brees — and that showed as soon as the playoffs started.

I was there in Mr. Benson's Superdome suite when the Saints crushed the Arizona Cardinals 45-14 in the NFC divisional playoffs, and then I came back the following week for the NFC Championship Game against the Minnesota Vikings. When Garrett Hartley kicked the forty-yard field goal to give the Saints a 31-28 overtime victory — and their first berth in a Super Bowl — I could scarcely contain myself.

Tom Benson had been praying for this every day for years, and I knew the Saints had a great opportunity to win the Super Bowl over the Colts, even though they were underdogs. Somebody joked that there's a great saying in Vegas: "Never bet against a ninety-six-year-old archbishop." I guess it worked.

What some people from around the country failed to realize was that this Super Bowl was much more than a football game. The emergence of the Saints was a tremendous, providential event for New Orleans. In the terrible aftermath of a succession of deadly storms — Katrina, Rita, and Gustav — we needed the Saints and other organizations to lift the spirits of the very poor and deprived of the area.

During the off week between the NFC Championship Game and the Super Bowl, I flew to Washington, D.C., to anoint my gravely ill brother, Denis, who was close to death. We visited quietly and shared some old WWII stories, especially the one my mother liked. Somehow, my Army assistant, Jack Ospital, was able to track down Denis during the war, and we got to spend several days together. Then I was able to reassure my parents that Denis was in great shape. Three days after I anointed him, Denis died peacefully in his sleep.

Mr. Benson graciously offered to fly Archbishop Gregory Aymond and me to the Super Bowl on his private plane, and we arrived in Miami on the Saturday night before the game. I knew it would be a tremendous achievement for the Saints to win, and I remained hopeful. You can't understand the emotional lift given to the spectators and the general public unless you are part of the crowd. Regardless of the score, the crowd rollicks with shouts of "When the Saints go marching in" and "Who Dat say they gonna beat dem Saints?" It's all foolishness, but it's a lot of fun.

The morning of the Super Bowl, Archbishop Aymond and I concelebrated Mass for the Bensons and more than five hundred Saints officials and friends at the Hotel Intercontinental in Miami. Archbishop Aymond struck the perfect note, I thought, when he predicted the Saints would win because history indicates "that many of the saints of old went into battle for the faith. And when they did so, they rode on colts. In the battle, the colts got wounded, but the saints had victory in eternal life. So, the Saints will win."

That really brought down the house. Then Mr. Benson got off a good line. He stood up before the Mass and said, "There will be no collection."

The Super Bowl was amazing, and I must say I watched it in almost stunned disbelief. The Saints' victory was a metaphor for everything New Orleans has been through — even in our darkest hour, we kept the faith that we could overcome anything. And, we did!

In addition to the contributions of the Saints, New Orleans also is blessed to have the fabulous example set by the Manning family. Archie and his wife Olivia have reared three sensational sons, and Peyton and Eli were the quarterbacks on back-to-back Super Bowl championship teams. I don't think we'll ever see that again. I'm sure Archie didn't feel too badly that his sad-sack Saints had finally become champions of the world at the temporary expense of his son Peyton.

In the midst of the deepest depression this city has seen, the post-Katrina decision by Tom Benson to keep the Saints in New Orleans despite a series of very tempting offers from other cities such as San Antonio provided heartfelt relief to a beleaguered city.

I always had the faith I would be able to say these words: "The Saints have come marching in!"

Who dat? We dat!

My good friend, Saints owner Tom Benson, his wife Gayle, and granddaughter Rita Benson LeBlanc really got into the swing of things during the closing song of the pre-Super Bowl Mass in Miami. We were all singing at the top of our lungs, "O, When the Saints, Come Marchin' In" ... and they did!

CHAPTER 16

Television, Politics, and Abortion

No one has to convince me about the overpowering influence of television. If St. Paul were alive today, I have no doubt he would be using television and the Internet to instantly spread the Good News to Christian communities across the globe.

We always will need the written word to express and explain complex ideas with nuance, clarity, and substance. But nothing rivals TV for its ability to communicate visually and immediately to a far-flung audience. With a few notable exceptions — such as Archbishop Fulton J. Sheen and the feisty Mother Angelica, who in 1981 with no real money of her own started a worldwide Catholic television and radio network in Birmingham, Alabama — the Catholic Church in America has been woefully slow to embrace television and other forms of electronic communication as critical tools responding to the Gospel imperative to evangelize the world.

Yes, television is extremely expensive, which is why most bishops have been reluctant to commit to its use. But not having a viable, effective television presence in every diocese is an incredibly shortsighted stance.

Actually, my idea of getting into TV in a big way began in the dark recesses of the catacombs. As a seminarian in Rome in the 1930s, I had fallen in love with the catacombs because they represented a stunning visual history of the faith and the devotional practices of the early Christian church. There was a seminary rule in those days that a group of seminarians — called a *camerata* — had to take a daily walk together. Naturally we visited a lot of ancient churches, but once I saw the catacombs I was mesmerized. I believed deeply in them. They are my spiritual home in a way that no cathedral or basilica can match.

The catacombs proved that the governance of the Church was exactly the same in the early Church as it is today. The catacombs were much more than underground burial places on the outskirts of Rome. They were living museums and classrooms. Their frescoes served as a visual catechism in the same way the stained-glass windows of the gothic cathedrals of Western Europe taught the faith.

My introduction to the majesty of the catacombs came in 1936 when I met an Austrian priest, Father Wilpert, who was an acknowledged authority after having spent forty years walking through the miles of underground corridors. His explanation of the symbols contained in the frescoes was so intriguing that I knew a wider knowledge of the catacombs would benefit all Catholics.

One of the most important frescoes Father Wilpert discovered is in what is known today as the Greek Chapel. The fresco is the oldest picture of the Mass as it was celebrated — with people seated around a table on which there are loaves and fish. The earliest Greek symbol for Christ is the fish — "ICHTHUS" — which also was a secret acronym. Each letter stood for a Greek word in the phrase: "Jesus Christ God's Son Savior." We know that fresco dates to about A.D. 100 because of the hairstyle of a prominent woman in the picture, who Father Wilpert said probably was the person who allowed her land to be used for the building of the catacombs. She is seated at the center of the table, with the priest right next to her. The catacomb walls also bear inscriptions of Jesus Christ as the Good Shepherd and Noah's ark, a symbol of the waters of Baptism. There are many more symbols directed toward St. Peter than to St. Paul, because St. Peter was the "big boy" — the Rock — of the early Church. Also depicted is the crowing rooster — the symbol of forgiveness

An executive with Capital Cities Television meets with Pope Paul VI in 1968 to discuss "The Secret of Michelangelo: Every Man's Dream," an hour-long color television special based on Michelangelo's frescoes in the Sistine Chapel. I was able to pave the way for filmmakers to gain access to the chapel. The Pope had one condition for the filming: "One thing I don't want is for you to make a big deal of the Swiss guards. Everybody does that. That's not essential to the workings of the church."

— and pictures of the Blessed Mother holding the infant Jesus in her arms. Baptism was represented by Noah's Ark. The Sacrament of Penance was represented by a fresco of the cripple cured by Christ, as related in Scripture: Is it easier to restore life than to forgive sins?

In 1950, several hundred Catholics from the Archdiocese of Washington joined Archbishop O'Boyle and me on a Jubilee Year pilgrimage to Rome. When I interviewed the pilgrims on the way home about what most impressed them, virtually every person said they were transfixed by the catacombs. Years later, when I started WLAE-TV in New Orleans, I knew our first documentary had to be an insider's look at the catacombs. I may not have known much about television at the time, but I knew plenty about the catacombs.

Shortly after coming to New Orleans, I became aware of the city's rich history of religious broadcasting. As far back as the 1920s, WWL Radio, one of the few 50,000-watt stations in America, was owned by the Jesuits of Loyola University, and its powerful signal could reach nearly the entire country at night. During the 1938 Eucharistic Congress held in New Orleans, Pope Pius XI communicated with the faithful by means of WDSU Radio. Archbishop Rummel made an arrangement with WDSU Radio in 1945 and with WDSU TV in 1949 to broadcast the Christmas Eve Midnight Mass live from St. Louis Cathedral.

In later years, commercial television stations in New Orleans exhibited extreme generosity by offering free time not only to Catholic causes but also to nonprofits. In 1963 Archbishop John Cody worked with WWL-TV general manager Mike Early to air the first Sunday TV Mass for shut-ins. Because of the camera angles in the studio — which was outfitted with faux stained-glass windows — WWL probably had the first head-on shots of a priest celebrating Mass long before the Second Vatican Council dictated that coverage!

WLAE subsequently picked up the Sunday Mass, and I'll never forget Mike Early telling me that by reaching fifteen thousand households — and multiplying that number by a factor of between 2.75 to 3 persons per household — we were reaching forty to forty-five thousand viewers. "It would take quite a few Masses and churches on Sunday to gather forty-five thousand people," Mike said. In 1965, WWL-TV even helped Archbishop Sheen tape twenty-six shows — "The Fulton Sheen Program" — for syndication throughout the country. He commuted from New York and taped two shows a week in front of a two hundred-person audience. It was a very simple set. Sheen insisted that WWL provide a vase with a single rose in it. He was a master showman.

In the 1970s, economics began to play a larger role in the programming decisions of local broadcasters. Nondenominational televangelists were willing to pay big money for Sunday morning air time on local channels, and that income wasn't something the stations could ignore. Thus, the Catho-

A 1975 Mass in the Louisiana Superdome where Archbishop
Fulton Sheen spoke

lic Church's ability to air low-cost programming became more limited and
restricted to off-peak hours.

For many years — going back even to the time I spent in Washington as
editor of the *Catholic Standard* and as producer of a TV show — I was determined to start a television station at my earliest opportunity. I couldn't realize
the dream when I first came to New Orleans because the archdiocesan debt
was significant and other needs had to be addressed first.

In the early 1970s I was named to chair the U.S. Bishops' Committee on
Communications. We started the Institute for Religious Communication, a
summer program at Loyola University that helped train religious men and
women from across the country in public relations, written media, film, radio,
and television. I even got twenty-nine bishops to join me for a communications seminar by promising them free tickets to Super Bowl IX in New
Orleans in January 1975. I was determined that the Church not only get "on"
television but also that we get "into" television in a big way. I spoke frequently

about my dreams to the bishops at our annual meetings in Washington, D.C., but I'll admit it was a very tough sell.

In 1980 I brought together various local media officials, including Mike Early of WWL and Lou Read of WDSU, and Xavier University president Dr. Norman Francis to discuss the possibility of the archdiocese getting into television. An attorney involved in the initial meeting discovered that a license had been set aside in the 1950s — but had gone unused — for UHF Channel 32 to serve as a second educational television station in the New Orleans area. That excited me because I had always intended our station to have an educational component that could serve the entire community.

In 1981 we legally constituted the Educational Broadcasting Foundation, with Dr. Francis as president of the board, with the expressed mission of expanding educational programming on TV in the New Orleans market. A majority of our board of trustees were Blacks and Hispanics.

I also knew a crucial but often overlooked factor in having a successful TV station was the location of the broadcast tower. In this area, there really was only one location where a tower might be built, and the man who owned the land at Bayou Bienvenue and Paris Road in Chalmette wasn't very interested in selling any of his land. I went to see him and told him what I needed, and he said, "All right, let's talk it over. First of all, I like golf, so you've got to come play golf with me." So, eventually, I did. He gave me a one hundred-year lease on sixteen acres of land for $1,000 a year. Since the land we leased was marshy, the massive one thousand twenty-foot tower had to be designed in such a way to enable it to stand firm. That meant using very strong guide lines. We were able to defray some of the cost of building the tower by renting out space to a couple of radio companies that needed the high location for their own broadcast equipment.

As with any major deal, there were a few thorny issues that needed to be resolved. Although WYES, the lone PBS station in the New Orleans market, had not objected to our license application with the Federal Communications Commission within the allotted time period for public comment, it eventually raised some questions about our application and asked the FCC to delay the licensing process. We held a joint meeting in September 1981 to discuss the WYES board's concerns. University of New Orleans chancellor Homer Hitt, the head of the WYES board, said he was concerned primarily about two things: that WLAE might duplicate WYES's programming and that we might cut into their local fund-raising efforts. We gave them assurances that we would not harm them in either area, and the WYES board followed up by sending a letter to the FCC expressing no objection to the processing of our application. Mike Early of WWL had suggested hiring his station's Washington-based attorney, Robert Marmet, to handle all the licensing matters with the FCC, and Marmet did a fantastic job. He knew the procedures inside and out.

As I mentioned, getting into television is not for the financially faint of heart. The archdiocese initially loaned WLAE $1 million to get the station off the ground, and the Catholic Foundation and several benefactors helped raise an additional $1 million. The archdiocese added another $3 million in start-up costs, which included renovating St. Joseph Hall at Notre Dame Seminary and purchasing equipment for the studio. That kind of price tag didn't exactly make me a popular bishop with my priests. They thought I was crazy spending $5 million on television, but I figured that if a station was run well, it would minister to the old people sitting in their homes. No one would squawk if I spent $6 million to build a high school or two high schools, and certainly the old folks would not profit from that. Of course, I couldn't convince Monsignor Charles Duke, our finance chairman, of that rationale. I just had to tell him: "Look, I've made up my mind and that is that." He was very obliging.

One of the best moves we made was applying for membership in the Corporation for Public Broadcasting, which encourages programming that addresses the needs of underserved audiences, especially children and minorities. We also asked for the right to air PBS programs. By airing instructional programs during the school day, we received badly needed revenue from the state of Louisiana and helped keep the budget in check. Our special focus during the day was educational programming, with particular emphasis on elementary and secondary students.

Although we started each broadcast day with the recitation of the rosary at 7:45 a.m., followed by the Mass for shut-ins, the thrust of the WLAE programming was not explicitly religious. We included several ecumenical programs, but more than half of the programming was educational in nature. Considering our community's high rate of illiteracy, we also made sure we aired adult remedial classes that helped persons prepare for the General Educational Development (GED) tests. We also were able to gain access to several PBS programs that WYES — which had the right of first refusal — was not running. The *MacNeil-Lehrer News Hour* and other news programs were among our most popular offerings. I don't know why WYES wasn't interested in those programs. That decision was a miracle for us. They let me have their best program. It's a weird world, in case you didn't know.

In my opinion, the mission of running a television station is utterly consistent with our efforts in other important areas such as education, housing, and health care. If we are truly Catholic, then we should serve our neighbor and enhance the common good, even if the means we use are not explicitly Catholic. Loving our neighbor by providing quality, uplifting, inspiring television constitutes a blessed activity. It is no different than the Church's historic role in educating students of all faiths, not just Catholic students. Our efforts in education have touched an entire region, and that's as it should be.

I always looked for ways to develop interesting religious programming. I went on a retreat once and was enthralled by the director, a Capuchin priest from New York by the name of Father Benedict Groeschel. He had a Ph.D. in psychology, but he was so funny and down to earth in his storytelling that I spent most of my free time during the retreat trying to recruit him to tape a Lenten series for WLAE. "I've been on television before, but I was a terrible flop," Father Groeschel told me, shaking his head.

Then he described the style of his TV show: He stood behind a lectern for thirty minutes, virtually chained, and didn't move.

"You couldn't have been anything but a flop the way you presented it," I told him. "With your natural technique — which is very attractive not only to priests but to everyone — you should simply be yourself. You also need to play off an audience and have them respond to your sense of humor." I arranged to have him tape six half-hour shows for Lent. We brought in an audience that consisted of permanent deacons and their wives. Father Groeschel did two tapings — one on Saturday and another on Sunday. The Saturday crowd was so enthralled by his performance that most of them showed up again the next day. Father Groeschel is a natural.

Catacombs Documentary

The three-part documentary on the catacombs in the mid-1980s was my maiden effort in television, and I will always be proud of the way we were able to pull it off. I had checked with Vatican television officials before going over to Rome to see if they had any comprehensive catalogue of films or images of the catacombs, but to my utter amazement, nothing had been catalogued. That meant we would be on our own. After paying a hefty access fee, I got permission from the Christian Archeological Society to spend three days in the catacombs with my camera crew, but the logistics of shooting were so difficult we needed extra time. Since everything was at least seventy feet underground, we needed to use battery power, and in those days the batteries didn't last a long time. At the end of three days, we had shot only half of the material we needed.

I went to the Polish priest who was on the catacombs staff and begged his indulgence for more time. In Rome, you never know how the church authorities will respond, but I told the priest we needed extra time because this documentary would be shown to every child in New Orleans and would be a real boon to evangelization. The priest went to bat for us with his boss, telling him: "I don't care what the permission papers say. This guy from America is the only person who has taken a camera crew down there, and he needs a little extra time. He ought to be able to stay here as long as he wants." We got the extension. Because of that, we have the only existing film made on the catacombs, because now it is completely against the rules to have television

POLITICS

President Dwight D. Eisenhower and I at a reception in the
Mayflower Hotel in Washington, D.C.

Hale and Lindy Boggs of Louisiana were among
my closest political friends. Lindy later became
U.S. ambassador to the Vatican and still keeps in
touch with me

In February 1967, Speaker of the House John McCormack and Mrs. Harriet McCormack received from me the Cardinal Newman Award in ceremonies held in the rotunda of the U.S. Capitol. The National Newman Club Federation presented the award annually to an outstanding Catholic lay person. McCormack never went anywhere in public without his wife. McCormack was a champion for public housing in Boston. Harriet was never bashful about making requests, even to Washington Archbishop Patrick O'Boyle, asking him to provide more comfortable kneeling pads at the Communion rail in St. Matthew's Cathedral. McCormack later told Archbishop O'Boyle, "Don't pay any attention to her."

On Thanksgiving Day in 1967, President Lyndon Baines Johnson and his wife Lady Bird attended the annual Pan American Mass which was held at St. Patrick Church for representatives of all Latin American countries. Archbishop Patrick O'Boyle and the apostolic nuncio, Archbishop Luigi Raimondi were also in attendance.

I got along well with Vice President Richard Nixon. After losing the presidential
election to JFK, Nixon spoke at a Catholic event at the Hilton Hotel on 16th
Street in Washington. I sat next to him to make sure no ill-tempered remarks
were directed his way. By temperament, Nixon's wife, Pat, was a Catholic.
Her mother had raised her as a Protestant, but she always had respect for the
Catholic Church. Nixon was a Quaker and attended a church fifteen miles from
Washington, but he was very much pro-Catholic

Greeting Vice President and Mrs. Richard M. Nixon and banker Mr. Reilly

Letter of appreciation from President
Ronald Reagan to me

THE WHITE HOUSE
WASHINGTON
June 10, 1985

Your Excellency:

It is with genuine regret that I see your leadership role at
Catholic University, as a trustee and Chairman of the Board,
come to an end. As an individual who has served his Church
and his country in innumerable ways, you can take great satisfaction from this phase of your lifelong achievement.

Your service to our country in World War II is well known to
anyone familiar with the history of the 82nd Airborne Division.
Your dedication to the Church has been even more outstanding
as Auxiliary Bishop of Washington and, for the past 20 years,
as Archbishop of New Orleans.

Your leadership on the governing board of The Catholic
University of America here in Washington for 19 years, although
less well known than other elements of your biography, has
been equally significant. I understand that Pope John Paul II
welcomed you in Rome two months ago in your capacity as board
chairman of Catholic University, which he called America's
"fundamental Catholic university." Truly you are a religious
leader who brings strength to the people and institutions you
have been privileged to serve.

Thank you for doing so many things so well. I regret that
you will no longer be making regular trips to Washington for
Catholic University business. I hope you will visit here often
just the same, for we will always need your presence, your
prayers and your generous dedication to all that is good for
America.

Again, congratulations on all you have accomplished on behalf
of Catholic University and Catholic higher education.

Sincerely,

Ronald Reagan

The Most Reverend Philip M. Hannan
Archbishop of New Orleans
New Orleans, Louisiana 70118

THE WHITE HOUSE
WASHINGTON
June 16, 1987

Dear Archbishop Hannan:

Thank you for your letter and your words of encouragement
and support. I deeply appreciate them.

Bill Casey built his life around the responsibility of free
men to aid the innocent victims of persecution and unjust
aggression. He was meeting that responsibility at the time
of his death, just as he did over 40 years ago when Europe
was in turmoil. I know that he prayed a time would come
when a peace founded on justice and respect for the dignity
of each person would prevail in every nation. If that day
should ever arrive, Bill Casey will be counted among the
first rank of those who made it possible.

Again, my heartfelt thanks for writing.

Sincerely,

Ronald Reagan

The Most Reverend Philip M. Hannan
Archbishop of New Orleans
7887 Walmsley Avenue
New Orleans, Louisiana 70125-3496

Note from President Ronald Reagan relating to the death
and life of Bill Casey

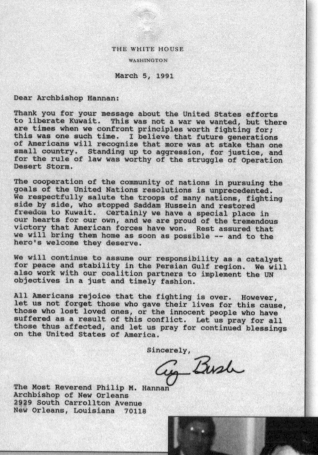

THE WHITE HOUSE

WASHINGTON

March 5, 1991

Dear Archbishop Hannan:

Thank you for your message about the United States efforts
to liberate Kuwait. This was not a war we wanted, but there
are times when we confront principles worth fighting for;
this was one such time. I believe that future generations
of Americans will recognize that more was at stake than one
small country. Standing up to aggression, for justice, and
for the rule of law was worthy of the struggle of Operation
Desert Storm.

The cooperation of the community of nations in pursuing the
goals of the United Nations resolutions is unprecedented.
We respectfully salute the troops of many nations, fighting
side by side, who stopped Saddam Hussein and restored
freedom to Kuwait. Certainly we have a special place in
our hearts for our own, and we are proud of the tremendous
victory that American forces have won. Rest assured that
we will bring them home as soon as possible -- and to the
hero's welcome they deserve.

We will continue to assume our responsibility as a catalyst
for peace and stability in the Persian Gulf region. We will
also work with our coalition partners to implement the UN
objectives in a just and timely fashion.

All Americans rejoice that the fighting is over. However,
let us not forget those who gave their lives for this cause,
those who lost loved ones, or the innocent people who have
suffered as a result of this conflict. Let us pray for all
those thus affected, and let us pray for continued blessings
on the United States of America.

Sincerely,

George Bush

The Most Reverend Philip M. Hannan
Archbishop of New Orleans
2929 South Carrollton Avenue
New Orleans, Louisiana 70118

Letter from President George H.W.
Bush on Kuwait

President George H.W. Bush and I during a meeting with
religious leaders in Washington, D.C.

President George H.W. Bush with me at the National Prayer Breakfast

Note from then-Vice President George H.W. Bush

lights of any kind down there out of fear the lights will harm the frescoes. The reason the frescoes have lasted so long is the paint they used contained no oil — oil did not come to be used in paint until the Renaissance. The frescoes were painted when the plaster was fresh, and the paint bonded into the plaster.

The catacombs were ingeniously engineered. Every so often there was an opening where you could look up and see the heavens, and that provided the ventilation. The catacombs were protected by Roman law, which permitted the establishment of organizations for the purpose of burying the dead. Anybody who belonged to that organization had the right to be buried under its auspices. Father Wilpert estimated that at least five hundred thousand people were buried in the one hundred miles of underground chambers uncovered so far. The catacombs were carved out of a unique substance called tufa. You can dig through it fairly easily, but after it is exposed to the air it hardens quickly. That's the reason there was no need for structural supports inside the catacombs. The tufa rock also made the walls very strong burial places, and the whole purpose of the catacombs was to preserve and protect the bodies. The sanctity of the body was a precious concept in the early Church because the body and the soul were to be reunited at the time of the "general judgment." The early Christians never wanted to move a body that had been buried. The catacombs were such a labyrinth that Father Wilpert himself got lost for two days and almost died there. He told me he almost gave up hope of finding his way out. That proves the extent of the catacombs.

The mapping of the catacombs began in 1865 through the efforts of a young archeological student, Giovanni Battista de Rossi, who stumbled across a piece of marble that was part of the burial stone of Pope Cornelius. The stone fragment read "NELIUS MARTYR," which de Rossi knew from his studies probably belonged to Cornelius, who died in exile in A.D. 253. That find eventually led to the discovery of the chapel of the popes in the catacombs of St. Callixtus, where fourteen popes were buried.

Naturally, I figured we could sell this three-part series to every church and school in the Archdiocese of New Orleans because it was so rich in spiritual and historical information. I gathered the priests for a meeting and tried to persuade them that this might be a new way for them to teach their students and children about the faith. I even offered them a very good discount on the tapes. And do you know what happened? I sold exactly three sets! After that, I told myself, "Man, you're in bad shape in this archdiocese in terms of catechetics." It wasn't so much a personal comeuppance as it was a revelation to me that people are hesitant to embrace anything new. It was as if they had said, "Don't bother us. The kids aren't learning that much, but that's just the way they are."

I figured the only way to succeed was to go over their heads and really make a go of a television station. It was around the same time that the U.S. bishops decided they should have a national network presence and that every diocese, where possible, should have a TV outlet to spread the faith. In order to encourage dioceses to develop their own TV stations, the U.S. bishops promised to send three to four hours a day of quality Catholic programming. That sounded good to me, but as soon as we began to receive the programs, Jerry Romig, general manager of WLAE, came to me with the sobering news that the quality of the programming was awful — the sound and picture quality were poor and the programs were simply not well done. As a result, we dropped out of the national Catholic network, which was called the Catholic Telecommunications Network of America.

The real difficulty was that the bishops talked only among themselves and not to the lay TV experts before launching their expensive initiative. Detroit Cardinal Edmund Szoka, the head of the National Conference of Catholic Bishops committee for TV matters, went about it the wrong way. There was a good practicing Catholic who owned ABC, and I asked him if he had ever been contacted by the U.S. bishops for input into starting a national Catholic network. To my utter amazement, he said no. He would have been very willing to give any advice, free of charge, but we didn't even talk to him. I knew from that one story that we would not succeed. We spent $17 million and came away with nothing to show for it.

Several things doomed CTNA. Cardinal Szoka had the signal scrambled so that cable companies could use it only with the permission of the local bishop. CTNA also was not set up as a nonprofit, which would have allowed it to accept tax-deductible contributions from viewers. That was one of the great attributes of Mother Angelica's Eternal Word Television Network, which was fully supported by viewer contributions. In fact, Mother Angelica even offered to give the U.S. bishops several hours a week of free air time on EWTN, but the negotiations got sticky when EWTN insisted on the right to determine which programs it would and would not run. Mother Angelica didn't want to run a lot of social justice programs. Eventually, everyone agreed that a five-member appeals board of bishops — with the majority appointed by the USCCB president — would review any programs that EWTN refused to air. The bishops finally pulled the plug on CTNA in 1995 when there was no support for continuing the mounting financial losses. The bottom line: The bishops did not produce quality programming, and if you don't have good and attractive programming, you don't have television.

We've made so many missteps in TV it's hard to count them all. New York Cardinal John O'Connor told me once that he had a TV interview show from a studio set up in his rectory. The show only took about fifteen or twenty minutes every morning, but he decided to stop it after awhile. I asked him why. "It was a pain in the neck," he told me. "Every time I gave a talk, I got a lot of bad calls. I've had it." A Protestant television executive, who owned a number of TV stations, said he offered one channel free of charge to the Archbishop of

St. Paul-Minneapolis in the late 1950s, and the archbishop turned him down. I asked the executive if his offer was still good. "Not now," he said. Boy, we did some dumb things.

The reason Mother Angelica succeeded where the U.S. bishops failed was the strength of her ideas. She got good ideas, and then she produced them, and she had nobody to interfere with her vision. Deep in her heart she knew there was a big elderly population that was craving good Catholic programming, and she catered originally to that age group and then branched her way out to other age groups as EWTN got its sea legs. Pope John Paul II indirectly supported her efforts, even when she got into trouble with Los Angeles Cardinal Roger Mahony for questioning his statements about the Real Presence of Christ in the Eucharist. The Vatican didn't respond to Cardinal Mahony's complaints, and Pope John Paul II later presented a monstrance to Mother Angelica for her new chapel in recognition of her contributions to the Church. Certainly, the hand of the Lord was with her by virtue of the contributions she received to keep her television apostolate going.

Heroic Military Chaplains

Quality programming is the key to any television effort, and I think we were able to provide several documentaries and news reports that not only entertained but also enlightened our viewers. Because of my military background as a paratroop chaplain, I have been inspired by stories of heroism and faith, and those two qualities are exhibited brilliantly in the lives of two chaplains that I was able to profile — Navy chaplain Father Vincent R. Capodanno, who served with the Third Battalion of the Fifth Marines in Vietnam and whose cause for beatification has been opened by the U.S. Military Archdiocese; and Army chaplain Father Emil Kapaun, who was captured, imprisoned, and executed during the Korean War and whose cause for beatification is being promoted by the Diocese of Wichita.

Father Capodanno, who was born in Staten Island, was known as "The Grunt Padre." His religious community, the Maryknolls, was totally against the Vietnam War, but he insisted on serving as a combat chaplain and even requested an extension after completing his first tour of duty. If his unit was not involved in combat, he would simply walk to the next unit and find the combat action. He finally died on September 4, 1967, when he tried to rescue a medic who had been injured in no-man's land. Father Capodanno went to pull the soldier to safety, but he didn't see a machine gun nest and was riddled with twenty-nine bullets. When I went to interview soldiers who had served with him, they were reverential in their respect. The Protestant chaplain, a Presbyterian minister named Eli Takesian who was the regimental chaplain and Father Capodanno's superior, talked for six minutes without taking a break. "If I ever was an artist and wanted to paint a portrait of Christ," he told me,

"I'd use his eyes. His eyes were the eyes of Christ. He speaks like Christ. For me, he is Christ."

The other chaplain, Father Kapaun, stayed with his men in North Korea when the enemy broke through the American lines and had our forces surrounded. Our soldiers had to surrender because they didn't have a chance to escape. The Communists marched our soldiers to a POW camp, and anybody who couldn't make the journey on foot was shot. Father Kapaun knew this, and when he saw a wounded soldier who couldn't walk on his own, he brushed aside the rifle of the Communist soldier pointed at the wounded man, lifted him, put him across his shoulders and carried him for thirty miles to the prisoner of war camp. That soldier, a Baptist, is still alive. When I interviewed the survivor, I told him, "You've just told me a story that is humanly impossible." He replied, "Yes, sir, I know that. But I'm telling you, it was God who gave him the strength to do what he did. Nobody could have done what he did."

Another incredible attribute of Father Kapaun was his boundless compassion. A fellow POW — an officer who had graduated from West Point — held out under the Communist torture as long as he could, but he finally broke down. The North Koreans had beaten him almost to death, hung him by his thumbs, and put him in a cell so narrow that he couldn't lie down to sleep — he had to stand erect. They simply wore him out until he finally capitulated to their interrogation. When the officer was finally released and sent back to his fellow prisoners, he felt ashamed for having broken under the torture and

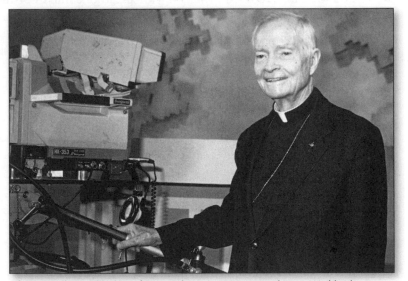

After I retired as archbishop of New Orleans in 1989, I started Focus Worldwide Television Network and traveled extensively to bring Catholic issues, personalities, and history to light. I'm still convinced that St. Paul would have chosen to use TV as his major evangelizing tool if he were alive today

having used the name of the chaplain to benefit his situation. As soon as the officer returned to the general prison area, Father Kapaun rushed up to him and threw his arms around him. "Never will I think ill of you for breaking; we are proud of your bravery," Father Kapaun told him. Then the priest turned to the other prisoners and said, "I don't expect anyone here to suffer physical harm in order to save me or my name."

When Pope John Paul II accepted my retirement in 1989, I knew immediately that my successor, Archbishop Francis Schulte, was not going to be interested in the archdiocese maintaining ownership of WLAE. In the original deal, I had arranged that the archbishop of New Orleans would be the president of the Educational Broadcasting Foundation — which is as it should have been — but Archbishop Schulte was naturally concerned about the long-range liabilities of running the station, even though PBS would defray a large percentage of the indebtedness each year. Archbishop Schulte didn't think the size of the WLAE audience justified the investment, and thus another deal was struck. Since WLAE was an educational station, it could not be sold on the open market. Therefore, the Willwoods Community, a group of private Catholics headed by Deacon Paul Nalty, and Louisiana Public Broadcasting agreed to a 50-50 ownership share in the station.

I was still doing my own programming, but I concluded that the only way to continue in television was to form my own corporation — Focus Worldwide Television Network. Our major emphasis was producing a weekly news show, with Mary Lou McCall, and documentaries with a Catholic interest. Among the excellent documentaries we made was one on Nicaraguan dictator Daniel

In 1991, Mary Lou McCall and I traveled to Nicaragua to interview Sandinista leader Daniel Ortega for WLAE-TV. Noriega got so flustered with some of Mary Lou's questions that he cut the interview short, saying he had to go to a baseball game

Ortega in 1991 — which was so good the federal government asked for permission to make an unlimited number of copies to give to their embassies across the world — and another on the first Mass celebrated in Siberia by its new bishop.

Mary Lou really got under Ortega's skin, but he was a real rascal. She asked him, point blank, "How many people did you murder?" And, he didn't answer. He finally got so flustered that he cut the interview short because he said he had to go to a baseball game!

The documentary we did from Russia and Siberia was particularly interesting to me. A politician I knew from Lithuania gave us inside information about the amazing standoff in Russia in August 1991 when hard-line Communists tried to stage a coup against Soviet president Mikhail Gorbachev by having him placed under house arrest and then circling the Duma — the parliamentary building — with tanks. The hard-liners had taken over control of the radio airwaves, and they were blocking any radio contact that Duma members had with the outside world. A Lithuanian member of the Duma had broken the communications blockade by hiding radio broadcast equipment inside a potato truck, allowing him to smuggle the equipment past the guards. We got to interview him a few years later, but we had to do the interview in the middle of a forest. "I can't tell you anything unless we go out to the woods," he told us. "Everything around here is bugged." That smuggled radio helped break the back of the blockade because Gorbachev could talk directly to the people.

On that same trip we traveled to Siberia, to a town called Magadan that had been completely controlled by the Communists. We were able to film the first Mass celebrated by the new bishop of Siberia at the Church of the Nativity. Before the Mass, we were in the town square and met some of the people who were milling about in the open market. "What do you think about the Pope?" we asked one woman. "Who is he?" the woman asked, incredibly. One person did know who the Pope was, but the fact that the Pope was a fellow Slav didn't mean much to him. "The trouble with him is that he's a Pole," the man said. Even more sobering was our interview with people who had uncovered a mass grave in Kiev in southern Russia. We found evidence of a terrible slaughter, and the victims were simply dumped into a common grave. The explanation given by the Communist government was that they were all brigands, but we got one doctor to identify some of the bodies, and he told us a number of these brigands were ten-year-old girls!

Abortion Issue

I have never been afraid to tackle an issue head on, and perhaps my most newsworthy stance came in the fall elections of 1996 when Mary Landrieu, the daughter of former New Orleans Mayor Moon Landrieu, was running for the United States Senate. I had been a close personal friend of the Landrieus and their nine children since coming to New Orleans in 1965. Moon had been a stalwart in pushing for civil rights for African-Americans and included them in his administration. I admired him for his bold stance, which alienated him from so many in the white power structure of New Orleans.

However, the issue of abortion — the civil rights issue of our time — played out in big way in the 1996 election. Mary, who was raised a Catholic, clearly had stated that the she was "pro-choice," strongly believed "in a woman's right to choose," and did not support "any attempt to weaken the Supreme Court decision in Roe v. Wade." She also was supported in her Senate bid by Emily's List, a political action committee that supports only pro-choice Democratic women in their quest for political office.

At a news conference on October 30, 1996, I issued the following statement: "Abortion is a detestable crime, its particular malice deriving from the very helpless condition of the unborn baby. Unfortunately, legalized abortion pertains to every unborn baby, from the first moment of conception to its actual birth. Therefore, even partial-birth abortion is legally permitted owing to the veto by the President (Clinton) of the ban on partial-birth abortion.

"Legislators have a solemn duty to protect the life of the unborn at every stage. It is a deception to say that one is against certain kinds of abortion. Legalized abortion is permitted for every type of abortion in virtue of the Roe vs. Wade decision."

I added that no Catholic should vote for any officeholder who believes in abortion, which included President Clinton and Mary Landrieu. Mary was clearly on record as supporting Roe v. Wade as a legal right for

Praying during a protest against abortion

women, and I felt it was necessary for Catholics to be aware of Mary's position regarding abortion. In a question-and-answer period that followed, I said: "If a person actually believes in Catholic doctrine, I don't see how they can avoid it being a sin" to vote for Landrieu.

As you can imagine, my announcement created an uproar within both the political and the religious communities. My decision to go public so forcefully was particularly difficult for me because I really like everyone in the Landrieu family, and that made it sad.

I decided to speak out unequivocally after receiving documents that could not be refuted — Emily's List had provided Mary with $300,000 in contributions for her Senate race against Woody Jenkins. Since Emily's List contributed only to Democratic female candidates who supported abortion rights, that fact belied Mary's comments during the campaign that she was "pro-choice, but not pro-abortion." Mary also said during the campaign that she supported President Clinton's veto of the partial-birth abortion ban.

To me, the issue simply cannot be danced around. Abortion strikes at the fundamental right we all have — the right to life. There's no use worrying about welfare or health care or education for a baby who is dead.

I knew my speaking out just before the election would ignite a firestorm, but I did what I thought was right. In my opinion, many Catholic bishops across the country did not oppose abortion vigorously, saying they neither endorsed nor opposed candidates for political office but adding they did consider abortion the defining moral issue of our time that needed to be opposed. How do you oppose something without taking a firm stand against it?

Of course, Americans United for Separation of Church and State issued a formal complaint to the Internal Revenue Service that the Archdiocese of New Orleans had engaged in illegal political activity. I expected that. My conscience was clear.

Even though I was condemned in many quarters, the Landrieu flap had an interesting fallout. Every time I went into a Catholic church after that, the whole congregation got up and applauded, which tells me priests haven't been preaching to their parishioners point-blank about the horrors of abortion.

After I made my statement, Moon came to see me, and he insisted: "Mary is for life. She supports life." I replied: "Well, all she has to do is vote for it."

Then Moon told me about Mary as a child. "When she was a little girl she would come home after school, and if there was something wrong with a kitten she would pick it up and comfort it," Moon said. "She would bring home a little bird if it was injured. She was always for life. She is completely for life." I didn't argue with him because we were way past that point. "I'm just talking about legislation," I finally said. "We judge legislators on the laws they support."

With the passing of time, I think some of the wounds have begun to heal. Moon called me a few years ago and said he wanted to apologize for some of his comments, which probably were the result of his wounded, paternal pride. I told him it wasn't necessary for him to apologize and that I had admired the tough political stands he had taken over the years, especially regarding integration.

I've always been perfectly proper with Mary. When we meet, we shake hands. I think she understands my position that I am simply teaching what the Church has taught for centuries. There is nothing new in this teaching. She recently voted against partial-birth abortion, which is an encouraging sign. However, I don't know if she fully understands the full scope of what she voted for. If you're against partial-birth abortion, then you're against abortion.

People ask me all the time to reflect on the Supreme Court's 1973 decision in Roe v. Wade that invented a constitutional right to privacy and gave legal protection to abortion through all nine months of pregnancy. I was not surprised at all by the decision because the Catholic Supreme Court Justice appointed by President Eisenhower in 1956 — William J. Brennan — was a rebel from the very beginning. Eisenhower thought he had made a shrewd move by making Brennan a recess appointment. Brennan was a Catholic Democrat from New Jersey who was the second of eight children in a large, Irish immigrant family. But Eisenhower made a fatal mistake — he never checked out Brennan with his bishop, Archbishop Thomas Boland of Newark, who could have told him to steer clear of him because he was way off base about abortion.

I had a few occasions to interact with Brennan after the Roe decision, and I remember him telling me, "In today's world, we can be more adventurous than we used to be."

The strange thing is the person who introduced me to Brennan was Chief Justice Earl Warren, who was not even a Catholic. I got along great with Warren because he loved to attend the Pan American Mass we held annually around Thanksgiving at St. Patrick's Church for the ambassadorial community. We always invited Chief Justice Warren, and he never missed. After a few years, he enjoyed the Mass so much that he invited me to his office for some informal conversations. He had enough respect for the Church that he wanted to know what we were thinking. Right after Brennan was named to the court in 1956, Chief Justice Warren told me, "You have to meet the new justice." He seemed surprised that I had never met Brennan, especially since Brennan was a Catholic.

We walked down the hall and knocked on Brennan's office door. I'll never forget the look on Brennan's face — I don't think he ever expected the Chief Justice of the Supreme Court to know a Catholic bishop! I always wished Archbishop O'Boyle had gone to see Warren more often. It could have done so much good, particularly in the area of integration, because the Archdiocese of Washington had done a masterful job of integrating its schools without major incident and had a real success story to share.

Warren wasn't the only chief justice I got to know. I also became acquainted with Chief Justice Warren Burger, who unfortunately voted with the majority in Roe v. Wade, which recognized a broad right to "privacy" that prohibited states from banning all abortions. In 1979 when Pope John Paul II made his first trip to the United States, the Holy Father celebrated Mass in Washington and issued unequivocal admonitions against abortion and birth control. He didn't sugarcoat a thing. After the Mass ended I walked over to Chief Justice Burger and said, "I know the Holy Father expressed some views that you don't agree with. What, in general, did you think of his talk?"

Burger replied: "I do disagree with him about abortion. It's something that's so obviously a part of the Constitution." I thought to myself, "What part of the Constitution are you talking about?" Then Burger continued: "I think that he performed a real service in stating the beliefs and the doctrine of his Church so that we can compare our convictions with those of the Church."

I don't care what any legal scholar might have to say in support of Roe. It's an abominable opinion that has no recognition of the law of nature and human life, and it has caused immeasurable harm to society. It has devastated our teenagers, because now the Constitution is interpreted to allow public schools to distribute condoms to any student without parental consultation. The decision has ripped apart families and destroyed family rights. Now the United Nations is espousing abortion as if it were a "human right" and insisting that U.N. funding be tied to a country's legal acceptance of abortion.

Canon 2350 states: "Whoever procures a complete abortion is automatically (*latae sententiae*) excommunicated." The Church has a duty to stand by canon law. The Church has made it clear for centuries that anyone who procures an abortion — and that doesn't mean just the surgeon, it means anyone who helps to procure a completed abortion — is automatically excommunicated. That means the bishop does not have to make a public statement about excommunication. It is automatic, and it's been that way for centuries. The Second Vatican Council did not change that teaching one iota. So here we are, wasting our time wondering if we can afford to hurt the feelings of a Catholic congressman or congresswoman who supports abortion rights through a very public vote. If these Catholic lawmakers support abortion rights, they are automatically excommunicated.

Abortion also runs counter to the Declaration of Independence, which has a clear message to the world that all human rights — life, liberty, and the pursuit of happiness — are bestowed by God, not by the state. Anybody who reads the Declaration of Independence ought to understand that the United States, from its founding, considered life as a gift from God. Abortion is murder, and I don't care what anyone else calls it. Before the operation you have a live person and after the operation you've got a dead corpse. Anyone who believes in murder does not belong in any high office, especially the White

House. I have often made this statement, and frequently I am told that the word "murder" is too rough. It is a fact.

The Church's condemnation of abortion stretches back to the very first catechism that was written before the year A.D. 100. In those days the early Christians knew about abortion. Under Roman law, the father of a child had the right simply to let a baby die for any reason whatsoever. The Romans had a custom of depositing unwanted children in two places in Rome that were well-known to Christians. That enabled the pope to tell the Christians that they should go there and pick up the babies and adopt them, and they did.

There's an incredible inscription in the catacombs that illustrates the value the early Christians placed on the God-given gift of human life. The inscription is on the grave of a man who was one of these abandoned babies that a Catholic family adopted and then raised as its own. In the inscription the man recognizes his parents, and then there are a series of dates — his birth into this life, then a dash and then the date of his birthday in heaven (the day of his death). He thanks his parents not only for life in this world but also for eternal life.

We must change the culture of death, which is rampant in our country. The reason we have so many murders and terrible crimes involving violence — even to point of mothers beating their own children and letting them die — derives from our legally allowing a mother to kill her child. We are in such bad shape that we have national leaders pushing for passage of the Freedom of Choice Act that would extend the possibility of abortion to the time of viability, even to the time when a living, breathing child is outside the womb. This is not freedom of choice — it is license to commit murder.

For months before the presidential election in 2008 I made this simple and concise statement about abortion. Your vote should be cast as a matter of morality, not as a matter of deciding which political party you favor.

Abortion is basically the murder of an unborn child. No person believing in abortion — a murder — should be elected to a high political office in our country, especially to the presidency.

Voting for abortion is not only against our moral code; it is also against the basic moral principles of our country as stated in the Declaration of Independence, which states that our basic human rights — life, liberty, and the pursuit of happiness — come from God, not from any political organization. The people always agreed with that declaration, and it was the linchpin of President Kennedy's famous inaugural address.

The bottom line is the Roe decision was an awful mistake. Brennan's selection to the court was, in my opinion, a huge mistake. I am hoping that eventually, some day, another case will make it to the Supreme Court so that the court can express itself again and abortion-on-demand can be revoked. We owe it to our Creator to fight for those who have no voice.

When I was a pastor at St. Patrick's Church in Washington, I went to the home of an elderly woman on a sick call. As I entered the room, she looked absolutely horrid, and she asked me urgently to hear her confession. "Don't you want me to call the doctor for you?" I asked. She replied, "No, the doctor doesn't know my trouble." I knew then that this was a case of conscience, and I immediately asked everyone to leave the room. As soon as we were alone, she said, "I am seventy-two years old, and I can't clear my thinking that when I was twenty, I had an abortion. I just can't forget it." I talked to her and gave her absolution. Can you imagine what this woman had to deal with her entire life? It is an absolute lie that a woman will "get over" or "forget" her abortion. That's not my experience with people. We need to develop a culture of life.

When I was a young priest, there were not many women who even considered having an abortion because they knew at the core of their being that it was wrong. My brother Frank was a superb family practice doctor, and one of his greatest joys was delivering babies. He told me that none of his colleagues would even consider such a practice. Abortion is not health care. It's a death sentence. And we need the American Medical Association to stand up and say that again. We need leadership at all levels to say that. We have to pray the culture will change, and we must change the culture. It will happen.

We need to be that voice of truth, freedom, and life. And, believe me, we need to embrace the power of television to inform, inspire, and persuade so that the truth will be told!

CHAPTER 17

Pope John Paul II's Historic Visit
to New Orleans

In 1986, Father Robert N. Lynch, the associate general secretary in charge of public policy matters for the National Conference of Catholic Bishops/ United States Catholic Conference, flew from Washington, D.C., to pay me a visit. We chatted for a few minutes, and then he zeroed in on the purpose of his visit.

"This is no indication whatsoever from the Holy See that there will be a visit by the Holy Father to New Orleans," Father Lynch told me, "but is it your opinion that such a visit would be beneficial to the city and the surrounding area?"

Right then and there I knew, despite Father Lynch's diplomatically chosen words, that New Orleans was on the cusp of one of the most historic events in its nearly three centuries of existence.

Pope John Paul II was coming to New Orleans! Of that, I was certain.

In answer to Father Lynch's question, I really poured it on. I reviewed with him the Catholic history of New Orleans and talked about how the Catholic culture permeates our region, how St. Louis Cathedral dates back to the 1720s and serves as an icon for the city, how we had the largest concentration of black Catholics in the United States.

When Father Lynch was about to leave, he ended with a cautionary note: "There is absolutely no proof that the Holy Father is coming here, and don't believe any rumors that indicate he is definitely coming." Right then, I knew the Pope was coming. It was simple common sense. Why would the NCCB have its official representative make a trip to see me and ask all of these questions if the Pope wasn't coming to New Orleans? He was coming, and I knew it.

Of course, I couldn't tell anybody anything about the potential visit because nothing had been confirmed. A few weeks later I heard through the grapevine that, unlike his previous visits to the United States, Pope John Paul was not going to be meeting with any specific ethnic groups — such as black Catholics — but would visit cities that the NCCB/USCC would decide would be best for him to visit. Right then, I got concerned that New Orleans might fall out of the loop, and I thought we had to counter that.

From its beginnings — dating back to the sad institution of slavery — New Orleans had the most black Catholics of any area in the country. I also knew that slavery and racial discrimination were of such import that they deserved to be considered as the focus for any papal trip to the South. The Pope needed to talk about race relations, and where better to do that than in New Orleans?

Eventually, the Holy See convened a quiet meeting in Rome of U.S. bishops whose dioceses were being considered for his 1987 visit. The Vatican already had released a statement that the Pope planned a U.S. visit sometime in 1987 but had not indicated the cities he would visit. The bishops "in the running" for his visit got to meet personally with Pope John Paul II in his office. The only other place in the Deep South the Holy Father seriously considered going in 1987 was Mobile, Alabama, which was considered to be important because it was older as an archdiocese (established in 1829) than New Orleans (elevated from a diocese to archdiocese in 1850). I will always be grateful to Mobile Archbishop Oscar Lipscomb, who viewed the event through the prism of a true Southerner, and insisted that New Orleans and its Catholic history deserved the honor of a papal visit. I wrote Archbishop Lipscomb and thanked him for his graciousness.

At the Vatican meeting, the Holy Father was very frank. "I don't want to make this visit an occasion to visit with various groups," he said. "I think it

Pope John Paul II and me at St. Louis Cathedral in New Orleans

would be better if we did not do that." But about five minutes later, the Pope said he wanted to make an exception to that. He said the last time he had come to the United States he regretted not being able to meet with Polish Catholics in Chicago and Detroit. "I'd like to go there and make them happy," Pope John Paul said.

Then he said he had not been able to visit with Native Americans, and he also wanted to consider doing that on the upcoming trip.

Immediately, I sensed my opening. I spoke up: "If you don't mind my asking, Your Holiness, you said you weren't going to visit with any particular nationalities, and now you're saying you're going to visit with Polish Catholics and Native American Catholics in our country. One of the biggest questions in the United States is the issue of race relations between whites and blacks, and in New Orleans we have the largest number of black Catholics in the country. This is the place you ought to come to talk about race relations and show black Catholics how much you care for them."

After a prayer service with priests and religious at St. Louis Cathedral on September 12, 1987, Pope John Paul II and I ride in the Popemobile down Decatur Street toward the Superdome. An interesting battle of wills ensued. The Secret Service agents in charge kept telling the driver to step on the gas; I countered by asking the driver to slow down for the crowd to get a better chance to see the Pope

I guess my forthright nature, which goes back to my childhood, served me well. The Pope smiled and said he liked my proposal. That's when I really knew he was coming to New Orleans! I certainly was worried that he might say no, but I also said to myself, I hadn't lost anything by asking. I could sense that the other bishops in the room were reluctant to speak up, and I thought that was my perfect opportunity. I knew race relations was an entrenched problem in our country, and this was a chance for the Pope to address it head-on during his eleven-day trip to the United States.

During the course of the meeting and in the months that followed when I had a chance to see the Holy Father, I always addressed myself to him simply as "New Orleans." I didn't use my last name — I wanted him simply to remember where I was from — New Orleans. That was more important than anything else. He kept calling me, "New Orleans, New Orleans."

After I returned from Rome, I knew we had a monumental task ahead of us, and if our preparations were to lead to a successful visit, it was going to be necessary to get the laity involved from the outset. I spoke to Monsignor Roger Morin, who was executive director of the Office of the Social Apostolate, and asked him to serve as the coordinator of the papal visit, which would entail months of meticulous and even tedious planning.

One of the first major things we had to determine for the September 11-13, 1987, trip was the site of the September 12 outdoor papal Mass, which was expected to draw a crowd of more than 150,000. That was too big even for the Superdome, which could accommodate about 80,000 or 90,000.

The committee that Monsignor Morin charged with recommending an outdoor site did an ingenious thing — it hired a helicopter to get a bird's-eye view of the entire metropolitan area. As it turned out, the best place was the University of New Orleans near Lake Pontchartrain, which had plenty of land and just a few buildings dotting its expansive east campus.

Of course, the University of New Orleans is a state university, and celebrating a papal Mass on public property might have caused a stir among the litigious, church-state separationists. But I will never forget the welcoming attitude of UNO Chancellor Gregory O'Brien, who himself was a Catholic. Rather than create any roadblocks — as the chancellors of other public universities in California had — Chancellor O'Brien and the entire university opened their arms to the Pope and even declared a university holiday to help ease the flow of traffic. O'Brien turned over all of the university's buses to us and made sure the parking lots were cleared so that they could accommodate Mass attendees from around the South. No other university head in the country had done that. That's why I tip my hat to the entire New Orleans community. Even non-Catholic entities exceeded my fondest expectations and did whatever they could to welcome the Pope — for example, *The Times-Picayune* printed a complete Mass booklet for us as part of its pre-trip coverage.

By way of thanks, I placed University of New Orleans Chancellor O'Brien in a reserved section close to the altar, and after the Mass, I introduced him personally to the Holy Father. "These are the people who through their goodness made this public campus available to us and allowed us to put up a building and an altar for you," I told Pope John Paul II. The laypeople pulled us through.

One of the laypeople Monsignor Morin identified as invaluable to our papal preparations was Anne Milling, who is one of those rare people who simply know how to get things done in a first-class manner. I first spotted Anne's impressive abilities at the inauguration reception for New Orleans

Mayor Sidney Barthelemy, who had succeeded Dutch Morial. Anne was hospitality chairwoman for the inauguration, and she carried out every detail beautifully. I remember being struck by her relaxed wit evident in her public remarks. She had an elegant charm, and it was clear to me she knew how to organize much more than a two-float parade.

Anne also was a great Catholic volunteer, so she was a natural to assume responsibility for the minutiae of this historic state visit. When Monsignor Morin approached requesting her help, Anne instantly agreed to handle all of the papal protocol attendant to the Pope's two-night stay at my residence adjacent to Notre Dame Seminary.

One of Anne's first jobs was to prepare for the luncheon I was to host at my residence for the Pope, his traveling staff, and the bishops of Louisiana. We knew that the honor of preparing the luncheon for the Pope — especially in a city with such a revered reputation for superb food — was incredibly prestigious. How would we be able to decide which restaurant would receive that honor?

The committee felt the only fair way was to present the honor to New Orleans' oldest continuously operating restaurant — Antoine's — which opened in 1840 and has served impeccable French Creole cuisine to presidents, heads of state, governors, and Hollywood and Broadway stars. That settled, one big problem remained, Anne discovered. After taking one look at the mismatched china I had in the kitchen cabinets, she said, "This simply won't do. Not for the Pope."

On her own initiative, Anne contacted Stafford Sweatt, the president of Lenox China, and pleaded her case. "We do not have the proper plates for the Holy Father," she told him. Somehow Anne was so convincing that Lenox agreed to create, free of charge, a limited edition of twenty-four settings of gilt-edged china, complete with the papal monogram and the coat of arms of the Archdiocese of New Orleans. In order to guarantee that the china would be unique, Sweatt agreed to break the mold Lenox had used to make the plates. After Anne got approval for the dinnerware, she had the guts to call Lenox back and say, "The Archbishop doesn't have the proper wine glasses for the dinner. Can you help us?" Incredibly, she got three glasses for each place setting.

Choosing Xavier University

Another sensitive issue we had to decide was which Catholic college would host the Pope for his important message on Catholic higher education. It came down to a choice between Loyola University, founded by the Jesuits, and Xavier University of Louisiana, established by then-Mother Katharine Drexel of the Sisters of the Blessed Sacrament, a Philadelphia heiress who had used the considerable fortune of her banker-father's estate to start Catholic schools and churches for African-Americans and Native Americans across the country.

To me, Xavier University was the easy choice for a number of reasons. For one, the Holy Father was coming to New Orleans to address the issue of racism, and Xavier University was the only historically black Catholic university in the Western Hemisphere and was unsurpassed in creating harmony and understanding among the races. I wanted to support Xavier in every way possible. I was a long-time friend of Dr. Norman Francis, the first lay president of Xavier who also was the first black to graduate from Loyola Law School. Norman had studied law in the 1950s for the very reason of serving the cause of justice as the United States worked through the painful experience of ensuring civil rights for all of its citizens.

When the superior of the Sisters of the Blessed Sacrament called me in 1968 because she was considering Norman to become Xavier's first lay president, she wanted to know what I thought. "Would you be opposed to our naming a layman as president?" she asked me. I asked her whom she had in mind, and she told me it was Norman. "That might be the best idea you've ever had in your life," I replied. "Please act on it immediately."

Part of the Pope's visit would be to address the leaders of the more than two hundred thirty-five Catholic colleges and universities across the United States, and I wanted that address to be at Xavier. On the day we announced a detailed agenda for the papal trip — including the various venues for the major papal addresses — I got a call from a reporter at *The Times-Picayune* because he thought the information he had received about Xavier hosting the

Papal Mass at the Lakefront – University of New Orleans

higher education talk was incorrect. "Isn't that a mistake? Isn't Loyola going to be the location for the Pope's talk?" the reporter asked me. "No," I said. "I didn't make a mistake." I think Loyola completely understood, and there were no hard feelings.

I told Norman that since Xavier was the only Catholic college the Pope would be visiting in New Orleans, he ought to capitalize on the honor by stressing Xavier's track record of success not only to alumni but also to foundations and corporations across the country. Subsequently, after the Pope's visit, Norman launched a capital campaign, raising nearly $18 million, and he got nearly twice as much as he asked.

By early February 1987, our preparations were beginning to come together. However, looking over the Mass readings for Saturday, September 12 — the vigil Mass for Sunday — they appeared to only concern sin. How would the Pope be able to weave an uplifting message to hundreds of thousands of people suffering in the midst of a severe economic collapse? I called in Father Kenneth Hedrick, the director of our Office of Worship, who nearly collapsed when I suggested that we ask the Holy See to substitute that day's readings with something more positive for people who are hurting. But the designated readings prevailed.

Our advance team was extremely involved in making sure all the logistical issues were handled at each site of a major papal address, but my biggest concern was far more pragmatic — people wanted tickets to the events, and they wanted them right away! They didn't care about how the Superdome was going to be decorated. Who cared? They wanted tickets! What amazed me at the morning meetings we held was that nobody except me was bringing up the subject of tickets. I got the impression that the whole event was being planned for the benefit of the Secret Service and its worthy mission to control the crowds and keep the Pope safe. Meanwhile, there wouldn't be one person at any event if we didn't distribute the tickets.

The host committee unveiled two officials posters — one by former WWL-TV anchorman Garland Robinette and the other by Jean Seidenberg — at a special gathering at One Canal Place, which drew a tremendous crowd, proving again the incredible charisma of the Holy Father. At the unveiling, people had one question on their minds — how could they get in to see the Pope? As one woman put it: "Can we even stand in the same room with him? We know we couldn't shake hands, but just to be in his presence." As much as I wanted, of course, I couldn't promise.

The unveiling of the two portraits was so successful that many bought both, perhaps urged on by salesman Hannan assuring them that "every great event deserves a great souvenir. And the Holy Father in New Orleans has brought out the best efforts in two artists. Rest assured, that I am merely quoting Scripture when I say that, though man does not live by bread alone, he does live by bread, which we need — two million dollars worth, to be exact — in order to defray the cost of the visit. Though originally we planned to do one poster, we decided it better to have two, which means there's a special blessing for those who buy both." The crowd roared — and, happily, bought five thousand copies over the next several weeks.

The budget for the trip was something of a moving target. We figured it would cost about $2 million, and we were correct. The City of New Orleans thought it might be able to profit from the visit and figured that since it needed more police barricades for crowd control, the archdiocese ought to pay for them. As soon as we heard that, Alden "Doc" Laborde, who was part of our finance team, went personally to see not only Mayor Barthelemy but also the police chief to bring them back to reality. "You didn't spend one dime to bring the Holy Father here," Doc told them. "Every hotel in the city is going to profit from his presence here. You owe Hannan a big debt of gratitude." That was the last time the city asked us for a dime!

Papal Altar

One of the most expensive projects was designing and building the papal altar at UNO. The architectural firm of Walk, Haydel & Associates — headed by my good friend Frank J. Walk — won the contract to design the sweeping, elevated altar, built to withstand winds of 200 m.p.h. as well as provide extra protection for the Holy Father in case of a terrorist attack. The plywood altar was reinforced underneath with thick steel plating in case, due to an air attack, the Secret Service agents had to shove the Holy Father inside a four-foot opening.

The sturdiness of the altar turned out to be a critical factor — as well as a source of pride since, just before the September 12 Mass, an intense thunderstorm blew across the Lakefront campus and, happily, the altar and its yellow canopy more than held its own, unlike the Miami and San Antonio altars erected for the Pope, which had been obliterated by strong winds. At a closing meeting in Detroit before the Pope flew back to Rome, Frank and Monsignor Morin had a chance to shake hands with Pope John Paul II, who told them with a glint in his eye: "Ah, New Orleans — you built your altar big and strong, and it stood up against the wind and the rain!" Did that ever make Frank blush!

As another safety feature, the Secret Service demanded that we install an asphalt roadway on the grass field east of the Lakefront Arena, which would allow the Pope to make a quick, emergency getaway in case of any trouble. The Pope's security was paramount. Bulletproof glass shielded the sides of the altar platform. In case the Secret Service needed to shuffle the Pope away quickly in a James Bond-style water escape, the back stairs were just a short distance to the protection levee of Lake Pontchartrain. We installed a ramp up the levee and down the other side, and we kept a boat ready in the lake to get the Pope out that way if we were forced to do so.

By August, everything was nearly in place for the Pope's visit. We weathered some unflattering publicity — the media were questioning whether or not we had made arrangements for sufficient medical facilities to handle any eventuality at the outdoor Mass, which, of course, might be plagued by very hot temperatures. So when I went out to UNO to officially bless the eight-foot-by-twelve-foot metal cross that we placed by crane atop the altar canopy, nobody paid much attention at all. All the reporters wanted to know about was: Do you have enough health facilities, water, soft drinks, food, and toilets to take care of everyone? They especially wanted to know what we would do with people who might faint or have a more serious condition during the Mass. I repeated what I had been saying for months — we would have more health facilities available on site than any other place in the city. "So if you feel sick or even have a heart attack coming on, the place to go is out to the Mass," I said. Well, everybody got a ruffle out of that!

After I got finished with those interviews, the foreman in charge of placing the large cross above the altar motioned me over to talk to him privately. He told me everyone had praised him for the way the cross fit perfectly. He said to me: "I didn't put that cross on for the first time today. I put it on yesterday two times! I surely wasn't going to get embarrassed by anybody out here." He got a big belt out of that, of course. The cross was grooved so that it had to be installed in a certain way or else wouldn't fit. There was so much talk about

Pope John Paul II and I celebrating Mass at the University of New Orleans

health concerns and the placement of the cross that nobody even noticed that it was put in place without a blessing. So that was it.

We finally started sending out tickets to all the parishes about a month ahead of the visit, and most pastors seemed to be very pleased that we had decided to give a certain number of reserved seats to each parish so that they could take care of the people who were their leaders. Every parish has a band of loyal volunteers, and those are the people who should be rewarded at such an historic event. Of course, I didn't have enough tickets for everybody to be taken care of in the special seating area, but we did the best we could do.

On the eve of the Feast of the Assumption — August 14 — I flew to Washington to attend the funeral of my former archbishop, Cardinal Patrick O'Boyle, who had died at the age of ninety-one. I had seen him just a few days earlier when he was in a coma in Providence Hospital. When I went into his room, he perked up just a bit, and I was able to tell him, *"state in fide"* (his episcopal motto was "stand fast in the faith, keep on fighting") and then give him a blessing. That evening I was back in New Orleans for a small dinner party at the home of Anne and King Milling. The purpose of the gathering was to meet Stafford Sweatt, the president of Lenox China, who came to New Orleans to present the new papal china, which was gorgeous. I gave him a medallion as a token of our esteem. Anne presented me with several things, climaxed by a navy blue windbreaker that was monogrammed above the insignia of the Secret Service with the words, "The Arch." Everybody got a howl out of that.

The dinner was such a joyful event that it seemed to me we were being blessed by the Holy Spirit long before the Holy Father came to town. Anytime you work with Christ, and work with people who believe in Christ, the whole of life is a joyful celebration. What links us together is a commonality — faith in Christ — which brings us closer and closer every time we meet. In a way, I was enjoying the Pope even before he got here.

On August 15 at St. John the Baptist Church, we had a dress rehearsal for the papal Mass with a rousing performance by a three hundred fifty-person archdiocesan-wide choir, directed by Dominican Sister Hilary Simpson. They were absolutely splendid. The few people who were there for the normal vigil Mass were astounded because of the surprise choir in their midst. I told Sister Hilary that we needed to keep the choir together long after the Holy Father's visit. I felt if the choir stopped after September 12, they would be disappointed that their efforts had come to an end. I suggested that we throw a buffet for them and then have them make a transition into a permanent archdiocesan choir. Sister Hilary loved the idea. Some choir directors can be opinionated and difficult, but Sister Hilary was one of the easiest people to be around, and everybody liked her.

Meanwhile, I got the reports I had expected regarding the way in which some parishes were distributing — or, to be more precise, not distributing — tickets to the papal Mass. I found out that the pastor of St. Gabriel the Archangel Parish, located about a mile away from the site of the papal Mass, was stringing along parishioners with promises to distribute the general admission tickets on an unnamed, upcoming Sunday. In other words, the parishioners who literally lived closest to where the Pope would celebrate Mass had to show up each weekend in order to be sure they would get tickets. It wasn't as though there was a limit on these tickets — these were general admission tickets and a parish could get as many as it needed. But I'm glad we got the ticket process going as early as we did so we could handle any recalcitrant pastors who came up with a "clever" distribution process.

During the lead-up to the papal visit, we were treated to the "instant analysis" that the national news media like to trot out before a major Catholic event. Even locally, where our Catholic-educated journalists should have known better, we had a WWL-TV documentary that insisted that St. Peter's Basilica was built on money paid for by indulgences and other practices. The 1980s was a schizophrenic age in which people were greatly interested in the Holy Father, except, of course, for the usual number of dissenters. At the same time, the media seemed compelled to criticize the papacy for its financial dealings, even though it had nothing to do with Pope John Paul II, who was one of the simplest men ever to inherit the chair of Peter. He was a lover of humility and poverty, so unlike some of the televangelists who loved to flaunt their gold rings and wealthy lifestyles as a way of proving that God had prospered the work of their hands.

Fortunately, we were also beginning to get articles from even the large secular magazines such as *Time* and *Newsweek* about the necessity to have more stable marriages and the hopeful sign that the divorce rate was decreasing slightly. They pointed out that people must learn to discipline themselves, that they need responsibility and commitment. The Catholic Church has been emphasizing the virtue of sacrifice for millennia, and it is a bitter truth to someone who chooses not to accept it. I've always said the religious life is an example to lay people of the meaning of responsibility and commitment. Lay people see the example of religious commitment, and that encourages them to make the same kind of commitment, according to their proper calling in life.

Of course, sprinkled in with the positive articles were the ones that seemed to revel in promoting discord among Catholics regarding Church teaching. A group of nuns was determined to hold a "counter" prayer service on September 12 at the same time as the papal Mass to call attention to issues, such as women's ordination, that the Church was opposed to. Many people responded by writing letters to *The Times-Picayune* in which they made the basic point that morality is not something to be voted on. Critics of the Church made the

Pope John Paul II and I embrace at the Sign of Peace during the Papal Mass at the University of New Orleans on September 12, 1987

charge that many Catholics would defect because of Church teaching on birth control, abortion, and women's ordination.

I have a simple answer for all those so troubled. Suppose for a moment that the universal Church had given in to the American Church in the 1940s, 1950s, and 1960s in regard to integration and racial justice. Would we not have been discredited before the world? The fact is that at the time about 80 percent of the people in the Archdiocese of New Orleans opposed Archbishop Rummel's decision to insist on racial justice — and the Church now benefits from that. Those who went along with the feeling of the times are the ones who are now discredited.

Of course, human nature persists in its course during the life of the Church. At my daily meetings, a nice nun kept asking me for a map to show her exactly where the papal altar was. I said, "Sister, why don't you ride out to UNO and take a look!" I also was bombarded with questions about where Mass attendees could park and how far they would have to walk. It's so hilarious. People will park miles away on the street when they attend a Saints game at the Superdome, and they'll be sure to arrive early. They don't ask anyone to take care of them. But if you ask someone to walk a few hundred yards to attend a papal Mass, the objections flow. Each year at Mardi Gras hundreds of thousands people walk for miles to participate in the festivities, and that minor inconvenience doesn't keep them from having a great time. But if they have to walk to see the Pope, they want to know how much refreshments will be on hand. That's human nature!

Almost daily I was the conduit for material gifts that were flowing in for the Holy Father. One was from a Native American who braided a ceremonial sweatband that he wanted the Pope to wear on his forehead! Another package contained a crate of beer from Dixie Brewery, which was struggling to stay alive. The gifts kept piling up, but it gave people the feeling that they were contributing to the Holy Father's comfort. One person called to suggest we put together a youth soccer match between teams of ten-year-olds for the Holy Father to watch. I didn't think we could slip that into the program. Mother Mary Rose de Lima Hazeur, the superior of the Sisters of Holy Family, asked Sister Mary Guadalupe, my housekeeper, if she could send over one of her fruitcakes for the papal luncheon. Of course, I welcomed that gift. I said, "Sure, fine, send it over." I don't think the Holy Father had a bite. Another friend sent over twenty-four commemorative golden coconuts, beads, and doubloons from the Krewe of Zulu, the oldest African-American Carnival organization in New Orleans.

The entire community was becoming galvanized. The president of the New Orleans Baptist Seminary wrote a piece in *The Times-Picayune* thanking the Catholic Church for helping to change the face of ecumenical relations in New Orleans. He had come to New Orleans, a predominantly Catholic city, in the late 1940s and he recalled the strain between Catholics and Protestants. Quite often Catholics were inhospitable toward their Protestant neighbors. But he said the change in relations began when the Archdiocese of New Orleans "got interested" in charities that helped the entire community.

On September 4 — one week before the visit — my schedule was packed, and I was expecting a few peculiar things to happen. I wasn't disappointed. Tom Finney, the communications director for the archdiocese, called me late in the afternoon to tell me the city had signed a contract with Boh Brothers Construction Company to fix potholes on several roads around the Superdome on September 12 and 13! The Pope was coming to town for the first time in history, and the City of New Orleans was going to choose that occasion to get serious about fixing potholes. I got on the phone immediately and got Bob Boh, a good Catholic, to get the city to delay its big dig. Then I got several phone calls from movie director Robert Evans and his friends, who were trying to convince me to introduce Evans to the Holy Father so that he could personally present him with the thirty-eight-minute video he was trying to market across the United States. He actually asked to sit down with the Pope while he watched the video! I even got a call from actor Ricardo Montalban, a good Catholic, imploring me to get Evans a brief papal audience. That was impossible, I said, and I promised to present the video to the Holy Father myself.

That evening, I had dinner at Commander's Palace with the Pope's master of ceremonies, Monsignor Piero Marini, and Father Ken Hedrick, who was heading up our liturgy committee. As soon as we sat down, Monsignor Marini told me, "I'm afraid we can't use the cross that was made for the papal altar because it has no corpus on it." Up to that point, I had just seen the cross on TV. The rubrics of the Church insist that the cross used in the liturgy should have a corpus, and I totally agreed. "We'll have the crucifix just the way the Holy Father wants it," I told Monsignor Marini. I could see that Father Hedrick had been badgering Monsignor Marini to accept the cross, and afterwards Father Hedrick told me I gave in too easily.

As we left the restaurant, I thanked Monsignor Marini for his final visit and said, "Look, whatever the Holy Father wants, that's exactly what we're going to do."

Shepherd I Lands

At 9:30 p.m. on Friday, September 11, 1987, a TWA commercial airliner nicknamed Shepherd I touched down at New Orleans International Airport following a two-hour flight from Columbia, S.C. I walked up the stairs and entered the aircraft to personally greet the Holy Father. I was concerned about the Pope's stamina because he had just run the gauntlet in Miami and South Carolina. A violent thunderstorm blew through Miami and did so much damage to the altar structure in Tamiami Park that the outdoor Mass had to be canceled due to the threat of lightning. I also heard there had been a problem with the air-conditioning in the Pope's living quarters in Miami. He was tired after meeting in Columbia with former President Jimmy Carter, a meeting that had been rescheduled at the last minute.

My suspicions were confirmed when I saw the Pope in the first-class section at the front of the plane. He looked dead tired. One of the flight attendants told me he was so tired he could barely keep his eyes open. He was slumped in his seat against the wall, and we had to awaken him. I said, "Your Holiness, welcome to New Orleans, and thank you for coming here." He finally stretched and stood up, but as he walked down the aisle, he walked shakily. I said to myself, "How will this work out?"

As soon as the Holy Father emerged from the front door and faced the muggy September air, he raised his arms skyward to accept the thanks of the crowd gathered below on the tarmac, and he seemed to be buoyed by the reception and the bouncy strains of "When the Saints Go Marchin' In" by the Olympia Brass Band. When he came to the bottom steps, Angelika Kokoszka, a four-year-old Polish girl dressed in her native garb, rushed over and presented him with a bouquet of flowers. All the Pope did was kiss Angelika on her head. Right away, the Polish people standing nearby knew he must have been totally exhausted because if he had an ounce of strength, he would have picked up that little girl and given her a big hug. Something was wrong. He was exhausted.

The Pope acknowledged the small group of city and state dignitaries and chatted briefly with the band members. Trumpeter Milton Batiste offered the Pope a purple-and-white umbrella with a dove at the top. The Pope smiled and handed the umbrella to an aide before slipping into the waiting limousine.

I had prepared a list of questions for the Holy Father, but as soon as he sank into the padded leather seat of the limousine he nodded off instantly. He slept for the entire twenty-five-minute drive from the airport to my residence at Notre Dame Seminary. When we reached the house, a thousand people were waiting outside, including a group of seminarians that the Pope greeted. But as soon as he entered the house, the Holy Father could barely drag his feet across the carpet.

His traveling secretary, Father Roberto Tucci, had told us the only thing the Holy Father wanted — and he was very specific about this — when he arrived at the residence on Friday night was a cup of hot tea and a few cookies. The lead waiter from Antoine's brought the small platter to the Pope's bedroom, which normally served as my bedroom. The waiter told me later when he delivered the tea and cookies that as tired as the Pope was, he had on his nightstand a book about ecumenism and another theology book in German.

Originally, I had planned for the Vatican Secretary of State, Cardinal Agostino Casaroli, to occupy the bedroom next to the Holy Father, figuring that was the proper protocol. But during his pre-trip visit, Father Tucci changed all those arrangements. He said the Holy Father's valet needed the room next door because he was entrusted with all of the gifts the Pope would be handing out to special guests. Father Tucci asked me to place Cardinal Casaroli with other Vatican officials and U.S. bishops at the Windsor Court Hotel, where we could secure an entire floor. I followed his instructions and escorted the Secretary of State out of the residence! Naturally, security was incredibly tight. We provided a bedroom for the head of the Swiss Guard and, in keeping with the Lateran Pact signed between the Vatican and Italy, we also provided a bedroom for the director of Italy's national police force. One of the two men was required to be stationed directly outside the Pope's bedroom throughout the night, and there was a Secret Service guard a few paces away. I figured there was only one foreigner in the house that the Vatican could be concerned about getting to the Pope — and that was me! I thought the security plan was a little over the top, but when in Rome... (well, even when not in Rome)!

I slept in the smallest bedroom we had, and I was glad to be able to hang on to it! I slept quite well. On Saturday morning I awakened early, about 5:15 a.m., and went to the second-floor chapel to say my morning prayers. To my surprise, Father Tucci was already there, celebrating Mass. What I saw next will stay with me for the rest of my life. Off to the side in the front pew was the Holy Father. At the presentation of the gifts, Pope John Paul II got up and brought the wine and water to the altar and then returned to the credence table to take the finger bowl and towel to Father Tucci so that he could wash his hands. The Pope was serving the Mass! At that moment, I came to fully appreciate the papal motto: "Servant of the Servants of God."

With just a few hours sleep, the Holy Father seemed totally rejuvenated. We ate a simple breakfast, and as we entered the limousine in front of my residence for the short drive to St. Louis Cathedral, the weather was warm but bright and sunny. But as they say in New Orleans, if you don't like the weather, stick around for a few minutes because it's sure to change. More on that later.

The Pope's first stop was Place Jean Paul II, the cobblestone area between the cathedral and Jackson Square that was renamed in his honor. Inside the cathedral were more than one thousand clergy and religious from Louisiana, Mississippi, Alabama, and Florida. Oblate Father Gerard Barrett, rector of the cathedral, greeted him at the door and presented him with holy water, and the Pope made the Sign of the Cross as he came down the marble main aisle, pausing to greet and shake hands with the nuns and priests who were leaning out from their pews to touch him. A *prie dieu* was set up in front of the altar, and the Pope knelt there in silent prayer. "Inexpressible pleasure," I said to those assembled. "This is the day the Lord has made." The Pope then read the following proclamation:

> "This temple of God, this house of prayer and gate of heaven stands as the central point of the City of New Orleans, and from this place all distances are measured. Here Christ dwells in your midst, present in word and Sacrament, making this a place of grace and blessing for all the People of God. Here God the Father is adored in spirit and truth (cf. Jn 4:23); and here the Holy Spirit is always at work in the hearts of the faithful, preparing them for the glory of the heavenly Jerusalem.
>
> "And just as this Cathedral of Saint Louis is the focal point of the City of New Orleans, so too Christ is the very center of your lives. Christ is for you 'the beginning and the end' (Rev 21:6); he is for you 'the way, and the truth, and the life' (Jn 14:6). So closely are you identified with Christ that each of you can say, as did St. Paul: 'The life I live now is not my own; Christ is living in me. I still live my human life, but it is a life of faith in the Son of God.'
>
> "Just as the Cathedral of St. Louis is the focal point of the City of New Orleans, so too Christ is the very center of your lives.
>
> "The Church in Louisiana owes a great debt of gratitude to the many priests and religious who have labored here from the beginning.

That tradition of heroic dedication in proclaiming the Gospel of Christ by word and deed continues today in the service that you render to the People of God. Always remember that the supernatural effectiveness of your service within the Church is linked to the witness of your life lived in union with Christ."

During his address, the Holy Father appealed for unity among the clergy and religious modeled after the unity of the Holy Trinity.

Upon entering the cathedral, the Pope had walked down the right side of the aisle shaking hands with the sisters in the pews. The clergy were in the pews on the left side of the aisle. The priests were perturbed, wondering whether the Pope would exit the cathedral on their side of the aisle so that they could shake hands with him. As the Pope was finishing his prayer at the altar I told him of the anxiety of the priests, and he allowed me to announce to the priests that he would exit on their side of the aisle.

After his talk, we processed out to the front of the cathedral, where Mayor Barthelemy greeted the Pope. I announced to the crowd gathered behind the barricades that the portion of Chartres Street running directly in front of the cathedral had been renamed Place Jean Paul II in his honor. The Pope smiled and said, "There's one thing I've learned about New Orleans. It's hot here!"

The Pope had whispered to me as we were walking out of the cathedral that he had never seen the Mississippi River. "Is there any way I could walk over and see it?" he asked me. I didn't think there would be any problem fulfilling his request. The river was no more than a two-minute stroll from the plaza, and it wouldn't have resulted in a scheduling delay of more than five or ten minutes to grant the Pope his lifelong wish.

But as soon as I mentioned the request to Mike James, the lead Secret Service agent in charge, I received an emphatic "no." "There's absolutely no way," Mike told me. "I have enough agents to cover only about 50 or 60 yards. I don't have enough agents to cover that space. It's not part of the plan." That was one of many tussles Mike and I had over security. I could understand his mission, but sometimes I think he was a bit unreasonable. For instance, when the Pope came to Notre Dame Seminary, I thought it would be nice for him to address the crowd from a second-floor balcony, but Mike thought that elevated position would leave him too exposed to a sniper. The Secret Service also had warned the residents of the Pontalba Apartments that flanked both sides of Jackson Square not to come out onto their balconies during the Pope's visit to the cathedral because they might risk being shot by security personnel.

The Secret Service insisted on us installing an asphalt road at the site of the outdoor Mass at UNO to provide a hard surface for a quick automobile escape. I found out later that such a road, which cost about $50,000 to install, wasn't even necessary because the Popemobile was built to such high standards by Mercedes in Germany that it could go from 0 to 60 mph in six or seven seconds. It had plenty of ability to get out of the way quickly.

Mike and I made up at the end of the trip, but I guess we had different agendas. I wanted to make the Pope happy; he wanted to keep the Pope alive!

There are actually two Popemobiles, and both were used on his eleven-day trip to the United States. While the Pope is using the Popemobile No. 1 in the city he visits first, Popemobile No. 2 is already staged in the city he will visit next. Then Popemobile No. 1 is airlifted to the third city on the trip, and so on. Mercedes makes sure it sends not only a chauffeur but also a master mechanic in case anything goes wrong. As we drove in the Popemobile down Decatur Street toward Canal Street en route to the Superdome for the massive youth rally, it was unlike any Mardi Gras parade I have ever witnessed. The crowds on both sides were screaming and waving yellow-and-white papal flags. I kept leaning over and telling the driver, "Go slower, please, slower!" And right away, the Secret Service agent in charge yelled out, "Faster, faster!" It was like a crazy vaudeville routine. We kept this up virtually the entire way. Finally, the agent told me, "Look, we're at exactly opposite poles here. We're trying to get rid of the Holy Father as fast as possible to make sure no one gets hurt, and you're interested in keeping him here as long as possible so the people can see him." That was about as accurate an analysis as I've ever heard.

The Holy Father's first of three addresses at the Superdome was to an assembly of the eleven black Catholic bishops in the United States and one thousand eight hundred other black Catholics gathered in the southwest quad-

Pope John Paul II greets a line of worshippers following the September 12, 1987, Mass at the University of New Orleans

rant meeting room. He very directly acknowledged the sin of racism and the history of African-American suffering through slavery, and he praised their resilience in overcoming such inhumane treatment and holding fast to the faith. The symbol of the meeting was the African acacia tree, which is the tree used to build the Old Testament Ark of the Covenant.

At one point in his address to the black Catholics, the Pope said forcefully: "It is important to realize that there is no black Church, no white Church, no American Church; but there is and must be, in the one church of Jesus Christ, a home for blacks, whites, Americans, every culture and race." Those words sparked a rousing response from the assembly. They stood up and shouted: "Hallelujah! Hallelujah!"; "Say it again, brother!"; "Right on!"

Their response completely surprised the Pope. He looked toward me to get some indication whether the shouting was positive or negative. When he saw me clapping and shouting with them, he became very joyful, responsive, and at ease.

The Pope told the assembly of black Catholics: "Today as we recall those who with Christian vision opted for nonviolence as the only truly effective approach for ensuring and safeguarding human dignity, we cannot but think of the Reverend Martin Luther King Jr., and of the providential role he played in contributing to the rightful human betterment of black Americans and therefore to the improvement of American society itself."

He also offered strong words against racism in American society and encouraged black Catholics to continue serving the wider Church with their many gifts. "Even in this wealthy nation, committed by the Founding Fathers to the dignity and equality of all persons, the black community suffers a disproportionate share of economic deprivation," the Pope said.

After that thirty-minute talk, the Pope strolled just a few yards to another large meeting room to address one thousand eight hundred people involved in Catholic elementary, secondary, and religious education. Members of the National Catholic Educational Association greeted him and showed him two short video presentations on Catholic education in the United States. In his remarks, the Pope alluded to the rich Catholic educational history in New Orleans.

"It is fitting that we should be meeting in this historic city, itself the meeting point of several rich cultures, where the Capuchin Fathers and Ursuline Sisters founded schools at the very dawn of your emergence as a nation," the Pope said. He also addressed the responsibilities of parents. "Parents need to ensure that their own homes are places where spiritual and moral values are lived," he said. "They are right to insist that their children's faith be respected and fostered." As usual, the Pope knew his audience well. At the end of his talk, he playfully suggested that as a student in front of so many teachers, he wondered how his address would be graded. "But I am hopeful," he said. "I am hopeful."

The Main Event

From there the Pope went to his main event at the Superdome — an address to an estimated sixty thousand young people of high school and college age. He entered the Superdome in the Popemobile, and we circled the floor of the dome once. Sister of Mercy of the Holy Cross Pat Cormack had planned the music selections, and against my better judgment she decided to feature Christian rock singer Tom Franzak. I wasn't too thrilled with the style of music because I thought we could do better. In fact, Dana Rosemary Scallon, the Irish singer who had begun to make a name for herself, gave a thrilling rendition of *"Totus Tuus"* ("Totally Yours"), which was the Pope's motto, and she brought down the house.

The Pope showed me that day how he could electrify a crowd with his charisma and actor's instincts. When Bing Crosby told me in 1975 that no single performer could ever really touch a crowd's heart inside the massive Superdome, he had no idea that one day a Pope would prove him wrong. Pope John Paul II's God-given gifts as a communicator were on full display that day. When I had cautioned Father Tucci about my fears during his advance site inspection, he smiled and told me not to worry. I found out that day what Father Tucci already knew — that John Paul II was an absolute genius in sizing up a crowd.

The platform from which the Pope would speak had about five or six steps. John Paul decided to take one step, and then he stopped and looked up and smiled and waved at the cheering crowd. Then he took another step and did the same thing. Every time he took a step and stopped, the crowd got wilder and wilder. He was in total contact with the young people by the time he reached the platform. I thought, "The Pope really knows his business in handling the crowd."

The Holy Father then went on to give what I thought was a superb talk. Once again, he never beat around the bush. He also was a brilliant tactician. I knew his speech was scheduled to go on for a long time, so I suggested he might want to deliver it in two parts, separated by music. Instead of dismissing the idea, the Pope was very agreeable and sensed it would work out better that way. He adjusted right on the spot. He told the young people to remember that they had to remain pure. He told them that if they made a habit of breaking the sixth commandment ("You shall not commit adultery") that it could one day result in ruining their marriage. He urged them to remain pure. And guess what? They stood up and cheered. Their response so surprised him that he stopped and smiled back.

"Jesus and his Church hold to God's plan for human love, telling you that sex is a great gift of God that is reserved for marriage," John Paul said, waving his hand for emphasis. "The message of Jesus is clear: purity means true love and it is the total opposite of selfishness and escape.... You young people are proud to live in a free country, and you should be grateful to God for your freedom. But even though you can come and go as you like, and do what you want, you are not really free if you are living under the power of error or falsehood, or deceit or sin."

During a mini Mardi Gras parade, Patricia Marie Baham of Xavier Prep presented Pope John Paul II with a Mardi Gras headdress that had plumes of purple, green, and gold. The Pope tried to put it on, but it didn't fit. The crowd loved it. As a native Washingtonian, I grew up observing the public persona of every president since Calvin Coolidge, and I don't know of any president who could handle a crowd the way he could. The Pope didn't have public relations experts advising him on what to do. He simply trusted his instincts, and those never failed him.

After the youth rally, we drove back to my residence for a small luncheon for the Pope and the bishops of the Province of New Orleans. The midday break also allowed the Pope to rest before his outdoor Mass later that afternoon. Before we sat down to eat, Houma-Thibodaux Bishop Warren Boudreaux, who loved to sing, asked me privately if I thought it would be okay for him to serenade the Pope with a song at the end of the meal.

I was seated next to the Pope, and as we were served our dessert, I said to him in a voice loud enough to be heard by everyone in the room, "Your Holiness, we have a bishop here who is a good singer and has a favorite song he would like to sing in your presence. Do you have any objections?" The Pope smiled and said, "No, I love singing."

Then Bishop Boudreaux stood up. He was a very respectful person, and he was quite frank. "I feel very nervous," he said. "I've never sung in the presence of the Pope. As a matter of fact, I'd better sit down and drink another glass of water." Which he did. Then he stood up again and performed a great rendition of his favorite song — "To Dream the Impossible Dream" from "Man of La Mancha." He was really on, and the Pope thoroughly enjoyed it. We all gave him a rousing round of applause. Of course, Father Tucci was outside the door chomping at the bit because we were behind schedule, and he sent in a note that we had to bring the festivities to a conclusion. He also said the Pope was so late that he would have to skip the brief nap that had been built into the schedule.

As we opened the dining room door to enter the parlor, I knew the Pope was very tired. So I told him, "Your master of ceremonies insists that you not take a siesta, but I think you should forget that advice. Of all the one hundred fifty thousand people who have gathered for the Mass, there isn't one who would not want you to take a siesta. Why don't you take a forty-minute nap?"

I hosted a luncheon at my residence for the Pope and Louisiana bishops. At the end of the meal, Houma-Thibodaux Bishop Warren Boudreaux asked and received permission from the Pope to sing Bishop Boudreaux's favorite song, "To Dream the Impossible Dream," from *Man of LaMancha.*

The Pope smiled and said he'd take the nap, and I think that was the right thing to do. He awoke completely refreshed and continued with great vigor for the remainder of his ambitious schedule.

The original plan called for the Pope to travel to the Mass site by helicopter from the lawn of St. Mary's Dominican High School, which was one block from my residence. But a violent thunderstorm and lightning in the area forced us to change those plans, disappointing the hundreds of girls who were lined up to wave to the Pope. Instead, we traveled by motorcade to the lakefront, a trip that took about twenty minutes. On the ride to UNO, the Pope was obviously refreshed and in a great mood. He was bantering back and forth with his personal secretary, Monsignor Stanislaw Dziwisz, about the day's events, and he seemed struck by the great reception he had received from the black Catholics at the Superdome. Every now and then, Dziwisz would turn around and say, "Brother, say it again! Hallelujah!" They both broke out into great laughter.

As we drove through the pouring rain, I reflected about all of our unfounded fears about the crowd suffering from heat prostration. Now the one hundred fifty thousand Mass-goers were going to be part of the biggest swamp Mass in the history of the Archdiocese of New Orleans! I had never seen so many umbrellas in one place in my life, and the multicolored patterns created a spiritual kaleidoscope. No one in the crowd was about to leave — they were as wet as they could possibly be, so a little more rain would have absolutely no effect on their enthusiasm. Fortunately, as soon as the Pope walked onto the elevated platform to the altar to begin Mass, the rain stopped completely.

Because of the weather, we had to skip the planned procession. Everyone — from priests to deacons to sacristans to bishops — simply got into their places as quickly as possible so the Mass could begin. I walked up to the elevated altar platform and greeted the crowd. In the distance, I could see the wind and rain abating, and I told the people their prayers were lifting the clouds. I welcomed the Pope: "We defy the weather to be here with you, to show you that you are our father. Today we are all members of one parish, with you as our shepherd.... We are thankful to the Lord that he has spared us from the heat!"

The theme of the Mass was based on the Church's regular readings from the Old and New Testament: "Forgive us as we forgive." The Pope compared human justice, which is often characterized by hatred and revenge, with divine justice, which is filled with mercy and love.

"The human standard is inclined to stop at justice alone," Pope John Paul II said. "Refusal to forgive is not in keeping with the true nature of marriage as God established it and as he wants it to be lived."

He ended his homily with a specific reference to St. Paul's First Letter to the Corinthians, Chapter 13: "Love is patient and kind... it does not rejoice at wrong, but rejoices in the right.... Love never ends." And then he told the crowd, "Yes, love is supreme!" Then he gave a definition of love. "Love is not just a moment of emotion. Love is a deliberate decision, a commitment of service to another for the rest of life." Later I heard those words repeated often by young people.

During the Presentation of Gifts at the Mass, we were treated to performances by two of New Orleans' pre-eminent musicians. Clarinetist Pete Fountain intoned a soulful version of "Just a Closer Walk with Thee," and trumpeter Al Hirt hit clarion tones in his rendition of "Ave Maria." We had one thousand eight hundred Communion ministers distributing the Eucharist across the waterlogged field.

"I have always heard of the beautiful music of New Orleans," the Pope said. "Today I have been able to hear it and admire it personally." At the end of the Mass, the Pope took a detour from the procession of cross and candle bearers and made a beeline to the crowd, who were calling out to him, "Come to us!" He did and shook hundreds of hands.

The Pope's final major address came that evening at Xavier University of Louisiana to representatives of the two hundred thirty-five Catholic colleges and universities in the United States. A year earlier in Rome, the Holy Father had beatified Mother Katharine Drexel, the foundress of the Sisters of the Blessed Sacrament and who had personally established Xavier University in 1925. As he spoke, a soft rain fell. The Pope spoke about theological reflection as a gift of the Holy Spirit for the good of the entire Church. "Bishops, united with the pope... need the assistance of Catholic theologians, who perform an inestimable service to the Church," he said. "(But) theologians also need the charism entrusted by Christ to the bishops and, in the first place, to the Bishop of Rome.... The fruits of their work must ultimately be tested and validated" by the Church.

At the end of his talk, the Pope, on his own, began an impromptu rendition of *Salve Regina* in his great baritone voice. I will never forget the opportunity I missed — what a dummy I was. I had the Pope right next to me, booming out *Salve Regina* in beautiful style, and I did not have a recording of it. It would have been a great souvenir of his presence with us. It was a solo by the Pope, and I flubbed it!

That might have been the only misstep of the entire trip. I will be forever grateful to the people of all faiths who drew together and made the Pope's visit so memorable. The committee of bishops in charge of that visit remarked that there was more cooperation here for the Pope's visit than in any other city in the United States. People here, people of all faiths, are naturally hospitable, and they responded heartily to the Pope. Likewise, the Holy Father really had an affinity for people. We had the right temperament for him.

The American Civil Liberties Union even showed some uncharacteristic decorum. The organization that historically has been prickly when it comes to the separation of church and state waited until Pope John Paul II had moved on to San Antonio to ask that the large cross be removed from the papal altar at UNO. We took the cross off immediately, and it rests today atop the new church at Ascension of Our Lord in LaPlace. We were prepared to tear down the entire altar structure, but the university officials said they might be able to put the first-floor building to good use as a day care center for children, and that structure remained for more than twenty years until the ravages of termites and Hurricane Katrina dealt it a final blow. The plywood that formed the altar and the canvas material that formed the altar canopy were cut into small pieces and given away to people as keepsakes of the Pope's visit.

The Pope returned to my residence about 10:00 p.m. for some well-deserved rest. Before he could get into my front door, he was serenaded by a throng of Polish Catholics who had practiced several hymns that they wanted badly to sing for him. The limousine pulled up near the crowd, and I opened the door to allow the Holy Father get out — only to have the Secret Service agent slam the door shut. This went on for a second and a third time. Finally, they simply would not let us vary from the prescribed routine. The official said very deliberately, "This stop is not on the program, and we do not have enough of our men to guard him. We cannot permit this stop." If I had insisted any longer, it might have embarrassed the Pope, so I stopped my efforts. The Holy Father simply waved to the crowd and gave them a nice blessing — but he wasn't allowed to stay outside for their short concert.

The Pope told me in my residence, "Job well done." New Orleans' preparations for the outdoor Mass – building an altar to withstand hurricane-force winds – paid off when a major thunderstorm blew through the city just before Mass, but the altar remained intact

The Holy Father had given me the word that the next morning before he left for the airport to fly to San Antonio, he would personally receive the people who had been especially helpful in planning for his trip to New Orleans. That gave me a chance to invite some of those who had worked especially hard. The head of Antoine's took a few liberties by bringing all his little children with him so that they could meet the Pope, and predictably the babies drew the Pope's complete attention! My secretary, Emily, who is of Polish descent, was so enthralled to greet the Pope that she clasped his right hand firmly with both of her hands. She wouldn't let go! This was the first time in history, I think, that a Pope had to bless someone with his left hand! We have an excellent picture of this unique handshake!

As we arrived at the airport, the farewell ceremony was just as emotional as the other events of the two-day visit. The Pope shook hands with everyone in sight, even with the members of Dejean's Olympia Brass Band, who were so befuddled that they did not know what to do. One trumpet player was so shaken up by the prospect of meeting the Pope that he didn't know if he should keep playing his horn. He was fidgeting with his other arm, trying to pry a rosary out of his pocket! I told him, "Just stop playing for a few seconds and you'll be fine!" Just when it looked like the Pope was determined to leave — he was halfway up the airplane steps — he spotted a group of police officers and rushed to thank them and give them a blessing. That certainly taught me a lesson about taking care of the desires of the people. God knows he extended himself to the absolute limit in shaking hands with people, and that's the reason people loved him so dearly. He was a real person to them, the servant of the servants of God.

I am often asked if the Pope showed any of the initial signs of the Parkinson's Disease that years later so disabled him physically. I can say I saw nothing in him but amazing stamina and strength. He went through a tremendous physical ordeal — five major talks in one day — and he met thousands of people. If anything was wrong with him physically, it should have been apparent.

The visit of John Paul II to New Orleans, without question, was the highlight of my life as a priest and bishop. Reflecting on the trip, I cannot see how it could have gone much better. No one could have found a Pope who was more accommodating and obliging to serve his people.

His visit created a level of zeal that was manifest even years later. Loyola University political science professor Ed Renwick did a revealing poll a year after the Pope's visit concerning the effect of the Pope's visit on their spiritual lives. Seventy-five percent of the people who responded said they were still practicing their faith more fervently as a direct result of the Pope's visit. It is difficult to imagine someone having that kind of lasting effect, but he was a special Pope who will be known one day as John Paul the Great.

After the Pope left town, the laypeople with whom I came in contact were on fire. Their only question to me was: "Isn't there some great, big thing you can give us to do? The Pope is gone."

Pope John Paul II was at least the greatest Pope of the last century and a half. In all of his travels, he expressed to bishops and priests exactly what they should do, from the top of the educational system all the way down. Nobody stated it as well because he was both an intellectual and a pastoral person. He knew that true knowledge was not measured in the number of degrees a person had but by the way in which that person would live his life. He insisted that Catholics need to change the culture. I am blessed to have known him and to have shared his presence with my beloved New Orleans for one cherished moment in time.

The visit of Pope John Paul II has remained with us as a constant blessing. May God continue to bless us as he did during this unforgettable visit!

Changes in the Province
of New Orleans

After arriving in New Orleans in 1965, it didn't take long for me to realize how overextended the Province of New Orleans was. It comprised not
only the dioceses of Louisiana but also the dioceses of Mississippi, Alabama,
Arkansas, and Oklahoma. There was a historical reason for this far-flung
ecclesiastical structure: The Diocese of Louisiana and the Floridas had been
established in New Orleans on April 25, 1793 — making it the second-oldest
diocese in the present-day United States, second only to Baltimore in 1789.

The diocese originally encompassed the entire Louisiana Territory, which
stretched from the Gulf of Mexico to the Canadian border and also included
Florida, and the Gulf Coast of Mississippi and Alabama. That original diocese
was the mother diocese of more than fifty dioceses stretching up the Mississippi River Valley as far north as Minnesota.

Over the decades, of course, as more Catholics moved into once sparsely
populated areas, the Church needed to erect new dioceses to serve the people
more effectively and to foster vocations to the priesthood and religious life.
The principle of subsidiarity — which holds that people are better served at
the local level — helped the Church fulfill its teaching and sanctifying mission. One reason the Province of New Orleans still included the territories of
five states as late as 1965 was because the Vatican respected the long and heroic
tenure of Archbishop Joseph Rummel, who had had served as archbishop of
New Orleans from 1935 until his death in 1964. It was well understood that
the Province would be divided shortly after his death.

When I became archbishop in 1965 I totally supported paring down the
size of the Province. It was geographically too large to administer properly.
Catholics in parts of the province constantly asked me to visit them for special
liturgies and meetings, and I knew I had more than enough to handle in New
Orleans. Thus, in late 1972, the Province of Oklahoma City was established,
which included the Archdiocese of Oklahoma City and the dioceses of Little
Rock, Arkansas, and Tulsa, Oklahoma. In 1980, the Province of Mobile was
formed from the eastern side of the New Orleans Province, and its territory

included the Archdiocese of Mobile and the dioceses of Birmingham, Alabama, and Biloxi and Jackson, Mississippi.

I know the decision to scale back the Province of New Orleans probably did not make everyone universally happy. After all, the old and venerable province once was one of the largest in the entire country and did occupy a position of pre-eminence. However, I always liked to look to the future. I heartily endorsed the idea of giving smaller geographic areas a greater sense of responsibility so that they could better develop and nurture the faith. That's the reason I kept sending letters to the Holy See in support of the realignment. In the long run it benefited the souls of the Catholics in those states and created a renewed spirit of evangelization.

Today the Province of New Orleans includes the seven dioceses of Louisiana: New Orleans, Baton Rouge, Houma-Thibodaux, Lafayette, Lake Charles, Alexandria, and Shreveport. Three of those dioceses were created during my tenure as archbishop of New Orleans: Houma-Thibodaux in 1977, Lake Charles in 1980, and Shreveport in 1986.

Actually, it was Archbishop John Cody who was the original catalyst for the eventual establishment of the Houma-Thibodaux Diocese. Cody thought he needed someone to serve as his personal agent down on the bayou, and he assigned Monsignor Gerard Frey as pastor of St. Francis de Sales in Houma, the premier parish in the area. Monsignor Frey did so well in his spiritual and administrative work that Cody thought it would one day be very easy to establish a separate diocese for Houma-Thibodaux. Although Frey never held the title of "bishop" in Houma, Archbishop Cody had given him free rein to administer the area, and he did a great job.

I kept an open mind on the subject of a new diocese for Houma-Thibodaux, but I wanted the request to come from a majority of the priests. A few years later, I began to get more entreaties to establish a separate diocese. Monsignor Francis Amedee, in particular, was very forceful in stating the opinion that a new diocese was needed. The proponents of a new diocese told me they thought vocations to the priesthood were being adversely affected because young men who hailed from the bayou were not very inclined to enter Notre Dame Seminary if they did not know for sure that they would be assigned after ordination to churches in their home area. They thought creating a separate diocese would spark an abundance of local vocations to the priesthood. If that was the major reason for creating the new diocese, it never really worked out that way. I don't think vocations were enhanced by the creation of the new diocese, but I do believe the establishment of Houma-Thibodaux helped serve local Catholics in a positive way and built up the life of the Church.

Monsignor Frey left St. Francis de Sales in 1968 when he was appointed Bishop of Savannah, Georgia. In 1972, I appointed Father Joseph Latino as rector of St. Francis de Sales Cathedral. As I expected, Father Joe's magnetic, joyful personality and competence served him well at the cathedral, and when the Holy See did create the new diocese of Houma-Thibodaux in 1977, Father Latino became incardinated in the new diocese and served eventually as its vicar general. He recently was named bishop of the new diocese of Jackson, Mississippi.

Bishop Warren Boudreaux was bishop of Beaumont, Texas, when Pope Paul VI appointed him as the first bishop of Houma-Thibodaux in 1977. I had been familiar with Bishop Boudreaux for many years, dating back to his attendance at all four sessions of the Second Vatican Council in Rome and to his service as auxiliary bishop of Lafayette under Bishop Maurice Schexnayder in the 1960s.

Bishop Boudreaux assisted me immeasurably in resolving a very delicate race relations issue in Lafayette in May 1969. Monsignor Richard Mouton, superintendent of Catholic schools in the Lafayette Diocese, went before the local school board and proposed a way to begin the integration of parochial schools. He suggested starting in Opelousas by doing something very bold. Directly across the street from each other were two Catholic churches and schools, one predominantly for African-Americans and the other predominantly for whites. The black school was Holy Ghost, staffed by the Sisters of the Holy Family. The white school was the Academy of the Immaculate Conception, run by the Marianites of Holy Cross. At the time, Bishop Schexnayder was extremely reluctant to move forward in integrating the schools because he felt separate schools for black children actually were better for them and would be financially feasible.

Mouton's idea was to have five Holy Family sisters and five Marianite sisters switch schools and therefore ease the path to integration. But after the proposal was brought up publicly, Schexnayder vetoed it, and that ignited a firestorm that flashed all the way to the National Conference of Catholic Bishops in Washington. D.C. I got an urgent call from the head of the NCCB imploring me to get Bishop Schexnayder to change his mind. The last thing the NCCB needed was for the Church to be sued for failure to integrate its schools and then be forced to accept some kind of court-ordered desegregation plan. In the middle of the summer I went to Lafayette along with an NCCB attorney to meet privately with Bishop Schexnayder, Auxiliary Bishop Boudreaux, and Monsignor Mouton. For three hours, the attorney, Bishop Boudreaux, and I took turns trying to impress upon Bishop Schexnayder why he had to withdraw his veto and allow Monsignor Mouton's desegregation plan to go through. His only argument for opposing the plan was, "I know it won't work." Finally, Bishop Boudreaux somehow was able to get through to him, and Bishop Schexnayder capitulated.

I know Bishop Boudreaux's exhibition of prudence and grace under fire won him many plaudits in Washington. In 1969–1970, both schools in Opelousas were racially mixed: one school served students in kindergarten through fourth grade, and the other served students in fifth through eighth grades. It was an excellent solution. All schools in the Lafayette Diocese eventually were paired and integrated without the courts having to get involved. Bishop Boudreaux's ability to broker a resolution to the problem stood out in my mind, and he was an easy choice to become the first Bishop of Houma-Thibodaux. He was a natural. He was a likable person, he spoke French, which endeared him to the Cajuns, and he loved to sing.

Today, Houma-Thibodaux Bishop Sam Jacobs is trying to encourage vocations to the priesthood among some of the young men by doing a lot of youth outreach and gathering them for dinner meetings in the rectory so that he can get to know them better and judge their aptitude.

Diocese of Shreveport

In 1986, the Holy See created the diocese of Shreveport by carving out territory from the diocese of Alexandria. All the preparations went like clockwork. The invitations were sent out to all the bishops, and Cardinal Pio Laghi, the Apostolic Pro-Nuncio, confirmed his presence for the special Mass during which the new diocese would be formally established and Bishop William Friend confirmed as the first bishop of Shreveport. I traveled to Shreveport the day before to meet with Cardinal Laghi, who had the responsibility of conveying the papal appointment of the bishop and offering him the Pope's blessings. At the beginning of the Mass, the new diocesan consultors are supposed to examine the papal "bull" — the formal church document, signed by the Pope, that establishes the new diocese and authenticates the new bishop. "Bull" is the English word for the Latin *bulla*, which was a seal appended to the end of an official document for authentication purposes.

There was only one problem. The bull had not arrived. "Your Excellency, do you have the bull?" Cardinal Laghi asked me. I looked at him quizzically and replied, "No, Your Eminence, it didn't come to me. I thought you normally bring it with you. Don't you usually give it to the metropolitan archbishop when his province is going to be dismembered?" To my astonishment, he replied, "No, I don't have it. Somehow it was misplaced." Then he smiled and said, "Well, you know Latin very well. You can draw it up tonight." So that night, I leaned on every ounce of Latin training I had taken in the seminary and drafted a papal bull. The most difficult aspect of crafting a bull is to accurately account for the regions in the new province, and I knew the regions.

I made it short and sweet for fear I might make a mistake. I wanted to make sure that after I drew up the bull, Cardinal Laghi would indicate that he was the representative of the Holy See and that he agreed to state that the bull, as I drew it up, would be accepted as the official document of the Holy See. At least he didn't find any errors. I was told later by Bishop Friend that the Holy See had furnished him with a new and formal document of establishment of the new province with its dioceses. That was quite a way to conclude my duties as metropolitan archbishop of the Province of New Orleans.

During all of my time in New Orleans I was pleased to find that the priests of the Archdiocese generally liked each other and were very cooperative. For a bishop, that's not always the case. For a brief time after the retirement of Baton Rouge Bishop Robert Tracy in 1974, I served as the administrator of the Baton Rouge Diocese. I had a few meetings with the priests, and it was obvious that there were large differences of opinion among them. I called one meeting to see if I could ameliorate the situation, but in the midst of the discussion a veteran priest stood up and said, "Why get into all this discussion? We were happier when we belonged to the Archdiocese of New Orleans. Why don't we just ask to discontinue the Diocese of Baton Rouge and go back to New Orleans?"

Of course, I had absolutely no authority to suppress the Diocese of Baton Rouge!

Obviously, my attempt to calm any ill feelings on the part of the Baton Rouge clergy fell flat. But several years later — in 1983 — I did succeed in changing the outlook of many priests by securing the appointment of Bishop Stanley J. Ott as the Bishop of Baton Rouge, succeeding Bishop Joseph Sullivan. Working with him for several years when he served as auxiliary bishop of New Orleans, I knew Stanley Ott as perhaps the most kind, loving, and pious priest I had ever encountered. He completely changed the fractious attitude of the Baton Rouge clergy. He brought a peaceful presence to the Baton Rouge Diocese, and his priests grew to love and respect him. Stanley showed God's grace in bearing his suffering from inoperable cancer. At his funeral, St. Joseph Cathedral was filled with tearful clergy and laity, including myself.

Stanley's only fault was his habit to consult with me and often with the Apostolic Delegate about his many decisions. If that was his only fault, he was a walking saint. His piety convinced me to suggest him as the chaplain of the Magnificat women's group that was formed by Marilyn Quirk in the Archdiocese of New Orleans and has now spread across the world. In addition to his piety, Stanley knew all the good restaurants in New Orleans. About once or twice a month he went out to dinner with his friends. Any time I had an inquiry about a "good" restaurant, I simply introduced the person to Stanley and he took it from there. He was better than any Michelin guide. No priest dared to argue or disregard the counsel of such a holy man, and his nearly ten years as Bishop of Baton Rouge had a calming effect on everyone who encountered his spirit-filled presence.

I am often asked if there was ever a consideration of my being elevated to cardinal as archbishop of New Orleans. On one hand, I have to honestly say that I am surprised the Archdiocese of New Orleans did not merit that distinction long before my arrival because of its history. It unquestionably was the Catholic center of the south-central part of the United States, and I thought for that reason alone it would be proper and fitting to have a cardinal as its bishop. Somewhere along the line, the Holy See decided that St. Louis would qualify for that honor.

I understand my good friend Hale Boggs, the long-time Louisiana congressman, made several impassioned pleas with the Apostolic Nuncio for the Holy See to recognize New Orleans and its history, but for a man so politically astute, he was barking up the wrong tree. You can't put pressure on the Vatican about something like that.

I still believe New Orleans deserves such an honor largely because it would reflect very well on the black Catholics who have made their home here and battled so many injustices throughout the generations. To this day I think New Orleans is much more significant than St. Louis in terms of its Catholic history and culture, but I'm admittedly biased. I was not surprised when in 2007 the Archdiocese of Galveston-Houston received the honor of having its archbishop, Daniel DiNardo, named a cardinal because Texas is such an important state. Perhaps one day New Orleans will be equally honored.

CHAPTER 19

Hurricane Katrina and Its Aftermath

I hate hurricanes, but my life as an archbishop has been inextricably linked to them and to the extraordinary cooperation I have experienced in their wake.

From Betsy to Camille to Katrina, the people of south Louisiana and the Mississippi Gulf Coast have been put to unimaginable tests since 1965. They have responded in faith by clinging to the promise, first delineated by St. Paul, that all things work together for good for those who love God.

Is finding God easy in the midst of immense suffering? Not always. For someone who has lost a loved one, a home, or a way of life due to a natural disaster, the best the Church can offer is the promise of God's help and a tangible experience of the love of Christ, exhibited by neighbor caring for neighbor.

When two hijacked planes flew into the twin towers of the World Trade Center in lower Manhattan on September 11, 2001, it was natural to ask, "Where was God in this evil act?"

I would suggest our Catholic faith teaches that God was present in the resolute steps of the firefighters, police officers, and emergency medical personnel who ran into instead of away from those burning, crumbling, smoke-filled buildings.

God was there, as well, both during and after Betsy, Camille, and Katrina. It is the responsibility of the Church to seek the lost and bind up their wounds, which is both a physical and a spiritual response.

Coming to New Orleans as I did in the immediate aftermath of Hurricane Betsy in September 1965, I learned quickly about the resilience of the people of the Archdiocese of New Orleans. People often tell me that our response after Betsy — simply going out and being with the people — meant more to them anything else. When I was a pastor in Washington, D.C., I made it a rule that all of my associate pastors were to stand outside of church after every Mass greeting the people as they left Mass. If people need to see their priests during normal times, that basic need is exponentially greater in the midst of crisis. People need to see their priests — their Church — after a major disaster. Any priest who does not understand this is not worthy to wear the collar.

After Hurricane Betsy in 1965 I was constantly amazed at the resilience of the people of south Louisiana. There was no moaning and groaning. Rather, there was a collective spirit of neighbor helping neighbor.

My first real experience with a hurricane as an archbishop came four years later when Hurricane Camille, a brutal Category 5 storm, went ashore east of New Orleans and devastated the Mississippi Gulf Coast. Bishop Joseph Brunini, the bishop of Natchez-Jackson, was north of the impact area, so I sent Monsignor Clinton Doskey and several archdiocesan priests and employees to the Gulf Coast to see what we could do for the people. The biggest immediate problem was the lack of drinking water, and we were able to distribute vital supplies as quickly as possible. I credit that to the training Monsignor Doskey and his fellow priests in the Social Apostolate had in responding to emergency situations.

Although Camille dealt a wicked blow to the Mississippi Gulf Coast, we were spared in the Archdiocese of New Orleans except for lower Plaquemines, where both protection levees were breached, which led to massive flooding. In the months after Camille I went to visit the parish president and urged him to rebuild the levees and to use this disaster as proof that the main highway in lower Plaquemines needed to be elevated to provide an emergency escape route for people. He told me, "Absolutely not. It's going to take too much money, and we don't know whether or not we'll have another storm as strong as Camille."

When I visited the Mississippi Gulf Coast, I was struck by the incongruous sight of what used to be a bank building. The only things left standing on the cement floor were the massive safety deposit boxes. In terms of water and wind, Camille was every bit the equal of Katrina thirty-six years later. I shudder to think what would happen to New Orleans if a Camille ever scored a direct hit on the Crescent City. The biggest difference in hurricane response back in the 1960s was that the federal government pretty much stayed out of the picture — the municipalities and states had to fend for themselves, and that's what we tried to do.

In 1984, New Orleans had another brush with major flooding when Tropical Storm Juan's heavy rains inundated parts of the West Bank. There was a break in one of the levees, and I got an urgent call at my residence about two o'clock in the morning that the water was rising fast. I told the man I'd try to round up some seminarians and any other able-bodied men I could find to get over there and help out. I kept a pair of overalls in my closet — along with my old Army combat boots — for emergency situations. I dressed quickly and got a few seminarians to join me. Putting on my boots took me back more than forty years to the time I broke in those same elk-leather boots by wearing them in the shower for forty-five minutes and then letting them dry to fit snugly the curvatures of my feet. Those size 8 1/2 boots still fit perfectly!

When we got to the West Bank, an engineer on the scene determined the best place to drop the sand bags, and we immediately became part of the sandbagging crew. I'll always treasure the photograph that was taken of the sandbagging team and me, working in a common mission to save what we could. People often have remarked how much they appreciated our efforts. I learned a vital truth: If you make a decent effort to help, even if it turns out to be an utter failure, people will give you credit for trying. People have a right to expect that you will become involved in their problems.

Then came Katrina. Believe me, I was not trying to be a risk-taking hero when I decided on August 29, 2005, to remain inside my Focus Worldwide Television studios on Metairie Road as Hurricane Katrina approached the metropolitan New Orleans area. Yes, I was ninety-two years old at the time, and I knew I probably was going to be staying by myself in a four-story building, but I considered myself very safe.

At the time I was living at St. Pius X Church rectory in Lake Vista — just a few hundred yards from Lake Pontchartrain. Monsignor Doskey, the pastor, was absolutely convinced that the new gymnasium building he had erected was going to be strong enough to sustain hurricane-force winds. That's where he determined to ride out Katrina. I told him, "Clint, I'd like to stay with you, but I've got to go to Focus to protect all of our television equipment." We parted very amicably on Sunday afternoon, about twelve hours before landfall.

I made the fifteen-minute drive to the Focus studios in Metairie with some emergency supplies — I had enough water, peanut butter, and crackers to last a couple of weeks. I forgot to bring with me a battery-powered radio, which I would regret after the storm passed.

I know most of my family thought I was crazy — in fact, they probably thought I was going to be hunkering down with my staff. But even if I was alone, I was convinced of the safety of that building, which was built almost like a fortress. It once had served as the headquarters of AT&T and had been overbuilt with the strongest foundation and thickest walls you could ever imagine. It was three stories tall but had been designed to accommodate a fourth floor if ever needed. Before I bought the building to house the Focus studios, I had my architect friend Frank Walk examine the building. Frank told me, "This building was built like no other I've ever seen. AT&T certainly spared no expense."

As the storm progressed, I could look out the windows and see trees being twisted in the wind, but I couldn't hear a sound. That's how thick the walls were. Also, I knew the building was on some of the highest ground in Metairie, and it wound up not getting a single drop of water inside. I heard Jefferson Parish President Aaron Broussard talking about trying to find a safe haven for his essential personnel during a hurricane. He couldn't have done any better than the old AT&T building. It was a bunker.

I was the only one there. I was comfortable, for the most part, until the electricity went out and the temperature rose to about ninety-five degrees. It was as hot as the devil. I slept on the floor, but that was no problem — the floor in my office had a nice rug.

Of course, by the Tuesday after Katrina, my cell phone was not operable — no one could get calls in or out — and my family in Washington, D.C., was absolutely apoplectic with fear. I found out much later that my dear niece Peggy Hannan Laramie sent a frantic e-mail to *The Times-Picayune*'s website on September 1: "Please help us rescue retired Archbishop Philip Hannan, who is at his Focus TV office in Metairie at 106 Metairie Lawn Drive (perhaps 3rd fl). He's alive and has food, but along with others in the building — a former Verizon substation — needs rescue. Any info? Call his niece, Peg.... God bless you."

I was fine. In addition to the peanut butter and crackers, I had bread in the kitchen. By Wednesday night, I was confident there wouldn't be any looting. The only person who entered the building during the entire four days I was there was a computer technician who had some very expensive equipment stored on the third floor that he wanted to take with him to Baton Rouge for safekeeping. He just broke down the door and got into the building. He hauled out his equipment, loaded it in his car, and took it to Baton Rouge.

There was only one flaw in my entire plan. We had a backup diesel tank on site that had a one-month supply of fuel for the generator that would be triggered in the event of a power outage. Well, when the power went, the generator worked for awhile, but a small connection in the fuel line gave way and the flow of fuel stopped.

People often ask me what I might have been able to do if, in fact, someone had tried to come in and loot the building. I found a good wooden club, which I could have used as a weapon. I could've stood behind the door and clobbered someone if he had tried to gain access to the building. I admit I don't have the strength I once had, but I did have one big advantage. Anyone who tried to bust in would not know where things were inside because it was so dark, and I knew the floor plan so well I had a big advantage. I would have had the looters at my mercy. I wasn't afraid at all. Thank God, I didn't have to test my reflexes!

On the Thursday morning after Katrina — four days after landfall — I decided things were quiet enough at the office that I could try to make it across the Causeway in my car. My initial idea was to offer spiritual guidance and moral support to the people in the church parishes and the emergency personnel on the Northshore. Of course, when I drove my car to the south tollbooth of the Causeway, the police stopped me at a barricade because the twenty-four-mile bridge was closed. One of the officers was a good Catholic, and he recognized me. "I'm sorry, Archbishop, the bridge is closed." I replied,

"I know it is, but I simply want to go to the other side. I've got to get to the parishes so that I can help the people over there." Without giving it a second thought, he smiled and waved me through, telling me to be careful.

Actually, I've never had a better ride across the Causeway. I didn't encounter a single car on the entire length of the bridge. I had it entirely to myself. My only concern was whether or not I had enough gas in my tank to make it across, but I took courage from the fact that the police were so obliging, and I knew they would be able to give me more gas in case I ran out.

My first stop was St. Peter Church in Covington because I knew that parish had a big rectory. But when I got there the pastor already had taken in two priests. I wouldn't have minded sleeping on the couch, but by that time a nice woman came by and suggested I travel a little farther north to St. Joseph's Abbey. I wasn't sure if I had enough gas, but she agreed to follow me in her car, and we made it by snaking our way through felled trees of every description. The great news was that the abbey's backup generator was working, and thus I had an air-conditioned room and all the food I could eat.

The first thing I did was to take a long, hot shower. That reminded me of the war when after a major campaign we finally would be able to get a proper shower. It felt so wonderful, and I was so thankful. During the Bulge campaign in 1945, I went six weeks without a shower. People asked me, "What about your skin? Weren't you worried about catching a disease?" I told them, "The only thing I was worried about in regards to my skin was if there was a hole in it. As long as I didn't have a bullet hole, I was happy."

Aftermath of Katrina

The Benedictines and the seminarians could not have been more accommodating and hospitable to me. I had a perfect situation, and it was a good home base for me to begin traveling around St. Tammany Parish to visit with both old and newly arrived parishioners. I was able to contact Archbishop Alfred Hughes, who had gone to Baton Rouge with Archbishop Francis Schulte, and I told him I would try to stay in the Northshore area and offer whatever ministry I could. He was very grateful to hear from me, and it was good to talk to him, as well.

Only later did I hear some of the worst stories of what my priest friends and others encountered during and after Katrina. Father Dennis Hayes, who was pastor of St. Louise de Marillac in Arabi in St. Bernard Parish, was holed up on the second floor of his school building with dozens of neighbors, and they saw the water rise fourteen feet in one hour. He eventually managed to go by boat to the Mississippi River levee and actually walked for miles with water up to his chin. After getting into downtown New Orleans, he thought it might be best to try to make it to Notre Dame Seminary. He got as far as the C.J. Peete Housing Development on Earhart Boulevard, where the water again was impassible. The only person to help him was this incredible black woman who told him to come up to her second-floor apartment so that he could rest. He was totally bedraggled, and she took care of him!

The saddest story for me was the drowning death of Father Arthur (Red) Ginart, the pastor of St. Nicholas of Myra Church in Lake St. Catherine. Red had a great knack of speaking to people, especially to older people, and he was extremely popular. He tried to speak simply to people in words they could understand, and that endeared him to his parishioners. A number of people reported to me after his death that they had gone to him when the storm was getting ready to make landfall and practically begged him to leave. He always said the same thing: "I've been through this before." That was his typical bravado coming through. "I know the situation," he told his parishioners. "When all of you come back after the storm, I'll be here greeting you." The people could not understand why in the name of God he would not evacuate, even if just to please them.

Surveying the damage in the aftermath of Katrina (Photo by Sean Harrison)

St. Nicholas of Myra Church was destroyed by the storm surge, and Father Red's body was never found. A few days after the storm, I was able to make it by helicopter to the eviscerated shell of St. Nicholas Church. There on the ground was Father Red's mud-covered, purple stole. Placing the stole carefully around my neck, I opened my book of blessings and offered a soft prayer for the repose of Father Red's soul.

There were some reports that people had seen his body, but that was never confirmed, and I never spoke to anyone who had seen his body. At the height of the surge, the water was estimated to be thirty feet high. Red had no chance. The only things left of the church were some structural steel beams. Everything else was gone. I'm sure Red's body was washed out to the Gulf of Mexico. May God grant him eternal life.

One of the most incredible rescue stories to emerge from Katrina involved the efforts of two fishermen from St. Bernard who had a twenty-three-foot boat named "The Big Fish." It was said that nothing would stand up to the force of Katrina. But the indomitable will of Jimmy Pitre and his close friend Donald Colletti did exactly that. The two friends performed a nine-day crusade to save dozens of lives. They knew Katrina was going to be bad, so the night before the storm hit, they loaded their boat with every ounce of gasoline that would fit in the tank. It cost them every cent they had — about $300 — but it was worth it considering what they were able to do in their incredible rescue mission.

Unfortunately, Jimmy's mother, an invalid, was with him at the house. On Monday morning, Jimmy and Donald got a cell phone call from a fishing friend in Alexandria in central Louisiana, who told them the storm surge had already inundated Arabi with eight feet of water. At first Jimmy didn't believe the report because his house was high and dry and there were only two inches of water in the street. The first sign that something was wrong came from Jimmy's dog, who was running nervously through the house and finally hid under the bed. Perhaps the dog could sense the wall of water that was only minutes away.

The water began rising furiously, minute by minute, and Jimmy and Donald tried desperately to get Jimmy's mother into the boat. "She saw us struggling and she just said, 'Let me go!'" Jimmy said. But finally they were able to battle the current and the wind to get her into the boat. The men heard the cries of neighbors about six houses away. They struggled to get them into the boat, and in the midst of all of this, Jimmy turned to his mother and saw that she had died. It was a terrible shock. Donald gave Jimmy a hug.

They covered her body, and as they were making their way through the water, the men saw other neighbors who needed to be rescued. Jimmy said, "We're going to save as many people as we can." Under normal conditions, the boat could hold about five people comfortably. But this was a crisis. Jimmy and Donald maneuvered their boat through the flooded streets, hearing the screams of stranded neighbors. At one point they crammed twenty-seven people into the boat. The fishermen used all of their wiles to maneuver the boat to a dry spot where they could unload the survivors as well as the body of Jimmy's mother. Along the way the boat kept bumping into all kinds of things that were floating on the dark surface of the water. The fishermen couldn't fathom this, but all around them were entire houses that had been uprooted and were floating freely in the water. It took all of their seamanship to avoid the houses and keep the boat from capsizing in the half-light.

The men kept up the hunt for survivors for several days. They scoured the entire length of St. Bernard Parish because they figured no one else was in better position to save people's lives. They made more than twenty trips and averaged about twenty to twenty-five people per trip. That means they saved at least four hundred people!

I did a video interview with the men, and I asked, "Did you do any praying during this time?" One fisherman replied, "My God, we didn't do anything but pray! Somebody would say an 'Our Father,' and someone else would say another prayer. Everyone was praying."

They were able to get food for the people they rescued by wading into a grocery store and grabbing whatever canned goods they could find. People ask where God was during Katrina. These men — these heroes — were God's hands and feet.

The day after I arrived at St. Joseph's Abbey in Covington, St. Tammany Parish Sheriff Jack Strain found out I was there and asked if I would be available to give some pep talks to his personnel, who by this time were exhausted and operating strictly on fumes. Of course, I agreed to help him in any way I could. I went to the sheriff's headquarters, and he had sent out the word to assemble as many personnel as could make it for a brief meeting. The sheriff introduced me to the assembly.

"You've done a wonderful job," I told the weary group. "You've stayed at your duty and done your tasks remarkably well. But, please remember to do one thing for me. Please remember to tell your children about these days so that they will remember and tell their own children about how men and women of honor sacrificed and did their duty to protect a community. The only way we will build up this community again is to have our children inspired to follow your example. They need indoctrination into the sacrifices that are required to have a good, decent community. Never forget this, and never forget to tell your children and grandchildren so it will be in their memories."

Sheriff Strain was doing exactly the right thing in that situation. He knew his deputies and other support staff needed a pep talk, and he showed great leadership in keeping them all together. He was able to get practically

Two weeks after Hurricane Katrina, I greeted Archbishop Paul Joseph Cordes of the Pontifical Council Cor Unum for Human and Christian Development, the Vatican's humanitarian arm, following a Mass celebrated at St. Joseph Cathedral in Baton Rouge, Louisiana. Archbishop Cordes's visit marked the first time the prefect of Cor Unum had ever visited the site of a natural disaster in the United States

everyone who worked for him at the meeting. There was a lot of emotional reaction to my talk, and it humbled me to be able to help in some small way.

The only thing I asked of Sheriff Strain was to arrange a helicopter ride for me so that I could get a bird's-eye view of the devastation. That helicopter did not have the equipment to rescue people from their rooftops — that was the job of the Coast Guard — but we were able to assess the area from St. Tammany all the way down to St. Bernard Parish.

Everywhere I looked there was nothing but water, as though the Gulf of Mexico had shifted sixty miles to the north. We saw people stranded on rooftops, and I felt desperate for them because I figured that almost none of them knew how to swim. If any wind came up and they slipped off the roofs, I knew they'd be in terrible shape. I felt helpless because I saw the situation and couldn't do anything immediately to help.

Devastation

One of the first sites of devastation I witnessed was Our Lady of Lourdes Church and School in Slidell. The storm had blown out a side window of the church, and the differential in air pressure between the inside and outside of the church was so great that the roof simply collapsed to the floor. I was able to talk briefly to Father Adrian Hall, who had stayed at the rectory during the storm, and the police were able to pick him up and find him a temporary place to live. I also got a good look at Archbishop Hannan High School in Meraux, which was utterly devastated by the floodwaters.

In the meantime, the U.S. Coast Guard performed brilliantly, not waiting for any orders to come from on high. The Coast Guard knew people were sitting on rooftops and dying in attics, and they began a rescue mission unrivaled in any other natural disaster.

I've never been fond of Monday morning quarterbacking, but the overall response by city, state, and federal officials during and after Katrina was abysmal. First of all, President Bush asked Governor Kathleen Blanco to incorporate the Louisiana National Guard with regular Army soldiers, and she refused. Her refusal really shook the president — that refusal was probably unprecedented after a major disaster — and nobody knew what to do.

Given the fiasco of the evacuation process, I have never understood why Governor Blanco and New Orleans Mayor Ray Nagin — in the assessment of what went wrong — could not get together on a simple plan that would save lives. If a major storm is approaching, the city and state should mobilize every bus at their command to take people to Army camps in other parts of Louisiana. There are numerous Army camps within the state with plenty of room for thousands of evacuees. The only thing needed is a little foresight to prepare the extra facilities. Using Army camps also would eliminate one of the big problems that was experienced in the aftermath of Katrina — families being

Archbishop Cordes greets Louisiana bishops in Baton Rouge: From left (partially hidden) Auxiliary Bishop Roger Morin of New Orleans, Baton Rouge Bishop Robert W. Muench, me, Archbishop Cordes, and New Orleans Archbishop Alfred C. Hughes.

split apart and being sent to locations far away from each other and far away from home. We sent people to Duluth, Minnesota! That was a great disservice to many people. In our own state we have plenty of facilities to handle such a crisis. Maybe it's too simple an idea, but I know it would work.

I can only imagine the fear people had loading buses to go somewhere — anywhere? — out of town. The people asked where they were being taken, and no one would tell them anything. If anyone insisted on being told where he or she was being taken, the person was told to get off the bus and wait. That's why families were scattered to the four winds. Just about anything that could have gone wrong did go wrong.

A crisis situation demands leadership. I kept saying to myself, "I wish I knew where the mayor was because I would tell him that all he needed was one order from the president, and the mayor would have been allowed to use any Army facilities he needed." I finally learned that the president himself gave the order to send parts of the 82nd Airborne down to New Orleans. I wrote him a note of thanks later and congratulated him on his decision and said he did the right thing. I suggested that in the future the president of the United States ought to mobilize the Army after any major disaster. The military has an established chain of command, and no one will walk off duty when the going gets tough as, unfortunately, some of our police officers did. All the commander has to do is give the order, and everybody down the line must obey it. That's the type of command needed in a crisis.

82nd Airborne

I knew some of the members of the 505th Regiment of the 82nd Airborne Division who came down to New Orleans. I was the chaplain for that regiment in World War II. In one day they rid the area of looters. Their mere presence calmed the situation. All they had to do was walk the streets with their rifles at the ready and festoons of bullets draped on their shoulders. I know there were shootings after Katrina — we probably will never know the exact number — but the city police, with their little revolvers, were no match for the criminals and the addicts in withdrawal who were heavily armed.

One of the first things the paratroopers did when they arrived in New Orleans was to secure St. Louis Cathedral and the area around the cathedral. I eventually got down to the cathedral, and someone had let them know that I was an 82nd chaplain during WWII. I asked the general in charge, "What gave you the idea to secure the cathedral?" He looked almost insulted by my question. "That's our standing orders," the general said. "Whenever an area is turned over to us to stabilize, if there is a building that symbolizes the area or is something of special value that people really look up to, that's where we go. I knew St. Louis Cathedral was not only the symbol of the city but of the entire state of Louisiana. That's why we immediately came down here with our men and engineers and removed the fallen trees next to the cathedral."

I was on the ground in Biloxi, Mississippi, to greet the delegation from the Vatican as they toured the devastated Gulf Coast of Mississippi with Biloxi Bishop Thomas Rodi, a New Orleans native. One of the stops was St. Michael's Catholic Church on Highway 90, where the water surge blew out the windows and lifted pews completely out of the church

In St. Anthony's Garden behind the cathedral, a huge oak tree had fallen in such a way that it brushed the large statue of the Sacred Heart of Jesus but otherwise left it standing. The only damage to the statue occurred when a falling branch clipped off two fingers of Christ's upraised hand. The general sent his men to search carefully around the base of the statue, and sure enough, they found the two fingers and presented them to me. The soldiers could not have been nicer.

They asked if I needed transportation to any place in the city, and I told them I would appreciate any tour I could get that would let me know how badly our churches and schools were damaged. I was in good shape. The colonel in charge had a Humvee equipped with a GPS system. All I had to do was tell the soldiers the location, and we could get there. The Humvee could operate in four or five feet of water.

Back on the Northshore, I visited hospitals and spoke both to the patients and to the staff that was working so valiantly to care for the large influx of people. The hospital assembled far more people than could comfortably fit into a room, so we went into a large central area and I went around giving blessings and shaking hands. I must have blessed at least a thousand people. There was only one fellow — an atheist — who refused my blessing, but he was a very nice man. Meanwhile, as soon as I blessed someone, a voice from across the room would call out for me to come over and confer a blessing. If I missed a group, they were sure to let me know, and I doubled back to take care of the oversight. I was thoroughly impressed by the total dedication of the doctors and nurses.

About two weeks after the storm, I heard that Pope Benedict XVI was dispatching Cardinal Paul Josef Cordes, president of the Pontifical Council Cor Unum, to bring papal blessings and offer spiritual and financial support to the people of New Orleans and the Mississippi Gulf Coast. Cor Unum is the arm of the Vatican specifically charged with caring for the needy and providing

The 82nd Airborne Division assisted in retrieving the finger of the statue of the Sacred Heart of Jesus in the rear garden of the St. Louis Cathedral after Hurricane Katrina

I am addressing parishioners of St. Anthony Parish, a Vietnamese parish in Baton Rouge

humanitarian assistance, and this was the first time in its thirty-four-year history that it was responding to a natural disaster in the United States.

Part of Cardinal Cordes's mission was to take a helicopter tour of the affected areas. I knew he would be landing in Biloxi, Mississippi, first, so I drove over to the Gulf Coast with a seminarian and was able to meet the Cardinal and his traveling party when they arrived. I was quite impressed with Cardinal Cordes's pastoral sense. He met first with Biloxi Bishop Thomas Rodi and his diocesan staff, but what he really wanted to do was to tour the area and meet the people. We visited a Vietnamese parish in Biloxi, and Cardinal Cordes did something I thought was quite unusual. He sang for them a Vietnamese song he had learned years ago, and it really touched them. The Vietnamese took over the program and sang "God Bless America" and "America the Beautiful." Their soulful singing made such an impression on Father Larry Snyder, the head of Catholic Charities USA, that he cried. Imagine that — these people were in such desperate straits, and the first thing they thought about was to sing "God Bless America."

Because of my background of welcoming Vietnamese Catholics to the Archdiocese of New Orleans, I was asked to say a few words to the people. I told them, "We came to your help when you were in very bad shape and we were delighted to help you, and you've been a tremendous help to us. Now we are in a difficult situation. Are you going to leave us or stay with us in our time of troubles?" They were so enthused they jumped up and started clapping. A little while later I went over to meet the pastor to ask him if the church was cleaned out yet. "Not yet," he said. Then he walked over to a group of Vietnamese parishioners and asked them to get in the church and finish the cleanup, and they did it just like that. Nobody told the Vietnamese people the government was supposed to help them. They were well-organized and did most of their recovery work on their own. They are an amazing people.

Even with the advantage of hindsight, I do not know how to squarely answer the question: Is it safe to live in New Orleans? From our experience of Katrina, I would have to say it is not. I would hope to God that the levees hold next time, but you have to remember that a hurricane is a force of nature. Katrina lasted for about twelve hours, and that's the reason why our levees were under such enormous pressure, and they failed. Who knows if the next storm is going to last twelve hours or more? If you assess the worst-case scenario, no, New Orleans isn't a safe place to live. I hope to God the next storm will be more like Betsy, which really lasted only a few hours. I don't think it's possible to say categorically that everything and everyone in New Orleans is safe from future hurricanes. That's why I think it's prudent that anyone who

THE WHITE HOUSE

WASHINGTON

October 3, 2006

His Excellency
   the Most Reverend Philip M. Hannan
Covington, Louisiana

Dear Archbishop Hannan:

It was a pleasure to see you in New Orleans. Thank you for taking the time to say hello. St. Louis Cathedral was a good place to commemorate the first anniversary of Hurricane Katrina, and I appreciated your warm welcome.

Laura and I send our best wishes.

Sincerely,

George W. Bush

Note from George W. Bush on Katrina anniversary

can get out of town in advance of a major storm should do so even before a mandatory evacuation is called for. I think politicians ought to be very candid with citizens and tell them that what they can do on their own is a whole lot better than what the state or city can do for them.

I am glad that unprecedented efforts are being made to build stronger levees and restore the vanishing south Louisiana coastline. The Netherlands has shown it can marshal the financial and political resources to build a levee system that can protect a below-sea-level population from flooding. The challenge for Louisiana will be to make the case to the nation why preserving south Louisiana is critical to everyone's national security and economic outlook. We create and distribute oil and gas for the country, and we have one of the country's largest ports. The problem for Louisiana is simple — the Netherlands is one country, and everyone's survival rests on that levee system. Louisiana is one of fifty states and does not have the political clout to make the case that a natural disaster in New Orleans can affect the cab driver in Duluth, Minnesota. Well, how does $6-a-gallon gasoline sound?

We need effective leadership to make the case for Louisiana with facts and figures. God give us that leadership.

CHAPTER 20

Stroke and Recovery

In March 2007 I attended the annual retreat for Louisiana bishops at the Rosaryville retreat center near Ponchatoula. I was having some severe stomach pains, and Archbishop Hughes saw that I was physically in distress.

I couldn't figure out where the pain was coming from. Archbishop Hughes suggested that I go to the emergency room to be examined, and I was feeling so bad I knew that was the best course of action. Eventually, I went to St. Tammany Hospital for treatment.

I was told that I could expect to have an operation, but as soon as I was seated I was told by Dr. Angela Buonagura, "I don't think you need an operation. Tell me what happened." As soon as I began to tell her, she said, "I think your trouble is not in your lungs but with your throat. I think you have diverticulitis." A further examination did, in fact, show that I had diverticulitis. I remain deeply grateful for having her expertise.

Another of my doctors, Dr. Billy Barfield, also has been exceptionally helpful whenever I needed assistance, especially for my sinus trouble, a lingering result of my Army duty. At the time of my discharge from the Army, the Army doctor said my sinus trouble was so bad that it was incurable. But Dr. Barfield has been very helpful to

I wildly exceeded doctors' expectations when I rebounded quickly from a serious stroke in 2007 at age ninety-four. I was back walking and exercising within weeks of the scare. My daily exercise consists of walking in the Courthouse in Covington, Louisiana

me, not only in treating my sinusitis but also for his ability to treat other illnesses. These doctors have helped me remain so active in my ninety-sixth year.

A few weeks after my diverticulitis attack something much more serious occurred. On March 30, 2007, I began to feel some unusual sensations. I slipped to the floor and must have hit my head. Fortunately, I have a big skull — that's not a joke — and the skull must have absorbed a great deal of the force and did not sustain a fracture. I really do believe my head is harder than concrete. The bad fall was troubling to my doctors, however, because they could see on the imaging scans that I had suffered bleeding to the brain.

For a few weeks, it was touch and go. I had what doctors call "full-body" weakness, but the effect of the stroke was particularly noticeable on my right side. I had the doctors extremely worried right after the stroke because I was so weak and lethargic.

But week after week, I started to improve. I began to work on my motor skills, and I began to walk again with the assistance of a walker. I continued taking physical and occupational therapy and do some light exercise. The doctors said in late April that it would take another four to six weeks to determine whether or not I could resume a normal work regimen.

One of the amazing things was how my brain bounced back. The part of my brain that was not affected by the stroke began to absorb the blood that had pooled on the brain from my fall. It's almost like a miracle the way my brain reacted. The doctors told me they were amazed by my progress because they had never seen such a recovery in a patient of my advanced age. I had never had a really difficult illness or disease in my entire life, and I was absolutely determined to beat it.

After I returned home from the hospital, I resumed a regular exercise regimen. Kent Bossier, who is my primary caregiver and lives with me at my home in Covington, figured the easiest way for me to get some excellent exercise was to go over to the St. Tammany Parish Courthouse, which has a grand series of steps at the front entrance and another main staircase inside the building. From top to bottom, it's sixty-two steps — and I try to do that six times. When I came home from the hospital I was taking sixteen different pills for different symptoms, and they were really tying my stomach in knots. After a few weeks, I was in such good physical shape that my doctor told me to stop taking all the pills he had prescribed for me except for my vitamins and my blood-thinning medication. I am walking instead of taking pills.

In addition to the exercise, the best part of climbing the courthouse steps is interacting with so many people from the community. Some of them know who I am, but some don't. An elderly woman came up to me one day and asked, "How old are you?" When I told her I was ninety-four, she said, "Well, I can't believe it. If you can do this, I can, too!" Now I'm starting to see all kinds of people walking the courthouse steps for exercise. It really does work. If your heart can stand it — and thank God, I've got a very strong heart — exercise does you a lot of good. I didn't expect anyone to come and copy us, but they are. That's pretty good encouragement right there.

The only complication of doing my exercise routine at the courthouse is the natural tendency to run into lawyers. On two occasions I was asked not to give testimony but to simply sit in the courtroom so that the judge might be persuaded to give his client a lighter sentence. I did it, but it didn't work at all. The judge did his proper duty, and that was the end of my sit-in appearances in court.

My big preoccupation now is to watch my balance, because I don't want to fall. That's one thing I learned during my recuperation. I needed to get a little more rest. I'll take a nap in the afternoon, but I've got to watch that I don't nap too long. If I do, then I'll have trouble sleeping at night. I've never needed more than five or six hours of good sleep to function well. I inherited that from my mother. My father slept an awful lot to make up for my mother's lack of sleep.

My family's genetics seem to indicate the possibility of living a long life. Both my mother and father lived until they were ninety-three. My mother walked until the last day

I walk the steps of the St. Tammany Parish Courthouse in Covington every day for exercise, drawing cheers and looks of amazement from courthouse visitors. I have been known to climb the sixty-two steps six consecutive times. At my age, you have to earn feeling good

of her life to make sure her legs did not get cramped. That became part of the Hannan family lore. I try to take care of my body. I never smoked — except for once when I was eight or nine and got sick taking a puff of a cigar. My advice to elderly people is to decide the most pleasant exercise for them — something that is fun for them and can be accomplished in nice surroundings — and then stick to a regular schedule. You've got to keep the body moving and the brain occupied. I'll lift some light things around the house just to make sure my shoulders don't get tight.

I tell people that you have to "earn" feeling good. You've got to do something positive. The best thing any elderly person can do is to exercise regularly and do as much exercise as the doctor permits.

I have been so extraordinarily blessed by God with good health throughout my life. God's grace and the work of so many good doctors, nurses, and

At his installation as archbishop of New Orleans in 2009, I passed along to Archbishop Aymond a diamond and emerald pectoral cross that was given to me by the Cosgrove family on the day of my ordination as bishop in 1956

This picture of my parents and me at my installation as archbishop of the New Orleans archdiocese on October 13, 1965, was used for the celebration of my ninety-fifth birthday at St. Louis Cathedral on May 25, 2008. At the installation, my mom delighted local reporters when they said to her, "Well, you must be very proud of your son," and she replied by asking, "Which one?"

aides helped me recover from a medical condition that is extremely serious. I appreciate what's happening to me, and I also thank all the people who sent me cards and prayed for me during my illness.

The power of prayer can never be underestimated. I have visited hundreds of sick people in hospitals and their own homes over the years, and I take that Gospel imperative very seriously.

In 1980 I recall going to visit Father Skelly in the hospital. He had been diagnosed with brain cancer and was in a coma. He didn't recognize anyone. When I went to his room, strangely enough, he knew who I was, and we had a pleasant talk for a few minutes before he began to wander. The response of the sick is something that is very edifying and sometimes frightening. It gives me a sense of the obligation and the power of the episcopacy. Time and again I've been told that people in a coma won't respond. I will come in, whisper in their ear and tell them who I am, and for a few moments they are lucid. This certainly implies a very serious obligation on the part of all priests and bishops to visit the sick as much as possible. Father Skelly's nurse told me that someone mentioned to him that I would be coming, and he seemed to be waiting for me. As tired as I was during that day, it would have been a terrible thing if I had not come. Would not each of us want that compassionate visit if we were in that bed?

So the next time you think about how important it would be to visit your sick aunt or grandfather, don't just think about it — do it!

In front of my house in Covington, Louisiana

CHAPTER 21

Pope John Paul II the Great

I am convinced that the Holy Spirit was present and moving like a fiery wind inside the Sistine Chapel in 1978 when the conclave of cardinals elected Cardinal Karol Wojtyla as Pope John Paul II. He proved to be the most outstanding Pope of the last one hundred fifty years.

Pope John Paul II, of course, followed the incredibly brief, thirty-three-day pontificate of Pope John Paul I, who before his election was Venice Cardinal Albino Luciani. Pope John Paul I gave only one major talk to a group of American bishops, and the subject was the dignity of the Catholic family.

The death of John Paul I, a native of northern Italy, shocked the world and led to some ridiculous speculation about the existence of a conspiracy to murder him. The first persons to realize the Pope had died were the Sisters who were in charge of the papal quarters and who had come into his bedroom in the morning to bring him a cup of coffee. The morning of his death, the Sisters came in to find him dead, sitting up in his bed. That spawned a bevy of rumors, none of them true.

The papal interregnum was a dramatic time for the Church. Catholics across the world were asking the question, "What kind of successor will we get?" Of course, the election of Cardinal Wojtyla of Krakow as Pope — the first non-Italian Pope in four hundred years — came as a complete shock. In the August conclave that had elected Pope John Paul I, there were two other Italian cardinals who had gotten significant support. Genoa Cardinal Giuseppi Siri, a conservative, is believed to have led the first count in the August conclave. Also garnering large support had been Florence Cardinal Giovanni Benelli, a high-profile moderate candidate with close ties to Pope Paul VI. Cardinal Benelli had supported Cardinal Luciani in the August conclave.

The trouble was Siri and Benelli could not agree on many basic things, and neither could their supporters. Initially, after one or two votes, the cardinals thought they might be able to unite behind one of the two major candidates, but it never happened because each candidate's core supporters were intransigent. That led to a search for a compromise candidate.

Cardinal Wojtyla began to emerge as that person. He had visited the United States many times to give theological lectures and was fairly well-known among American cardinals. He also had taught philosophy at Catholic University of America in Washington, and anyone studying philosophy was very familiar with his writings. He was a brilliant man who was fluent in several languages. His philosophy studies were the reason he learned so many languages. There were a couple of Spanish philosophers that he deeply respected, and he learned Spanish to be able to truly understand their works.

The papal conclave is supposed to maintain complete secrecy, but in Italy, nothing can be kept secret. It is well known that there is a secret code that is used by Vatican insiders to telegraph the results of the conclave long before the white smoke emerges from the Sistine Chapel and the balcony doors at St. Peter's Basilica swing open to announce: *"Annuntio vobis gaudium magnum... habemus papam!"* — "I announce to you a great joy... we have a Pope!"

The way it works is this: lay people offer bribes to the people who work inside the Vatican and they agree to stand at a window, or any place where they can be seen, and there is a special code to identify the candidates. It's very effective.

Sometimes, though, utter confusion reigns when a new Pope is announced to the world. I was present with hundreds of thousands of people in St. Peter's Square in March 1939 when Cardinal Eugenio Maria Giuseppi Giovanni Pacelli was proclaimed as Pope Pius XII. The cardinal who announced the name of his colleague who had been elected Pope said the name "Cardinal Eugenio..." The problem was this. There was also a brilliant French cardinal by the name of Eugene Tisserant, who was considered a leading candidate. When the name Eugene was announced, the French people near me began to cheer wildly, thinking that Cardinal Tisserant had become Pope. They were a bit let down when Cardinal Pacelli walked out onto the balcony.

For some reason, I was in Rome in October 1978 when the second papal conclave in two months was being held. I was going to stay in Rome as long as I needed to — after all, how often could you say you were in Rome when a new Pope was elected? I didn't think I would ever again have this wonderful opportunity.

Just as I did as a seminarian in 1939, I joined the multitudes in St. Peter's Square and waited. When Cardinal Wojtyla emerged from behind the doors and took the name Pope John Paul II, the buzz among the crowd, even among the Italians, was incredible. I will never forget his first words to the world: "Do not be afraid!" The non-Italians raised a real clamor. We didn't know it, but right after the new Pope gave his blessing, he disappeared and went by car to visit Polish Cardinal Andrzej Maria Deskur, who was in the hospital with a debilitating stroke that he had sustained during the conclave. Cardinal Deskur

Pope John Paul II leaving New Orleans after his visit in September of 1987

had been appointed head of the Pontifical Council for Social Communications in 1973, and it was through Cardinal Deskur's good will and offices that Cardinal Wojtyla had been well-known to so many cardinals.

Although I had heard of Cardinal Wojtyla, I had never really met him, and I wanted to learn more about his background. The word had been floating around that he was a real intellectual who could speak English well and had visited the United States several times. When Cardinal Wojtyla had come to Catholic University to teach philosophy during the summer of 1976, Jude Dougherty, then dean of the School of Philosophy, put him up at his home, and they became very good friends. Later, when the Pope made his first visit to the United States, the first place he went to was Catholic University, and he renewed his acquaintance with Dean Dougherty. It was obvious they had forged a good friendship. The only thing that got me upset about the Pope's first trip to Catholic University was the response he got from a group of nuns who upbraided him over women's issues. This was a real downer, especially coming right after the Pope had walked through a crowd of hundreds of cheering students who had stayed up all night in a prayer vigil in advance of his arrival.

The evening of the papal election, everyone was celebrating at the North American College in Rome. I wanted to talk to the priests and bishops there who might have insights on the new Pope. To me, his election was great for the Church because John Paul II was a "*tabula rasa*" — a clean slate. No one could place a claim on him. As a darkhorse candidate, he was totally his own man.

He went on to become John Paul the Great.

Pope John Paul II's teaching on the dignity of all human life — from conception to natural death — is both foundational and challenging to a world that so often seeks to deny God as the source of human life.

His unswerving, unrelenting proclamation of authentic human freedom led to the destruction of Communism without bloodshed. In 1979, when Pope John Paul II visited Warsaw, Poland, he shouted in Victory Square: "We want God, we want God, we want God in the family circle. We want God in books, in schools, we want God in government orders! We want God!"

He fought Communism in his own country long before the collapse of the Soviet Union. When the Communist government had determined it needed a new steel factory for Poland, it created a satellite industrial town called Nowa Huta on the edge of Krakow. In its original urban design, Nowa Huta lacked a Catholic church. Pope John Paul II rallied Catholic workers of the Solidarity movement, led by Lech Walesa, to stage a public demonstration demanding the government to relent and allow a church to be built — and it happened. The church is named Arka Pana — The Lord's Ark. The group of workers, named Solidarity, was one of the most effective groups fostering the Church and political freedom in Poland.

Pope John Paul II knew that if Solidarity ever resorted to violence to confront the Communist government, it would lose the moral high ground and give the state the excuse it needed to crush the worker movement. Cardinal Stefan Wyszynski, the primate of Poland, knelt in front of Walesa and grabbed him by the lapel of his coat and said, "I'm not going to stand up until you promise me that you are not going to resort to arms." Those were not simply the Cardinal's words but the words of the Holy Father. Finally, Walesa agreed to continue Solidarity's nonviolent approach. The meeting was so dramatic that it rallied the people to the side of the Church. It was a crucial event in the fall of Communism that many people forget, but it was directly from the provenance of Pope John Paul II.

Pope John Paul II, to be frank, expected individual bishops to follow his lead in promoting the Church's opposition to Communism, and I agreed with him completely. In Europe, where the two great world wars were fought, the people in general were united in their opposition to Communism. That's why the Pope got along so well with President Ronald Reagan. They saw the world through the same prism, and they both felt in their hearts that Communism was a tyranny against human freedom everywhere.

I was in my office in the chancery building in New Orleans on May 13, 1981, when I received the crushing news that the Pope had been gunned down by a would-be assassin following his general audience in St. Peter's Square. I was absolutely stunned. It was unbelievable. The second thought that emerged was that he had left himself completely defenseless to the deranged acts of evil people. He was always so open and so accommodating that, in a way, he was an inviting target. The public outpouring of sorrow and grief amazed me. For the next two hours, I did interviews with three television stations, seven radio stations, and the daily newspaper. I even offered prayers on the TV and radio for him.

We quickly arranged for a Mass that evening at St. Louis Cathedral to be celebrated for the intention of the Pope's recovery. My homily was simple: "John Paul II said human life was unintelligible without love, and in reality he is a martyr to love and charity throughout the world. This makes an obligation upon us: while we pray for him, we must live our lives in such a way that we merit to have our prayers heard by following his injunction. He's not the Holy Father just for the rest of the world; he is the Holy Father for New Orleans. We've got to make our mode of life his mode of life by trying to redress injustice, to guarantee peace, justice and love to all mankind, but especially to the poor. As the Holy Father was being carried to the hospital, he told his attendants, 'Tell my assailant that I am praying for him.' I ask all of you to examine your own conscience about whether or not you are worthy to pray for the recovery of the Holy Father by accepting his words. We can expect peace only if we really devote ourselves to peace. That doesn't mean peace in general. It means peace in our community — an end to brutality, an end to racism, an end to the hatreds that have divided us."

Then I asked the congregation to stand and sing the hymn, "Let There Be Peace on Earth." They were moved and sang with tremendous gusto. I had to confer Confirmation later that evening at St. Francis Xavier Church in Metairie, and I didn't get home until 10:30 p.m. I've always noticed those days which seem to exact an almost inhuman toll on you are the days when the Lord is really present. Sacrifice, it seems to me, is the necessary ingredient for success in the supernatural life. There simply is not in Christianity a victory without the cross. The cross must precede Easter. The sooner we learn that in the Christian world, then the more chance we'll have of really changing a world full of hate into a world full of love.

Catechism of the Catholic Church

Pope John Paul II also will be remembered through the ages for his foresight in compiling the critically important *Catechism of the Catholic Church*, an ambitious project that had been championed by Boston Cardinal Bernard Law. A new catechism was absolutely necessary, and I have to give Cardinal Law credit for his strong efforts in seeing the idea to fruition.

One of the real benefits of the old *Baltimore Catechism* was that it was condensed and gave direct, pithy answers that Catholics, even those with limited formal education, could memorize and learn. I had seen during World War II the effect of the *Baltimore Catechism* on our Catholic soldiers — they simply would not steal because they had learned from the catechism how wrong that would be. The *Baltimore Catechism* also made it easy to prepare students for first Holy Communion and for Confirmation, because the children were prepared to answer questions about their faith when posed by the bishop.

Vienna Cardinal Christoph Schönborn, who had the overall responsibility for producing the new catechism, came to New Orleans, and I took him to dinner and explained that as brilliantly designed as the *Catechism* was, I thought Catholics could really benefit from a shorter version that could give students a chance to memorize the most important elements. To this day I don't think enough has been done to produce a more concise version, but I still think it would be beneficial.

Pope John Paul II was brilliant because he understood what the faithful needed. He knew Pope Paul VI did not have the wide support of the people, and he was determined to bring that back. He knew as well as anyone that he had an abundance of charisma, and he decided to use that God-given quality to spread his teachings across the globe.

He was a personal Pope. He enjoyed people. He challenged people. He loved people.

I don't think the Holy Father got enough credit for his globetrotting style of evangelization. He was fearless in proclaiming the Gospel, even if it meant telling off a Latin American despot to his face. I will never forget the almost comical scene when Pope John Paul II made his historic visit to Cuba in 1998. At the last open-air Mass he celebrated in Cuba, the Pope drove through the throngs in his Popemobile, and right near the altar was a billboard-size portrait of revolutionary Che Guevara. Fidel Castro, a former Catholic, was seated in the front row in his general's fatigues. And then during his homily, the Holy Father unlimbered on Communism in a direct way that I had never heard before. It was all directed at Castro. The people, especially the young people, were enjoying the talk so much that they clapped, yelled, and carried on after almost every sentence. Finally, the Pope said, "Now wait a minute. You've got to stop all this applause because I've got something I want to tell you about." He was a master at becoming one with his audience.

One of the auxiliary bishops from Cuba was seated next to me, and I asked him what he thought about the Pope's pointed remarks toward Castro. "Look how miserable Castro is. I really enjoy looking at the face of that tyrant. This is great!" You could see that Castro was trying to remain implacable and immobile, but he must have been squirming inside! He had to be asking himself, "Who in the world ever gave me the advice to invite this guy?" He looked like he had swallowed a cigar.

As Pope John Paul II's physical infirmities became more apparent to the world, his shattered body became a prayer in itself. I will never forget when he visited the Holy Land and his aides had warned him that it would be impossible for him to access the Church of the Holy Sepulchre because he was so frail. But he managed to drag his body into the tight space, which almost everyone considered was a physical impossibility. On one of his final trips, using a cane, he walked slowly down the set of stairs that had been rolled up to the door of his jet. When he reached the ground, he raised his cane and then banged it into the ground as if to say, "Thank you, Lord, you did it!"

There may never again be a Pope like John Paul the Great. We were and continue to be blessed by his presence.

CHAPTER 22

A Few Final Thoughts

In August 1987, I visited Washington Archbishop Patrick O'Boyle, who, very ill, was being cared for by the Little Sisters of the Poor. Although close to death — and knowing it — he was in a very good mood. "I received calls this morning from two presidents," he happily announced, "our national president and the president of Catholic University."

Congratulating him, I noticed that he was struggling to recall something about the National Shrine of the Immaculate Conception, one of his great achievements and rightly a source of personal pride. But try as he might, Archbishop O'Boyle couldn't remember a thing. In the years after, I often replayed that moment in my mind. If the Cardinal had forgotten important memories surrounding one of the most satisfying moments in his life, what chance would I have to recollect the main events — albeit minor compared to his — of mine for those who might be interested.

As a result, approaching ninety years of age, I finally decided that it was high time I put my memories and thoughts down on paper before I no longer could. The result is this book which you have so kindly read to this point. However, being Irish, I not surprisingly still have a few more anecdotes, a couple more thoughts — many close to my heart — that I would like to add before my tale is finally told.

Hale and Lindy Boggs

I got to know Hale Boggs, a congressman from Louisiana, during my time as auxiliary bishop of Washington. Hale would come regularly to the Sunday morning Mass at St. Patrick Church, where I was pastor, and where Speaker of the House John McCormack, along with most of the Catholic congressional leadership, showed up, as well. Hale's wife Lindy meanwhile, staying home with the kids, attended a later Mass. The couple met, according to Lindy, at a Newcomb College dance in New Orleans. Hale broke in on Lindy's partner while they were dancing and before the night was over, Hale told Lindy he had decided he wanted to marry her! "I thought the guy was crazy," Lindy laughed. But he wasn't and after an appropriate courtship, the couple wed. Although Lindy was never a rough-and-tumble politician, she managed every one of Hale's campaigns, making her, in due course, as well known to Louisiana politicians as her husband.

By 1972, Hale was majority leader of the House of Representatives help- ing to push through most of President Johnson's Great Society legislation in the 1960s. But his sights were set higher — that is, to become Speaker of the House upon McCormack's retirement. After twelve terms, Hale's congres- sional seat was so safe he could spend the fall election period campaigning on behalf of other House Democrats in tight races. One such contest took him to Alaska where in October 1972 the twin-engine Cessna 310 in which he was traveling with Alaska Democrat Nick Begich disappeared during a flight from Anchorage to Juneau. (Though Begich was a sure winner, Hale was determined to show everyone that he would help any and all Democratic candidates.)

Immediately a massive thirty-nine-day search ensued during which I kept in daily touch with Lindy. Fed information from people in the oil and gas industry, I learned that though the pilot of the Cessna had a checkered past, nothing connecting his work history could be pinned to the crash, which didn't stop the spread of all kinds of other wild accusations. This was the time of Watergate, after all, and Hale was one of the leading Democrats harboring a special interest in seeing that President Nixon was investigated fully for his participation in the Watergate break-in. He was also an archenemy of FBI Director J. Edgar Hoover, who routinely tapped the private phone lines of just about every Democrat in Congress, compiling blackmail dossiers that might prove handy in the future. In fact, it was Hale who got up on the floor of the House and wagging his finger at the Director of the FBI, spat out: "I know what you're doing, J. Edgar Hoover!"

In the meantime, I was getting calls almost every day from psychics in California who claimed they knew what had happened to the plane. Lindy, beside herself and grasping at any straw, discounted nothing until I finally decided I needed to step in, telling her such reports were doing more harm than good since they got her so upset. Moreover, after checking them out, not a single tip had panned out. After awhile, Lindy understood, simply brushing them aside. In the end there was never proof that this was anything more than a tragic plane crash, the small Cessna apparently going down in seven hundred feet of water. Though oil men told me there was absolutely no sense in search- ing for either wreckage or bodies at that depth, Lindy refused to accept it, even going to Alaska to be close to search teams. Finally, thirty-nine days later, she reluctantly called off the search, and we began planning Hale's memorial ser- vice at St. Louis Cathedral.

On the day of the memorial Mass, Lindy asked me to stand at the receiving line and greet the mourners who turned out en masse (including Vice President Spiro Agnew sent by President Nixon to represent him). Following Mass, there was a reception at the Cabildo, where again Lindy asked that I stand next to her in the receiving line.

Though presumed dead, Hale won re-election for the thirteenth time. In 1973, Lindy won a special election to succeed her late husband, serving in Congress until 1991. Though she never spoke on the house floor, Lindy got things done, preferring to go through the committees where the real work was done anyway. A devout Catholic, she opposed abortion except in the case of rape or incest where exceptions could be made. Determined that men and women have equal rights when it came to bank loans, she passed legislation assuring just that. Whenever we needed help with any of our legislation, I always sought out Lindy who invariably made it happen.

One time Congressman Bob Livingston came to me asking a special favor. Though wanting Lindy's support on a bill, he didn't want to ask her directly. "Why?" I asked. "Because she'll talk and talk... start dropping that 'darling' stuff she likes to call everyone, and all of a sudden I'll give in." And, that's the way Lindy was. If she called you "darling" often enough, you felt ashamed not to be on her side.

After Lindy retired from Congress, Senator John Breaux approached President Clinton to put forward Lindy's name as the next ambassador to the Vatican. Lindy found out and called immediately, asking if the Vatican would have any objections to a woman serving as ambassador. I contacted the Apostolic Nuncio, who got in touch with Rome, and the word came back immediately that the Vatican would be delighted if she would accept the appointment. In short time, Lindy became the most popular ambassador to the Vatican, bar none, shaking hands and mingling with everyone, even if it meant staying up until midnight.

Insisting on attending every Vatican function to which she was invited, she was many times the only ambassador in the reserved section at St. Peter's Basilica. Any time the Holy See wanted an opinion about U.S. policy, Lindy dutifully delivered the requested information. In the end, Lindy Boggs was a treasure in her service to the people of Louisiana, the nation, and the Vatican. Even more importantly, she was a treasure as a friend.

Trip to Vietnam

In September 1978 I was asked by President Carter, the U.S. State Department, and Senator Edward Kennedy to join a delegation of Americans on a sensitive postwar visit to Vietnam. Thousands of Vietnamese refugees had

In August 1978, I (left) was part of an official U.S. delegation that visited Vietnam. I visited with Premier Pham Van Dong, right, to discuss the reunion of families. Also at the meeting was Dr. Jean Mayer, president of Tufts University, seated next to the premier. The premier gave lip service to the reunion efforts, although he did allow a few Vietnamese-American children to leave with me on the plane back to the United States

In 1978, I was able to bring home a Vietnamese-American child from Vietnam after I visited Vietnam on behalf of the U.S. government. She got tired of being with her mother on the plane ride home, so she ended up on my lap the entire time. She wouldn't leave me. How do you argue with a little girl? I don't know.

escaped their country and resettled in the United States, and our government was extremely interested in seeing if families could be reunited. We were getting official "promises" from the Communists in Vietnam that they would be willing to entertain permitting some family members still in Vietnam to immigrate to the United States to join their families in America.

I was chosen to go on the trip because the Archdiocese of New Orleans had accepted so many Vietnamese refugees, the first coming in 1975. I remember not having very high expectations for the trip. The Vietnamese priests in the archdiocese believed the Communist government would use the trip for political gain and would, at best, offer family reunification to a token few. Almost every Vietnamese parishioner I talked to said the trip would be useless.

Strangely enough, the president of Vietnam greeted us cordially. As the spokesman for the U.S. delegation, I pleaded with him to consider allowing as many Vietnamese citizens as possible to leave for the United States so that they could rejoin their relatives. He astonished me by agreeing with my premise, and he said the "natural law" supported what I had to say. He also said that as proof of his good will, he would allow a certain number of people to travel

Senator Edward Kennedy during a luncheon in Baton Rouge, Louisiana, before my trip to Vietnam in 1978

back with us to the United States on our plane. We returned with about thirty people.

I knew that this was all for public relations for the Vietnamese Communists, but even if we could reunite some families it would be worth it. One of the passengers on the return flight to freedom was a four-year-old girl who got it into her head that she had to sit on my lap for the entire flight home. Her mother relished this relief, but even though I begged her to keep her daughter, she couldn't restrain her from coming to me. Every once in awhile I needed a lap break, and I was delighted when she finally left. She and I became fast friends.

In Saigon I was allowed to celebrate Mass very early in the morning in a beautiful, gothic-style church built by the French. We had to celebrate Mass at 4:30 a.m. because the Communists ordered all the young children to attend indoctrination classes that began at 5:30 or 6:00 a.m. The Vietnamese Catholics simply moved up the starting time for Mass. Unbelievably, the church was crowded. The Notre Dame Basilica in Saigon was the only place where freedom of dress was permitted. Everywhere else the people had to wear the drab Communist outfits, but inside the church, there was a rainbow of colors displayed by the stylishly dressed congregation. I celebrated the Mass in Latin because that was the only language they had in their prayer books. After the Mass, piles of people descended upon me, and I was surprised by how well they spoke English. On a piece of paper, they wrote their names and the names of their relatives that they wished me to contact on my return just to let their families know they were okay.

The Communists held a sham conference for the American panel, and different people tried to answer questions about their country. I spoke up: "What do you do with all the people who disagree with you?" The moderator of the conference, a well-spoken graduate of a New York law school, got extremely testy. "Nobody disagrees with us," she said. "Those ideas that you Americans have are ridiculous. Everybody supports our system." This was a palpable lie because their premier agreed to discuss the demands of those who wished to leave. If, as the moderator suggested, there was universal "support" for that oppressive system, why would anyone want to leave?

At dinner one night I sat next to a Communist who was in charge of development for the southern part of the Republic of Vietnam. He got weary of all the official speeches and leaned over to me in a whisper: "If you and I could just get together and disregard all these dummies, I think we'd do a lot better in coming to an agreement. I know we absolutely need the United States for us to change our economic situation." I could hardly believe my ears, but I found out he had been drinking liberally, and his tongue had been loosened! He was the only Vietnamese person to speak any sense, and he was half-drunk. When I returned to the United States, I made a full report to the U.S. Congress.

1984 World's Fair

When New Orleans was chosen as the host of the 1984 World's Fair, I tried to make the Vatican Pavilion one of the can't-miss sites of the fair grounds. Enlisting Dominican Father Val McInnes, something of an expert on church art around the world, as my point person, I set out to convince the Archbishop of Turin to loan the Shroud of Turin to New Orleans for the fair. To get the ball rolling, I sent a request — and donation — to Cardinal Anastasio Ballestrero, telling him I would be coming to Turin to ask for a favor.

Undoubtedly, he knew what I had in mind. Cordially receiving Father McInnes and me, he volunteered to let us see the shroud. My pitch was that the shroud, the foremost relic in the Christian world, would be the perfect centerpiece for a Catholic pavilion at the World's Fair where millions would see it for the first time. "If you let me show it," I assured him, "you can do whatever you need to do. Come and stay with it around the clock if you like."

The Cardinal smiled, "If I were to touch that shroud," he said, "try to take it away from here, I'd be killed. The people would not hear of it. Period." So much for that idea.

Val, however, came up with a Plan B. In the Dominicans' major church in Rome — Santa Maria Sopra Minerva — was Michelangelo's famous statue of Christ the Redeemer. "I'm sure I can arrange to get you that for the fair," Val said. It sounded great to me. Knowing we needed government approval on something of this magnitude, I contacted the Italian president, Alessandro Ballestrero, a virulent anti-Catholic who agreed to let us borrow the statue. Taking every precaution, our treasure was to be wrapped with an abundance of caution as well, shipped transatlantically on a ship volunteered by the U.S. Navy.

The day that the statue was supposed to be moved from the church, Val was on the scene to make sure nothing went wrong. A large moving truck pulled up, and the driver handed Val a note. It was a message from the president of Italy rescinding his approval for the removal of the statue. Naturally, I put up a big squawk, but no matter how much I complained, we couldn't get that politician to change his mind. Hating both the Catholic Church and the United States, this was the perfect opportunity for him to tweak both of our noses.

Finally, the Holy See came to our rescue, making available to us some exquisite tapestries from the Vatican Museum. Happily, no one found out about our two earlier failures. As I learned as a child, you can't get something unless you ask and, in the end, the only thing we lost was the $30,000 we ponied up for boxing the statue.

Politicians, whether foreign or domestic, can be odious. My only consolation was that Alessandro Ballestrero got kicked out of office in the next election.

Sexual Abuse

To a man, the bishops of the United States got terrible advice when it came to reacting to the sexual abuse of minors by priests. The confusion began in the 1950s and 1960s when psychiatrists told the bishops that pedophilia could be treated and cured. As a result, these clergy spent hundreds of thousands of dollars on treatment that wasn't worth a plugged nickel, ultimately resulting in a myriad of children and families suffering unspeakable harm. Though the psychiatric world was certainly at fault, the blame ultimately lays with those bishops who relied on their advice.

Without offering excuses, let me explain how bankrupt professional advice was in those days. In New Orleans, hoping to be proactive, I brought in some so-called expert to hold a workshop for our priests. However, in talking with him before his presentation, I discovered that I had more experience dealing with abuse than he. And, yet, here we were, paying him to tell us what to do. Even before I came to New Orleans, I learned that pedophilia, for all practical purposes, is not curable. Even a man of God cannot be changed, no matter where you send him. At one point, the provincial of a religious community came to me asking that I help sue the psychiatrist who had assured him that pedophile priests could be rehabilitated. Guaranteeing positive results, they had lied. One priest, he recounted, having been given a clean bill of mental health, re-offended just two weeks later.

Quibbling over whether this predilection is innate or acquired is a waste of energy. The point is you have to deal with it. One afternoon in Washington, an old family doctor who took special interest in the subject of child abuse came to see Archbishop O'Boyle. "I'm hearing a lot of baloney from psychiatrists," he said, "about how this can be cured. But let me tell you something. I'm an old guy who has seen a lot of cases, and not one person ever got cured. Just take it for granted that once a pedophile, always a pedophile. Otherwise, you're a fool."

Consequently, when I came to New Orleans, I harbored no false assumptions about how to handle this problem. In one instance, a priest got in trouble, eventually leaving the priesthood. A few years later I found out that this same man met a bishop in the Midwest who was going to accept him into the diocese. Alarmed, I called the bishop, telling him directly that there was no way in the world this man could be, or had been, cured. His case was hopeless. Believing me, the bishop didn't give him an assignment. Doing something like that is hard, since people will badger you and try to sue. Bishops need priests. But you must follow your conscience. Whenever a bishop did not want to hear what I had to say on the matter, I cut to the chase: "I demand that you let me talk to your lawyer."

If I heard of a priest with this problem, meanwhile, I immediately called him in and said, "I don't think you understand how you got this way, but you have an absolutely intolerable and incurable difficulty. I can't be a bishop and appoint men whom I know can't take care of the people." According to canon law, bishops can suspend a priest's faculties for a certain length of time though not indefinitely. However, if a priest has committed these perverted acts, I'm not going to put him in a position where he is in charge of souls. Instead, I'll simply suspend him, and that's it. I would try to get him a job, but definitely not as a priest.

The case that I am most familiar with — garnering an abundance of unwanted negative publicity — involved a priest named Dino Cinel. Born in Italy, he was considered something of an expert in the immigration history of Italians to the United States, having written an award-winning book entitled *From Italy to San Francisco* outlining the history of Italians in that city. In the 1980s, Cinel moved to New Orleans to join the history faculty at Tulane University. Having taught a similar subject in California, he was highly regarded in academic circles. Before his arrival, Tulane got in touch to ask if I might continue my normal practice of assigning a priest into residence at a parish located near its uptown campus. Thinking that St. Rita pastor Monsignor Wegmann, up in years, could be relieved of celebrating some of his Masses, Cinel took up residence in the St. Rita rectory.

Neither Monsignor Wegmann, as conservative as they come, nor I, of course, had any inkling of the kind of evil lurking in this man's background. Per canon law, I wrote to the bishop in the California diocese where Cinel had taught, receiving back a glowing review. Reportedly, Cinel, a good priest in every way, was especially excellent with young people. The reality, we sadly came to find out, was the exact opposite. Granting permission for him to reside at St. Rita, he chose a room on the top floor of the rectory which, accessed via a rear staircase, allowed him to come and go without being seen by anyone in the main part of the rectory.

Nothing seemed amiss until December of 1988 when Cinel left for Italy to give a lecture. Dropped off by his future wife at the airport, she inadvertently locked the keys in the car. Calling St. Rita rectory, she asked if someone could look for an extra set of keys in his room. Obligingly, Father James Tarantino went upstairs where, searching through his desk drawers, he discovered, much to his horror, a huge cache of child pornography — pictures, magazines, and videos. When Father Tarantino informed me of this, I immediately called Cinel in Italy. "Look," I said, "having found this material in your possession, your position here is finished. You will not serve as a priest in this archdiocese or any place else in the United States. You should stay in Italy, because you're not coming back here."

Cinel's response was astounding: How dare we search his room! Clearly I had made a deal with Father Tarantino. How could anyone take the word of this man over mine?

When news got out about the pornographic materials in Cinel's room, I was accused of undercutting justice. In fact, one of the few who came to my defense was Jefferson Parish Sheriff Harry Lee. "You did exactly the right thing," he told me. "You don't want to have those people around here."

Of course, this was red meat for *The Times-Picayune*, who printed a story that I had offered Cinel a "deal" to stay in Italy so everything would be kept quiet. It was an absolute lie. I made no deal. Cinel was the liar, not I. Nevertheless, the *The Times-Picayune* would not back down. Counterpunching, I protested so vociferously to publisher Ashton Phelps that the paper finally sent a reporter to get my side of the story. For starters, I was not responsible for bringing Cinel to New Orleans. He had been contacted by Tulane University who gave him a teaching contract. We simply gave him a place to live, as we would any priest in good standing. The man had absolutely no shame. Eventually, after interminable controversy, Cinel, dismissed by Tulane, left the priesthood, married, and moved to New York.

In the final analysis, the sexual abuse of children by members of the clergy is a sin and a scandal. I pray every day for those who have been so harmed... their lives forever damaged by such revolting crimes.

"The Exorcist"

The Exorcist, the 1973 movie based on William Peter Blatty's novel, details the painful process of an exorcism of a twelve-year-old girl demonically possessed by the devil. The real story, however, on which the book was based, involved a thirteen-year-old boy who was living in Mount Rainier, Maryland, a Washington, D.C. suburb. Although the boy was raised in the Protestant faith, the lengthy exorcism process eventually led him to the Catholic Church, which, of course, was of special interest to the Archdiocese of Washington.

In 1949, the boy began suffering severe tribulations from the devil, who among other terrors, moved his bed across the floor at night. Fearful, his parents approached their minister, who came to their house and said prayers, albeit to no avail. The boy's situation merely worsened as marks akin to cigarette burns began to appear on his skin. Not knowing where to turn, his harried parents sought out a Catholic relative who suggested they approach the Catholic Church to undergo a formal ritual of exorcism.

The call came into the Washington chancery from a Catholic priest, who had been told that only Archbishop Patrick O'Boyle would authorize an exorcism. After listening to the story, the Archbishop told him, "I'm willing to do this, but on the condition that the boy first be examined by some of the psychiatrists at Georgetown University Hospital." Subsequently, undergoing psychiatric evaluation, the doctors reported that he was indeed perfectly normal and not imagining things.

Armed with medical verification, Archbishop O'Boyle appointed an old Jesuit to conduct the exorcism ritual — that is, special exorcism prayers that can be said only by a priest authorized by a bishop.

In the meantime, the boy's parents ever more desperate, thought that moving him to St. Louis, where the family had relatives, would not only keep the devil away, but give their son a better chance at recovery. But neither worked. Eventually, the old Jesuit priest suggested that the boy be admitted to a hospital run by a religious congregation, figuring that if the devil persisted in tormenting the child — sparking him to violent behavior — at least he would be monitored and helped medically.

As it turned out, he needed medical treatment. At times the boy got so violent that it took four Brothers to control and keep him fastened to his bed. In his quiet moments, the boy, after much reflection, decided that he wanted to become a Roman Catholic and began taking catechism lessons to learn about the faith even while the devil continued to besiege him night and day. Even when the Jesuit priest finally baptized him, the devil refused to relent. Deciding that the boy should receive his First Holy Communion on Easter Sunday, the priest presented the Host himself, whereupon the boy's violent torments ratcheted up yet another level. Nevertheless, the young man persisted and wore the devil down. Lashing out with one final act of body shaking defiance in his victim, the devil finally acquiesced, spitting at both boy and priest: "I'm leaving, and I'm not going to come back."

Subsequently, as required by the Church anytime an exorcism is performed, the Jesuit recorded every detail in an official journal of the Church which is kept in a secret file in the Archdiocese of Washington.

Freed from the devil, the boy tried to live a normal life. For his part, Archbishop O'Boyle, out of respect for the family, made it very clear that not one word was to be mentioned to the press. Eventually, however, word leaked out and the press, tracking down the boy's family, began reporting the story. In the end, it was a tough one to keep under wraps because the boy let things slip to his classmates. When they asked about his "trouble," he would tell the truth. Adding to his candor, the Jesuits, unfortunately, also decided to answer journalists' questions, and the floodgates opened.

The result was a book — *The Exorcist* — followed by the disturbing film seen by millions. Though the Archdiocese of Washington refused to cooperate either with the news media or movie producers, the Jesuits did. From my point of view, it should have remained a private matter. Eventually, the boy married and changed his name in order to live a normal life. The last time I heard from him, he was living in Virginia and was married with four children. Though he completely straightened out, his demonic possession continues to be a mystery. (In the Archdiocese of New Orleans, no clear-cut case of demonic possession was ever reported to me. Nevertheless, I authorized Father Denzil Perrera to perform the exorcism prayers, as well as heeding the wise counsel of Archbishop O'Boyle. If someone appears to be possessed, say a Mass for them first, followed by a psychiatric evaluation.)

Pope Benedict XVI

I first learned of Pope Benedict XVI when he was serving as the *peritus* — or theological expert — for Cardinal Josef Frings of Cologne during the Second Vatican Council. We met again during his 2008 visit to the United States where I had a brief audience with him in Washington, D.C. The purpose of my visit was to give him a donation to help defray the costs of the Catholic-Muslim dialogue currently underway at the Vatican. Moreover, I told him I'd be willing to launch a foundation whose mission it would be to find continued funding for this badly needed exchange. Accompanying me was New Orleans businessman Joseph Canizaro who presented the Holy Father with a check for

Me, Mr. Joseph Canizaro, Most Reverend Petro Sambi (Apostolic Nuncio to the United States), and Pope Benedict XVI during the Pope's 2008 visit to the United States. Mr. Canizaro had just presented a check for one million dollars to the Pope in his effort to aid in the construction of adoration chapels

$1 million to promote eucharistic adoration around the world. Needless to say, the Pope immediately brightened up.

A conversation with Muslim scholars is essential for the Church as we hold many things in common: a belief in one Almighty God who not only loves all people but told us to love one another. Moreover, I sincerely hope that Pope Benedict XVI will be able to follow up on Pope John Paul II's lead and visit New Orleans. Renewal since Hurricane Katrina has been steady, and his visit would give the entire area a much needed morale and financial boost. Symbolically speaking, Pope Benedict's presence would reinforce the message that when human beings are in crisis, the Church is there with them.

The Power of the Priesthood

I always tell seminarians and priests that as long as they wear the Roman collar, they have a chance at doing some good. Once time, in an Atlanta airport, my connecting flight delayed for two hours, I pulled out my breviary. Observing this, a member of the New Orleans Baptist Theological Seminary came over and said: "We're counting on you to get us through safely." "Well, then I'll be sure to include you in my breviary," I replied, "because, after all, we're all going to be on the same plane."

As indeed we are in life as well — fellow flyers, seatmates thrown randomly together for this most human and spiritual of flights. Just as you would instinctively reach out to pull a drowning child from a pool, so should we be prepared at any moment to reach out and help any co-traveler in need — as I was reminded later in the same Atlanta airport.

Walking toward my gate, I noticed a handsome, if distraught, young man barely old enough to be out of college. His frazzled demeanor shouted out that he was in some kind of trouble. Stopping, I asked if I could help. Immediately, he spat out his story. He was going to be indicted, following a friend already in jail for embezzlement. He wanted to go to Confession but having been so many years since he had, he barely remembered how. So we more or less did it on the spot. What he needed was to be straightened out… a good talking to, which I gave him.

Had this young man not recognized that I was a priest, seen my collar, we probably wouldn't have spoken. But seeing my collar, he came right over to me and made his Confession. Afterwards, I sent him away with a settled mind and the instructions that he had to straighten out his life. "You have a long life ahead of you, as well as parents of wealth and great understanding," I counseled, "you need to use the talents God has given you." He took it well.

Priests, in particular, must always stand firm in the belief that the priesthood, above all else, is service and sacrifice. When they start seeing a vocation as a service to themselves, they get off track. Though the Second Vatican Council declared that priests are to be coworkers with the bishops in serving the faithful, it is never to be forgotten that a coworker is also a *worker*! Whatever it takes to get the job done — often many jobs simultaneously — is what you have to do. Following Vatican II, the scales of the priesthood got tipped from not enough freedom to too much freedom. The system of rigid institutional discipline gave way to self-discipline — or lack of it, frequently resulting in unhappiness. One of the toughest problems I ever have to deal with is when a priest comes to me asking for a leave of absence, a dispensation from his vows so as to no longer be called a priest. In my experience, whenever a priest wanders from the path of dedication to his vocation, he invariably will veer off in the wildest possible ways — like a star or planet which, not staying its course around the sun, gets off track to cause destruction.

My long life as a priest has overflowed with an abundance of joy and wonder at the power of Almighty God — most particularly in everyday living. One day after Mass, a woman around fifty approached me. "You don't remember me," she said. "No, I really don't." Beside her, stood a girl of about twenty-two, her daughter who spoke slowly and walked haltingly as if she had polio. Nevertheless, she was obviously very intelligent. The mother continued. "You don't remember, but many years ago, you blessed my daughter who had a tumor on her brain. The doctors had given up on her completely, saying there was nothing they could do to save her. But you gave her a blessing, and here she is today, walking around!" It was a remarkable — humbling — story, reminding me yet again of the potential power of the priesthood in every transaction. In the midst of a day's turmoil, that conversation provided complete consolation.

In the final analysis, however, there is no one more important, or connected to Catholicism at its core, than those who serve on its front lines: the parish priest. Indeed, whenever I attend or see the inspiring *Urbi et Orbi* blessing of the Pope (to the city of Rome and world) I am again piercingly reminded of the contribution of these truly religious warriors. Delivered from the balcony of St. Peter's Basilica on important occasions, most particularly after the new Pope's election as Supreme Pontiff, His Holiness bestows this special blessing on an audience usually stretching from the courtyard of the Basilica through the Piazza and along the Via della Conciliazione (Street of the Conciliation) to the Tiber River. Crowds for the *Urbi et Orbi* blessing frequently number two hundred fifty thousand fervent people.

Though the glory of the occasion is the presence and blessing of the Holy Father, the faith of each person standing there is the work of the humble parish priest. Without his efforts and dedication, neither the streets of Rome nor the local cathedral would be filled with true believers in the Holy Trinity. For him we give our heartfelt thanks to God — Amen. Amen. Amen!

"Priests are in the Heaven Business," as my cousin Nancy Collins once put it. "What is it? Where is it? And how do you get there?" She's got a point. And having devoted years to the subject, you would think that by now I would be able to offer a precise, surefire answer on what to do down here to make it up there. Yet, even for priests, at least speaking for myself, this hopefully ultimate destination for all souls remains at times as intangible and mysterious as it does to those who haven't made it a lifetime, full-time study.

Having presided over thousands of deathbeds and funerals, it stands to reason that I might be uniquely qualified to offer a recipe guaranteed to get you to the Lord's Table. Yet, at ninety-seven, faced ever more personally with the question and reality of heaven, the only ingredient I know to be absolutely necessary is faith.

The road to heaven begins — and ends — with faith in God from whom all blessings, wisdom, tolerance, joy, and forgiveness have always — and will ever — flow. Consequently, I have come to believe that only when we actually get to heaven will we truly understand what we accomplished here on earth — especially when it concerns the priesthood. From my perspective, a priest — I will accomplish in death what I could not in life because as priests we are most fully alive when we die. If we don't feel that way, we certainly have not served the cause of Christ as we were meant to. In the final spiritual analysis, to fulfill the will of Christ, a priest must die in life as did his own Son. And when that time comes, with the grace of God, I am ready.

Recollections of the
Major Documents of Vatican II

Constitution on the Sacred Liturgy, *Sacrosanctum Concilium* (1963)

The Council discussed the Liturgy first because there were no general objections to it, but its paramount importance made the discussion the longest of any subject. Changes in the language of the Mass, the Sacraments and devotions were the central matters of discussion. Unfortunately, few realized that the first great change in the language of the Church, from Greek to Latin in the areas where Latin predominated in the third century, precipitated a momentous reaction and occasioned the election of an anti-Pope, Hippolytus, leader of the group favoring Greek. Later, he was reconciled and today is venerated as a martyr.

There were zealots on both sides of celebrating Mass in the vernacular, but many proponents were not in favor of using it for the whole Mass. I believe a majority of the American bishops favored using the vernacular for the section called the Liturgy of the Word and the Penitential Rite. Cardinal Spellman led those opposing any change. He cited, as an argument, the experience of many who traveled often and rejoiced in the unifying effect of the Mass celebrated in Latin. Many Europeans agreed, as well as many students of Latin.

I finally favored the use of the vernacular in the whole Mass, although I would have been satisfied with a reasonable compromise. There was no organized group of the "partial use" of the vernacular, but there was a tightly organized and vociferous group in the U.S. meetings advocating the total use of the vernacular. Atlanta Archbishop Hallinan was the chief U.S. proponent of the vernacular, and his constant cry was, "We believe that Latin is not the only language that God understands." That jibe always got a laugh, and humor is effective. For me, a decisive group in the vernacular discussion was the missionary bishops, who almost universally favored and demanded the use of the native tongue. Many of us felt very uneasy about opposing a measure that would help missionary work.

Eventually, the vernacular for the Mass, Sacraments, and devotions of the Church was approved. The final version of the section on the Liturgy is a balanced and reasonable document worthy of its sacred subject. Nobody should argue about it without reading it.

The Constitution, divided into seven chapters, makes it clear that the Sacred Liturgy is "sacred action surpassing all others" and "the summit towards which the activity of the Church is directed … the fountain from which all her power flows." It warns against innovations "unless the good of the Church genuinely and certainly requires them." To me, the key norm is Number 36: "Particular laws remaining in force, the use of the Latin language is to be preserved in the Latin Rite. But since the use of a mother tongue, whether in the Mass, the administration of the Sacraments, or other parts of the Liturgy, may frequently be of great advantage to the people, the limits of its employment may be extended."

In assessing the changes in the Liturgy by the Council, we must remember the Council's basic purpose. In convoking the Council, Pope John XXIII cited the need to confront a massive world crisis. He summoned the Catholic world to a renewal of faith — beginning with the changes in the Liturgy. Later the advocates of the "spirit of the Council" aimed at reform of the faith. Of course, we did not foresee the complications affecting the decisions of the Council — even in regard to the Liturgy — by the epochal change in society. We believed that the decisions of the Council would be implemented without any great influence by the prevailing morality of society. We were too optimistic. It is obvious, in the infallibility of hindsight, that more time should have been allotted for consulting with parish priests on the impact of the changes and for instructing the faithful.

There was a forlorn attempt made before the end of the Council to consult priests. To my knowledge, four priests from the United States were chosen and brought to Rome for consultation. One of them, Monsignor Gerard Frey, was from the Archdiocese of New Orleans, an excellent pastor and highly regarded by priests and his parishioners. When I met him, after the Council, in New Orleans, I asked him about their activity. He replied, "Well, they brought us to Rome, told us what they had in mind, but never had a meeting with us." Baffled, I said, "Didn't they ask your group to give an opinion about the pending changes?" "No," Monsignor Frey replied, "we didn't have a meeting about that at all." The pastors could have added valuable insight on the mentality of the people, and that would have helped us implement the changes.

Cardinal Cicognani, the former Apostolic Delegate to the United States, provided an insight into why the pastors may not have been asked their opinions. Many in the Roman Curia simply didn't want more changes, which would require more drawn-out consultations. He told me once during the Council, "Why don't you all go home and let us run this Church?"

The reaction to the changes in the Mass and other Sacraments was a major event in the Church in the United States. Remember, the document on the Liturgy was finished and promulgated by Pope Paul VI on December 3, 1963, just before the end of the second session of the Council. Of course, some time was allotted for explaining the "new Mass" and other sections of the Constitution before its use, but this was major change. The strife created in the third century over the change from Greek to Latin should have been a cautionary tale.

I was proud of our clergy and people for their comparatively easy acceptance of the Liturgy, especially of the Mass. The strength of their faith and stalwart obedience rallied their support. The priests, despite varied opinions, loyally and gracefully studied and accepted the changes, including "Communion in the hand" and "Communion under both species." Thank God, I often thought, for the "old-time" laity and priests.

Of course, this general and wholehearted acceptance of the changes did not mean there were no complaints, vehement at times. But the criticisms were balanced by very enthusiastic support.

The comments varied depending on the group:

- "Can't you get us older priests a dispensation to continue to use the Latin Mass? I've been saying Mass in Latin for forty-seven years. Why can't we older priests continue to say Mass in Latin? It's fine for the younger priests and people."
- "I think it's wonderful to have the Mass in English. We can all understand it, and my fifteen-year-old daughter is thrilled. Crowds of people will now want to hear Mass."
- "I don't like the idea of saying Mass in English. For years we've learned to follow it in our Missals. Why do you bishops think we're so dumb that we need it in English?"

Moving the Blessed Sacrament from the tabernacle at the main altar also created a firestorm. "We were taught to make a visit to the Blessed Sacrament," one man told me. "We taught our children to do the same. Now they can't find it."

Those favoring the changes were rhapsodic: "Now you'll see all those empty pews in the church filled at the Masses."

Unfortunately, the prediction that Mass in English would bring many more people to church was way off target. It was the greatest surprise — or disappointment — to find that it emptied many pews in our churches.

During this long discussion on the Liturgy, I often thought of Bishop John Carroll, the first American bishop (1789 to 1815), who advocated the use of the vernacular in the fledgling United States "because very few here understand Latin. But I won't suggest it unless the Holy See agrees." The Holy

See did not agree, any more than it did during the Council of Trent (1545 to 1563), when an effort was made to discuss it.

There was never any mention made during the Vatican II discussions about changing the Mass approved at Trent. Some of the repetitions in the Roman Mass could have been omitted, as I think Cardinal Alfons Stickler, a member of the Committee that submitted the text of the document, later suggested. I also wish to state very firmly that the English translation of the text of the Latin Mass was not submitted for discussion by Rome. The Committee to implement *Sacramentum Concilium*, under the direction of Monsignor Annibale Bugnini, later made an archbishop by Pope Paul VI, submitted the translation, which was finally approved by the Pope.

On two specific points, there was no discussion among U.S. bishops about omitting the phrase *mysterium fidei* from the words of consecration nor any approval of the translation of the words *pro multis* in the consecration as "for all" instead of "for many." These translations or omissions were and are decried strongly, but the validity of the Mass is not questioned. Bugnini was head of the Vatican commission that produced the *Novus Ordo* Mass, which moved the words *mysterium fidei* ("the mystery of faith") away from the actual consecration.

Of course, the texts of several new Eucharistic Prayers also were not voted on by the Council. They were approved *motu proprio* by Paul VI. Although they have brought benefits, the timing of their introduction is questionable. It suggested to many that change in practically everything in the Church was debatable and possible.

For me, one of the greatest surprises — and one of the mysteries of evil — was the marked decline of respect and devotion to the inexpressible Presence of Jesus Christ in the Holy Eucharist following the Council. Along with many bishops, I smugly thought the use of the vernacular would increase attendance at Mass and other Eucharistic devotions. We did not realize the growth of the deadly "*spirit* of the Council," which gave every Catholic the "right" to shape his or her conscience despite the teaching of the Church.

One element of this "spirit" was the development of the idea the Church was to become more "horizontal" and less "vertical" in its thinking and teaching. This meant less "vertical" respect and devotion to God and his Church and more "horizontal," or community-thinking, regarding the ideas and convictions of all people, no matter how weird. Ecumenism was stretched beyond any limits, and the preaching of the Gospel and the doctrine of the Church, as well as making converts, was diminished. This certainly was not what John XXIII had intended.

There was less rigorous deliberation about being in the state of grace, and almost everybody in the Church at Mass received Holy Communion, many without thinking enough about going to Confession. Despite the rampant evils such as abortion, drugs, premarital sex, sex outside of marriage, and gay "marriage," there were more people presenting themselves for Communion despite never having received sacramental absolution. I remember a flight attendant telling me after a flight that she had upbraided a priest in Confession, who told her she had to develop a right conscience about some of the sins she committed and confessed. She replied, "You're wrong. Making my conscience is my own business, not the priest's."

In addition to this autonomous "right to conscience," another false development was the feeling that everything was open for change. This spiritual barnacle apparently grew because the Council had approved many changes. At St. Patrick's Church in downtown Washington, we offered confessions either for the convenience of the hordes of shoppers or those who didn't wish to go to Confession to their local parish priest. We normally had long lines of penitents waiting outside four confessionals on Saturday from one-thirty in the afternoon to six o'clock and then in the evening from seven to nine. The number of confessions drastically declined after the Council.

The diminished use of the Sacrament of Reconciliation also has led to a decline in respect for the Holy Eucharist at Mass. This decline contributed to the occasional but abominable cases of impiety and possible desecration in the celebration of Mass. I learned from a layperson who attended such a Mass performed on a beach near Rome by a priest in beach attire, with a congregation of beach-attired persons using a soft drink cup for a chalice. Thank God, those days are over.

A lessening of respect for the Eucharist has led to diminished respect for the sacred character of the Church — wearing almost beach attire in summer and spending almost no time after Mass in thanksgiving. The loud talking inside the church leads to a general casual attitude that one expects only in a meeting hall, not the church. The church is the house of God, a place for worship and prayer.

This decline in respect for the Holy Eucharist has, of course, caused or contributed to a neglect of the Eucharistic devotions — Benediction of the Blessed Sacrament, Forty Hours Devotion, and other devotions. Paul VI made a futile attempt to halt this development by attending a National Italian Eucharistic Congress shortly after his election.

When the law of abstaining from meat on all Fridays changed in 1966 — shortly after the final session of Vatican II — I don't think we truly realized how sacrosanct that centuries-old tradition of penance had been. When that rule was relaxed, a lot of regular Catholics obviously said to themselves, "Maybe we ought to do a little more thinking on our own." The new law actually said that while the particular form of penance — abstaining from meat on all Fridays — was no longer obligatory except during Lent, Catholics who do decide to eat meat on Fridays should find some other penitential act to perform, because we are all obliged to do penance. Did people take that seriously? Not at all. The by-product of this was the thinking, "If this can change, anything can change." It became almost a law of laxity, and there was no way to reverse field once it was allowed.

The fallout from the elimination of obligatory abstinence got almost comical. A pastor called me one day and said his cook would not prepare anything but fish for him to eat on Friday, even though he insisted to her that the rule had changed. He handed the phone to the cook so she could talk to me. I tried to tell her what the Pope had decided, but she was so shocked by my explanation that she said, "Well, the Pope didn't tell *me* that, so I'm still going to give him fish!"

My big regret about the liturgical changes called for by Vatican II is that we did not specify more precisely certain things that should be maintained. I definitely feel the words of consecration should have remained in Latin. To this day, the Latin reverberates in my mind when the bread and wine is transformed into the Body and Blood of Christ. Gregorian chant and the Kyrie Eleison were also integral parts of the Mass. It's no secret Pope Benedict is trying to encourage the use of Latin in the Mass.

The efforts of Paul VI and John Paul II, with strong cooperation of clergy and especially the laity, have gone a long way in correcting the situation. The consecration of Jubilee Year 2000 to the Eucharist by John Paul II ignited a sacred fire. I love especially his words: "The worship of the Eucharist outside of Mass is of inestimable worth for the life of the Church.... It is the responsibility of pastors to encourage, also by their personal witness, the practice of Eucharistic adoration and exposition of the Blessed Sacrament in particular as well as prayer of adoration before Christ present under the Eucharistic species." There has been a marvelous growth of adoration of the Blessed Sacrament in chapels for adoration, devotion to the Benediction of the Blessed Sacrament, and the solemn celebration of Corpus Christi.

The liturgical changes engendered by the Council have taught us a great deal about the depth of devotion and piety in the psyche of man. The resistance to changing the language — from Latin to the vernacular — was more than a resistance to changing a long custom. The failure of this change in language to increase Mass attendance was another surprise, at least to me. The Latin Mass produced far more than cozy feelings of unity within a congregation of multiple cultures and languages. Frankly, I always felt the long list of remembrances of saints from the earliest apostolic years was a good part of the popular appeal of the old "Roman" Mass.

There is a greater depth and complexity than we have thought to the concept we call religious feeling or piety. Deep in the human soul there is a faculty or capacity to commune with God that goes beyond the power of language or custom. We are temples of the Holy Spirit, created by the unfathomable grace of God and fortunately responding to that grace by the countless means implanted in us by an omnipotent God. The saints, in their meditations and ecstasies, have shown us that truth.

I still believe we made the right decision in the Council concerning the vernacular in the Mass, but we have learned a great deal more about the nature of religion and piety from the results of that change.

At the end of the first session, John XXIII gave a paternal talk, thanking the members for their work, saying it was a good beginning that the "divergent views" were signs of a "holy liberty" and asking us to study diligently for the next session.

The discussion about the Liturgy extended beyond the first session in 1962. When we returned home in December, we met a baffled audience. They wanted to know why we didn't finish the discussion on the Liturgy and why we didn't get more done. Frankly, I think even the patient Pope John XXIII had some of those same feelings, and to show that we had achieved something he announced the additional invocation of St. Joseph to be added to those in the Divine Praises in Benediction, "Blessed be St. Joseph, chaste spouse of the Blessed Mother." Naturally, Archbishop O'Boyle directed the complaints and questions from the frustrated laity to me. I was hard pressed to satisfy them.

Another and more favorable reaction of the people happened at the end of the first session. The fathers of the Council became popular. Catholics considered us partly heroic because we were pioneers of a new Church, deliberating major changes. Many Protestants were surprised, somewhat shocked that the old, hide-bound Catholic Church was becoming so new and vital. Meanwhile, some writers began to hail this time as "the century of the Church."

It was obvious the American public had great interest in the Council. In turn, this nudged us bishops to become more active in developing and presenting our ideas at the Council. Also, lay Catholics became more involved. "Bishop, a group of Catholics and I want to see you about a good idea we have for the Council," one man told me after Mass at St. Patrick's. "We've really thought about this."

The Constitution on the Sacred Liturgy finally passed with an overwhelming majority of 2,147 in favor to four against, and it was promulgated by Paul VI on December 4, 1963. The landslide was attributed to the remarks made by some of the outstanding "elders" in the hierarchy. Cardinal Eugène Tisserant, Dean of the College of Cardinals, stated laconically and decisively that there had been changes in the language of the Mass ever since Sts. Cyril and Methodius, Apostles of the Slavic people, converted the Slavs in the eleventh century, using the Slavic language in the Liturgy.

Paul VI instructed that seminaries begin to implement the Constitution on the First Sunday of Lent, February 16, 1964. The date for the implementation of the Constitution of the Liturgy in parishes was set for September 26,

1964. In many parishes, this ignited the pent-up enthusiasm for the changes, often long before the required diocesan commissions to guide the implementation had been set up, including one for Sacred Music and one for Sacred Art.

In music, the guitar took over — despite the rule that the pipe organ was to be held in "high esteem" and other instruments were to be used "on condition that the instruments can be made suitable for sacred use." It also stipulated that Gregorian Chant should be given "pride of place" in the Latin Rite. In addition, the musical tradition in mission lands was to be recognized, and a suitable place was to be given it. The interpretation was unbelievable. My good friend, Monsignor Pete Rakowski, pastor of Mount Calvary Parish in Forestville, Maryland, asked for permission to celebrate a "Zulu" Mass. "Monsignor Pete," I asked, "How many Zulus do you have in Forestville?" "We just want to see what it's like," he said.

Archbishop O'Boyle took over decisions about the construction of new churches. A literal interpretation was made of the instruction that "great care be taken that they be suitable for the celebration of liturgical services and for the active participation of the faithful." No weird ideas were permitted, as happened in Berlin, where the good Cardinal Julius Döpfner, a classmate at the Gregorian University, determined to be more "modern" than the occupying Communists. The crucifixes in some of the new Berlin churches had the corpus (body) dangling from the wood. Some of my American friends, visiting Berlin, were so repelled they couldn't attend Mass in any of the new churches.

Dogmatic Constitution on the Church, *Lumen Gentium* (1964)

The discussion on the most important document of the Council, the Dogmatic Constitution of the Church (*Lumen Gentium*), began on October 17, 1963, and evolved into an historic evaluation of the position of the laity in the Church. Vatican II is the only Council in the history of the Church to set forth the layperson's rights and duties.

The young, charismatic archbishop of Krakow, Poland, Karol Wojtyla, was one of the first to suggest that the document use the image of the "People of God" in describing the Church. He also demanded a full response by the laity to their position in the Church. "The laity do not fulfill their duties as members of the people of God by being satisfied with the mere possession of the faith," the future Pope John Paul II said. Emphasizing the laity and not the hierarchy of the Church was a revolution, discarding the usual framework in defining the Church.

Archbishop Wojtyla's spark lit a flame. Archbishop Adam Kozlowiecki of Lusaka, Zambia, also of Slavic descent, said, "We (bishops) are not sufficiently aware of the limits of our power.... We speak too administratively of our relations with the laity. Not everything depends upon us bishops; many things depend upon the laity."

Archbishop Denis Hurley of Durban, South Africa, an ardent foe of apartheid, said, "Let us proclaim that the role of the Church is to form the consciences of the faithful, and let us trust the laity." The Melkite Bishop, Georges Hakim, Archbishop Maximos V, objected that there was no reference to women in the *schema*. "It is as though they did not exist and yet they are the first battalion (*primum agmen*) of humanity."

The one hundred forty-seven U.S. bishops were largely in accord with this thinking. Citing particular aspects of this approach, Baton Rouge Bishop Robert E. Tracy, speaking for the American prelates, asked that there be a solemn declaration against racism. I remember Bishop Tracy was searching for the right Latin word for "racism," and a priest suggested "*stirps*" (lineage). That word got put into the final document. The assembly of French Bishops, referring to another aspect of the "People of God," asked the leaders of the Young Christian Workers to address them.

Some bishops objected to certain words in the *schema*. Auxiliary Bishop Thomas Muldoon of Sydney, Australia, said the word "laity" was a harmful expression and pleaded that the words "People of God" be used in its place. Bishop William Philbin of the Down and Connor Diocese in Ireland objected to references to the word "world" as if it "were all evil" although it is the place "where our good people live."

It was generally believed that the primary focus of the Dogmatic Constitution was to be on the position of bishops, the ordinaries of dioceses, in relationship to the pope. Catholic magazines stated repeatedly before the Council that while Vatican Council I defined the authority of the successor of St. Peter (Vatican I was terminated abruptly by the attack on Rome by the forces of Victor Emmanuel Garibaldi), Vatican II should define the position of bishops, successors to the Apostles. In fact, Pope Paul VI spoke to this point almost immediately after his election.

In his speech at the beginning of the second session in 1963, Paul VI stated that the first question to be answered in the debate on the nature of the Church was the position of the bishops "to develop the doctrine regarding the episcopate, its function and its relationship with Peter."

The discussion of the relationship of the bishops with the pope was lengthy and controversial. At a certain point it was reduced to several different statements on which the bishops were asked to take a straw ballot. Every statement gained powerful support: Episcopal consecration is the highest grade of the Sacrament of Holy Orders (passed 2,123 to 34); every bishop in union with all the bishops and the pope is in the College of Bishops (2,049 to 104); the College of Bishops succeeds the College of Apostles and with the pope has full authority (1,808 to 336); the College of Bishops, in union with the pope, has power by Divine Right (1,717 to 408).

However, Vatican II did not delve deeply into the nettlesome subject of the relationship between the pope and the bishops. No one, I think, felt like opening up that subject because it might have been discussed forever. One idea that surfaced was to create a group of cardinals, stationed in Rome, who could bring to the pope matters of extreme importance that bishops throughout the world wanted to have discussed. Pope Paul VI turned that idea down, but issued the *motu proprio* (on his own authority) *Apostolica Sollicitudo*, establishing the Synod of Bishops to which the pope would invite bishops to meet in Rome to discuss matters — at the invitation of the pope. That was the key — the synod was not to be initiated by the bishops themselves. I think going the other way would have reduced the pope's ultimate authority.

There also was a discussion about the position of the priesthood, and a patriarch noted that diocesan priests have as much sanctity as priests of religious orders and bishops! There was a burst of applause for his remarks.

But in the end, this discussion was secondary to the debate on the laity. In the fourth chapter of the Constitution, the dignity of the laity is set forth: "Though they differ essentially and not only in degree, the common priesthood of the faithful and the ministerial or hierarchical priesthood are none the less ordered one to another: Each in its own proper way shares in the one priesthood of Christ. The ministerial priest, by the sacred power that he has, forms and rules the priestly people; in the person of Christ he effects the Eucharistic Sacrifice and offers it to God in the name of all the people. The faithful indeed, by virtue of their Royal priesthood, participate in the offering of the Eucharist. They exercise that priesthood, too, by the reception of the sacraments, prayer and thanksgiving, the witness of a holy life, abnegation and active charity... the sacred nature and organic structure of the priestly community is brought into operation through the sacraments and the exercise of virtue" (Paragraphs 10 and 11 of Chapter II of *Lumen Gentium*).

I was not certain that the document was specific enough about the duties of the laity, and I submitted an intervention that cited several of the duties incumbent on the laity. I emphasized their duties as parents and as members of the community, as well as their duties in their jobs. To be very effective, I said, "Bishops should set up special organizations to solicit ideas from the laity. What Canon 1520 prescribes for the administration of temporalities (competent laymen to advise the bishop in financial matters) should be implemented in spiritual and mixed fields." I had in mind several exceptionally well-educated and recognized laymen who thought they were doing their full duty by being helpful to their pastors in small matters. I thought their vision had to be enlarged. Later, after the Council was ended, I let the air out of the sails of a well-equipped layman, who boasted to me that he was doing his duty as layman by being a lector at Mass.

The laity also were interested in the restoration of the "permanent diaconate" for men who were properly trained. This debate elicited sharp differences in opinion among the bishops. Cardinal Spellman spoke against it, asserting it would reduce ordinations to the priesthood. A number of bishops agreed with him, but many supported the renewal. Cardinal Döpfner of Berlin said there could not be a discussion about the episcopacy and the priesthood without considering the diaconate. There was a general feeling among the U.S. bishops that we should support the renewal of the diaconate to help the Church in Latin America, but as a body, the Latin American bishops did not speak strongly in support of it. After the Council, we were surprised that the U.S. bishops were more interested in the permanent diaconate than the Latin American bishops.

The concept of the "common priesthood of the faithful" sent a buzz throughout the Catholic and Protestant worlds, as expressed by the observers at the Council. This was the first time many observers had heard the term, and they were jubilant.

An exaggeration of the relationship subsequently led to some trouble in the Archdiocese of New Orleans. Father Richard McBrien, a theology professor, had taught some New Orleans seminarians at the Pope John XXIII National Seminary in Boston that there was no essential difference in the common or general priesthood of the laity and the priesthood of the ordained clergy. A priest in New Orleans promulgated that false teaching on a Sunday, and I received a flurry of complaints from the people. When I called him in, he agreed he had taught and believed that there was no essential difference. I ordered him to correct this mistake, but four days later he left, telling me he had decided to leave my "organization."

Nevertheless, the "common priesthood of the faithful" was uplifting, but it was not completely new. Pope Pius XII had used it in his encyclical *Mediator Dei*, issued on November 20, 1947, and in his allocution *Magnificate Dominum* on November 2, 1954.

Probably the most misunderstood discussion of the Council dealt with the position of the Blessed Mother in the Church. The controversy came to a head with a headline in some of U.S. newspapers lamenting that the bishops had "downgraded the Blessed Mother." This produced a telegram to me from Father Sy Hoffman, the senior assistant priest at St. Patrick's Parish, in which he said: "What are you bishops doing? The lay people have lit all the vigil lights in front of the Blessed Mother's statue in the church."

The lay people, loyal to the Blessed Mother, had read a woefully inaccurate article in the newspaper about the decision not to publish a separate document on the Blessed Mother but to have a section devoted to her in *Lumen Gentium*. This decision followed a vote in the Council on October 29, 1963, in which the Council members voted by a small majority not to have the separate document, which originally had been planned. In A.D. 431, when the Council of Ephesus declared solemnly that the Blessed Mother was truly the Mother of God, the entire city broke out in a huge demonstration in honor of the Blessed Mother, including an eighty-year-old monk who left his cell for the first time to join the demonstration. The only difference, fifteen centuries later, was that the laity decided to light vigil candles rather than march.

The eighth chapter of the Constitution described "the role of the Blessed Virgin Mary, Mother of God, in the mystery of Christ and the Church." The news item that caused the commotion included the decision not to name the Blessed Mother the "Co-redemptrix." The decision was largely due to the fact that there had not been sufficient theological discussion of this title. Using the same reasoning, John Paul II made the same decision during his pontificate, despite his immense devotion to the Blessed Mother.

The eighth chapter states strongly the position of the Blessed Mother in the economy of salvation; it called for "probing" the Sacred Scriptures, both the Old and the New Testaments, as well as ancient tradition "to show the role of the Mother of the Savior in the economy of salvation in an ever clearer light and propose it as something to be probed into" (Section II, Par. 55).

The beautiful and inspiring description of the Blessed Mother's position did have a marked effect on many Protestant observers. I remember one saying, "I think we should give more attention to the Blessed Mother in the future." There definitely was a change in the attitude of the observers after listening to the very frank and open explanation of the deep veneration of the Church for the Blessed Mother.

The substance and effect of *Lumen Gentium* on Protestant observers and the rest of the world was splendidly expressed by Protestant ecumenist Albert C. Outler, whose appreciation of it reflected as much credit on him as on the Church. He said the document's "cardinal importance lies in its truly pastoral tone and ecumenical spirit. Here, in welcome contrast to the polemical tempers of Trent and Vatican I, we have a vision of the Church that enlivens the prospects of effective ecumenical dialogue: the Church aware of her mission under God and therefore capable of self-criticism; the Church in dialogue with the world and therefore capable of historical development; the Church in which all are called to holiness and therefore to Christian witness and service."

Vatican Council I was not undone but completed by Vatican II and its definition of bishops, clergy, and laity: All is accomplished by the Holy Spirit. No bishop belongs only to his diocese. No priest, no layperson, no Catholic organization belongs only to a parish. All belong to their part of the royal priesthood.

Dogmatic Constitution on Divine Revelation, *Dei Verbum* (1965)

I was in the coffee bar speaking to several Protestant observers when the announcement came that there would be discussion about the document on

Divine Revelation. The observers dropped their cups, as I did, to hurry as fast as our legs would allow to listen to the discussion. They were hoping the Church would accept the Protestant view that all revelation is contained in Sacred Scripture.

Of course, the Church did not change its doctrine that revelation is contained in Scripture *and* tradition. In fact, the final document on Divine Revelation encouraged scholars to discuss the scope of tradition, not ruling out the possibility that tradition might produce truths not contained in Scripture. The ecumenically significant subtext to the document was that it did *not* proclaim there were revealed truths transmitted only by tradition. Paragraph 9 states, "Tradition transmits in its entirety the Word of God which has been entrusted to the Apostles by Christ the Lord and the Holy Spirit. It transmits it to the successors of the Apostles so that they may faithfully preserve, expound and spread it abroad by their preaching."

The document also said unequivocally that tradition and Scripture make up a single, sacred deposit of the Word of God. Further, that authoritative interpretation belongs alone to the living, teaching authority of the Church.

The discussions had an effect on Protestant observers. In their conversations they admitted that the Church had developed the concept of tradition, which had to be considered. If they had any real hope of change in the Church's doctrine, their hopes were dashed by the final vote — 2,344 affirmative votes and only six negative votes. The Dogmatic Constitution of Divine Revelation was promulgated on November 10, 1965.

Decree on the Apostolate of the Laity, *Apostolicam Actuositatem* (1965)

The press in Washington, D.C., reacted very strongly in support of my interventions — and those of Bishop John Wright — about the role of the laity. *Washington Post* reporter Leo Wollemborg carried a long article on October 19, 1963, in which I said, "When it comes to judging how good a Catholic somebody is, we should ask not only whether he goes to Church on Sunday. This is the wrong approach, or at least it offers too partial a basis for judgment. To be sure, his going to Mass may provide him with a good inspiration for his daily activities. But our judgment must actually take into consideration what he does all day in the pursuit of his professional duties, as well as in his domestic, social and civic activities."

Wollemborg said the bishops should set up some machinery to seek actively the advice and collaboration of laymen, particularly of those who appear most willing and able to make a truly positive contribution not only in temporal matters as already prescribed by canon law but also in strictly spiritual and mixed matters. "Laymen are often hesitant to come forward as individuals with their suggestions but would gladly offer them if a specially organized unit served as a channel of approach to Church authorities," I told him.

At the same time, I said, Catholic laymen "should be urged to be genuine witnesses to the faith in their domestic, business, social and civic activities and to join organizations which can influence daily life: associations of parents interested in educational activities and organizations with professional, charitable and civic aims, not excluding participation in politics."

I mentioned that in areas of the country where Catholics are a minority, "our laymen (should) take part as Catholics in the active life of their communities rather than by setting up new and exclusively Catholic organizations." Bishop Wright declared that this was the first time that an Ecumenical Council had discussed specifically the role of Catholic laymen, who for "at least one thousand four hundred years have been waiting for an explicit vocation." The present text of the relevant chapter, Bishop Wright believed, represented "a substantial, hopeful beginning" in that direction.

At the same time, Bishop Wright openly voiced the hope that the Council would proceed even further and give a "positive, theological definition of what a Christian layman is." This was not only essential "to help fulfill the high hopes that Pius XI and Pius XII placed upon Catholic action but also would serve for building Christian society in the world tomorrow."

Bishop Wright's approach, which reportedly reflected the views of many other members of the American episcopate, was avowedly based upon the conviction that Catholic laypersons understood perfectly the distinction between their "priesthood" and the "fuller priesthood" of the ordained members of the Church, the clergy. Bishop Wright believed that a positive definition of the concept and role of the Catholic laity would also "dispel the prevailing erroneous impression that the Catholic Church is exclusively clerical, while the Protestant churches are more (non-clerical)."

The final vote of affirmation for the document was impressive — 2,340 affirmative votes and only two negative votes.

I fervently hope that the laity takes this ground-breaking document to heart. I remember one very unusual instance about the laity's role after I became archbishop of New Orleans. One night at about ten o'clock, a group of students from Loyola University in New Orleans banged at the door of my residence and requested strongly that I help them in a critical matter. My niece Peggy, a student at Loyola, was among them. Their concern was that a professor had told them that given a continuance of the present economic situation in the United States, they would not receive the full payment of their Social Security funds when they became old enough to need them. Of course, they all ended with, "The Church ought to do something about this."

"You are Catholic citizens," I told them. "You have a right and duty to do something about this. Why don't you form a group of students to make a presentation of your thoughts to your congressmen? Peggy, you're from Washington, and you certainly know how to get an appointment to see your congressman." Peggy was very gracious in shaking her head in assent. Finally, one of the students said, "Well, thank you." Ironically, Peggy eventually went to work for the American Association of Retired Persons, which certainly has as its main goals protecting the rights of seniors.

Declaration on Religious Freedom, *Dignitatis Humanae* (1965)

This Declaration on Religious Freedom was of intense interest to U.S. bishops, and it highlighted one of our weekly meetings held at the North American College in the Vatican. It featured a presentation by Jesuit Father John Courtney Murray and a planned rebuttal by the redoubtable Father Joseph Clifford "Butch" Fenton of Catholic University. Father Murray of Woodstock College was the principal architect of the Declaration on Religious Freedom. The most important element of the Declaration, which must be constantly emphasized, concerns the relationship of persons — and their religious convictions — with the state. It does not concern the relationship of the person with God. The person has a duty of conscience to determine his relationship with God.

Father Murray had devoted his studies on religious freedom principally in regard to our American system, recognizing everyone's right as a citizen to have unfettered religious freedom. His counterpart in Rome was Irish Cardinal Michael Browne, the official theologian of the papal household. In the summer of 1965, before the fourth session of the Council, Father Murray went to Rome to discuss the issue with Cardinal Browne. According to Father Murray, Cardinal Browne said the "sticking point" was the principle that in religion, truth cannot recognize error. Of course, this principle considers the relationship of the individual person with God. This did not involve the principle concerning the individual's relationship with civil society, the state.

At the meeting at the North American College, Murray was allowed to speak first, with Fenton following him. Murray took almost the full hour assigned to the discussion, and Fenton was able to speak for only a few minutes. The vast majority favored Murray, including Archbishop O'Boyle, who at that time was the president of the National Catholic Welfare Council (later the National Conference of Catholic Bishops).

The Council fathers indicated strongly their support of the following concept of religious freedom: "Religious freedom, in turn, which men demand as necessary to fulfill their duty to worship God has to do with immunity from coercion in civil society. Therefore, it leaves untouched traditional Catholic doctrine on the moral duty of men and societies toward the true religion and toward the one Church of God. Over and above all this, in taking up the matter of religious freedom this sacred synod intends to develop the doctrine of recent popes on the inviolable rights of the human person and on the constitutional order of society."

The popes to whom this section referred were Leo XIII in his famous 1891 encyclical *Rerum Novarum*, Pius XII in his Christmas address of 1942, and Pope John XXIII in his 1963 encyclical *Pacem in Terris*. Cardinal John Henry Newman wrote a book on the development of doctrine. No conciliar document so clearly stated that there was a development of doctrine. Even today, the opposition to the Declaration on Religious Freedom centers on the concept of development of doctrine. It also must be remembered that there was no mention of freedom of conscience in the declaration. That phrase, so open to so many interpretations, was carefully avoided.

The Declaration has provoked serious discussion, which must continue. Citing the need for further discussion, Father Murray wrote, "The notion of development, not the notion of religious freedom, was the real sticking point for many of those who opposed the declaration to the end. The course of the development between the syllabus of errors (1864) and *Dignitatis Humanae* (1965) still remains to be explained by theologians."

The Declaration dealt also with many concomitant rights of religious freedom flowing from the basic foundation of this right. "The right to religious freedom has its foundation, not in the subjective disposition of the person but in his very nature," it said. The Declaration stipulated that "the social nature of man itself requires that he should give external expression to his internal acts of religion, that he should participate with others in matters religious, that he should profess his religion in community."

"Government, therefore, ought indeed to take account of the religious life of the people and show it favor, since the foundation of government is to make provision for the common welfare," the Declaration continued. It also follows that a person has a right to act in "community. Religious bodies are a requirement of the social nature both of man and of religions itself."

The Declaration received many compliments from the press and governments across the world. I wondered if those complimenting it actually read it. There are many practices today in the United States that run counter to the Declaration.

In general, we American bishops thought we were the principal proponents of religious freedom, not because we were the only nation to practice it but because we practiced it with so many different opinions of religious freedom in our country. Our history proved, as we saw it, that religious freedom could be practiced on a vast and varied scale. In view of the need for the Declaration in world politics, Paul VI declared the Declaration was "one of the major texts of the Council."

Decree on the Mission Activity of the Church, *Ad Gentes* (1965)

This decree gets right to the point as to its purpose and content in its first sentence: "The pilgrim Church is missionary by her very nature." The Council fathers universally believed in the missionary activity of the Church. In fact, missionary fervor was a distinguishing mark between the Vatican Council I and Vatican Council II. In the first Vatican Council (1869-70) there were no native bishops from mission areas. In the Second Vatican Council there were 4 native cardinals, 41 archbishops, and 126 bishops from the mission areas, according to a report by Armenian Cardinal Agaganian, head of the Vatican's world missions.

The Decree was very practical in its statements about missionary activity, beginning with the personal character of the missionaries from non-missionary lands: they must have an appropriate natural disposition, a suitable character and talents, and special spiritual and moral training for their work. Missionaries also must have the proper respect for the culture of the people they are working with. "Let them share in the cultural and social life by the various exchanges and enterprises of human living." Missionary priests and laity must become "members of the group of men among whom they live." Cardinal Laurean Rugambwa, the first African cardinal, stressed the importance of these instructions. The instruction also emphasized the need for pre-evangelization, stating that Christ's disciples are encouraged to work among those whom they cannot immediately evangelize.

We were surprised by the attention paid to the development of the laity in mission lands. "The Church has not yet been truly established and is not yet fully alive... unless there exists a laity worthy of the name working along with the hierarchy," the Decree stated. A test of the stability of the local congregation is that the "congregation is now equipped with its own supply, insufficient though it be, of local priests, religious and laymen."

The mission decree was especially important to Bishop Fulton Sheen, who at that time was head of the U.S. Propagation of the Faith Office and was constantly besieged by missionary bishops asking for help. There was a growing anticipation of an intervention by Sheen on the floor of St. Peter's. Finally, during the discussion on the Mission of the Church, he was scheduled to speak. There was a series of microphones along the aisle, and a seminarian was appointed to be helpful at each microphone. Seeing Sheen approach the microphone, the seminarian dutifully asked, "Have you ever spoken with a microphone?" "Yes, I have," Sheen replied with a twinkle in his eyes. "Well," the seminarian said, "I must make sure that you stand in the right place and use it correctly." He then showed Sheen how to speak into the microphone! That was an enjoyable show.

Sheen did not disappoint the audience of bishops, delivering an impassioned plea for generosity to the missions in the person of Christ. He climaxed with a typically dramatic flourish, ending with the Latin plea, *"Misereor"* ("Have pity on us"). I greatly admired Sheen, who, in my opinion, was the most successful speaker in the Church in the United States. My Protestant relatives, along with so many of their friends, would reserve four o'clock on Sunday afternoon as a sacred hour — the hour to listen to Sheen. I agreed heartily with so many priests that there should be some effort made to secure a successor to him. Consequently, at the end of one of our dinners at the Hotel Eden, I told him, "You have been of such tremendous benefit to the cause of Christ that it seems to many of us that there should be a successor to you. Did you ever think of training someone to succeed you?"

Fixing his dramatic gaze upon me, he said: "This is learned only by fast and prayer!" Even today, I can hear him say, "Thank you, and good evening!"

Pastoral Constitution on the Church in the Modern World, *Gaudium et Spes* (1965): Advancing the theory of nuclear deterrence

The document that probably aroused the most interest in the world — and the one that captured my supreme interest — was the Pastoral Constitution on the Church in the Modern World (*Gaudium et Spes*). In the course of the intense debate, I became the defender of nuclear weapons and deterrence as a means of avoiding war. My intervention, together with the approximately four hundred fifty-one votes for my position, served its purpose — the deletion from the final document of a condemnation of the possession and use of all nuclear weapons.

The Constitution was conceived and developed during the course of the Council proceedings by Council fathers and by a strong demand from the Protestant observers. The demand from the Council members started with a statement by Belgian Cardinal Suenens on December 4, 1962, supported by Milan Cardinal Giovanni Battista Montini (the future Pope Paul VI) and Bologna Cardinal Giacomo Lercaro. In a nutshell, they believed the Council, in advising the Church and the world about morality, should be specific in its counsels.

Protestant observers were even more precise and blunt. In effect, they believed the Church had stated throughout the centuries and into modern times its doctrines and principles about the difficulties in the world. And now, they said the Church should offer to the world its solution to these difficulties and problems. What should we do? They wanted this pastoral Council to offer concrete advice to the world.

The Council seemed to have developed a maturity in its deliberations and now felt secure in addressing the whole world. *Gaudium et Spes* stated its purpose in its second paragraph: "Hence the Second Vatican Council, having probed more profoundly into the mystery of the Church, now addresses itself without hesitation not only to the sons of the Church and to all who invoke the name of Christ but to the whole of humanity. For the Council yearns to explain to everyone how it conceives of the presence and activity of the Church in the world today."

The document contained significant parts of the two encyclicals of John XXIII, *Mater et Magistra* ("Mother and Teacher") and *Pacem in Terris* ("Peace in the World"). The first part of the document consisted of the general principles of the Church in regard to the world, and the second part dealt precisely with the application of those principles to conditions in the world.

The fathers of the Council could agree on the doctrine and general principles of the Church, but the application of those principles to modern conditions in the world elicited a wide disparity of opinions. For obvious reasons, the discussion of the morality of nuclear weapons unleashed a whole gamut of disparate opinions. My experience as a paratroop chaplain and my firsthand knowledge of the horrors of war gave me the necessary background, I believe, to directly address this issue with the Council. That discussion has not ended to this day.

The Document was introduced on October 20, 1964. Cardinal Fernando Cento, spokesman for the Theological Commission and Commission on the Apostolate of the Laity, said the Church needed to "find answers in Christ for a world living in constant fear of an apocalyptic conflagration.... It must frame a message which can be sent not only to believers but to atheists as well."

The subcommission that drafted the Document was headed by Bishop Emilio Guano of Livorno, Italy, who said, "It does not concern doctrine or theological principles so much as the transition of the Council to the treatment of the problems that concern man today."

Eight cardinals spoke on the document; all accepted it except for Cardinal Ernesto Ruffini of Palermo, Sicily. Chicago Cardinal Albert Meyer called for a "compenetration" between the World and the Church. Archbishop Wojtyla of Krakow, the future Pope John Paul II, celebrated the Mass on October 20, feast of St. John Kantius of Poland. He urged acceptance of the document on October 21, saying "it should not speak only from authority, Scripture and tradition, but give clear and intelligent arguments from natural law and reason, leading the world to discover its own answers." Cardinal Bernardus Alfrink of Utrecht wanted the document to be an extension of *Pacem in Terris*, making a case for disarmament and "abolishing war altogether."

Despite a general agreement on broad political principles, there was sharp diversity of opinions. Cardinal Alfrink condemned the arms race but acknowledged that defensive war was permitted. Bishop Alfred-Jean-Félix Ancel of Lyon said two conditions were needed: an agreement by all nations not to go to war and an international authority that would have all arms and thus be able to stop any aggression. Benedictine Abbot Dom Basil Christopher Butler and two English bishops said deterrence and possession of nuclear weapons were wrong. Cardinal Achille Liénart of Lille and Montreal Cardinal Paul-Émile Léger opposed all nuclear arms. Cardinal Alfredo Ottaviani was cheered for his denunciation of all war. Archbishop Pedro Cantero of Zaragoza, Spain, said nations had a right to defend themselves, even if it meant possessing nuclear arms. Incidentally, Pope Pius XII, after World War II, had refused to accede to a demand that he condemn nuclear development, saying nuclear power could be used for peaceful and good means.

My interest in nuclear weapons stemmed from my military service during World War II. As Catholic chaplain for the 505th Parachute Infantry Regiment in the American sector of Berlin, I had direct, daily contact with the Russian Communist troops. We saw firsthand their brutal and merciless actions in governing the defeated Germans, especially their ruthless treatment of German women, who were assaulted and raped with impunity. I did not meet one German woman who had not been raped or brutally treated by the Russians, including the young woman who acted as my secretary. I am not saying American troops were without fault, but their misdeeds were punished, not permitted, by their superiors.

I also developed a friendship with the interpreter of the Russian command, Captain Igor Bevs, a good and intelligent man who did not approve the Communist regime. Naturally, our generals often discussed how we could cope with the Communist forces, because they openly professed their aim to conquer the world. Their resources and strategic position seemed to be impregnable. Nuclear weapons were the only deterrent to keep their ruthless power in check.

Later, I became friendly with General Joseph (Lightning Joe) Collins, chief of staff of our military, who agreed with the U.S. policy of deterrence. I also knew Thomas E. Murray, head of the Atomic Energy Commission and a very good practicing Catholic who believed in the development of nuclear weapons of a very small destructive power, capable of being used on a battlefield.

I also understood that it was difficult for most people to understand that deterrence did not mean retaliation. I was very much impressed by a U.S. general who was being interrogated by a small group of bishops. They posed the question, "What would you do if the Russians fired a nuclear weapon at one of our big cities?" The general replied quietly, "What would be the purpose of a reply?" The bishops then said among themselves, "See, he wouldn't say the U.S. would not fire a nuclear weapon in reprisal."

I groaned. The bishops didn't understand that the general could not say there would be no retaliation without destroying the policy of deterrence. Deterrence depended upon the enemy believing that launching a nuclear strike could or would trigger a nuclear response. Therefore, it would be in the enemy country's national interest not to develop nuclear weapons nor to even consider launching a nuclear attack.

The attitude of the United States toward nuclear weapons was evidenced before the Vietnam War, when the French Army asked the United States if it could use an American nuclear weapon to save its cause in Vietnam after their disastrous defeat at Dien Bien Phu. President Truman bucked the request to the Chiefs of Staff, who immediately rejected it and so informed the President. The United States was certainly not trigger-happy about nuclear weapons.

The majority of the Council fathers favored the condemnation of nuclear weapons. Their position was based on theoretical principles, which neglected any actual facts, including the peril of Communism then being waged in the Cold War. The bishops also did not know of the recent developments in nuclear production that could produce nuclear weapons of limited strength and could be used tactically against military targets without targeting entire cities and their civil populations. These were called "Davy Crockett rockets" — small, bazooka-launched, tactical nuclear missiles that were not weapons of mass destruction. (Try explaining a "Davy Crockett rocket" in Latin!)

The opponents of nuclear weapons were highly respected. Cardinal Alfrink quoted a passage from the *Pacem in Terris*, issued by Pope John XXIII, that condemned the use of all nuclear weapons. Patriarch Maximos IV Saigh claimed that the moral authority of two thousand bishops calling for peace and prohibiting nuclear weapons could "change the course of history and save humanity." Bishop Jacques Guilhem of Laval, France, contended that "no moral principle could justify" the use of nuclear weapons and that such genocide should be repudiated vociferously.

On the other hand, there were also many Council fathers — especially those in Italy, Western Europe, England, and the countries under Communist domination — who favored the U.S. position. They had seen the near annihilation of much of their territory, including their major cities, during World War II. Warsaw was almost totally destroyed by the Nazi and Communist occupation. Berlin and many cities in Germany were in ruins; when U.S. troops entered Cologne, formerly a city of almost nine hundred thousand citizens, only twenty-five thousand people climbed out of their cellars to greet the American troops. They saw the peril of Communism as described by British Prime Minister Winston Churchill, "If it were not for the nuclear power of the United States there would not be a single free citizen in Europe." They knew that eventually Communism would self-destruct from its own evils if it could be restrained by nuclear deterrence.

Nevertheless, I was nervous about making a statement in regard to such a momentous matter. Unfortunately, I could not find a senior — or any — member of our group, including Archbishop O'Boyle, who would make an intervention on nuclear weapons. By all rights New York Cardinal Spellman, as Military Ordinary, should have spoken up, but he didn't because he was so afraid of being wrong. Probably fewer than half the U.S. bishops agreed with me, but I couldn't bear the prospect of there being no statement about the morality and the effectiveness of deterrence, which I thoroughly supported.

It finally dawned on me that no one was going to speak up and that it would be a disaster for the Council to declare that even the possession of nuclear weapons would lead to war. From my discussions with the head of the Atomic Energy Commission, I knew about weapons development. From my days as an Army chaplain, I knew about combat. I also knew that deterrence did not mean the United States would have a blanket excuse to use those weapons. I was defending a program that I thought was absolutely essential for keeping the peace. After much prayer, I took the floor. My job was simply to knock out that one sentence that weapons would lead to war, and I knew the two thousand five hundred bishops in St. Peter's Basilica would be hanging on my every word. Forget about yelling "fire!" in a crowded movie theater — all anyone had to say inside St. Peter's was "nuclear," and he was guaranteed to have a rapt audience.

The substance of my intervention on November 10, 1964, which received the concurrence of about four hundred fifty members, was as follows:

> "In Section 2, there is a serious mistake of fact in regard to nuclear weapons, and therefore a false conclusion is reached. In the second sentence of this section it is stated, '... the use of arms, especially nuclear weapons, whose effects are greater than can be imagined and therefore cannot be reasonably regulated by men, exceeds all just proportion and therefore must be judged before God and man as most wicked.' But this affirmation is incorrect since there exist today nuclear weapons whose destructive force is narrowly limited. Some weapons of this type are mobile. Obviously, if these weapons did not have a very restricted field of destruction, the soldiers who fired them would be killed as a result of the explosion. There are smaller weapons now in use which have a range of 1.3 to 2.5 miles, and their missile has a destructive force of forty tons of TNT.

> "Although all such weapons — even those of low yield — inflict great damage, still it cannot be said, as the text does, that their effects are greater than what can be estimated. Their effects are within certain well-defined limits and can be entirely foreseen. Furthermore, it may be permitted to use these arms, with their limited effect, against military objectives in a just war according to theological principles.

> "Therefore, the whole section seems to ignore the common teaching of the Church and its norms that must be applied to the conduct of a just war.

> "The whole paragraph also would seem to imply that all nations have been equally negligent in fulfilling their duty to seek a common international peace. This is an unjust assertion and offended many nations and heads of governments who have expended great efforts toward securing

peace. It is especially injurious to nations which are now suffering from military aggression. The whole world knows the source of this aggression.

"The question of the greatest importance, now and for the future, is to avoid war and to defend both national and personal liberty. We must have complete and actual liberty to carry on a dialogue with militant atheists. No dialogue is possible if we fall into slavery. Because liberty is the foundation of human life, those who defend liberty should be praised.

"Therefore, since this *schema* deals with practical matters, we should at least say a word about the defense of liberty and a word of praise in favor of those who defend liberty, as well as those who freely offered their lives so that we might enjoy the full freedom of the sons of God.

"Therefore, in my humble opinion, this whole section should be completely revised."

Archbishop George Beck of Liverpool, England, speaking "in the name of many Bishops in England and Wales," jumped to my defense. He stated that in a just, defensive war, the use of limited nuclear weapons was permissible, and therefore the contention that the *possession and use* of all nuclear weapons as "intrinsically and necessarily evil" was wrong. He said the Council should not rashly condemn governments who had worked so hard to keep the peace. Beck said, "To turn the other cheek is a counsel of perfection addressed to individuals, not to governments that have a grave duty to defend the citizens entrusted to their authority." The *schema* was sent back for rewriting.

I remember my intervention received a generally good reception, and some members asked that I prepare a further *modus* requesting more changes. This second *modus* did not receive the same acceptance as the first, and Bishop Joseph Schroffer, the head of the subcommission dealing with Chapter V, and Toulouse Archbishop Gabriel-Marie Garrone, the General Relator of the Constitution, sent me and the other members who supported the second *modus* a detailed rebuttal. I decided not to contest their statement and not to press further an acceptance of the second *modus*. I was content that we had achieved our main objective, the deletion of the statement that any possession or use of nuclear weapons was absolutely wrong.

I had the support of many, but certainly not the majority, of American bishops. In a recess after the discussions, Archbishop O'Boyle, grim-faced and determined, said, "Phil, I am all for you, but many of our bishops are against you." My liberal opponents included Cardinal Shehan of Baltimore.

In the end, our efforts did eliminate a total condemnation of the possession and use of nuclear weapons. The end product was certainly acceptable: "Any act of war aimed indiscriminately at the destruction of entire cities or of extensive areas along with their population is a crime against God and man himself. It merits unequivocal and unhesitating condemnation. The unique hazard of modern warfare consists in this: It provides those who possess modern scientific weapons with a kind of occasion for perpetrating just such abominations" (Par. 80 Chapter V, the Fostering of Peace and the Promotion of a Community of Nations).

For me, the final form of Paragraph 81 was an important vindication of my position: "To be sure, scientific weapons are not amassed solely for use in war. Since the defensive strength of any nation is considered to be dependent upon its capacity for immediate retaliation, this accumulation of arms, which increases every year, likewise serves, in a way heretofore unknown, as deterrent to possible enemy attack. Many regard this procedure as the most effective way by which peace of a sort can be maintained between nations at the present time."

Obviously, our position was that deterrence — mutually assured destruction — would prevent such an abomination. I realized many of the bishops in Communist countries were silent supporters of my position. They could not risk any open support of my position for fear of being plastered by their governments. I didn't care about offending any Communist sensibilities.

Cardinal Ruffini from Sicily sent a messenger to ask me to come to his seat. He shook my hand and said, "Congratulations. Your position is just common sense." Many bishops thought, because I was from Washington, I was speaking on behalf of all American bishops and our country. Cardinal Amleto Cicognani, the former Apostolic Nuncio to the United States, summoned me and asked, "Is there any message in your statement from the President?" I replied, "No, not at all." This was my feeling about what was right.

The most satisfying support and biggest compliment I ever received came from the dean of the diplomatic corps of the United States, Ambassador Jefferson Caffery, a native of Lafayette, Louisiana, who came to see me in Washington after the final session and declared, "Without the policy of deterrence by our country, diplomacy would be dead." He cordially thanked me for my defense of it.

There was another section in the original *schema* that I criticized. It stated that any war that entailed the killing of a million people was automatically wrong. The losses in Germany in World War II were terribly higher than that. In the Rhineland alone, two million civilians were killed by the bombing and ground warfare. Russia never publicly quantified its losses, but the lowest estimate was at least twenty million killed. Using the logic of the *schema* as first proposed, Adolf Hitler would still be domineering Germany. Sometimes the free nations of the world must stand up to fight evil.

Our intense discussion of nuclear weapons at Vatican II was carried on in the context of the Cold War. Communist Russia, invigorated by its launching of the Sputnik satellite, was charging ahead with its propaganda, highlighted by Khrushchev's histrionic pounding of his shoe on the desk at the United Nations and shouting, "We will bury you!" Further, the Soviets had planted missiles in Cuba, just ninety miles from Florida, precipitating the Cuban missile crisis. We have long forgotten the result of this crisis in the life of Washington, D.C., which created a frenzy among the populace, who feared a Russian missile attack on the capital.

While all this was going on, there was a well-engineered Communist campaign among misled liberals and Communist propagandists that the United States alter its strict opposition to Communism. As usual, this effort found some success among the faculties in many colleges and universities.

The Church, meanwhile, under the guidance of Pope Paul VI, famous for his condemnation of all war, was undertaking a quiet policy of compromise with Communism. One of his actions was the removal in 1971 of Cardinal József Mindszenty, the symbol and heart of Communist opposition in Hungary, from the United States Embassy in Budapest, where he had taken refuge. All these factors were a part of my determination not to help the Communist propaganda by a condemnation of the "use and possession" of nuclear weapons in the Council.

Fortunately, the course of events in Europe, especially the increased pressure of the Communist Soviet Union, led to a reversal in the thinking of the free world in regard to deterrence. I made a collection of statements, filling a whole bushel basket, in support of deterrence in Europe in the decades following the Second Vatican Council. Today there is much greater tolerance and acceptance of the policy of deterrence — especially in the countries that opposed it in the 1960s — because of the horrible terrorist attacks on the United States in 2001, which caused more U.S. casualties than the attack on Pearl Harbor that propelled us into World War II. During the height of the Cold War, I did not think the cause of humanity, the cause of morality, nor the cause of Christian dialogue was forwarded by making ourselves defenseless in the face of nuclear threats from Communist aggression. No free and fruitful dialogue with the Communists would have been possible in a Communist prison. I was glad to see the overwhelming majority in the Council eventually agreed with me.

Recent popes, including Benedict XVI, have been heroic and intense in the quest for peace. They have initiated and supported proposals for the avoidance of war. Of course, they have continued to defend the right of a nation to self-defense, and during the frightful war of Serbia against Croatia and Bosnia-Herzegovina, Pope John Paul II instructed the Cardinal Secretary of State to appeal to any nation able to do so to aid the defense of Croatia and Bosnia against Serbia.

Naturally and properly, the Holy See continues to criticize the arms race and calls for an international solution to this immense expenditure of effort and finances for arms. While the discussion on arms was engaging the attention of the Council in 1965, Pope Paul VI made his famous trip to the United Nations in which he made his heroic plea, "No more war; war never again!" He returned to the Council in the midst of a General Session, walked up the entire length of St. Peter's to the standing ovation of the fathers.

The procession up the aisle was unique — the Pope was vigorous in his stride, but Cardinal Cicognani and the other elderly members of his group were puffing, exhausted, and lagging. Cardinal Cicognani remarked later to me, "The Pope likes to show that he is still young and active." He was not impressed, but I was.

These issues of life and death place the United States in a unique position of responsibility in world affairs. Can the United Nations come together to force a rogue nation run by a radical Islamic government, such as Iran, to give up a nuclear weapons program? I really believe that the good Lord gave the United States its abundance of resources to use for the cause of freedom. To me, those riches carry with it a concomitant obligation to protect the freedom of the world. Nobody else can do it — and the U.N. isn't going to do it. Unless we want to be totally incompetent, I think we've got to let it be known we will defend the freedom of the world.

Either we do it or it won't get done.

Love Is the Most Important Thing

One story that particularly stands out in my mind sums up the human condition. It has stayed with me since World War II. My assistant, Jacques Ospital, and I were in occupied Berlin after the war had ended. We had some time on our hands and, being nosy, we thought we would walk around the city. The city was busy. People from all over the countryside were making their way back into the city seeking shelter, although there was none.

A woman in her early thirties was pulling a wooden cart, which was not unusual, as there were no animals available for such duty. In the cart was her little boy, neatly dressed, sitting amongst all their earthly belongings. The woman was quite obviously distraught.

Jacques and I stopped her and, as best we could, using our poor German, asked her if we could help. We were hoping to point her in the direction of some of the aid that was available. Her heartbreaking response was, "All is lost. Everything is gone. You cannot help me."

In halting German, we tried to determine her trouble. "Have you no place to stay?... No food?... Are you or the child sick?" We stood together in the midst of the terrible desolation of a city utterly destroyed.

"You cannot help me," she cried. "My man has left me. There is no help that you can give me. There is no one to love me." She was inconsolable.

I was amazed. In the midst of such devastation, what grieved her most was that she had no one to love her. And, in the end, isn't that what it's all about anyway? Nothing matters without love.

The image of that woman in Berlin was formative to me. It has stayed with me for all these decades. We are dependent upon one another. When things are good, it is easy to lose that sense of dependence — especially in the present culture. However, when love is not present, we are adrift.

The ultimate and purest example of love comes from God. Throughout my priestly ministry I have tried to remember to let the pure love of God flow through me to others. I have tried to cultivate that love in others in their darkest hours.

In the end, all that matters is love.